# Legal Lessons

HARVARD EAST ASIAN MONOGRAPHS 411

# Legal Lessons

*Popularizing Laws in the*
*People's Republic of China, 1949–1989*

## Jennifer Altehenger

Published by the Harvard University Asia Center
Distributed by Harvard University Press
Cambridge (Massachusetts) and London 2018, 2021

Printed in the United States of America

The Harvard University Asia Center publishes a monograph series and, in coordination with the Fairbank Center for Chinese Studies, the Korea Institute, the Reischauer Institute of Japanese Studies, and other faculties and institutes, administers research projects designed to further scholarly understanding of China, Japan, Vietnam, Korea, and other Asian countries. The Center also sponsors projects addressing multidisciplinary and regional issues in Asia.

Library of Congress Cataloging-in-Publication Data

Names: Altehenger, Jennifer E., author.
Title: Legal lessons : popularizing laws in the People's Republic of China, 1949–1989 / Jennifer E Altehenger.
Other titles: Harvard East Asian monographs ; 411.
Description: Cambridge, Massachusetts : Published by the Harvard University Asia Center, 2018. | Series: Harvard East Asian monographs ; 411 | Includes bibliographical references and index.
Identifiers: LCCN 2017029701 | ISBN 9780674983854 (hardcover : alk. paper) ISBN 9780674251243 (paperback : alk. paper)
Subjects: LCSH: Law—Social aspects—China.
Classification: LCC KNQ68 .A44 2018 | DDC 349.5109/045--dc23 LC record available at https://lccn.loc.gov/2017029701

A previous version of parts of the material in this book appeared in Jennifer Altehenger, "Simplified Legal Knowledge in the Early PRC: Explaining and Publishing the Marriage Law." In *Chinese Law: Knowledge, Practice, and Transformation, 1530s–1950s*, edited by Li Chen and Madeleine Zelin, pp. 342–66. Leiden: Brill, 2015. It has been reprinted with permission of Brill Publishers.

Index by Anne Holmes of EdIndex
Printed on acid-free paper
First paperback edition 2021

Last figure below indicates year of this printing
28  27  26  25  24  23  22  21

For my parents

# Contents

Contents

## PART III   REVIVALS: 1970–1989

# Acknowledgments

Writing this book has taught me to appreciate and respect time. It is a pleasure to write this final bit now and thank the many people who generously spent time with me or for me. I fear I may, and probably will, fail to mention every debt I have accumulated over the past years, and so I would like to express my gratitude to everyone who has, at some point, been willing to talk to me about this project. They have helped me turn my ideas into an argument, a thesis, and eventually a book.

I thank my teachers first. Without Barbara Mittler's encouragement, I may not have embarked on this journey. I am grateful for her guidance, her patience, her infectious enthusiasm, and for her unwavering support at all times of the day. I could not have wished for a better Doktormutter. Gregor Ahn's door was always open for a chat and a laugh. He ensured that I looked beyond Chinese Studies, and he always had faith that this manuscript was worth writing. At the end of the thesis and the beginning of the book, Rana Mitter helped me find my way into the book and into life in UK academia. Without his sage advice, I would have made more than one mistake too many. Karl Gerth has been a wonderful mentor and friend ever since he chaperoned me through my first gig as a departmental lecturer.

Over the years, I was lucky to have many people whose scholarship I greatly admire take the time to read and comment on my work. The late Christina Gilmartin, Henrietta Harrison, Jiang Jin, Alison Kaufman, William Kirby, and Nicolai Volland made my book workshop at Harvard a mind-boggling and thoroughly enjoyable day. Many moons later, Karl Gerth, Charlotte Goodburn, Tehyun Ma, and Glenn Tiffert read the next draft of the manuscript and sent rich and incredibly helpful notes saving me from many an interpretive and factual error. Tim Cheek, David Edgerton, Lena Henningsen, Tim Hildebrandt, and Nicolai Volland thoughtfully commented on several individual chapters, and their suggestions pushed me to clarify my arguments and sharpen my analysis. The two anonymous readers for the Harvard University Asia Center Publications Program provided incisive comments that helped me work through the structure and argument of the book. I also thank Karl Gerth, Denise Ho, Jie Li, and Rana Mitter for many wonderful tips as I prepared for submission of the manuscript and then publication. I have been humbled by the effort and time they all invested in this work. They have set a model of friendship and collegiality to which I aspire. And although I have tried to do justice to everyone's comments throughout the chapters, I fear many questions still remain unanswered. Any remaining mistakes—factual, interpretive, or otherwise—are of course entirely my fault.

Many others have commented on parts of the manuscript and presentations I gave at workshops and conferences, have kindly invited me to participate in panels and workshops, have provided help in accessing archival collections, and have given advice over coffee and meals: Paul Betts, Jerome Bourgon, Pär Cassel, Janet Chen, Tina Mai Chen, Chen Xiaomei, Paul Cohen, Rob Culp, Hannah Dawson, Richard Drayton, Hilde de Weerdt, Neil Diamant, Joseph Esherick, Jacob Eyferth, Merle Goldman, Gail Hershatter, Joan Judge, Thomas Kampen, Margaret Kuo, Barak Kushner, Eugenia Lean, Benjamin Liebman, Chang Liu, Stephen Lovell, Luo Liang, Michael Lüdke, Gotelind Müller-Saini, Rebecca Nedostup, Priscilla Roberts, Shao Qin, Matthew Sommer, Julia Strauss, Hue-Tam Ho Tai, Eddy U, Hans van de Ven, Margaret Wan, Rudolf Wagner, Wan Li, Odd Arne Westad, Xu Lanjun, Wen Hsin-Yeh, Madeleine Zelin, and Harriet Zurndorfer. Their ideas, suggestions, and enthusiasm for the topic provided crucial encouragement and support as I worked on this book. I am exceedingly grateful to many colleagues in China on whose advice I have relied for years, whose support was crucial to my work, and who have been truly inspiring models of scholarship. I further thank audiences and participants at conference panels and workshops at the University of California at Berkeley, University of Cambridge, Columbia University,

Harvard University, University of Heidelberg, the Institute of Histori-cal Research, Lund University, and the University of Oxford for listen-ing to a presentation on law and asking very helpful questions. Li Chen and Madeleine Zelin in particular provided incisive notes on parts of the thesis that then became a chapter in their edited volume. Michael Schoenhals generously introduced me to a range of sources that I would otherwise not have known about, invited me to Lund to read them, and ensured that there was plenty of caffeine to keep my brain cells going. To them all, I owe an enormous debt of gratitude.

For their help in locating crucial sources and scholarship, I thank the librarians at the Beijing National Library, Berkeley C.V. Starr East Asian Library, Cambridge University Library, Harvard-Yenching Li-brary, Heidelberg University Library, Lund University Library, Oxford University Library and the Chinese Studies Collection at Oxford, Shanghai Municipal Library, and the Staatsbibliothek zu Berlin (in particular for hosting the unparalleled CrossAsia platform). Archivists in Beijing, Berlin, Hangzhou, and Shanghai were welcoming and helpful. A special thank you to Anne Labitzky-Wagner at the Library of the Institute of Chinese Studies at Heidelberg, who helped me find many of the sources on which the thesis was based. And to Nancy Hearst at the Fung Library at Harvard University who will see the footprints of the wonderful sources she suggested across this book.

Several institutions provided financial as well as other kinds of sup-port that enabled me to travel to all these libraries and archives to read documents without which this book would not have been possible and to participate in conferences and workshops. I thank the Cusanuswerk, the Graduate Academy of the University of Heidelberg, the Cluster "Asia and Europe in a Global Context" (now the Heidelberg Center for Transcultural Studies), the Fairbank Center for Chinese Studies at Harvard University, the University of Oxford, the British Academy, the Universities China Committee London, the Robert Bosch Stiftung, the Shanghai Academy of Social Sciences, and King's College London. The Fairbank Center provided generous funds and administrative help to organize a book workshop at the end of my postdoctoral fellowship. The Heidelberg Academy of Sciences and Humanities, moreover, awarded this work with the Academy Prize of 2015, and I thank the members of the Academy for their support. Given how tight funding is these days, I am doubly grateful to all these organizations for their confidence that I would eventually deliver on my research promises. I am grateful, moreover, to the anonymous reviewers who took time to read the proposals and who had faith that my (often vague) ideas would develop into something worth publishing.

Friends and colleagues made the attempt to figure out the academic yellow brick road so much more manageable and enjoyable. During my time in Germany, China, the United Kingdom, and the United States, I enjoyed the company of friends and fellow students of China and/or history, including Roy Chan, Aglaia de Angeli, Miriam Gross, Josh Hill, Jon Howlett, Huang Xuelei, Matt Johnson, Jennifer Johnson-Cooper, Annika Jöst, Cora Jungbluth, Alison Kaufman, Miriam Kingsberg, Konrad Lawson, Chris Leighton, Jie Li, Toby Lincoln, David Luesink, Marc Matten, Jennifer May, Tom Mullaney, Johanna Ransmeier, Ned Richardson-Little, Leon Rocha, Anna Ross, Marina Rudyak, Jon Schlesinger, Sun Liying, Heidi Tworek, and Mandy Wu. Friends in China, meanwhile, made each visit truly enjoyable, and I always look forward to going back there. I am also grateful to my colleagues at Oxford, Harvard, and King's College London for making my academic homes for the past years such inspiring and welcoming places in which to work and research. Last but most certainly not least, Felix Boecking, Arunabh Ghosh, Anke Hein, Lena Henningsen, Denise Ho, Rachel Leow, Tehyun Ma, Helen Schneider, Petra Thiel, Glenn Tiffert, and Nico Volland have been crucial sources of friendship, strength, and support. Thank you for everything you have done for me.

Since submitting the manuscript, I have been very fortunate to work with patient and resourceful editors who have guided me every step of the way. Bob Graham chaperoned the book through the review process, keeping me updated every step of the way. Nancy Hearst proofread the final manuscript with an eagle eye to detail. Kristen Wanner has been a more amazing editor than I could have ever dared to hope for, making the manuscript far more accessible than it was.

This book exists because of my family and it is dedicated to them. My wonderful parents Sherry and Bernd have always been by my side. With much patience and love, they made home a safe haven. They gave us shelter over the summers, sent care packages, stored more of our things than they had space for, and tirelessly tried to make our lives as easy as possible. My in-laws always helped in any way they could and provided plenty of food and homemade wine to sustain us along the way. Over the past years, Sebastian has made each day a little bit sunnier for me. Words cannot express how grateful I am to be able to walk through life together with him.

London, July 2017

# Illustrations

# Abbreviations

| | |
|---|---|
| BArch SAPMO | Federal Archives, Foundation Archives of Parties and Mass Organizations of the GDR, Berlin-Lichterfelde |
| BFB | *Beijing fazhi bao* (Beijing legal daily) |
| BMA | Beijing Municipal Archives |
| CARCDB | Chinese Anti-Rightist Campaign Database |
| CBSL | *Zhonghua renmin gongheguo chuban shiliao* (Historical materials on publishing in the People's Republic of China) |
| CCP | Chinese Communist Party |
| CPCDB | Chinese Political Campaigns in the 1950s Database |
| CRDB | Cultural Revolution Database |
| DXGHGW | *Dang de xuanchuan gongzuo huiyi gaikuang he wenxian* (Overview of and documents related to party propaganda work meetings) |
| DXGWX | *Dang de xuanchuan gongzuo wenjian xuanbian* (Selection of documents on party propaganda work) |
| GMRB | *Guangming ribao* (Guangming daily) |
| HMA | Hangzhou Municipal Archives |
| NBCK | *Neibu cankao* (Internal reference) |
| PA AA / MfAA | Political Archive, Ministry for Foreign Affairs, Berlin |
| PRC | People's Republic of China |
| RMRB | *Renmin ribao* (People's daily) |
| SMA | Shanghai Municipal Archives |

| | |
|---|---|
| XMB | *Xinmin bao* (New people's news) |
| XWRB | *Xinwen ribao* (News daily) |
| ZFB | *Zhongguo fazhi bao* (China legal daily) |
| ZGXGWX | *Zhongguo gongchandang xuanchuan gongzuo wenxian xuanbian* (Selections of documents on CCP propaganda work) |

# Introduction

"There is a law for everything. Right now it rains daily—how is it that there is no law to stop that?"[1] These were the words of an unnamed worker in Wuxi, a city some one hundred miles inland from Shanghai. A reporter from the Xinhua News Agency, the central news agency of the People's Republic of China (PRC), recorded them in 1954 when people across China's cities were asked to read, reflect, and comment on the draft of the country's first state constitution in what was called a national "discussion." The worker, disgruntled about having to read the constitution draft, felt that so many laws seemed pointless, unless they could start to control the dismal weather. He probably did not know that his words were being written down; nor could he have known that, together with hundreds of other people's responses, his words would be re-printed in the restricted internal circular *Neibu cankao* (Internal reference). Only central leadership had access to the circular, and they wanted to know how the dissemination and discussion of the draft was proceeding. To them it mattered greatly that ordinary citizens understood the constitution draft correctly and knew what it meant to abide by laws. And Xinhua News Agency had decided that they should know about the Wuxi worker's complaint.

The man's comment was recorded less than five years after the Chinese Communist Party (CCP) had come to power and had begun to reorganize public spaces, workplaces, schools, and—gradually—people's private lives. Under Mao Zedong's (1893–1976) leadership, the CCP had drastically altered some of the fabric of everyday life through a series of mass campaigns that famously targeted, in particular, counterrevolutionaries, intellectuals, the bourgeoisie, and capitalists.[2] Learning laws, as the descriptions in *Neibu cankao* richly document, was part of the way many people—particularly in urban areas—experienced this transition to a new political regime. To learn about laws was to learn about socialism. Yet compared to the political, economic, and sociocultural history of the PRC, much less is known about the history of its laws. This is remarkable because, I argue, the PRC stands out in the history of the modern state for its repeated attempts to mobilize China's citizens to learn laws during the 1950s and after the death of Mao Zedong in 1976.

This book explores the history of mass legal education in the two municipalities of Beijing and Shanghai between 1949, the year the PRC was established, and 1989, the year many people went to the streets in both cities calling on their government to live up to the legal promises made in the 1982 state constitution. I examine how state authorities and cultural workers attempted in different ways over the years to create effective "law propaganda" (*fazhi xuanchuan* or *falü xuanchuan*), how state officials disseminated basic legal knowledge among the general population, and how people learned or did not learn about laws. Getting the population to learn laws was a contested process that state authorities repeatedly initiated because of its anticipated merits, but also at times abandoned because of its unanticipated consequences. The trajectory of this process allows us to reassess the links between laws, state authority, and people, both under the socialism of the early Mao period and under the "new period" of socialism and economic reforms that followed after 1978.

Beginning in the early 1950s, the CCP tried to deliver parts of its socialist promise in legal form. During the early Mao period, the most important of these laws were called the country's "Great Laws." They included the 1949 Common Program, the 1950 Marriage Law, the 1950 Agrarian Reform Law, the 1950 Trade Union Law, the 1953 Election Law, the 1954 constitution, and the Organic Laws.[3] Widely announced in state media, these were the laws that citizens were required to learn about and read. After 1976, under the leadership of Deng Xiaoping (1904–97), the central government initiated a wide-ranging program of legal reforms, publishing in a mere decade a flurry of new laws intended to symbolize the transition to a new era. Citizens were now required to know even more about different laws, but the canon was still restricted to a selection that included the state constitution, Criminal Law, Marriage Law, and other laws the CCP determined to be relevant to citizens' daily life. Throughout these decades, a significant amount of widely available materials discussed the new laws. The pages of newspapers and magazines were covered with articles explaining different aspects of laws. Human interest stories about how good socialist men and women had used laws to reform their families, increase production, and better the quality of life in their communities were abundant. Operas and dramatic performances told such stories as part of educational entertainment for the masses. Cartoons, propaganda images, and picture stories visualized life regulated by state laws. Diverse in kind, propaganda materials all transmitted a similar message: laws were a "weapon" (wuqi) of the People (renmin), an expression of the "will of the People," and a product of CCP rule.[4]

The history of law in the PRC is therefore marked by extremes. Life was often lawless, as state agents and ordinary people broke or circumvented laws.[5] At the same time, people's daily lives were sometimes also over-saturated with laws and having to learn about laws. Depending on where he lived, where he worked, and the activities his work unit wanted him to join, the Wuxi worker may have had cause to be annoyed with having to hear about laws yet again. Because he lived in a larger city the constitution draft discussion could have been the fifth or sixth public study of a law that he had had to participate in since the CCP came to power. While he and others complained, still others were happy to study laws, and some believed that the existing PRC laws did not go far enough, were still too few, or needed much more and better explanation. People did not agree on how many laws New China needed and when. They also had different opinions about what laws meant, and what laws could and should do.

Because of this diversity of opinion, as this book shows, official promotion of mass legal learning posed a major dilemma for the CCP and the government. The CCP wanted to disseminate legal knowledge widely in order to persuade people to abide by laws. It also wanted to retain control of how laws were interpreted and how laws would serve the state. Control was hard to accomplish, though. The wider the dissemination of knowledge, the more difficult it became to supervise how people used this knowledge or interpreted what they learned.[6] There was no easy way out. Any attempt to guide how people understood laws had to involve telling them about the laws and what they meant. As the years passed, the dissemination of legal knowledge and the often unfulfilled promises of a more equal and just society led some Chinese citizens to believe in the possibility of seeking recourse in the law, while it led others to think of laws as "only words on paper" or as instruments of arbitrary state power. Given these challenges and risks, what made law dissemination nonetheless worthwhile or, at the very least, necessary in the eyes of party and government leaders at different times after 1949?

## A Complex Legal Inheritance

The laws that the CCP disseminated after 1949 were the product of legal developments that reached back to imperial times.[7] As in countries across the world, legislative activities in China precipitated or followed on the heels of tumultuous political transformations. For centuries, imperial China's elaborate legal codes formed the basis for imperial rule and for people to interact with state authority in its different local manifestations. In the nineteenth century, the process of instituting and negotiating extraterritoriality with foreign imperial powers furthered the formation of a pluralist legal order in China.[8] Following the 1911 revolution, the "new policy reforms" initiated by the late Qing provided the basis for a range of new Republican legislation modeled on Japanese, German, and Swiss legal influences and advice.[9] These formed part of the Nationalist government's Six Codes, promulgated under the Chinese Nationalist Party (Guomindang or GMD) and Chiang Kaishek, which included the Civil Code and the Criminal Code.[10]

In the dissemination of law, the formal and political process of lawmaking connected with social and cultural processes of laws in practice. Historians have investigated how ordinary people in imperial and Republican China engaged with, applied, and contested laws.[11] How people dealt with laws depended on what they knew about laws and how they obtained this knowledge. Successive imperial and Republican regimes spent considerable time and energy trying to convince or compel their respective imperial subjects and Republican citizens to abide by laws.[12] Government officials experimented with different types of public fora, lectures, publications, and images to convey essential information about the content of laws and how people might live by the letter of the law. Village lectures in imperial China informed residents that their state expected its subjects to obey the law.[13] Jingles and rhymes made laws memorable for the overburdened local official.[14] Republican governments and reformers told people that they should know something about their country's laws in order to be part of a modern citizenry; and they sponsored publishing houses that edited and printed affordable general leaflets and handbooks on laws.[15]

State projects to educate people in laws during the imperial and Republican periods were driven by a desire to impart any legal information that the authorities thought people had to know in order to be part of whatever the polity envisaged at that moment. State-led education in laws was also a quest to rectify what people knew. At the same time, imperial regimes, as Jeffrey Kinkley has pointed out, were "ambivalent" about exactly how much law people should know, though they were not so ambivalent about the requirement to know some laws. This ambivalence continued into the twentieth century.[16]

Chinese states, moreover, never had a monopoly over how or what people learned about laws. People interpreted laws in the context of their daily lives and in ways that best suited their interests. State officials had to compete with alternative sources of legal information that they constantly sought to survey and curtail. Many people wanted to know about laws, but they did not necessarily trust official sources and interpretations. Despite Confucian norms that stressed that people should only resort to laws if there was no other way to resolve a dispute, people were willing to use what information they could find about laws and legal means to deal with issues and disputes as they arose in their daily lives and to further their interests.[17] Qing China was awash with diverse and personal interpretations of what laws could do. Litigation masters, at many times operating illegally, helped those who either could not write or did not have a command of the language of imperial law to write legal documents.[18] Private legal specialists assisted magistrates in dealing with Qing law and wrote commercially available and privately disseminated handbooks both for official use and to help the literate elite.[19] Almanacs explained the essentials of imperial law to readers. Court case dramas and ballads made laws accessible and entertaining for their audiences.[20] And starting in the late nineteenth century, commercial newspapers interpreted legal developments and important court cases for their readers.

After the founding of the Republic, its flourishing world of newspapers, magazines, political pamphlets, and other media picked up on the calls of political reformers and newly minted legal professionals to use laws to serve the republic and its citizens. Many reformers had trained in China's new legal colleges or in institutions abroad in Japan, Europe, and the United States, and now debated how to modernize the country with the help of law.[21] Print media also readily provided readers with some of the legal information necessary for dealing with situations that arose in daily life, including updates about the Family Law, Criminal Code, and laws relating to commercial businesses. In the meantime, increasingly sensational court cases kept journalists busy as they penned titillating reports one after another, vying with each other to be the first to bring the newest stories about litigants, prosecutors, and victims to their readers' doorsteps. Readers hoping to hear the latest developments eagerly awaited the next newspaper or magazine issue.[22]

Over time, legal knowledge became, Chen and Zelin have argued, "an epistemological field whose modes of production, transmission, and contestation shape what constitutes law and justice and how the state is legitimized or imagined."[23] As state authorities sought homogeneity in the dissemination of laws, generations of people staked claims and understood laws and legal vocabulary in innumerable ways. These diverse interpretations could align or conflict with state norms, but they were—in some form or another—continuously connected.

## Law and the Socialist State

Though building on these historical legacies, PRC government campaigns to disseminate laws in the decade after 1949 were unprecedented in Chinese history, and they were exceptional even in the global history of twentieth-century civic education. Three aspects in particular distinguish law dissemination under the CCP from earlier efforts. First, party authorities insisted that learning about laws was a matter of class consciousness. Because laws were presented as an expression of the will of the People,[24] materialized with the help of the CCP, people were expected to embrace laws emotionally and to support and uphold the party-state that had helped create the laws. The CCP believed that class status (*jieji chengfen*) determined consciousness, and it followed that people with the correct consciousness would automatically welcome and embrace the new laws. Second, the party-state drastically expanded the simplification of laws and legal language. Laws were written to be read widely and to be flexible, even if that made their application in practice much more complicated. Third, the new regime decided to combine law dissemination with techniques of mass education and mass mobilization.

This does not mean that the CCP leadership had firm plans to disseminate laws more systematically and to mobilize the "revolutionary masses" to study laws when they assumed national control. While the dissemination of laws was part of mass education, the evidence does not suggest that the leadership had planned to organize mass campaigns to mobilize people for legal learning. Within three years of assuming national power, however, the central government decided to carry out a national mass campaign to study the 1950 Marriage Law, involving the population in legal learning for a defined period of time. That the central government became so active in teaching its people about laws was the result of a historical process in which the CCP's ideals of how to disseminate and redistribute legal knowledge and transform people's consciousness through laws clashed with the much more complicated realities of how to execute this dissemination of knowledge.

In order to trace this process, we need to connect it to the dilemmas the CCP faced upon assuming the reins of national governance.[25] Not only had the new government inherited the legacies of legal knowledge dissemination from its Republican and imperial predecessors, it also faced the daunting challenge of governing a population with diverse opinions on what laws were, what they meant, how they operated, and how the state should be involved.[26] Preferring not to engage with these diverse opinions and seeking a definitive break between life in "pre-liberation" China and life in "post-liberation" China, the CCP and the government proclaimed that it would form a "new society" on the basis of new laws and a new legal regime. Newspapers and educational materials presented the "Great Laws" as especially relevant to China's population because they would enable the broad masses to construct their new society. To learn them was to become trained in wielding a "weapon" the CCP had forged.

Adapted from the Soviet Union and from Lenin's writings on laws, the common practice of referring to laws as instruments and "weapons" during the 1950s linked laws to the "people's democratic dictatorship" (*renmin minzhu zhuanzheng*), the CCP's official mode of governance.[27] According to popular explanations of the people's democratic dictatorship, members of the People would be led democratically under the leadership of the CCP. Those labeled as reactionaries, counterrevolutionaries, enemies of the state, and others who were not part of the People would be controlled by dictatorial means. Discussions in newspapers and magazines about laws during the 1950s kept on emphasizing that laws were weapons of the ruling classes, which were now to be the People and the worker-peasant alliance. "Old" and "bourgeois" laws reflected the bourgeois political order and were to be replaced with "new," "New Democratic" (*xin minzhu zhuyi de*), and eventually "socialist" laws reflecting the people's democratic dictatorship. As weapons of the people's democracy, laws would help the People understand what behavior was legal and illegal. As weapons of the people's dictatorship over those who were not part of the People, laws would control crime and punish criminals.[28]

Law dissemination was thus designed to help clarify the link between state authority and society. It would help people understand that the new state guaranteed their legal rights but expected them to fulfill their legal duties. Education in laws promised liberation, and yet it also incited fear of legal retribution. This dichotomy between laws as empowering and constraining was central to the way laws were taught and legitimized. Propaganda presented legal learning for the People as a positive way of becoming a good citizen. Those who were not part of the People might better themselves through learning laws under state supervision.[29] Revolutionary justice, meanwhile, kindled fear. Local officials were encouraged and required to stage public trials and mass accusation meetings (*kongsu hui*). Members of the public were involved in trials, making denunciations, or as part of the observing masses. People learned about laws by participation.[30] Public trials showcased state authorities' power to unleash violence and mete out punishments. They illustrated what would happen to those who had "violated the law" (*weifa*). Tribunals, courts, prisons, and camps, and the men and women working in them, were the public—and sometimes not so public—face of criminal justice and political terror, especially during the first years of national Communist rule as the regime sought to stamp out revolutionary violence with the approval of an evolving, though still rudimentary, jurisprudence of terror. Hasty arrests, interrogations, mass trials, accusation sessions, public verdicts and executions were not divorced from law. The CCP presented them as manifestations of a decisive, efficient, swift judicial system that was in close touch with those whom it claimed to serve.[31]

## The Difference a Law Makes

To chart the development of law propaganda as a technique of CCP governance and to explain why people responded to it in different ways, I examine how the Marriage Law and state constitutions were disseminated over time, paying attention also to the popularization of the Regulations for the Punishment of Counterrevolutionaries and the Election Law. I illustrate how state attempts to find ideal ways to disseminate all laws regularly conflicted with the messiness of implementing each law. Particularly in the case of the early PRC, my analytical approach departs from studying how a law facilitated or hindered specific kinds of social and political change. This aspect of PRC history has been well covered. Scholars, for instance, have shown how the Marriage Law affected marriage customs, family and marital structures, and divorce patterns.[32] The Agrarian Reform Law has become part of the history of land reform and the reorganization of land ownership.[33] The Regulations of the People's Republic of China for the Punishment of Counterrevolutionaries are embedded in the history of political mobilization against "counterrevolutionaries" because they helped define, if very broadly, who could be labeled a counterrevolutionary and what could be classified as counterrevolutionary actions.[34] The 1953 Election Law has formed the basis for studies of the PRC's first elections and political reform.[35] And accounts of the PRC's first constitution have shed new light on its role in the longue durée of Chinese constitutional history, its impact on elite-level party politics, and the way in which it shaped how elites and ordinary people conceptualized the Chinese state and its revolution.[36]

Connecting these individual laws as part of a larger story of law dissemination suggests that many people experienced legal learning as something different from learning about other types of policies. CCP ideology saw politics, morality, and laws as intertwined. Laws were not above politics—they were an instrument of politics.[37] Public pronouncements about laws, propaganda materials, and group discussions constantly classified behavior as "lawful" (hefa), "unlawful" (bu hefa), or a "violation of law" and thereby established a normative framework for law dissemination and for the application of laws in daily life.[38] This normative framework was tied to and often, though not always, overlapped with moral frameworks of "right" and "wrong," "good" and "bad." Whenever the government called for laws to be disseminated, teaching the population about laws was therefore at once a matter of legal, political, and moral education.[39]

Archival documents and periodicals published for internal circulation demonstrate, however, that many residents, as well as local party cadres and government officials, in Beijing and Shanghai during the 1950s and after were puzzled by the demand to study laws. When residents learned about topics not clearly linked to specific laws—such as public hygiene—they were often unconcerned that making mistakes or refusing to participate would have legal consequences. They might be reprimanded, publicly criticized, or forced to assume extra chores, and many certainly worried about these possibilities. Still, studying laws was something different. When residents studied the Marriage Law, Election Law, or the Regulations for the Punishment of Counterrevolutionaries, many demanded that state officials should punish minor misbehavior with the full force of the law or, conversely, some began to fear that if they contravened these laws—even if accidentally and because they had not really understood what the laws meant—there might be severe legal retribution. The combination of the legal, political, and moral frameworks could provoke intense responses.[40] When, moreover, several residents repeatedly tried asking about the precise meaning of certain articles in the law, seeking some interpretive reassurance, most could not get clear answers from their local cadres, often because cadres could not get clear answers from their superiors.

This is not to say that popular understandings of PRC laws fit neatly into a binary of approval and disapproval. When legal terms and formulations became part of everyday vocabulary, people used this to varying extents to frame their relationships with each other and vis-à-vis state authorities at all levels of state and society.[41] Popular legal learning, moreover, generated a diversity of unofficial interpretations of what laws meant. How people interpreted laws depended on their locality and on their individual identities, which, as Jeremy Brown and Matthew Johnson write, were drawn from their social environments, family circumstances, religious beliefs, and roles in political life.[42] This wide range of legal interpretations shines through in officials' internal reports on how people understood laws throughout the 1950s and after, but also in the pages of internal periodicals such as *Gongan jianshe* (Public security construction) that instructed public security officials on how to deal with people's divergent takes on laws. Such interpretive diversity, however, was a problem for the CCP because it ran counter to its plans for unified and unifying study of selected laws.

## Transforming People through Law Propaganda

China's imperial, Republican, and socialist states all pursued a similar goal: knowledge of laws was supposed to transform people into subjects or citizens who knew that they had to abide by laws. Prior to the 1950s, law dissemination had been guided by the concept of *jiaohua*— transformation through education. *Jiaohua*, as Sarah Schneewind argues, was a governing process that "can be condemned as indoctrination to control the masses, or praised as a way of improving morality and broadening participation in the high-status pursuit of humanistic study and self-cultivation."[43] When Qing and Republican citizens learned something about laws, it was meant to lead to moral improvement and good societal conduct. The CCP expected the same of its citizens, but when it sought to mobilize them in support of a law, it extended and intensified this transformational process by embedding the study of laws within its propaganda system.[44] To disseminate laws to the masses was to conduct "law propaganda"— a complex process of controlled information dissemination and circulation about laws at different levels of Chinese state and society.[45]

If laws are created when they are written, printed, circulated, and otherwise solidified, then the CCP propaganda system did not merely disseminate socialist laws; it contributed to creating them.[46] James Scott's discussion of state-driven simplification provides a useful analytical framework to make sense of this process and why it resulted in unanticipated consequences.[47] High modernist states, as Scott outlines, seek to simplify knowledge transmission in order to make human behavior, social practices, and state-society relations more legible and easier to shape. In China, party and government pushed for a simplification of how laws were made, disseminated, understood, and applied. Already during the drafting process those who wrote the "Great Laws" took care to use legal vocabulary that they thought was simple enough to be accessible to the wider population and flexible in its application. This simplification of legal language then came to serve the dissemination of laws via the propaganda system in at least four ways. First, it could be used as a sign that the CCP had genuinely written a law for the masses. Second, it was supposed to enable party and government officials to use legal terms when they talked to people from diverse educational backgrounds because officials and ordinary citizens alike would have an easier time understanding these terms. Third, simplified terms promised to enable party and government officials to make people's responses and behavior more legible by allowing them to associate certain behavior or thought with legal categories.[48] This legibility would make it easier to structure and supervise people's understanding of laws via the propaganda system. And fourth, simplified legal terms could be better incorporated into the production of diverse law propaganda materials. Terms describing key legal concepts were short and could often be adapted to popular propaganda genres, such as storytelling, cartoons, songs, and opera. Simplification, in short, tied together state and people, law and politics, norms and practice, as well as legal texts and legal interpretations.

The agents of this simplification process were numerous, but propaganda and publishing authorities, as well as cultural workers, stand out because they were key links between state lawmaking and the general population.[49] Propaganda and publishing authorities included officials in the CCP Central Propaganda Department, State General Publishing Administration, Ministry of Culture, provincial and municipal party committee propaganda departments, local bureaus of culture, and news and press offices. These institutions wrote guidelines for law propaganda work, coordinated campaign plans, and surveyed as well as censored propaganda materials. Propaganda departments oversaw the "propaganda network" (*xuanchuanwang*). They also trained grassroots "report-givers" (*baogaoyuan*) and propagandists (*xuanchuanyuan*) who were employed by the state and carried out propaganda work in neighborhoods and work units.[50]

In the specific case of law propaganda, propaganda and publishing officials acted not merely as guardians of words and their meanings, but also as guardians of laws and their meanings. This was a new role—one they could not easily conceptualize at the time. Propaganda work as perception management required officials to promote the circulation of knowledge about party and state, help people understand CCP policies within a larger ideological context, identify incorrect usage and interpretations of official terms and "formulations" (*tifa*) that did not align with party ideology, and prevent the spread of incorrect information about policies and their meanings.[51] During the dissemination of laws, officials thus managed people's perceptions about what socialist laws were, why laws could not be separated from or stand above party and state, and how the individual could make use of laws in a socialist society. As guardians of the correct dissemination of laws and legal knowledge, they also became responsible for spreading what they determined to be correct facts about the laws, helping to explain what laws meant, and identifying wrong legal interpretations. Perception management and the task of explaining laws often overlapped in practice, and this could make it difficult for officials to judge

whether an interpretation of a law was correct. In the process of policing legal meanings, propaganda authorities took on some of the work
of legal authorities.

Cultural workers were the second group of people on whom law
propaganda depended. Publishing and propaganda authorities assigned the complicated task of creating educational materials to publishers, editors, writers, artists, playwrights, cartoonists, and others.
Because their work translated the plain text of any law into stories and
images, cultural workers became instrumental in influencing the way
people understood laws. They joined law and politics together, and
tied the definition of what constituted "lawful" and "unlawful" behavior more closely to moral and political categories of "right" and
"wrong." Propaganda materials gave legal validity to political ideology
because they explained laws within the confines of political ideology.
Stories were written to recount the lawful lives of male and female
models, whereas "bad elements" of society were described as "unlawful." Making use of standard repertoires of Chinese socialist propaganda art, artists who visualized individual legal articles depicted
scenes of the idealized everyday life of model socialist men and women
in the city and the countryside. A book explaining the 1954 constitution might contain illustrations representing citizens' freedom of
speech, press, assembly, association, procession, and demonstration by
showing, for example, a cadre studiously writing in the evening, a
group of people demonstrating for the liberation of Taiwan, men and
women joining the workers' union, or people signing a petition for
world peace (fig. o.1). Such propaganda materials suggested that to live
by the letter of the law was to conform to the pictorial and narrative
utopia of New China.

Transforming people by educating them in simplified laws, however, often did not work as the CCP envisaged. Just as in other examples
of state simplification, the case of law propaganda shows that the attempt to deal with the messiness of people's interpretations of and
opinions about law only led to more messiness and, above all, more
work for state officials.[52] Propaganda authorities spent much time correcting "erroneous" explanations of laws in internal letters and reports,
and in public newspaper and magazine articles. Although this was
their job, hints in the documents suggest that many felt exasperated at

Fig. 0.1 "Article 87" from the booklet *PRC Constitution Propaganda Images*. Article 87 of the 1954 state constitution outlines: "Citizens of the People's Republic of China enjoy freedom of speech, press, assembly, association, procession and demonstration." (Source: Liaoning sheng meishu gongzuo shi, *Zhonghua renmin gongheguo xianfa xuanchuan ce* [PRC constitution propaganda images], Shenyang: Dongbei huabaoshe, 1954, p. 58.)

times, having to intervene more often than expected. Because the CCP's ideological framework only allowed for a limited range of possible responses to the laws, which it had pre-classified as either a "correct" or an "erroneous" understanding, officials often had insufficient means to deal with the scale of individual legal interpretations that the party's own efforts to mobilize people to study laws generated.

The apparent simplicity of PRC legal language also complicated the work of cultural workers. The task of having to popularize laws placed cultural workers and propaganda workers in a difficult and unfamiliar position because it transferred to them parts of the responsibility for explaining laws. Simplicity in legal language allowed for ambiguity of interpretation, and so it often fell to cultural workers to address difficult questions of how laws could be applied in daily life—and these were questions that many a high-level cadre could not answer. Cultural workers made choices about how laws should be explained. Their works informed audiences about the importance of laws and helped to explain the exact relationship between laws and politics. At the same time, censors repeatedly held them responsible for "errors" and "shortcomings," even if these were the result of confusion about what the legal terms truly meant.

If the dissemination of law via the propaganda network was a novel task for propagandists and cultural workers during the 1950s, it was no longer as unfamiliar for those active in the late 1980s. By the 1980s, "law propaganda," a term frequently mentioned in 1950s government documents or reports about the need to popularize laws in order to strengthen the party's thought work, had come to denote a distinct, comprehensive system of mass education. Law propaganda and "legal system education" (*fazhi jiaoyu*) were to help turn people into good, law-abiding socialist citizens. A new official formulation known as the "popularization of common legal knowledge" (*puji falü changshi*— short: *pufa*) paralleled the well-developed framework for the dissemination of scientific knowledge (*kexue puji*—short: *kepu*).[53] The CCP had elevated law popularization to occupy a separate sphere within its propaganda apparatus.

## China in the Late Socialist Legal World

The CCP promoted popular legal learning during the 1950s in order to consolidate its rule. Starting in the late 1970s, law propaganda was resuscitated to serve a similar function—as an instrument to strengthen party-state rule following the official end of the Cultural Revolution (officially dated 1966–76). During the 1980s, the wide dissemination of legal knowledge became essential to party governance. The reason why is best captured in the description of law under a Communist regime written by Czech playwright and later president Vaclav Havel:

> If the exercise of power circulates through the whole power structure as blood flows through veins, then the legal code can be understood as something that reinforces the walls of those veins. Without it, the blood of power could not circulate in an organized way and the body of society would hemorrhage at random. Order would collapse. . . . Like ideology, the legal code is an essential instrument of ritual communication outside

the power structure. It is the legal code that gives the exercise of power a form, a framework, a set of rules. It is the legal code that enables all components of the system to communicate, to put themselves in a good light, to establish their own legitimacy. Without the legal code functioning as a ritually cohesive force, the post-totalitarian system could not exist.[54]

Published in 1978, the same year that the PRC carried out a new national campaign to popularize the new state constitution, Havel insisted that laws and the ritual communication of laws were essential to late socialist and more generally post-totalitarian regimes.

The CCP's return to state legality as of the late 1970s was a wide-ranging project to reinforce the walls of the regime's veins.[55] The story of law propaganda after 1978 therefore needs to be connected with the developments since 1949. During the late 1970s and 1980s several influential Chinese party-state elites (many of whom had already been active in this field during the 1950s) breathed new life into law propaganda as a component of civic education. Mass legal education during the 1980s vastly expanded the techniques of the 1950s. "Legal socialization," as James Seymour calls it, was institutionalized and regularized in schools, work spaces, and learning groups. These became crucial spaces in which citizens were inducted into the state's politico-legal culture.[56] Laws were now hailed as "scientific" means to order society and to help individuals better themselves to become good, productive, and law-abiding socialist citizens who had broken with the chaotic legacy of the Cultural Revolution. Chinese publications explaining law propaganda spoke of the need to social-engineer China's population.[57]

The PRC was not the only socialist country to rely on law propaganda, and the case of post-Mao law propaganda suggests new perspectives on the history of law in late socialism internationally. Notwithstanding the PRC government's minimal diplomatic relations with most socialist governments until the mid-1980s, its renewed endorsement of law propaganda also marked it as a late socialist state that shared commonalities with the Soviet Union and many socialist states in Eastern Europe. The Chinese state during the 1950s had pioneered mass mobilization for legal learning that went beyond Soviet practices of disseminating and discussing laws. Starting in the late 1960s, however, the Soviet Union and Eastern European regimes, notably the German

Democratic Republic (GDR), Poland, and Hungary, also called on their citizens to abide by and study laws more intensely than in past decades.[58] Most socialist regimes had come to see in law propaganda an essential instrument of socialist law and state-making. They also used it in late Cold War rhetoric to show that socialist legal systems were superior to liberal-democratic systems because they made legal knowledge accessible and available to everyone.

This "legal turn" of socialism reflected an international arena in which legal paradigms and the language of law were some of the dominant principles structuring national and transnational politics, even if only at the surface level.[59] By comparing the practices of law propaganda in China during the 1970s and 1980s with developments in other socialist countries, this book shows how the CCP became part of a socialist legal world that allowed it to forge a new narrative for one-party rule in an era when laws had become a global barometer to determine the legitimacy of any state.

Yet the history of law dissemination in China also provides an important corrective to the narrative of laws in the socialist world. In common with other regimes, the Chinese government had, as William Alford writes, "through its law provided a legal, moral, and political vocabulary with which those who wish to take it to task might articulate their concerns."[60] Unlike in China, most of the Communist countries that advocated and practiced law propaganda, including the Soviet Union, Poland, and the GDR, collapsed after 1989 when citizens took to the streets calling for their governments to honor the legal rights guaranteed to them on paper. Evaluating the fall of European socialist regimes, Willibald Steinmetz writes that "the linguistic routines which were meant to re-stabilize the ruling parties in the end contributed to destabilizing the regime."[61] In China, meanwhile, the linguistic routines of law propaganda led some people to believe in the efficacy and superiority of socialist law, some to doubt it or use it to challenge the state, and others to simply not care. Local state authorities used law propaganda efficiently in the aftermath of popular protests in China in 1989 to reinstate "order," thus complicating any analytical link between legal knowledge and popular desires for political reform. That the PRC government quelled the protests by force certainly determined historical developments and the influence of many other factors

is open for debate. But the fact that socialist regimes shared law propaganda techniques in common, were all confronted with protesters'
law-based claims, and yet developed in different ways is a reminder
that gaining knowledge of laws could have a range of outcomes.[62]
Many of these outcomes, as this book shows, do not find a comfortable
place on the axis of regime stability versus instability.[63]

## A Puzzle and Its Pieces

In 1978 Jerome Cohen wrote, "One of the major unresolved puzzles of
Chinese constitutionalism is to ascertain why these freedoms continue
to be asserted when to do so flies in the face of the everyday experience
of Chinese people." He concluded that for party leaders no risk was "as
great as the risk of immediate embarrassment that would be created by
failing to reassert the freedoms in question."[64] I argue that the wide
dissemination of laws, including the assertions of certain rights and
freedoms, has been intricately bound up with the CCP's use of laws as
an instrument of party-state governance at different times since 1949.

The three parts of this book highlight different facets of how learning laws became, by the mid-1980s, the task of every Chinese socialist
citizen, and ask what that meant in practice. The focus is on law propaganda in the municipalities of Beijing and Shanghai. While I consider examples of law propaganda work in other cities, these are not
examined systematically throughout the chapters. In the larger picture, Beijing and Shanghai are exceptional case studies and are not
representative of one Chinese urban experience of law dissemination—
not least because life in many of their outer districts would be better
described as rural than urban. The two cities spearheaded many of the
key legal developments of the twentieth century.[65] Beijing was the
center of state lawmaking. Shanghai was later one of the first cities to
have active bar associations and higher educational institutions for
legal learning. I have chosen to focus on the two cities because both
Beijing and Shanghai were centers of cultural production, especially
print publishing. Given this existing infrastructure, they became
centers of law propaganda production, with many of the internal discussions about print publishing and good law dissemination focusing

on the two cities. Finally, documents consulted for this study suggest
that urban law implementation during the 1950s was one of the major
contexts in which party-state authorities closely considered the problem of how to guide people's knowledge of laws.

The book draws from a range of sources produced by different
state agents and institutions. State archival documents—including
campaign reports, meeting records, propaganda plans, situation briefings, publication lists, and censors' notes—illustrate the workings and
discussions of local governments, party propaganda departments, bureaus of culture, news and publishing offices, and other local party and
government institutions as they tried to figure out what law propaganda was and how it should be conducted. Documentary volumes on
propaganda and publishing work, many issued during the 1990s, give
details about the discussions and decisions of national-level authorities, such as the Central Propaganda Department and the General
Publishing Administration, as they tried to steer the dissemination of
laws. Periodicals marked for only internal (*neibu*) circulation and reference are the third type of source used.[66] They include publications
issued by the Central Propaganda Department such as *Xuanchuan
tongxun* (Propaganda bulletin) during the 1950s and *Xuanchuan dongtai* (Propaganda trends), during the late 1970s and 1980s. These were
meant to inform party cadres working in the "propaganda system" of
how to conduct their work and which mistakes to avoid. *Neibu cankao*,
meanwhile, kept the central leadership updated with candid details
about anything that Xinhua reporters decided were mistakes made
by people, especially by local party and government officials. These
reports recorded the mood of the country, focusing predominantly on
what was not working.[67] They are read against a range of public newspapers and magazines, how-to guides for the local propagandist and
cadre, as well as propaganda works—from illustrated booklets explaining laws to opera and theater scripts, and from novels and short stories
to cartoon magazines and propaganda posters.

Because I focus on the discussions and work of state agents as they
tried to conceptualize and then carry out law propaganda, most of these
sources reveal the perspective of "the state" at different levels. Even the
reports about people's responses to legal learning were selected and

then recorded by state officials. Taken together, however, they make a compelling case for looking again at the political, institutional, and cultural history of law and propaganda as part of the history of the Chinese state at all levels.

The book's chapters discuss important moments in the politics of law under CCP rule, seen through the lens of propaganda and cultural work. Part 1 examines the challenges the young CCP regime faced when it tried to lay the ideological and practical foundations for law propaganda work at the national level between 1949 and 1954. How to deal with the dissemination of legal knowledge was, as party and government soon realized, a complicated question because laws did not fit neatly into any existing categories of the CCP's pre-1949 education and propaganda systems. Chapter 1 explores the ideas, discussions, and decisions at the national level that resulted in a more active dissemination of law and promotion of mass legal learning. Few of the people who were placed in charge of this propaganda work—publishing authorities, publishers, censors, and cultural workers—were ready to assume this responsibility. Yet the dissemination of legal knowledge relied extensively on published materials. Written and published texts were the authoritative source for many local officials who used them as a basis for their work. Chapter 2 traces some of the difficulties of setting up print propaganda for legal learning. Diversity in legal interpretations, I argue, was not merely the result of people's individualized understandings of law but also of the mechanics of a publishing industry that was not fully under state control.

Part 2 uses the case studies of the 1953 Marriage Law campaign and the 1954 constitution draft discussion to illustrate how law propaganda was carried out in Beijing and Shanghai. These were important moments during which techniques for law propaganda were developed and tested. Local governments then continued to use many of these techniques during the late 1950s and 1960s. Focusing on two famous national events in the country's largest cities means working along what Gail Hershatter has termed "campaign time" and campaign space.[68] I pay less attention to the social effects of the campaign and, in the case of law propaganda, also focus less on the more regularized day-to-day work of judicial workers as they responded to residents' personal legal queries outside of the "campaign moment." The two chapters position the national drives to study laws as moments during which propaganda officials, cultural workers, and others focused more intensely on legal learning, and this gives crucial insights into the rationale of law propaganda. The context of the campaign also brought to the surface some of the paradoxes and problems inherent to mass legal learning. At times, to be sure, these could be exaggerated. Censors, for example, were more alert during these weeks and months. Still, the campaigns helped define law propaganda as a field of cultural production and propaganda work.

As laws became largely absent from official discourse during the 1960s and early 1970s, so did mass legal learning. Part 3 of this study shows how and why law propaganda developed once again into a technique of socialist governance by the mid-1980s. As chapter 5 outlines, this development had its early origins in 1970 when a new state constitution draft was publicly discussed. This 1970 discussion, though quickly aborted together with the draft and almost erased from official historiography, was not erased from many people's memories, and was the first of four national constitution discussions transcending the 1978 divide into 1982. Chapter 6 examines the post-Mao high tide of law propaganda, known as the first five-year plan for the "popularization of common legal knowledge." By that point, the central government's continuous attempts to control the dissemination of legal knowledge had led it to advocate for a long-term plan that allowed for a better institutionalization of law dissemination and for more structured control of how legal knowledge was spread and by whom. The plan was not the beginning of a new type of law dissemination: it represented the continuation and institutionalization of a long-standing practice.

The seventh five-year plan for the popularization of legal knowledge was rolled out in 2016. If we take a bird's eye view of the more than sixty-five years of CCP rule, then law propaganda has been part of people's lives for much of this time. For this reason alone, the popularization of law deserves to be featured more prominently in writings on the history of the PRC. Tracing law dissemination across several decades illustrates how the CCP conceptualized and implemented laws. It highlights the role of popular legal learning as well as propaganda and education about laws in the party-state's overarching vision of transformational governance. It also reveals deep-seated paradoxes in the socialist claim of making laws more accessible than other non-socialist regimes. The legal lessons learned by state authorities and citizens cut both ways, and their history offers fresh perspectives on how the CCP dealt with questions of knowledge simplification and redistribution when it tried to use laws to govern.

# PART I

## PREPARATIONS: 1949–1954

# 1     No Legalese, Please

## Why the Dissemination of Laws Became a Problem

I n the months before and after the establishment of the People's Re- public of China on 1 October 1949, the CCP leadership moved quickly to break with the country's legal past and replace the "old" system with a "new" one. The CCP's official view of the legal system it had inherited was simple: because laws were always an instrument of the "ruling class," it followed that they had been an instrument of oppression before "liberation." Pre-liberation laws were complicated to read and inaccessible to people. Moreover, an elite group of legal experts com- manded specialized knowledge of a thick bulwark of laws, regulations, legal interpretations, and procedural norms, and "the masses" of ordi- nary people were told only to obey these laws. In "New China," by contrast, the CCP and the central government announced that they would help make laws into a "weapon" wielded by the masses. New laws would have to be accessible to the ordinary citizen, without the need for legal professionals to mediate.

This transformation was easy to proclaim but difficult to accom- plish. On paper, "old" laws were swiftly abolished. In February 1949, the "Directive on Abrogating the Book of Six Codes of the Guomin- dang and on Fixing the Judicial Principles of the Liberated Areas" made—at least in rhetoric—a clean break with any Nationalist legal leg- acies.[1] Party leaders explained that this was a crucial step that paved the way toward a legal system focused on protecting the People rather than on maintaining bourgeois privilege. In September 1949, Arti- cle 17 of the new Common Program of the Chinese People's Political

Consultative Conference reiterated this break: "All laws, decrees, and judicial systems of the Guomindang reactionary government that oppress the people shall be abolished. Laws and decrees protecting the people's judicial system shall be established."[2] It took the central government much more time, though, to decide on the details. The men and women charged with developing a new legal system for the young People's Republic busily drew up plans for a legal framework suited to a people's democratic dictatorship in the stage of New Democracy (*xin minzhu zhuyi*).[3] Next to major foundational laws, including the Common Program, the Organic Laws, the Marriage Law, the Agrarian Reform Law, and the Trade Union Law, the various committees with oversight of legal matters spent the first years after 1949 drafting a myriad of regulations, guidelines, temporary procedures, and directives to govern the country. In practice, the break with the past was much less clear-cut.[4]

In particular, the claims that "Great Laws" would be accessible to the people and would serve as a "weapon of the masses" complicated the government's work. What exactly would the dissemination of these laws involve, and how would people know how to use this weapon correctly? Party-state magazines discussed these questions with growing urgency in the years after 1949. Disseminating laws was not like the other kinds of knowledge dissemination work that the CCP had carried out over the years. The study of political theory and the popularization of scientific knowledge, for example, were much better established. Already during the early 1950s, as Sigrid Schmalzer writes, "science dissemination crystallized into a clear position that was well articulated, given a specific name (and even a well-known abbreviation), and provided with specific organizations to carry out its mission."[5] This was not so in the case of law dissemination, which seemed to operate on makeshift techniques and solutions that produced many unanticipated results.

Finding a place for the dissemination of laws in the wider repertoire of CCP governance was a difficult task for the government. Laws had to be accommodated in the CCP's policies that were, in turn, based on the ideological framework of the Marxist-Leninist canon and Mao Zedong Thought. Yet the canonical writings had comparatively little to say about laws.[6] Another hurdle was that the work of law dissemination had to be carried out by government and party officials across the country, many of whom were unfamiliar with or uninterested in teaching laws. Each law that the central government decided should be taught, moreover, posed a different challenge, as officials soon discovered. The Agrarian Reform Law and the Regulations of the People's Republic of China for the Punishment of Counterrevolutionaries could not be taught in the same way as the Marriage Law. More refined approaches were needed. The process by which the party and the central government came to recognize and deal with these challenges is the subject of this chapter. It is a story told in fragments because there was no single causal chain of events and decisions that led to a master plan for the popularization of legal knowledge. Yet by 1954, when the party and government involved much of China's urban population in a national discussion of the new constitution draft, law dissemination had become part of the repertoire of Chinese socialist governance.

## The Politics of Access: Common Legal Knowledge before "Liberation"

Though unacknowledged, the central government based its plans for the dissemination of laws on Republican blueprints for civic education. During the Republican period, politicians, intellectuals, and legal experts had promoted the need for people to know and understand laws.[7] In the areas under their control, both the CCP and the GMD regularly propagated new laws and regulations, to varying degrees and with varying effects. Both parties looked to Sun Yatsen, who had advocated a period of "tutelage" during which the revolutionary government would help people raise their civic consciousness prior to the transition to constitutional government.[8] The overarching message was that citizens of Republican China had the right to benefit from and the duty to abide by the laws of their country. Treatises written by well-known intellectuals amplified this message, and textbooks repeated it for students of all ages.[9]

Beyond the space of the classroom and the pages of schoolbooks, the business of printing legal knowledge for everyday use was lucrative. During the 1920s and 1930s, a busy and mostly commercial publishing sector in Shanghai and Beijing made significant investments in the production of popular guidebooks that explained everything from criminal to civil law, family law, and any aspect of law considered relevant to the newly minted citizens' lives. Starting in the late 1910s, customers could pick up *ABC* guides that advised readers about what they had to know in order to file a lawsuit and make use of Republican laws. These manuals advised how the judicial process worked and also explained the language of the law.[10] By the late 1920s and early 1930s, with new civil and criminal legislation in place, urban residents were offered even more *ABC* and "how to" guides that promised to help them navigate an increasingly difficult landscape of different legal institutions and, in the case of Shanghai, different legal jurisdictions.[11]

In all of these materials, authors reminded their readers to strive to acquire "common knowledge" (*changshi*) of the law. Common knowledge did not mean that people should have a comprehensive understanding of all laws; it meant having a basic understanding of the most important legal norms pertinent to daily life, orderly conduct, and citizenship. It often also included useful bits of information to help readers secure their interests in an increasingly complex legal world. Some of the publications written by politicians, legal experts, and others debated the best approach to disseminating common legal knowledge. That legal knowledge should be democratized in some way was a point of consensus across most publications, yet the politically and ideologically charged question was how and to what extent.[12]

Writing on this question in the 1930s, Li Yizhen identified two different approaches to law in his book *Marriage Law and Marriage Problems*. Broadly speaking, one approach held that law should serve everyone but should be administered by a group of trained legal professionals. Li thought that this approach would probably ensure that laws would benefit those who had access to professional legal help. The other approach posited that if laws and knowledge of laws were widely popularized, then everyone would benefit. To achieve this, writings about law would have to be truly "popular" (*tongsu*) and intelligible to readers who had no legal training or advanced education. Li did not seem very hopeful that this could be achieved, though. In his opinion, most legal professionals and politicians disdained writing popular tracts. And those authors who did write accessible works often did not know enough about laws, were too opinionated, or made too many obvious mistakes. An inclusive approach to legal learning seemed to have few advocates and even fewer helpers.[13]

The GMD government focused mostly on implementing the first approach Li had outlined. It pursued the path of legal professionalization by adapting the format of German and Swiss civil codes, and modeling formal legal education on Japanese, US, German, and other foreign legal models. The Nationalist government advocated and slowly put in place a structure in which legal professionals would mediate and navigate the law on behalf of citizens.[14] This was not to happen outside the realm of politics, however. Starting in the late 1920s, legal professionals were expected to align closely with the GMD; a process labeled the "partification" (*danghua*) of law.[15] In an ideal scenario, then, through legal professionals, the government and party would be able to structure and influence legal processes and how people understood the law. Similar to later CCP ideas, Nationalist citizens would be given access to legal knowledge in order to make it easier for them to abide by these laws and use them in an orderly manner under the supervision of legal professionals.[16]

In the Communist-controlled areas, by contrast, the CCP's policies mirrored the second approach Li had outlined, of more popular inclusion and less professional control of legal knowledge. CCP jurists experimented with methods of adjudication that included the so-called masses. Many championed "Ma Xiwu's Way of Judging," a combination of community-based mediation and adjudication in which local officials worked in close cooperation with local residents to assemble the facts of a dispute and then find an equitable solution. Ma Xiwu's Way was, as Xiaoping Cong writes, "a system that tried not to create antagonism in communities and to build on the broad participation and consensus of the masses, while ultimately achieving justice."[17] In the case of legislation, those writing in the late 1940s the drafts of what would become the PRC's first laws operated on the assumption that accessible legal knowledge required accessible laws. This meant that laws would have to be written not merely with an eye to legal process and validity but with a general readership in mind.

The drafting of the 1950 Marriage Law is one example of a process that put this approach into practice. In late 1948, a group of prominent women, most of whom had no formal legal training, gathered to draft this law. The group included Deng Yingchao (1904–92), a prominent women's rights activist who was also Zhou Enlai's wife; Yang Zhihua (1900–1973), a feminist veteran of the May Fourth Movement who would become a leading figure in the All-China Women's Federation after 1949; Wang Ruqi (1912–90), a Fudan University Law School graduate soon to be one of the PRC's foremost women legal experts; and Luo Qiong (1911–2006), editor-in-chief of the CCP's magazine *Zhongguo funü* (Women of China).[18] Feminist and Republican ideas of knowledge democratization and constitutionalism inspired and drove their work.[19] During the writing process, Wang Ruqi, the only group member with legal training, put the group's ideas into writing. Together, the group ensured that the law's language was as simple as possible.[20] Under their pen, phrases that had until then not been part of official legal language—such as "buy and sell marriages" (*maimai hunyin*)— became legal terms.[21] Yet linguistic simplification, as the group members later stated, was only the first step; the larger question was how to make this language and the ideas it embodied fit into the ideological framework of New China.

## In Theory: Finding a Place for Laws in Ideology

Having gained experience working in the CCP base areas and elsewhere, many trained jurists and party officials working in legal affairs knew that it would be difficult to explain the meaning of both freedoms and duties, enshrined in laws, to the newly minted citizens of the People's Republic.[22] Beyond the elite world of formal law and revolutionary jurisprudence, any major law the central government passed had to be explained within the ideological parameters on which the People's Republic was founded. This included the people's democratic dictatorship, the mass line, and categories of the People and class. As it turned out, it was not always easy to accommodate laws within these parameters.

On paper, the new state expected everyone to abide by laws. Article 8 of the Common Program stipulated, "It is the duty of every national (*guomin*) of the People's Republic of China to defend the fatherland, to abide by the law, to observe labor discipline."[23] The CCP legitimized the implementation and enforcement of PRC laws, however, on the basis of the people's democratic dictatorship. Read in the context of the political framework of the people's democratic dictatorship, everyone may have been a national but not all nationals were the same; they were divided into the People and non-People. The People broadly encompassed peasants, workers, intellectuals, the poor, the urban petty bourgeoisie, and the national bourgeoisie. The landlord classes, bureaucrat-bourgeoisie, the "running dogs of imperialism," and GMD reactionaries were not part of the People. This distinction between People and non-People was central to explaining how laws should work and how party and government would police who abided by laws and who did not. Party officials saw laws primarily as instruments to punish violations committed by non-People. They were supported in this view by Mao who, at the second session of the first National Committee of the Chinese People's Political Consultative Conference in June 1950, made clear that laws were something that non-People should be forced to abide by under the people's democratic dictatorship.[24] Non-People needed to know the laws because, by default of their class status, they were most in danger of breaking laws.

This does not mean that punishment under the law was restricted to non-People. Laws would also punish members of the People, but, as Mao Zedong explained in June 1949, only in selected cases when "anyone among the People" had broken the law. The theoretical assumption was that few members of the People would ever break the law:

> The people's state protects the people. Only when the people have such a state can they educate and remold themselves by democratic methods on a country-wide scale. . . . Here, the method we employ is democratic, the method of persuasion, not of compulsion. When anyone among the people breaks the law, he too should be punished, imprisoned or even sentenced to death; but this is a matter of a few individual cases, and it differs in principle from the dictatorship exercised over the reactionaries as a class.[25]

The 1949 Common Program may have therefore required all "nationals," which included People and non-People, to abide by laws, yet Mao's words made clear that the law's focus at that moment was on non-People.[26] They might eventually, with the help of state-led reform through education and work, rehabilitate themselves. But the education of non-People, including instructing them in the laws by which they should abide, would not be the same as the democratic methods of education and learning to which the People would be led.

In speeches and writings, other party leaders and intellectuals at the time also stressed the role of laws as the expression of the ruling classes' will and an instrument of punishment. Peng Zhen (1902–97) was one of the individuals most instrumental in crafting the attack on counterrevolutionaries in 1950 and 1951. He envisioned laws, as Pitman Potter writes, as a "statement" of political and ideological goals. The CCP saw these goals as representative of "public interest." Laws, by extension, became an "organizational framework for carrying them [the goals] out." Peng, too, used the Leninist language of laws as weapons of the People as the new ruling classes.[27] A piece on the history of Chinese law and jurisprudence written by Yang Shaoxuan for the magazine *Xin jianshe* (New construction), meanwhile, argued that New Democratic laws could be used to educate people who had committed crimes, helping them to reform their ways.[28] And early 1950s popular dictionaries such as the *Newspaper Readers' Dictionary* explained that "laws are a manifestation of the will of the ruling classes, and the ruling classes also use laws to make the ruled classes follow their will."[29]

If writings on laws explained clearly how non-People should engage with laws, they were less clear about how much legal education members of the People required and how they should be educated. That the People had to be educated in laws in some way followed from the policy of the mass line outlined by Mao in 1943:

All the practical work of our Party, all correct leadership is necessarily "from the masses, to the masses." This means take the ideas of the masses (scattered and unsystematic ideas) and concentrate them (through study turn them into concentrated and systematic ideas), then go to the masses and propagate and explain these ideas until the masses embrace them as their own, hold fast to them and translate them into action, and test the correctness of these ideas in such action. . . . And so on, over and over again in an endless spiral, with the ideas becoming more correct, more vital and richer each time. Such is the Marxist theory of knowledge.[30]

As expressions of the will of the People, the CCP's laws were seen as products of the mass line. They were the People's ideas, needs, and desires synthesized into legal form. Wang Feiran, president of the Beijing People's Municipal Court, affirmed this in April 1950 when he explained to audiences in a broadcast of the Central People's Broadcasting Station that the Marriage Law was the first law to take the mass line as its "legislative principle" (*lifa fangfa*).[31] It followed from Mao's conception of the mass line that the masses would have to study these laws, but by default of their "good" class status they would naturally be more inclined to "embrace them as their own." In the pages of CCP theoretical writings, the People would voluntarily cultivate themselves through study and learning, including learning about laws.[32]

Such was the ideological basis of laws and law dissemination. Although the CCP expected everyone to learn and know laws, it emphasized the education of non-People. It also emphasized laws as an instrument of punishment and control. Within less than two years, the CCP realized that both emphases were problematic for several reasons. The distinction between the People and non-People was messy in practice, making it less clear who actually needed what kind of legal education. Many people, moreover, did not understand that not all laws were about punishment, and this was a problem for implementing those parts of the law that were meant to regulate, not punish, socialist society. And irrespective of class status, most people were not naturally inclined to want to learn laws. Members of the People, officials soon discovered, would need to be told how to study laws in order to understand how to "translate them into action" in accordance with the mass line.

## Law, Punishment, and Mass Campaigns

The CCP's focus on laws as punishment in theoretical writings and party discussions translated into the way many residents of Beijing and Shanghai experienced laws during the first three years of CCP rule.

Laws were instruments of punishment, and they went hand-in-hand with mass campaigns. Between 1950 and 1953, the CCP carried out fervent mass mobilization campaigns targeting enemies of the people, including anyone labeled a landlord, counterrevolutionary, reactionary, or *tewu* (which included spies and Guomindang special agents).[33] During mass campaigns, public trials and mass accusation sessions (*kongsu hui*) became important sites of mass mobilization and a crucial channel to disseminate schematic knowledge of laws. Beyond the physical spaces of trials and struggle sessions, party and government bureaus worked to turn trials and verdicts into propaganda materials for wider circulation. The propaganda bureau of the national Ministry of Justice coordinated with state newspapers and magazines to draft articles that described trial proceedings, and verdicts were published in local and national newspapers. Trial reports detailed the crimes committed and the choreography of trial proceedings. To ensure that verdicts were accessible to the masses, *Renmin ribao* (People's daily) regularly evaluated verdicts. Articles sometimes publicly admonished judges to write in a more accessible style and to make their verdicts easier to understand for a broad readership. At the municipal level, people's courts set up propaganda and education sections (*xuanjiaoke*) that compiled documents, took photographs of trials, and supplied informational materials to newspapers and broadcasting stations.[34] Authorities considered such materials vital because trials and mass accusation sessions illustrated vividly what would happen to those who dared to break the law.

In no uncertain terms, propaganda materials told their audiences that the new government would punish any violations of its laws and regulations.[35] Explaining the language of official publications, popular dictionaries such as the pocket-sized *People's Study Dictionary* explained to their largely urban readership that laws such as the Agrarian Reform Law and the Regulations for the Punishment of Counterrevolutionaries were "laws to protect the people's interests; anyone who violates the people's interests will receive the punishment of the law."[36] Behavior that violated the law could be broadly defined, and might include any behavior past or present that officials thought contravened the schematic and ambiguous stipulations of laws and regulations—from counterrevolutionary acts to rape, petty crimes, or illicit sexual relations.[37] At the grassroots level, local police and public security officials became important guardians of laws and arbiters deciding what was and what was not a violation of law. They registered people's class status and gathered information about how mass campaigns were progressing locally and how people were responding to new policies, laws, and regulations.[38] They also dealt with many everyday disputes and they apprehended and punished so-called enemies of the People.[39]

Across the country, people experienced the process of identifying and punishing violations of law in different ways. Rural residents witnessed revolutionary justice in the context of land reform and implementation of the 1950 Agrarian Reform Law. Having designated—sometimes with great difficulty—certain individuals as "landlords," "bandits," or "local tyrants," local activists, work teams, and cadres carried out mass accusation sessions, denunciation meetings, and public trials.[40] "Speaking bitterness" (suku), people shared stories of their past hardships, of being wronged and oppressed by the accused.[41] In the urban districts of Shanghai and Beijing, residents witnessed or were implicated in the Campaign to Suppress Counterrevolutionaries between late 1950 and 1951.[42] During this campaign, the CCP expected everyone to help find counterrevolutionaries and bring them to justice. Participation was often not voluntary, as some local officials measured residents' allegiance to the new regime by their enthusiasm for the campaign.

Public trials and struggle as well as accusation sessions created space for the performance of revolutionary justice, and laws and regulations were essential props to make the performance both effective and legitimate. In the case of the suppression of counterrevolutionaries, the CCP created the legal framework for the campaign in February 1951, several months after the campaign had begun, when it published the Regulations of the People's Republic of China for the Punishment of Counterrevolutionaries that vaguely defined categories of counterrevolutionary crimes.[43] Once published, however, the regulations had an important function both as an idea and a propaganda object. The regulations were printed in newspapers, read out in radio broadcasts, and published as little bound volumes at print runs of hundreds of thousands of copies. By summer 1951, even if they did

Fig. 1.1. "Harm the People and you will not escape the net of law!" 1951. (Source: Private Collection, International Institute of Social History [Amsterdam].)

not know the precise content of the regulations, most residents knew that the regulations existed and one needed to avoid violating them.[44] Posters and cartoons hung up along the streets helped people visualize the link between knowing the regulations and identifying counterrevolutionaries in one's neighborhood. The regulations became a noose with which to trap counterrevolutionaries, a larger-than-life book protecting the People and smashing enemies trying to escape, or a knife to cut through the organic tissue that connected counterrevolutionaries, bandits, reactionary sects, and secret agents to Chiang Kaishek on Taiwan and President Truman in the United States (figs. 1.1, 1.2, and 1.3).

To engage with the regulations was to engage with the campaign. In Beijing, local officials wrote internal reports that recorded how residents read the regulations and how they responded. One report noted that local residents in Beijing were satisfied with the way the state was hunting down enemies on the basis of the regulations.[45] Another described how a worker from a leather factory had told local

Fig. 1.2a-b. (a) De Wei, "Chop It"; and (b) Zhen Hua, "Two Paths for a Counterrevolutionary Element," 1951. (Source: *Manhua yuebao* [Cartoon monthly], no. 13, June 1951, pp. 6 and 23.)

officials, "Of the large numbers executed today, all had been sentenced according to the 'Regulations' and not one has been wronged."[46] One *tewu*, who had already made a confession and had been registered with the authorities, had been "pacing up and down in his home" after reading the regulations, worried that he would be subject to more

Fig. 1.3. Xin Dao, "Illustrated Explanation of Article 2," 1951. (Source: *Zhonghua renmin gongheguo chengzhi fangeming tiaoli: Tujie tongsuben* [Regulations of the PRC for the Punishment of Counterrevolutionaries: Illustrated popular explanations], Shanghai: Huadong renmin chubanshe, 1951, p. 6.)

police action.[47] "Some representatives and activists," another report detailed, "asked the local police station to explain the 'Regulations on the Punishment of Counterrevolution' and to assist them in their studies" in order to be sure that they would not interpret anything wrongly.[48] To hunt counterrevolutionaries was now to follow the law. Laws and regulations had provided a legitimizing canvas for persecutions, arrests, and executions.[49]

With revolutionary justice and the fight against enemies present in the everyday lives of many urban residents, state media also adjusted its coverage of any laws that were less punitive, such as the Marriage Law. Between late 1950 and 1952, implementation and enforcement of the Marriage Law was caught up in this web of volatile political mass campaigns. Connecting what they had learned about the Agrarian Reform Law with its attack on landlords and rich peasants, and the regulations with its attack on counterrevolutionaries, people interpreted the Marriage Law as another law-based attempt by the CCP to forcibly weed out enemies. Husbands who had beaten their wives, mothers-in-law who bullied their daughters-in-law, family members who had forced widows to remarry, and others were accused of having violated the provisions of the Marriage Law. District and local neighborhood committees organized public trials and mass accusation meetings at which daughters-in-law and wives spoke bitterness.[50] In Beijing and Shanghai, in particular, people were told that bourgeois and capitalist lifestyles resulted in violations of the Marriage Law.[51] Meanwhile, in the countryside land reform and the Marriage Law were explained together as core components of the fight against feudalism. Traveling exhibitions about land reform often included a room with educational materials and posters explaining the Marriage Law and recounting trials against offenders.[52] Although that was not the original intent of its creators, the Marriage Law was set in a context that emphasized violent punishment and strict enforcement of the law. And at first, the central government permitted this more aggressive interpretation of the Marriage Law, partly because it served to mobilize women, a core constituency of the socialist revolution.

By late 1952, however, central ministries began to change course in their general approach to the dissemination of all laws. They demanded that government officials, capitalists, and intellectuals study laws more carefully, in particular the Common Program. Study materials for three new campaigns—the Three Antis, the Five Antis, and Thought Reform targeting these three groups—explicitly included the Common Program as a core text.[53] Lead editorials in *Xin jianshe* magazine argued that it was crucial for everyone to study the Common Program as the country's "fundamental law."[54] Intellectuals and capitalists, many of whom were members of other democratic parties as part of the United Front, were told that to study and abide by the Common Program was to show their patriotic allegiance to the CCP and the country.[55] To this effect, for instance, Mao in early September 1952 rewrote a speech drafted by Huang Yanpei for the meeting of the Beijing branch of the China National Construction Association, one of the United Front's democratic parties. Whereas Huang's draft had demanded that capitalists be educated in "working class thought" to help them "reform their thinking," Mao instead called for them to be educated in "patriotic thought and 'Common Program' thinking," urging capitalists to "reform that evil thinking, that thinking that does not harmonize with patriotism and with the Common Program."[56]

## Judicial Reform and the Dissemination of Laws

The CCP's search for a more regularized approach to disseminating legal knowledge thus intensified in the summer of 1952. Work on conceptualizing and drafting the Election Law and state constitution slowly began during this time.[57] The central government and Ministry of Justice also initiated the Judicial Reform Movement to rectify and cleanse the judiciary. At a meeting of Zhou Enlai's (1898–1976) Government Administrative Council on 13 August 1952, Minister of Justice Shi Liang (1900–1985) explained that the judicial field urgently required thought reform and a reform of work processes. She drew a warning picture of "old legal outlooks" rampant across those working in people's courts at all levels, from county and district to municipal and provincial courts.[58] With such "old legal outlooks," she reasoned, laws could not be properly implemented and people's lives and livelihoods were endangered.[59] Old legal outlooks included the notion that law transcended class and politics, as one article in *Xin jianshe* explained, and the belief that the administration of cases was a matter of technical work. Such ideas were considered harmful to socialist justice.[60]

Judicial reform was carried out in several phases: the first phases focused on re-educating clerks, judges, and judicial cadres in municipal, county, and provincial people's courts. The later phase aimed at educating the general population about the legal process under CCP rule and had implications for how laws were disseminated during the movement and thereafter.[61] The different phases promoted talk of learning about laws, studying the Common Program, and reforming one's thoughts through criticism and self-criticism. Judicial reform continued discussions about the importance of accessible laws and the need for ordinary people to be able to engage with laws and legal institutions. It called for a simplification of legal procedures, after the different mass campaigns and the promulgation of the Marriage Law, as the Beijing municipal government wrote, had led to a massive backlog of cases that courts were not dealing with sufficiently swiftly.[62] The public performance of the movement therefore also propagandized the central government's intent to revolutionize the legal system from the roots up and to change how people interacted with laws.[63]

Why knowing and abiding by laws should become part of a socialist person's consciousness and should define what it means to be a member of the People was explained in an article that Xie Juezai, Minister of Internal Affairs, wrote for the magazine *Xin guancha* (New observer). Published in August 1952, and written to support the beginning of judicial reform, Xie's one-page manifesto, "One Should Study Law and Propagate Law," opened with a mention of the foreign accolades PRC laws had recently received. The recent Stalin Prize winner Heriberto Jara, a Mexican revolutionary and general, had publicly stated that the Chinese people had been able to base their plans for construction of the country on the basis of new and reasonable laws that were, Jara emphasized, not merely fair but also implemented immediately. Yet Xie did not present this as cause for celebration. PRC laws, he wrote, may be "praised by people across the world," but at home Chinese people, he thought, still neglected to study laws. Old legal personnel, who were the focus of judicial reform, were an obvious problem for Xie, but his criticism was not only about them. No matter how much they claimed to do so, ordinary officials could not serve the people if they knew little of laws or refused to learn them. Everyone should read important new laws and regulations, and then help teach others. This was particularly important for those offices charged with implementing laws. Xie called for more and better propaganda work. "As long as it [law] is propagated," he wrote, "people will understand and accept it. . . . The words of the law are both simple and clear, workers with little culture will all understand it at their first read. To say that the laws are hard to study, that is the talk of old judicial personnel that deceives people."[64]

Old legal outlooks—thought to be harbored by old legal personnel and those whom they had trained—were a recurring term that could be difficult to decipher. Articles in *Xin jianshe* explained that a revision of legal outlooks would ensure that law was understood as a product and instrument of class struggle. Study of the works of Marx, Lenin, and Mao Zedong, so the magazine asserted, would allow anyone to learn how to distinguish "old" from "new" legal outlooks and to understand how law could truly represent the will of the People.[65] Reports in Xinhua News Agency's *Neibu cankao*, meanwhile, showed how party and government officials made sense of the abstract concept of old and new legal outlooks in concrete terms that were not part of the canonical works. Journalists, for instance, reported that people in the East China region used terms such as the "five shields," the "five nots," the "three not-satisfieds," and the "three softs" to describe old thinking about laws. The "five shields" referred to shielding counterrevolutionaries, bandits, landlords, illegal capitalists, and drug dealers.[66] The "five nots" denoted not understanding, not propagating, not asking, not adjudicating, and not enforcing the law.[67] The "three not-satisfieds" included not being satisfied "with land reform, with the suppression of counterrevolutionaries, and with the Three and Five Antis." The "three softs" described those with a soft tongue, a soft hand, and a soft pen, meaning that they would lie, take bribes, and write verdicts accordingly.[68] Such habits and practices were linked to class consciousness and thus to the crucial factor that, in the eyes of many, distinguished the laws of capitalist countries from those of socialist societies.

In larger cities such as Beijing and Shanghai the movement served the propaganda purpose of drawing a closer connection between the legal field and the people it claimed to serve. People who were accused of harboring particularly egregious old legal outlooks were dismissed from their positions or reassigned.[69] Courts retried selected cases that had been filed following the promulgation of the Marriage Law, during the Campaign to Suppress Counterrevolutionaries, and during the Three Antis and Five Antis. They also retried cases that participants claimed had been mishandled by judges with old legal outlooks.[70] Judges in Beijing's courts were criticized for wrongly assuming that the principle of "everyone is equal before the law" applied and that this might give capitalists a benefit over the masses seeking redress.[71] When judges in question thought that the defendant had been wrongly accused of being a counterrevolutionary and that this was, as one report cited a judge, "wicked and cruel," they handed out lesser sentences.[72] Reports, conversely, interpreted this as inappropriate leniency. In the

North China region, party officials accused several judges of opposing freedom of marriage because they refused to grant people who had filed cases under the Marriage Law their legal rights.[73] Under the report-writers' pens, old legal personnel, much as the pre-liberation society with which they were associated, became a group that the masses needed to scrutinize more closely.

To do so, the Judicial Reform Movement's last phase focused on public engagement and the laws' public accessibility.[74] The CCP argued that there had been an unnecessary distance between the legal and non-legal spheres of society. Judicial reform was meant to reduce this. At the same time, party officials also worried that if they did not carefully propagate what judicial reform was all about, people might direct their anger at the whole of the judicial system and not just at, as the Beijing municipal government called it, a "small number of degenerates."[75] Radio broadcasts and newspaper reports called on everyone to participate and increase what they knew about laws. Officials in Tianjin municipality estimated that for one of their major broadcasts about judicial reform, about 130,000 people listened.[76] In Shanghai, local radio broadcasts included conversations about "Why should we have judicial reform?" These conversations used concrete examples to increase people's understanding of "old legal outlooks" and the work of the judiciary.[77] In Beijing, reports noted that people had approached court cadres and asked them, "Have you undergone judicial reform?" and "There's been judicial reform and it's still like this!"[78] Publicity that accompanied the movement spread the message that "legalese" and unnecessarily convoluted technical terms were unacceptable and that people should be responsible for knowing the necessary basics about law in order to be able to criticize those who maintained old legal outlooks.[79]

If the formal legal system continued to play an important role, the reform stressed that everyone was to be involved in some kind of legal work, even if they only participated as onlookers in public trials or local mediation processes.[80] Cadres leading the movement explained that dealing well with cases and reducing backlogs would reduce the distance between the law and the people, and would improve public engagement. Letters of complaint about local judicial work reinforced the propaganda message that judicial reform was aimed at improving matters for the People. In North China, cities set up "people's reception rooms" and installed letterboxes to allow people to submit written complaints and inform on others. In Beijing municipality, the number of letters received during the two months of the campaign's last phase increased six-fold.[81] Officials consulted with people who felt wronged by recent court verdicts. Beijing's district courts reported that they had met with over 2,800 concerned parties and had received more than 700 pieces of information about mistrials and poor conduct on the part of judges and legal personnel. Those who came forward were praised for their enthusiasm, heroism, and their "willingness to inform on others."[82] Local party offices then used these submissions to conduct internal investigations.

The central government had increased its efforts to disseminate laws as part of judicial reform, and the reform paved the way for a mass campaign to implement the Marriage Law that followed shortly thereafter. Although concluding nationally in spring 1953, judicial reform was completed in Beijing and Shanghai municipalities by the end of 1952. In December 1952, the central government resolved to dedicate the month of March 1953 to the new campaign on the Marriage Law. Divorce cases and other cases related to the Marriage Law were among those that had significantly contributed to the case backlog at local courts. Using the format of the mass campaign to shape what people knew about the Marriage Law, and how they interpreted its provisions, seemed one way to reduce the number of cases filed.

## Hidden Legal Innovators:
## Women Activists and the Marriage Law

If judicial reform called national attention to the need to disseminate laws better, it only served to amplify the voices of women reformers who had for years already belabored this point. The All-China Women's Federation was among the most vocal proponents of legal learning, well before law dissemination became part of a national campaign. Between 1950 and 1952, the federation consistently advocated engagement with the Marriage Law and with other laws related to it.[83] Over time, the federation's insistence that more should be done to implement the Marriage Law, and its members' experiences having popularized knowledge of the law among less-educated and illiterate women, influenced the design of law propaganda.

Concern with legal knowledge was a logical development of the feminist agenda. Women's liberation had historically been closely tied to knowledge of laws. Many of the leading women in the federation were instrumental in the movement for women's suffrage and women's rights before 1949. They included Lei Jieqiong, He Xiangning (1878–1972), Deng Yingchao, Luo Qiong, Wang Ruqi, and Shi Liang, all of whom had either drafted the Marriage Law or would soon sit on the 1953 national committee for the Marriage Law campaign. Shi Liang, as Minister of Justice, was the most visible link between the world of women's affairs and law. But the other women were also placed in high positions across the new government, its mass organizations, universities, and research institutes. Many of them had written and published on constitutional matters, organized conferences on women and the constitution, and advocated legal gender equality.[84] And they continued to do so into the early 1950s.[85]

As Mao, Zhou Enlai, and other party leaders later proclaimed repeatedly, the Marriage Law was different from other laws because it concerned matters among the People as opposed to matters between the people and their enemies. This realization, however, took some time. While the central government instructed local governments to send reporters and propagandists in 1950 and 1951 to spread word about the Regulations for the Punishment of Counterrevolutionaries and the Agrarian Reform Law, the Women's Federation had conducted much of the propaganda work for the Marriage Law in 1950. Despite the central government's repeated public affirmations that the Marriage Law was about everyone, the fact that the federation conducted much of the propaganda work sent a different message, as did some of the government's own statements. On 1 May 1950, for example, the day the Marriage Law was promulgated, a central announcement listed the appropriate propaganda slogans to be used for the country's first International Labor Day celebrations: slogan no. 25 out of a total of thirty-eight, ranked in order of importance, announced, "China's women actively participate in industry and agricultural production, and strive for women's rights in production! Implement the new

Marriage Law, remove women's feudalist fetters!"[86] This was the only slogan to mention the Marriage Law.

When the central government instructed local governments in late 1951 to begin countrywide investigations into how the Marriage Law had been enforced since 1950, Deng Yingchao could already say with some certainty in her speech "On the New Marriage Law" that a large part of the problem was a failure to educate the populace adequately.[87] The first phase of implementing the Marriage Law, she explained, had led to "chaos in marriages" as well as high divorce, suicide, and homicide numbers.[88] One problem was insufficient knowledge of the law. Another, far more severe, problem was that many people misinterpreted the law. Local cadres and activists who failed to study the law carefully, Deng argued, and who did not conduct "thought struggle" to grasp the essence of the law, would often either "just use the articles" to enforce the law—meaning that enforcement would be much too harsh and show little regard for personal and family complexities—or they would not enforce the law at all. Keeping with the logic of the people's democratic dictatorship, cadres and activists would have to help people voluntarily understand and implement the Marriage Law. Structured study was needed to raise the "consciousness of the masses" and help them solve their own problems.[89]

Deng's speech suggested that she knew that there were many obstacles to the kind of legal learning she envisaged. The omnipresent reference to crime and punishment was a major impediment to Marriage Law implementation in the areas where investigation and propaganda were actually carried out.[90] Moreover, the law's simple language and flexibility—the major accomplishment of the Marriage Law's feminist authors—opened up space for people to interpret the law in the context of their individual circumstances. Investigation reports in early 1952 revealed the extent to which people had used the ambiguous language of the law to stake claims and to change their lives, often with tragic consequences, as the rise in the number of homicides and suicides indicates.[91] Women and men who had taken up the promise of the law to legitimately seek legal protection, file for divorce, or marry a partner of their choice, found themselves in bitter fights with their families and at odds with their social environment. To their dismay, many found that government cadres to whom they looked for help favored local stability, even if it meant ignoring the central government's instructions to implement the law and to help people find legal protection.[92] Conversely, examples also abounded of people who were emboldened to use the law to divorce unwanted partners, sometimes for no reason other than they deemed their partners unattractive, or people who had married and divorced spontaneously, with little regard for the social consequences and the CCP's desire for societal and family harmony.[93]

A larger pattern emerged out of these individual applications of the Marriage Law that was deeply problematic for CCP rule.[94] The law was being disseminated in most areas, but the central government found it difficult to direct popular interpretations of what the law meant and the practices of how it was applied. When it spoke of "thorough implementation," the central government meant that the Marriage Law should be circulated, but it also meant that it should be implemented in a way that ensured "correct" understandings. At least on paper, correct understandings of the law would be those that linked the simple, yet vague, legal terms to the CCP's political ideal of a citizenry focused on improving production, raising socialist morality, and working toward the goal of communism. As Deng had outlined, further education was the only way to implement the Marriage Law properly and work to ensure that people would eventually understand the law correctly.

## The Unfamiliar Campaign

In late 1952, as judicial reform drew to a close and the investigation into implementation of the Marriage Law was completed, mass education in one law accelerated to mass mobilization. On 26 November 1952, Mao approved the draft of the internal directive that announced the CCP's decision to stage a national campaign to implement the Marriage Law.[95] The CCP's approach to law dissemination had shifted. The directive explained that this mass campaign would be unlike any previous mass campaign. Because implementing the Marriage Law was now more than ever before considered a "matter among the People," the logics of the people's democratic dictatorship required careful and repeated propaganda and education.[96] If members of the People committed serious violations of the law, they would be punished in court, but all the documents emphasized that such cases would be the exception.[97]

Shortly thereafter, the party and government set up the institutional framework for the campaign. National mass campaigns required a national committee with oversight of campaign activities and control over the work of local campaign offices. The Central Marriage Law Implementation Campaign Committee was announced in January.[98] The committee was made up of high-ranking representatives from the Women's Federation; the Ministries of Culture, Justice, and Internal Affairs; the Youth League; the Trade Union; the Propaganda Department; and leading national newspapers.[99] Shen Junru (1875–1963), the president of the Supreme People's Court, presided, and Liu Jingfan (1914–90), a long-time CCP member who at the time was first deputy director of the Central People's Control Commission, carried out the day-to-day work.[100] As the national node for the campaign, the campaign office would maintain oversight of the campaign's development across different provinces, coordinate national news reportage on the campaign, and prepare a regular situation briefing with information about the campaign's progress—collated from reports submitted by regional offices—to apprise the senior leadership of progress.[101] Meanwhile, Zhou Enlai publicly announced the mass campaign in a national directive in February 1953. "On the basis of the mass campaigns against feudalism," Zhou wrote, it was a good time to have a "large-scale mass campaign to propagate the Marriage Law and to investigate the situation of Marriage Law implementation."[102] Presenting this decision as the culmination of the party's previous efforts at implementation and enforcement of the law since 1950, he drew a narrative arch that began with the law's promulgation mere months after liberation and led through to the investigation drive of late 1951 and early 1952, the findings of which had compelled the party and government to rethink and now give implementation a decisive month-long push.[103]

The central leadership's decision to announce a "mass campaign" (*qunzhong yundong*) on a "grand scale" (*da guimo*) was of great significance. There had been many campaigns since 1949, but most ordinary people associated the term "campaign" with the three "great campaigns" (*da yundong*): land reform, the suppression of counterrevolutionaries, and the Three/Five Antis. The label therefore elevated the intense study of the Marriage Law to national importance, but it sent conflicting messages. Zhou's directives may have advocated education and propaganda among the People, but the campaigns people most vividly remembered had also called for education and propaganda— only to then focus mainly on widespread political mobilization, mass violence and executions, mass accusation meetings, public trials, speaking bitterness, and swift punishments.[104] Moreover, it did not contribute to greater ideological clarity that Mao had, separate from the Marriage Law, written another intra-party directive in January that announced the "New Three Antis" to combat "bureaucratism, commandism, and violations of law and discipline" and to "comb out the violators of law and discipline" among party officials.[105] The specific policy focus of each directive may have been different, but the language of campaigns and combatting "violations of law and discipline" suggested that the party still focused on enforcing laws as an instrument of punishment.

Trying to gauge how people read Zhou's directive, *Neibu cankao* recorded a variety of responses within the weeks following its publication. Many people, particularly female cadres, were enthusiastic. In Jiangxi Province, female cadres were excited that Marriage Law implementation was now to be conducted as part of a "great campaign."[106] The national People's Press adapted this language in its *Introduction to the Marriage Law*, printed in January 1953, which opened with a chapter on "Why carry out a great campaign to implement the Marriage Law?"[107] But the reference to a "great campaign" was also worrying for some, particularly those who had just weathered other campaign storms. In the South-Central region, families who had been labeled capitalists asked whether this new "great campaign" was going to be the same as the three other great campaigns.[108] Associating the term "grand scale" closely with earlier violent campaigns, many people were certain that they were being asked to repeat techniques they had picked up in previous campaigns.[109] Women's Federation cadres and activists, municipal and county governments, and people's court personnel began to prepare line-ups, speaking bitterness sessions, denouncements, and mutual comparisons. In some areas where the local government instituted test sites (*shidian*) to decide which propaganda strategies would work best during the full campaign, panic broke out because cadres and activists conducted these preliminary tests in the violent style they thought was expected of them, and with the expectation that they should get ready to do this much more widely.[110]

Shortly thereafter, the CCP Central Committee responded to these internal reports and issued a supplementary directive on the front page of *Renmin ribao* on 19 February 1953.[111] This supplementary directive was meant to be an important corrective and clarification on how the campaign should be carried out and what it sought to achieve.[112] The Central Committee urged everyone "not to carry out enforcement among the general masses of the people." It reminded readers that the campaign was to be "limited" to "propaganda among the masses."[113] Six days later, the campaign office issued a "Propaganda Outline for Marriage Law Implementation."[114] The outline reinforced that the campaign was intended to reform people's thoughts and explained that "although implementation of the Marriage Law is a reform against feudal society, it is different from land reform and other kinds of social reform; it is not about attacking people, but is mainly about changing people's own old thinking and old habits." Everything would focus on the law's "basic spirit" (*jiben jingshen*). The directive urged people to read the law and "use the method of self-education and self-reform" to implement it.[115]

Instead of providing clarification, in some places the supplementary directive complicated preparations for the campaign even further. Information materials that had already been disseminated had to be corrected, and this was difficult.[116] Provincial and regional governments had to revise and re-issue their campaign directives. In Jiangxi Province, a regional directive on the Marriage Law campaign that had been circulated in November 1952, well before the two official central directives, had told people to prepare for a campaign in the "spirit" of the Three Antis and the Campaign to Suppress Counterrevolutionaries. Many officials thereupon presumed that "if you do not kill a few, then you cannot eradicate a several thousand-year-old feudal marriage system."[117] Now they had to rethink everything. Mistaken instructions such as this would sometimes be reprinted in the reference materials issued for the campaign by the local Marriage Law campaign office, which then had to be revised.[118]

Moreover, if the language of campaigning led readers to make automatic assumptions about what that label meant, the same happened with the supplementary directive when readers misinterpreted the term "supplementary." Once the campaign was underway, internal reports showed that in many places, people either did not respond to the party leadership's attempts to control and calm it, or they interpreted the focus on propaganda to mean that they did not have to take the campaign as seriously as previous campaigns. In Shanxi, cadres who had been unenthusiastic about the campaign from the start took the directive as an invitation to take it easy.[119] In Shandong, the majority of cadres did not properly engage with the directive because it was only supplementary. All they took away from the instruction to focus on propaganda and education was the message that they needn't work so hard because "Party Central's policy has changed, the demands are no longer high."[120] Some people concluded that the new basic spirit of the campaign would be to "propagate it [the Marriage Law] once" and that would do.[121] Others said that all they would need to do now was "propagate, propagate" (xuanchuan xuanchuan). It was, they explained, just like learning from the Soviet Union, simple and familiar enough for most people that one could minimize trouble (mafan).[122] In Yantai, a coastal town in Shandong Province, people explained that they would have to "just listen to some reports and that is enough," while they told activists to "just shout with all your strength and that's it."[123] In Beijing's downtown Qianmen District, local officials, too, decided that they could take propaganda easier this time because it was just about education.[124] In Wuhan, some cadres thought that the easiest way to meet the new demands was to take a newspaper and read the sections called "Marriage Law propaganda materials" out loud, sentence by sentence.[125] Cadres in the South-Central region, meanwhile, thought that if propaganda was everything that was needed, then people could read the text just once. Why waste time studying it in detail? After all, one cadre was quoted, "the materials are very simple."[126]

The idea of using a mass campaign to study a law seemed an oddity given the major role that mass campaigns and state violence had played in the consolidation of the CCP. The head of the propaganda group of the Guizhou Provincial Marriage Law Committee likely spoke for many people across the country when he complained that they no longer knew how to propagate the Marriage Law.[127] In Wuhan, some people asked what they should do when they went to people's homes to educate them, as they were still expected to do. They thought it was inevitable that people would want to discuss individual problems, or compare experiences and speak bitterness.[128] It all did not seem to make sense. People preparing in evening schools for the campaign had gathered that "this is not permitted, that is not permitted," but they were also not clear about what was permitted beyond propagating the law.[129]

The central government's extensive and sometimes contradictory attempts to plan the Marriage Law campaign had become part of the problem. Nowhere was this more obvious than in its decision to discourage local governments, cadres, and activists from using mass accusation meetings and trials to teach people about the Marriage Law. When they first heard about the campaign, numerous cadres and activists presumed that the campaign label had to mean that there would be executions and public trials for those who had committed crimes under the Marriage Law.[130] People organizing the campaign locally liked planning these meetings and trials because they were an ideal educational tool to help residents understand laws and the consequences of failing to abide by them. Some counties in Jiangxi Province established extra "marriage courts" (*hunyin fating*) in addition to the normal people's courts, and this really scared people, particularly since in the case of Jiangxi these marriage courts often handed out harsh sentences. In an instance reported in *Neibu cankao*, a man was sentenced to one and a half years in jail for having beaten his wife.[131] But, as with other types of propaganda techniques from previous campaigns, the problem was that these techniques were considered "one sided" because, as one report commented generally, they "only criticize the bad, [and] do not praise the good."[132] Trials and accusation meetings were to be used sparsely and only to show cases of severe violations of the Marriage Law. In Zhejiang Province, this puzzled some people who did not understand how there could be a campaign without speaking bitterness and without mobilizing people against each other.[133]

The decision took many officials by surprise as they were preparing for the campaign. Several weeks earlier, during the Judicial Reform Movement, public trials had still been a common and popular propaganda technique. Why the sudden change? As late as December 1952, the Beijing party committee was still instructing local courts to select good example cases from the Judicial Reform Movement and to use them during the new campaign.[134] They would still use some of them, but it was not clear which and how many. In Guizhou, many cadres thought it was not fair that the central government would change its mind in this way.[135] Cadres who had spent days and weeks preparing cases that could be used for public trials as a useful way of educating residents were disillusioned that all they needed to do now was "spend a bit of time understanding the spirit and that'll do."[136] In the city of Yantai, people's courts, too, had spent weeks preparing cases as campaign "study materials," drawing up lists of who would attend, and documenting how the trials would take place and what people would say. After learning of the supplementary directive, many did not want to hold the trials anymore, arguing that "the regulations state that during the campaign month they [the cases] do not need to be processed."[137] Local Women's Federation cadres had to implore court officials several times in writing before they agreed to process the cases. Being more cautious about accusation meetings and trials may have transported the message that implementation of the Marriage Law was focused on propaganda and education, yet those officials, cadres, and activists at the grassroots level who wanted to heed the newest central directives and instructions were no longer able to make extensive use of some of their most effective propaganda tools for legal learning.

## Conclusion: The Conundrum of Law Propaganda

The CCP regime broke new ground with its decision to conduct a campaign focused in theory, though not always in reality, on the study and dissemination of laws. In the Soviet Union and the GDR, for example, the central governments had publicized new laws, but they had not combined law dissemination with mass campaign mobilization. When the

GDR promulgated its new labor and family laws during the 1950s, there had been discussion groups and newspaper reportage, but none of this reached the intensity of the 1953 Marriage Law campaign carried out in the PRC. The CCP had developed a new technique of mass mobilization for the study of a law.[138]

The theoretical unease with laws remained, however, as the following chapters show. By 1954, once the new constitution had been promulgated, legal experts would argue that the state constitution signaled a new phase for popular engagement with laws. The constitution, after all, was the "mother law" (*mufa*) and the ultimate product of the mass line. It behooved everyone to abide by it, because not to abide by the constitution was akin to not abiding by the will of the People.

During the early 1950s, meanwhile, the central government's shift to emphasizing more law dissemination and legal learning brought new problems not only for local officials but also for propaganda authorities. Published materials became the basis for learning about laws and a crucial vehicle for the transmission of "correct" legal interpretations. Propaganda producers, however, had little time to prepare for this new role. They had developed effective techniques for mass mobilization propaganda in the case of the Resist America / Aid Korea Campaign, land reform, and the suppression of counterrevolutionaries. How to produce propaganda for a mass campaign that was all about disseminating and teaching laws, however, puzzled them as it had puzzled local officials. Yet many more propaganda materials were needed if the campaign was to be successful. Publishing authorities, moreover, would have to increase their control and regulation of the publishing sector to ensure that those producing law propaganda had access to the necessary guidance, information, and vocabulary in the form of written materials. In other words, propaganda workers needed instructions before they could teach others. As the next chapter shows, demands made on state publishers to respond swiftly—within just a few months—to the focus on education revealed many questions about who would and should publish and write about laws.

# 2    Paper Trials

## How the Publishing Field Adapted to Law Propaganda

Writing and publishing on New China's new laws turned out to be an unexpectedly complicated task. Once the Central People's Government adopted a new law, the next day, newspapers, magazines, and radio broadcasts informed people of this law and its content.[1] The Marriage Law, for example, was announced on 16 April 1950 on the front page of *Renmin ribao*. On 30 May 1950, daily papers proclaimed the Agrarian Reform Law. Most newspapers printed the full text of the law on the front or second page, accompanied by a special editorial and a notification by the central government that exhorted everyone to help implement the law.[2] Publication for the general readership symbolized laws' accessibility and reinforced the party's and government's repeated statements that laws were for the People. It also served as a reminder that the government expected people to have encountered any laws publicized in this way. People had both the right and the duty to know their country's "Great Laws."

In publicizing these laws, the government had two connected goals: to make laws more accessible through the propaganda system and to bring the circulation of legal knowledge under state supervision. When the Marriage Law and the Agrarian Reform Law were passed in 1950, some people were interested in reading them, while others were not. Many residents in Beijing and Shanghai had to read the newspaper announcements during their work unit's study sessions. Others participated in neighborhood reading groups or literacy classes, or listened to radio broadcasts in group sessions. But this was only the first step. Realizing that merely learning about laws did not result in a correct understanding even among those of "good" class status, and desiring more influence over how people learned and therefore interpreted laws, the people's government sought control over the entire field of law publishing. This included materials aimed at high-level cadres as well as "popular" (*tongsu*) readings for the general population, from rural to urban readers, from males to females, and from young to old readers.[3] The government's publishing authorities also insisted that all publications on law—be they stories, novels, cartoons, or theater scripts—should disseminate reliable legal information. Every bit of printed material could potentially matter in how people understood laws.

In pursuit of this ambition, publishing authorities tried to establish who should write about and publish on laws.[4] Publishers meanwhile tried to adapt to these requirements, which were often unfamiliar. In the days and weeks following the promulgation of a law, editors commissioned stories from neighborhoods and work units telling readers how fellow residents received and implemented the law. Publishers issued paperback books with additional discussions of the new law, as well as short stories, novels, comic books, and songbooks that explained it in an entertaining and accessible format. The production and dissemination of propaganda materials, however, required far more coordination than the central government's directives often suggested—far more, even, than studies of law dissemination in the early 1950s have often presumed. Publishing plans and authors' ideas determined what kinds of materials became available, but so did production capacities and the structure of a publishing field in transition after 1949. The country's publishing sector in the early 1950s was made up of a mixture of state publishers, joint private-state publishers, and private publishers. Between 1950 and 1953, private publishers in particular had a certain amount of independence, if only because their publications were often censored after publication, not before. Publishing officials therefore did not have full control over the publishing sector during this time.[5] While the government wanted flagship state publishers to be the public face of reliable law propaganda, in reality it was often smaller and private publishers that had the capacity to deliver print matters for law dissemination.

The Communist regime's desire to assume more control over law publishing was not unique in Chinese history. In the late Qing and Republican periods, government officials had been wary of commercial publishers' increasingly close involvement with law publishing. The "commodification and privatization of legal knowledge" had already intensified over the course of the Ming and Qing.[6] In the late Qing, commercial publishers in the publishing centers of Beijing, Hangzhou, and Suzhou dominated a lively book market with their reprints of the Qing Code.[7] Official copies of the code, issued by the Qing court, often took years to complete, even if new statutes had been added in the meantime. Circulation was restricted to a limited readership made up of magistrates and state officials.[8] Commercial publishers, by contrast, made their products widely available to anyone who could afford to purchase copies, with private legal advisors among their most avid customers. Advertisements for such volumes promised that they were continuously updated, unlike official copies of the code, and assembled as quickly as possible to meet customers' needs.[9] Supplementary information, as Ting Zhang writes, included "cross-indexes, leading cases and administrative regulations."[10] Commercial publishers also printed independent commentaries and case collections written and assembled by private legal advisors.[11] In the Republican period, commercial publishers became even more powerful and ubiquitous. Shanghai was by then the leading center for China's polyglot and "modern" publishing world.[12] While commercial publishers did much law-related publishing, including commentaries on legal reforms, reprints of new codes, legal self-help guides, and "common legal knowledge" readings aimed at non-specialist literate and educated readers, commercial newspapers and magazines ran special columns explaining laws as well as legal knowledge for their readers as part of their regular and often sensationalist reportage on ongoing court cases.[13]

If the Communist regime continued the tradition of Chinese state authorities seeking more control over formal law publishing, its close and systematic attention to controlling popular readings of laws was extraordinary and set it apart from earlier governments' efforts. This had wide-ranging implications for the dissemination of legal knowledge. When publishing officials working in the General Publishing

Administration and the Central Propaganda Department tried to bring *all* publications about laws under governmental purview, they vastly expanded the group of people who were responsible for producing reliable law-related publications that could withstand the test of state censorship.[14] They also greatly increased the quantity of materials that censors had to scrutinize and engage with.

To understand how and why the party and the government came to be so careful about popular explanations of laws, and why this was, as the next chapters illustrate, a matter of managing explanations at the level of individual words, this chapter traces the mechanics and structures of law publishing during the early 1950s. Starting in 1950, it first maps the field of law publishing. By 1951 central leadership increasingly called for more popular and accessible publications addressed to all readers, expert and illiterate alike. Two law propaganda booklets, one explaining the Regulations for the Punishment of Counterrevolutionaries and one outlining the Marriage Law, circulated widely across the country during this time. Their story gives us a glimpse into the production and dissemination of publications; a task easier at some times than at others. The work of publishers and publishing officials intensified in the context of the Marriage Law mass campaign in 1953, yet it made the need for better supervision all the more evident as the publishing field prepared for the country's first constitution draft discussion.

## Established Channels of Law Publishing

Once newspapers published laws, the rest of the national publishing industry went to work. "Great Laws" were printed, reprinted, and circulated. They were part of annual compendia, handbooks, and collections of national laws and regulations.[15] For everyday use, they were available as separate bound volumes (*danxingben*); these were convenient, small, and thin paperback books available for purchase at an affordable price. They circulated at print runs of several hundred thousand and sometimes several million copies.[16] After the national People's Press was set up in 1950 as a venue for publishing key political and legal documents, it took on a leading role in publishing reprints of laws and compendia.[17] Newly established regional People's Presses soon became responsible for commissioning reprints of single-volume editions.[18]

Besides single-volume editions, laws also circulated in other official materials.[19] In the weeks following the publication of a new law, editors at regional People's Presses compiled supplementary readings, which often came in the form of small paperback books for daily use. Next to the full text of the law in question, these books contained other so-called relevant documents (*youguan wenxian*), meaning party-state directives that accompanied the law, leading editorials from *Renmin ribao* and other national or regional newspapers, important speeches, and further readings. Having everything in one booklet, officials would not miss out on crucial directives and editorials that gave important interpretive context. Without these, editors cautioned, officials might be in danger of misunderstanding the law's stipulations. Official report-givers, propagandists, and, to a lesser extent, general readers could arm themselves with manuals to conduct and participate in newspaper reading groups, report meetings at which report-givers explained a new law, and small group meetings to discuss individual laws. Propagandists and grassroots cadres could copy some of books' content onto blackboards in neighborhoods, alleys, factories, and other public spaces. Wanting to ensure that potential customers were made aware of their products, presses regularly advertised in local and national newspapers as well as in the back matter of other publications.

The growing system of open and internal reporting was a third source of legal information. Higher-level officials who read the bound volumes and books containing relevant documents often also read policy magazines such as *Xin jianshe*. This openly published magazine included commentaries on laws that gave ideological context and explanations, penned by legal and non-legal experts. Officials, judges, and clerks in the government's judicial branches, in courts and procuratorates, perused *Zhongyang zhengfa gongbao* (Central bulletin on politics and law), which became a monthly periodical in 1953. More periodicals became available as law publishing was regularized during the mid-1950s, including the periodicals *Zhengfa yanjiu* (Political-legal research, from 1954) and *Faxue* (Jurisprudence, from 1957). Internal bulletins at municipal, provincial, and national levels circulated status reports and regular work reports about local legal and political work.

They kept judicial workers who had access to the reports up to date with statistics on cases filed, judicial work conducted, and the kinds of violations of law that were being registered at local court levels.[20]

Although advertisements praised the publications of the national and regional People's Presses as accessible to all government workers, most of these materials did not cater to ordinary readers. They mostly focused on grassroots and high-level cadres who were working in the quickly expanding state apparatus. Manuals and publications presumed high literacy levels, moreover, and this often precluded even the large audience of grassroots cadres who did not find them accessible and useful. Dense layouts, small fonts, and little spacing between lines marked them out as publications read mostly by the educated or the very studious reader. For certain laws to be as accessible as the government claimed they should be, more popular publications were needed that could appeal to a broader audience with lower literacy levels or altogether illiterate. The definition of reading and therefore readable materials on laws had to be expanded.

## Popular Readings and the Problem of Private Publishers

Calls for more popular publications on laws were part of wider demands for popular materials. In April 1951, Lu Dingyi, head of the CCP Central Propaganda Department in Beijing, gave a summary report on the department's first meeting to discuss "popular" periodical and book publications. Lu thought that publishers were not producing nearly enough "popular readings," by which he meant materials written for adults who had received primary school education or had passed through state-sponsored literacy training, and whose literacy levels were elementary, with a vocabulary range of some 2,000 characters or more.[21] Because popular readings covered writings on the sciences, technology, literature, and the arts, they were crucial for all aspects of mass education. But instead of focusing on this essential task, Lu thought that publishers, intellectuals, and many of those working in the central and regional publishing authorities had lost touch with their most important audiences: workers, peasants, and soldiers. So clear was this rift, Lu remarked, that it was "as if they were another country."[22] Publishers had printed plenty of new readings, but they had neglected popular readings.

What China needed, in Lu's opinion, was more periodicals and readings for peasants and workers. Such new readings would include a limited amount of accessible discussions of national topics, enough to inform but not overwhelm the reader. Popular periodicals would be printed in larger type using basic vocabulary, with publications for peasants printed in larger type than those for workers. Prices could be kept low if periodicals came out every third day rather than every day. Lu thought this would give Xinhua Bookstore time to carefully plan distribution.[23] All publishers were told to set up sections to edit and write popular readings. Where necessary, government officials could seize some private publishers who were successful in this field and use their infrastructure to publish good popular readings quickly.[24]

Demand for more popular publications was growing more urgent by the day because materials were needed to accompany mass campaigns and general mass education. By April 1951, the Resist America / Aid Korea Campaign was in full swing, commanding the greater part of state publishers' attention. As one report explained, by mid-1951, publishers had brought out 900 new readings intended solely for this major campaign. Some eighty new readings accompanied the Campaign to Suppress Counterrevolutionaries, and some fifty were produced to accompany land reform.[25] Every bit of the CCP's mass education work, moreover, required materials because without them the popularization of science, the study of political theory, and the study of policies and laws could barely work.[26]

Yet, Lu lamented, not only were state publishers not delivering, but they were being outperformed by private competitors. In 1950, the Propaganda Department still counted more than one thousand private publishing businesses in major cities across the country, not including bookstalls and kiosks.[27] For this reason, the activities of private publishers received a great deal of attention from national, provincial, and local publishing authorities. Speaking at the first national meeting on the administration of publishing in late August 1951, Ye Shengtao, then vice-director of the central government's General Publishing Administration and not a CCP member, reminded his colleagues that

the good news was that many private publishers were small businesses.[28] Only three private publishers, Commercial Press, Zhonghua,
and Kaiming, were large enterprises; and these soon transitioned to
joint state-private management.[29] Ye, however, warned that even
though many private publishers were small, they often had several
years of experience and an "entrepreneurial spirit."[30] They also had
the capacity and experience to meet governmental demands for more
popular publications. By mid-1951, of all the books published, private
publishers occupied 57 percent of the market in terms of publication
variety, meaning they had a much wider portfolio of offerings, including popular readings on laws.[31]

Private publishers were therefore an important part of the story
of law dissemination. They were vilified and yet needed because state
publishers had insufficient resources to cover all publishing demands.
Several factors explain why private publishers fared well at first.
Many used materials they had developed during the Republican
Era—including picture books, primers, short stories, novels, and
songbooks—and amended them quickly to better suit the demands
of the new regime.[32] Private publishers also had good connections with
writers and often had a network of readers who kept up to date with
their publications.[33] Moreover, private publishers could bring their
products to the bookshelves well before regional state publishers could
because state publishers often suffered delays when their readings for
mass campaigns were held up in the internal vetting process.[34] Private
publishers, for instance, published some of the first popular materials
on the Marriage Law in the summer of 1951 to accompany the investigation into Marriage Law implementation. Many of these were in the same
formats Lu had demanded from state publishers. Shanghai's Tongli
Press released its *Marriage Law Three-Character Classic*, which was
filled with plenty of pictures, big readable characters, and rhymes, in
summer 1951.[35] New Masses Press published Miao Peishi's *Freedom of
Marriage Song* at a high print run of 500,000 copies in December
1951.[36] In the same month, Yuanchang Press brought its *People's Thousand-Character Lesson: The Great Event of Marriage* to the market. It
contained pictures and memorable rhymes explaining the law in the
format of a classic Confucian thousand-character lesson.[37]

## The Two Sides of Campaign
## Propaganda Bestsellers

Private publishers were influential in 1951, and publishing authorities worried that they needed more and better oversight over popular readings on politics and law. The promulgation and dissemination of the Regulations for the Punishment of Counterrevolutionaries in February of that year was one reason. Another factor was the central government's announcement, a few months later, that it would investigate the enforcement of the Marriage Law across the country. If propaganda materials to accompany both the law and the regulations contained faulty information of any kind, this would harm propaganda work. Still unable to outperform their private competitors on publication diversity, state publishers decided that they had three crucial advantages: they could dominate in high print-run numbers, they had access to official distribution networks, and they enjoyed official patronage. Rather than focusing on publication diversity, publishing authorities therefore honed in on publishing singular model works at high print runs.

In 1951, the East China People's Press successively edited two volumes that state authorities then helped—at least temporarily—turn into law propaganda success stories: the *Regulations of the People's Republic of China for the Punishment of Counterrevolutionaries: Illustrated Popular Explanations* (*Illustrated Regulations* hereafter) (fig. 2.1) and the *Marriage Law: Illustrated Popular Explanations* (*Illustrated Marriage Law* hereafter).[38] How they were produced and disseminated reveals the process and hurdles of popular law publishing. At the same time, their example shows that readers during the early 1950s could also forcefully reject model works, regardless of what their local cadres were telling them and regardless of how many copies they received as part of the official distribution network.

East China People's Press began working on the *Illustrated Regulations* in February 1951. Its editors wanted to produce a volume that would help readers make sense of the regulations and of the legal framework they outlined, and that would also help people understand how the regulations and the ongoing suppression of counterrevolutionaries

Fig. 2.1. Cover page of the *Illustrated Regulations*, 1951. (Source: *Zhonghua renmin gongheguo chengzhi fangeming tiaoli: tujie tongsuben* [Regulations of the People's Republic of China for the for the Punishment of Counterrevolutionaries: Illustrated popular explanations], Shanghai: Huadong renmin chubanshe, 1951.)

were connected. Pocket-sized, the booklet featured large images with captions that explained individual articles of the regulations. Editing followed a carefully laid-out process. Many of the images, painted by ten leading artists who had transferred from the Artists' Association, were first serialized in Shanghai's daily newspaper *Jiefang ribao* (Liberation daily). Meanwhile, under the leadership of the director of the East China People's Press, Ye Laishi, editors finalized the accompanying texts. Once completed, the deputy head of the East China regional propaganda department, Feng Ding, scrutinized the draft and then forwarded it to the Central Propaganda Department in Beijing where Wang Ziye, former Xinhua News Agency cadre and now a member of the department's publishing committee as well as a vice editor-in-chief of the People's Press, gave the final approval for printing.[39] This process took several weeks.

Public accounts of the *Illustrated Regulations* at first chronicled many happy readers and record sales. As a *Renmin ribao* article wrote, people liked the book because, as one customer reportedly explained, "I previously did not understand the country's laws, but now that I have read this book I finally understand."[40] One much-touted advantage of the booklet was its price. Marketed at only 800 yuan per copy, *Renmin ribao* announced that—in the words of the male and female customer respectively—one "only has to smoke one packet [of cigarettes] less and can buy the book," or one could have one's chicken lay two more eggs in order to cover the cost of the book.[41] In only a few months, statistics announced a staggering print run of over ten million copies. The other two propaganda publications that East China People's Press edited for the campaign, the *Popular Introduction to the Suppression of Counterrevolutionaries* and a songbook called *Law and Order: The Suppression of Counterrevolutionaries Songbook*, had only come out with comparatively low print runs of 300,000 and 200,000 copies respectively. Even if the numbers were exaggerated and the actual print run was only a fraction of the stated number, the *Illustrated Regulations* still had one of the highest print runs of the early 1950s and was one of the model stories of 1950s propaganda publishing for years to come.[42] Combining images with simplified explanatory captions, the format was accessible, and as one article wrote in support of the book, one could "see the images, know the words" (*kan tu shi zi*).[43]

Print-run statistics for the *Illustrated Regulations* indicate the scale at which it was distributed. Xinhua Bookstore's East China main branch determined that printing the *Illustrated Regulations* was the core task for June 1951. Making it a core task meant that production capacities were exploited in full to support the printing of the booklet, which, in turn, supported the Campaign to Suppress Counterrevolutionaries.[44] Bookstore branches determined how many copies were supposed to be sold or distributed. According to one memoir, the East China Xinhua Bookstore branch at first decided that its affiliates should distribute approximately 1,500,000 copies. Zhejiang Province would receive 300,000 copies, the Jiangnan area and Subei would each receive 200,000 copies, and Shanghai municipality's quota would be 260,000 copies. Memoirs recounting the booklet's sale note that from the beginning, the Shanghai Xinhua Bookstore branch decided that it was going to exceed the quota it had been given. It planned to sell about 500,000 copies. To achieve this goal, the branch assigned quotas to all wholesale points, as well as to its stores, such as the one on Fuzhou Road, which was then Shanghai's main street for bookseller and publishers, and its store in Tilanqiao District, which was home to Shanghai's largest prison and a place that Xinhua Bookstore officials seemed to think required particularly large numbers of copies. More copies would go to the section in charge of organizing mobile supplies (*liudong gongying*); these were salespeople on bike or foot who went to people's homes outside of the main urban areas to peddle books. Further downtown, people could also purchase copies at local bookstalls and book kiosks, and at stationery stores, department stores, and in cinemas. Salespeople went door-to-door and called up schools and work units to encourage telephone orders. They made special visits and calls to municipal mass organization branches to encourage them to buy large quantities of books and hand them out to their local representatives. Bookstores prioritized sales of the *Illustrated Regulations* as well as the other two volumes and actively promoted them to anyone who walked into the store.[45] By the end of July, in the Shanghai and Jiangnan areas, both belonging to the East China branch, one in eleven people reportedly had a copy. In Nanjing, reports claimed that one in five people had a copy.[46]

The scale at which this volume was distributed could overwhelm local publishing officials. Xinhua Bookstore's main branch admonished some regional branches for a lack of "foresight" and for failing to replenish stocks in time. They thought the North-East China branch could have done better and criticized their colleagues for not preparing for the "high tide" of the Campaign to Suppress Counterrevolutionaries. After the regulations were promulgated in late February and after the publisher had advertised the upcoming publication of the *Illustrated Regulations*, the North-East branch ordered only 4,000 copies. It had to commission an additional 10,000 copies on 7 May, a further 100,000 copies on 9 May, and yet another 200,000 copies a week later.[47] In Shandong Province, the Xinhua Bookstore branch first ordered 100,000 copies. Then it sold out. It reordered 20,000 more copies, and even the eventual 80,000 copies it ordered "still did not satisfy people's demands."[48] In the end, within four months, East China People's Press issued the booklet in six editions, shipping it to destinations across the country or allowing local printing facilities to reprint the booklet.[49] Judging merely on the basis of quantity, this was one of the highest print runs in PRC history, leaving aside the Little Red Book and its more than one billion copies.[50]

In summer 1951, East China People's Press decided to use the experience of writing *Illustrated Regulations* to help with the investigation into the Marriage Law's enforcement by editing the *Illustrated Marriage Law*. The *Illustrated Marriage Law* eventually outperformed the *Illustrated Regulations*, with an estimated print run of 11.5 million copies between late 1951 and the spring of 1953.[51] The first print runs arrived in Shanghai bookstores on 19 November 1951. Fourteen national newspapers and magazines serialized and reprinted the *Illustrated Marriage Law*. Cadres and mass organization activists used it in reading groups. Party propaganda bureaus wrote to the editors to ask for permission to reformat images and reproduce them as posters to be displayed in factories, alleyways, at roadsides, and in shop windows.[52]

Impressive print-run statistics tell only part of the story, however. In 1951, publishing authorities might have been very positive about both booklets and their bestseller status. No doubt the booklets did sell, and at least some of the people who purchased or obtained a copy leafed through or read it. Yet, only a few months later, the General Publishing Administration became more cautious when it learned that many more copies had been printed than were actually required. As East China People's Press's editors were recounting their success story in *Renmin ribao*, internal reports shed light on what had actually happened to many volumes once they were printed and shipped. The success story, if there was one, was mostly urban. And even then, the success story concealed a wider panic that had ensued among Xinhua Bookstore staff trying to trade off and disseminate as many copies as possible to meet and outstrip distribution quotas.

Beyond the major urban centers, both the *Illustrated Regulations* and the *Illustrated Marriage Law* were part of a wider scandal surrounding forced propaganda allotment. The problem lay in the way mass campaign publications were distributed. While legal education materials published by private publishers were available for purchase or subscription, state publishers' law propaganda materials were also distributed nationally on the basis of a propaganda material allotment system. Local governments determined demand for these materials by statistical calculations, based on the number of households in each village and district. Local county and village cadres received boxes of new materials, which they then delivered to households. Allotment was supposed to guarantee that areas with poor access to bookstores and peddlers obtained propaganda materials. It was also meant to ensure wide dissemination of state-published readings.

This system of allotment could pose a significant risk to successful propaganda, as the examples of the *Illustrated Regulations* and the *Illustrated Marriage Law* showed. Booklets were not handed out for free. Every village household had to pay for the readings they received; payment was crudely determined by household numbers and, sometimes, by general literacy levels. In Shanxi's Baode County, for instance, one village had sixty-three households. The primary school instructor was the only adult in the village who could read. Regardless, between April and September 1952, the village received nine issues of the *Illustrated Marriage Law*, fifteen issues of the *Current Affairs Handbook*, and nine issues of the *Handbook for Propagandists*. The costs for acquiring these materials were divided among households, and every household was asked to pay its share of 2,000 yuan.[53] In the South-West administrative region, Xinhua News Agency reporters found districts that had required households with one literate family member to purchase one copy per household. Households that did not have a literate family member had to share costs, with two households paying one fee. Several counties expected that every police officer, by virtue of his occupation, would purchase a copy of the *Illustrated Regulations*. One county compelled everyone—including the illiterate, elderly, children, and babies—to buy one copy per head.[54] In the East China region, people jokingly started to call the local government a "book warehouse."[55] The General Publishing Administration's own investigation report wrote that "mass distribution" had turned into "mass overstocking," and "focused distribution" had become "focused allotments."[56]

Pressure to distribute volumes was immense. Local cadres had to make sure copies were delivered and paid for. Pressure on cadres and officials to meet quotas often meant they pressured residents to buy more books. Some cadres claimed that anyone who refused to buy a copy of the *Illustrated Regulations* would be registered as sympathizing with counterrevolutionaries. Given such tactics, residents quickly began to think of compulsory allotments as a new kind of concealed tax. Some started calling it a "book tax" and complained, "The Guomindang sent down taxes, the CCP sends down books."[57] Allotment made demands on what little money many people had and seemed yet another way to repackage familiar state claims on people's savings. In one incident widely discussed within the General Publishing Administration, a man in Hebei had angrily tossed the *Illustrated Marriage Law* to the ground in front of the village cadre's feet.[58]

The story of these illustrated booklets reveals the challenges of propaganda circulation. The published and internal reports show that government officials cared about reader responses and that readers could not easily be forced to read whatever they were given. Officials in the General Publishing Administration worried that people would lose trust in the new government if cadres did not respect the principle that people should purchase books freely. Model works and other propaganda were useless once they were disseminated by force because they disgruntled readers and made it even more difficult to educate them about the new laws and regulations. Local government officials had to explain to people why they should bother to read official materials at all, especially given these experiences. Being forced to purchase materials about law and politics certainly did not help to promote political and legal learning, even if it often seemed to be the only way to engage people.

As a short-term solution to fix some of the damage, Xinhua Bookstore's main branch instructed those who had forced books onto local residents to go and apologize. Naturally, not everyone was pleased to do so.[59] Local cadres were also told to announce that people could return their books and get a refund. At the same time, apparently wary of accidentally suggesting to cadres that allotments were now a problem, the General Publishing Administration also cautioned that this should not turn into a "campaign" to get people to return books. Anyone happy to keep their books should be allowed to keep them.[60]

## Regulating Campaign Publishing

The apparent success story of the illustrated booklets and the controversies surrounding allotments both unfolded between late 1951 and spring 1953. Coincidentally, when the new Marriage Law mass campaign was announced in late 1952 the General Publishing Administration was just in the middle of dealing with the allotment problems. In light of all these difficulties, the campaign offered an opportunity to coordinate materials and distribution more carefully. It was a chance to improve on two years of, as administration officials saw it, poor publishing coordination during which publishing authorities had given publishers little guidance on how they should organize their work.[61] Yet the new campaign also posed a risk. In a situation where administration officials were already having difficulties controlling the circulation of reading materials, this renewed push for campaign-style study of a law threatened to compound the problem.

The central government had, however, in the meantime also put in place better national regulations on publishing that would now help coordinate the publication of materials on laws. In the summer of 1952, it promulgated the "Provisional Regulations" on the Administration of Book and Periodical Publishing, the Printing Industry, and the Distribution Trade.[62] Article 8 limited who could publish the full text of laws: "The rights to publication of legal documents of the people's government at all levels rests with the People's Press (all levels) and its licensed publishers. Other publishers may not publish or reprint [laws]."[63] Unless they obtained a license, private and joint private-state managed publishers could no longer publish, edit, or republish the full text of individual laws.

Article 8 was more of a problem for non-licensed publishers than might be apparent. The central government and the General Publishing Administration had from the beginning restricted private publishers from reprinting speeches by national leaders, key policy documents, and theoretical writings by party leaders.[64] But the situation was less clear in the field of law. Plenty of private publishers had in previous years sold popular legal education readings that included the full text of laws. These materials now had to be reprinted in order to comply with the new regulations, a process that was costly and used up parts of publishers' limited paper quotas. Not having the full text of the law as an appendix to a serial comic or a collection of stories, moreover, separated the popular explanation of the law from its full text. People either had to buy a copy of the law or keep the newspaper copy, if they wanted to read a book by a private publisher and consult the original law at the same time. Or, more conveniently, they could buy a licensed volume containing both the law and explanations. If the regulations could not easily rein in materials already sold and in circulation, they could delimit future publishing work.

The consequences of these new regulations first became evident during the preparations for the Marriage Law campaign, which formally began in early December 1952. In an internal notification sent to publishers, presses, and bookshops, the General Publishing Administration instructed state publishers and joint state-private managed publishers (but not private businesses) what kinds of provisions were needed.[65] As guidance for regional presses, the national People's Press was preparing formal educational materials and compendia updated with new editorials and speeches made since 1951. New textbooks and introductory explanations were also in the making. Because these were to be published by state publishers, they would include the full text of the Marriage Law. Textbooks were one of the core segments of state publishing, carefully guarded from any influence by private publishers. Once completed, these materials were to be sent to regional state publishers to help them determine their own campaign portfolios.[66]

Following Lu Dingyi's call for more popular readings, publishers were told to make these the focus of their preparations. In late November, the Art Workers Association met and drafted a plan detailing what kind of materials were required. New images were needed by early January if they were to be incorporated into "small people's books" (xiaoren shu). Images for newspapers were needed by early February. The association organized fieldtrips for artists to visit districts where the Marriage Law had been particularly well implemented.[67] The China Youth Press, also a national publisher, was working on two volumes of Russian translations on love and marriage during the time of socialism. And copying the format of the Illustrated Marriage Law, the People's Arts Press and China Youth Press were cooperating to produce a pamphlet called Talking about the Marriage Law.[68]

Editors and artists at the People's Arts Press prepared collections of propaganda posters. Once completed, these could be purchased in stores or reprinted in local newspapers and reproduced as posters for image-based Marriage Law lessons.

The principle for the production of new materials, as the Shanghai Propaganda Department explained, was "few but colorful," meaning that state publishers should not try to come up with too many formats but should focus on getting a selected amount of new materials right.[69] Even so, the General Publishing Administration estimated that the country's needs for new propaganda materials to accompany the campaign could only be met if existing materials were reprinted. The notification therefore also explained how best to control reprints and direct publishers in the selection of materials for reprint. Only readings that tied the articles of the Marriage Law to the CCP's goals of production, social harmony, and happiness should be reprinted. Any materials, for instance, that mainly discussed divorce, bigamy, the marriage customs of ethnic minorities, or criminal cases involving the Marriage Law were not to be reproduced.[70] Publishers, moreover, were supposed to select only those readings that organized information clearly and accessibly by focusing on the law's essential articles and "basic spirit." Publications that overwhelmed readers with information were not considered useful. Small fonts and dense narrow lines, too, were ill-suited to the majority of readers; publications formatted in this way did not meet the campaign criteria and should be barred from reprint. Transcripts of radio broadcasts aired between 1950 and 1951 could be reprinted, but editors had to attach notes explaining why older broadcasts were still relevant in 1953. Bookstores could resell some of the remaining stocks from the 1951 investigation drive, as long as they carefully checked that these stocks conformed to the new requirements.[71]

The notification pushed for central and hierarchically organized control of print propaganda. All editors were directed to coordinate closely with their local propaganda departments and publishing bureaus. Pressure to meet the government's requirements and still deliver goods on time was now on publishers. The notification was circulated in early December, and publishers were supposed to have materials ready by late January 1953. Figuring in time for revisions, this meant that publishers had to rush to get first drafts ready by early January at the latest. Presses needed time to print volumes and distribute them if materials were to appear on bookshelves and be delivered to subscribing work units, neighborhoods, schools, and mass organization branches in time for March, the official campaign month.

## What Went Wrong?

The administration's carefully laid out plans did not materialize. From the perspective of publishing authorities, the Marriage Law mass campaign became a model case showing how much work needed to be done to improve law propaganda and to bring it under the purview of the state. Municipal and provincial publishing authorities had tried to promote state-published materials as much as possible during the campaign. Reminded that they should strive to ensure quality standards among the materials they gave to their residents, work units were told to give preference to publications by People's Presses. The propaganda bureau of the Shanghai textile sector, for instance, had followed these instructions and advised its constituents that they should search for and order state-published materials.[72] Work units subscribed to Xinhua Bookstore and duly waited for campaign materials to be delivered once they became available. State publishers, however, could not always deliver as planned.

Production statistics collated after the conclusion of the campaign highlighted the shortcomings of state publishers in trying to disseminate the Marriage Law. If the Shanghai Propaganda Department had still advised state publishers to limit variety but ensure that publications were good and colorful, the General Publishing Administration took a different stance now. In autumn 1953, Chen Kehan, vice head of the General Publishing Administration and also editor-in-chief of Xinhua News Agency, addressed what he felt was a lack of variety in his report on the state of publishing in the first half of 1953. Of some 1,948 different kinds of popular readings published during this time, only 4.3 percent came from national publishers. Regional state-owned publishers issued 50.2 percent of the available books, joint state-private managed companies were responsible for 3.5 percent, and private publishers edited and printed as many as 42 percent of all publications for the campaign.[73] In terms of quantity, state publishers outperformed their private competitors by far, even if many publications had been delivered too late. But in variety, state publishers still fell short of private publishers, although they did slightly better now compared to 1951 when private publishers comprised 57 percent of the portfolio. Although he referenced the numbers for the field of popular readings in general, Chen singled out the Marriage Law campaign for detailed criticism. Since the majority of popular readings published during the first half of the year were associated with the campaign, the overall numbers were taken to reflect what had happened in the particular case of Marriage Law print production.

Private publishers, who had not been included in the General Publishing Administration's directive of late 1952, had come to the rescue of the campaign, accounting for a great majority of campaign publications. Despite or perhaps because private publishers filled this gap so prominently, they became the scapegoats for publishers' errors and Xinhua Bookstore's distribution shortcomings. In Chen's opinion, private publishers were the reason why print materials had failed to meet national standards:

> Due to the fact that state publishers' resources are thin and the masses' demands for popular readings are again urgent, private publishers have profiteered on a large scale, with the result that a lot of popular readings that are shoddily manufactured and full of mistakes are flooding the market. They copy and paste and plagiarize, unscrupulously and recklessly change the original texts, publish a lot of books that carelessly interpret government policies, laws, and decrees, publish many poisonous so-called "thought reform books," and they publish many common knowledge questions and answers, school guidelines, adaptations of famous Soviet literary works, and other such kinds of books.[74]

Chen argued that local and regional state publishers' failure to meet targets had given private publishers an easy opportunity to benefit. In addition, among the "small volumes" published by regional state publishers that explained the Marriage Law, he complained, "almost all had some kind of fault."[75] Errors of fact or interpretation abounded.

The former were fairly easy to identify. They included typographical and spelling errors, wrong presentations of the details of the law, and poor formatting. As the next chapter illustrates in more detail, however, what constituted an error of interpretation was difficult to determine. Different people working in the publishing authorities would not necessarily easily concur whether a particular interpretation of the law was erroneous.

Small errors in individual volumes, moreover, were just one concern. Another concern was the failure of the broader plan to gain control over law publishing at large. The publishing field had been ill-prepared to meet the demands of a state that not only wished to determine official publications on laws, but that sought to direct all publications on and interpretations of laws. Publishing authorities had managed to gain control over most publications in the field of politics and theory shortly after 1949. But that was partly due to the fact that they had done so right from the founding of the PRC in 1949, continuing the control and censorship mechanisms that the CCP had established in Yan'an and in the base areas during the 1930s and 1940s.[76] Because control over legal publications was only established slowly after the PRC was founded and the big push for centralization came a mere few months before the Marriage Law campaign, oversight was more difficult to achieve. If the Marriage Law campaign had meant to showcase a unified propaganda voice popularizing clear and "correct" understandings of the law, it had fallen short of expectations.

What exactly had happened in the preceding months that led to Chen's candid criticism? One explanation was that most publishers and presses were simply overwhelmed by the amount of demands sent down from Beijing, from the regional publishing authorities, and from municipal bureaus. Although the Marriage Law campaign was the primary focus for propaganda production during the first months of 1953, publishers also had to produce materials for other campaigns. Readings were needed for the campaigns to promote patriotic hygiene and physical education, and the government had also commenced preparations for the upcoming campaign to promote the Election Law. Most of the authors had to devise new materials for each new initiative or campaign, as there were only a few existing publications that could be copied. Because the same editorial teams often wrote, drew, or edited for different campaigns, they could quickly become overtaxed. When Stalin unexpectedly passed away in early March, moreover, publishers had to issue many different commemorative pieces on very short notice.

Similarly, government officials across most departments lamented that their respective units were understaffed and unable to complete all the tasks mandated by their superiors. Regional state publishers had been established swiftly in the months before and after the founding of the PRC. They were given no time to consolidate before campaign demands required them to produce materials at full capacity. Because publishing authorities were particularly concerned with popular readings, the strain on these departments was even higher. By the autumn of 1953, for instance, the North China region had four state publishers, but only twenty-seven people plus the head of publishing across the region worked above the common editorial level and could provide guidance to authors. And only a fraction of them worked on popular readings. This was also the problem in the South-West China administrative region, which had five state publishers, yet only twelve individuals above the basic editorial level. Shanxi People's Press and Yunnan People's Press were particularly problematic examples: Shanxi People's Press had one director and three assistant editors. Yunnan People's Press, at one point, only had one Youth League member who coordinated editorial work.[77] Regional party committees could have given guidance to publishers, but in actuality they left much up to the editors to decide.[78] It was difficult for these regional People's Presses to compete with the long-established private publishers and the larger joint private-state managed publishers, many of which were in a better position to respond to calls to publish swiftly, despite the increasing demands the new authorities made on them.

Finally, few writers, editors, and even censors had much training in the law. Many had received about the same amount of education as the people they were trying to teach through their writings. This made the task of writing about law and finding the correct interpretation all the more challenging, as the next chapter illustrates. Many publishers and their staff had just undergone the arduous period of the Thought Reform Campaign and were well aware of the need to get propaganda right.[79] Writing acceptable pieces was not a matter of implementing national guidelines, but—as authors were repeatedly reminded—it hinged on their own "educational levels." But what exactly differentiated "correct" and "erroneous" interpretations, beyond avoiding the most obvious examples of capitalist and feudal ideology? Political authorities were in a position to argue that anything they thought was an erroneous interpretation of the law in popular readings came as the result of insufficient training on the part of the author. Or, conversely, they could argue that erroneous interpretations were evidence of an author or editor's poor political consciousness. In October 1952, for example, Xinhua News Agency reporters had accused reporters at Shanghai's *Xinwen ribao* (News daily) and *Wenhui bao* and Tianjin's *Dagong bao (L'impartial)*, of creating rumors, singling out sensational stories of marriage and divorce court cases, and fabricating stories in order to sell more newspapers. These were some of the country's largest newspapers that had also actively published information on the Marriage Law. Reporters had to fear allegations of forging readers' letters, vulgarizing political news (including the manner in which reports discussed policies and laws), and publishing carelessly with only an interest in high sales numbers and profit-making.[80] Under these circumstances, writing on a law of national importance, or trying to explain an unprecedented and unfamiliar new mass campaign, was no trivial matter for writers and editors.

## Production and Distribution Mayhem

Problems with the printing and distribution of readings had also slowed down provisions for the Marriage Law campaign. The General Publishing Administration's notification in December 1952 on preparing publications for the campaign had been too optimistic. Publishers followed the plans and commissioned advertisements for their upcoming Marriage Law publications in all major newspapers from February 1953 onwards.[81] By late March and early April 1953, well into the campaign, however, readers reportedly sent letters to their local newspapers and bookstores complaining about inadequate provisions. In response to a reader's letter, Xinhua Bookstore's main branch wrote an open letter published in *Renmin ribao* that showed that this problem was taken seriously and that a reply was considered relevant for a wider audience of readers. Xinhua Bookstore officials explained that they were indeed experiencing delays and that some publishers had difficulties printing materials on time. Trying to deflect, they also pointed out that this problem pertained to only a small number of volumes and that there were lots of other state-published Marriage Law readings one might consult; with some 12.6 million volumes published only for the campaign, readers should surely be able to find something.[82]

Seeking to understand these local problems, Chen Kehan left on a longer trip to inspect bookstores in East China and South-Central China in spring 1953. Reporting back in regular letters to his colleagues, he wrote that delays at the printing plants were common, but they were not the only problems. Campaign readings printed on time could be delayed because they waited in storage facilities. When materials remained in storage for too long, they reached subscribers late even though there had not been any delay in printing. Sometimes bookstores failed to place copies on their shelves for customers to peruse, even if they had received stock. While surveying bookstores in South-Central China, he found that the regional Xinhua Bookstore branch still had some 40,000 copies of the booklet *Freedom of Marriage* in stock even though it was published in January 1953, well in time for the campaign.[83] In this case, the problem was poor coordination between the staff at storage facilities and bookstores.

This was not a new issue.[84] In late 1952, an investigation carried out by the Beijing Xinhua Bookstore branch had identified problems in the coordination of supply, marketing, and retail sales. Across the city, there had been about 5,513 different kinds of books available on the shelves in August 1952. By December, investigators reportedly only found some 1,400 different kinds of books. Not a single copy of Mao Zedong's *On the People's Democratic Dictatorship,* which was part of the reading syllabus for middle- and higher-level cadres for the Marriage Law campaign, was on the shelves. Nor could readers find copies of the novel *Happiness,* even though this was one of the recommended readings to accompany the Marriage Law.[85]

Timing had been a pervasive problem affecting print distribution during the campaign. In Shanghai, several work units and neighborhood committees had set aside parts of several days for activities that promoted study of the Marriage Law. Yet the state-published materials to which they had subscribed often only became available for collection from the local post after the groups had completed their study activities. When cadres in these work units and neighborhood officials realized that several of the advertised readings would not become available in time for them to carry out their work according to the education plans they had submitted to their superiors, or when delivery of new books failed, they decided to copy and reprint materials they already had.[86] Some of these reprints were based on inadequate or older materials, and as a result, according to Chen, mistakes multiplied.[87] Even so, Chen thought such practices should not be forbidden in the future, because that would only make life harder for grassroots cadres. At the same time, he did want local propaganda bureaus to supervise such "loose-leaf" republications of existing works. That way, loose-leaf materials for study and teaching could be made available locally, but people would theoretically be prevented from illegally copying entire books or copying the wrong bits, as had been the case during the implementation of the Marriage Law.[88]

Examples such as the "loose-leaf" reprints illustrate that the push to get reading materials into people's hands at times led authorities to turn a blind eye to exactly the kind of errors they had warned people about in newspaper articles and internal reports. Chen and his colleagues may have identified shortcomings in some of the publications for the study of the Common Program and in the provisions for the Marriage Law campaign, and they may have called for comprehensive organizational solutions, but they were willing to make concessions as the campaigns unfolded. The majority of privately published materials were permitted to circulate even if they contained minor errors of fact or interpretation. Plenty of them, some of which are discussed in the next chapter, were later criticized. Yet few publications were actually recalled.

This disjuncture between stated policy and practice greatly confused local propaganda authorities. How exactly were they to police campaign publications, authorities wondered, and how were they meant to strike a balance between publication diversity and "correct" content? Local publishing officials also feared that any major "errors" in publications produced by publishers within their geographical remit would reflect poorly on their propaganda work for the campaign. When in doubt, these officials thought it was preferable to shut down publications, an approach that the General Publishing Administration often found too hasty. In the summer of 1953, for example, the Beijing Municipal News and Publishing Office found several typographical mistakes and wrong explanations in the newly published songbook *Singing the Marriage Law* by Xinghua Bookstore, a private publisher. The booklet also contravened the 1952 regulations because it republished the entire Marriage Law and had accidentally added typos in the reprint of the law. The News and Publishing Office wanted to close Xinghua Bookstore and have its remaining holdings sold off and its publications no longer fit for circulation recycled to make new paper. Errors aside, it considered the entire project of explaining a law by a song, with the few words that the song lyrics could accommodate, to be an easy recipe for "distortions."[89] The General Publishing Administration was of a different opinion, though, and told its local Beijing colleagues to send a cadre to speak to the bookstore owner and ask him to revise the volume and to cease selling faulty stock. He was to be warned that if he committed another mistake of this kind he would not be treated with such leniency again.[90]

Because production, distribution, and supervision of propaganda materials could create diverse problems, readers were often put in a position of having to spot some of the errors in the campaign materials that were in circulation. Yet most readers were clearly not equipped to identify errors and the danger was high that they took mistaken information as correct. Once publications were sold and circulated it could become very difficult to instruct people about potential misinformation in the books they had purchased, aside from the minority who diligently read newspapers and regularly consulted the book criticism columns in newspapers such as *Guangming ribao* (Guangming daily) to keep themselves informed about such issues. Government and party officials were often poorly informed, as were average readers who did not work in the publishing industry or have much contact with officials involved in propaganda publishing and who could not easily identify private publishers and their products.[91]

## Conclusion: Applying Lessons Learned

The internal discussions about law publishing in 1953 served a political purpose. Officials at the General Publishing Administration kept on complaining that publishers and presses that produced materials for the Marriage Law campaign often failed to meet set targets. Yet many of these targets would have been difficult to fulfill under the best of circumstances. By tying shortcomings in campaign materials to staff and resource shortages and by blaming many of the problems on private publishers, the administration was able to make a compelling case for increased centralization of publishing activities.

Chen Kehan and his colleagues successfully used the shortcomings in politics and law publishing to lobby for a new national press with a mandate to publish popular materials on politics and law. The Popular Readings Press took up work in early 1954, in time to start preparations for the upcoming constitution discussion.[92] Plans for the press stated that about two hundred staff members were to be allocated from other work units. One of six editorial rooms was to be dedicated to material on law and policy.[93] The Popular Readings Press was not the only new press, moreover. In December 1954, the new national Law Press took over from the national People's Press responsibilities for the publication of laws, commentaries, and compendia. Together, these two publishers could service most of the demands for law-related readings. When they did not actively commission themselves, they helped regional presses decide on their print portfolios and took over some of the coordination work for publishing popular readings about laws.

This new arrangement placed the General Publishing Administration in a much stronger position to supervise and limit the circulation of legal information. By the time planning was underway for the creation of propaganda posters, comic booklets, and other popular literature to accompany the constitution draft discussion, the administration could much better delimit private law publishing. When administration officials began to prepare for the constitution draft discussion in spring 1954, they notified all regional and municipal publishing bureaus of much stricter regulations to manage private magazine and book publishers. Private publishers were not permitted to publish any legal texts, nor were they permitted to print interpretations of the articles and the words of the constitution because, the administration explained: "the constitution is a basic national law and the right to interpret it belongs to the state; the right to interpret the constitution draft belongs to the Constitution Drafting Committee of the People's Republic of China."[94] Allowing private publishers to print texts about the PRC's new laws, administration officials reasoned, had only created havoc in past years because they would not cease to try and interpret government policies, decrees, and laws.

In a change from previous years, regional and municipal publishing authorities were told to assemble all individuals responsible for private magazine and book publishing either on the day of the promulgation of the constitution draft or several days before, and to notify them of what types of materials they could and could not publish. Private businesses were only permitted to print research about the constitution draft, writings on constitutional theory, and reflections on how the national discussion was going. The notification left unresolved where the dividing line would be between official legal interpretations and unofficial reflections on the national constitution discussion. This forced private publishers who were careful about such matters to avoid these topics altogether. It also gave the General Publishing Administration more flexibility in determining whether private publishers had contravened the regulations.

Earlier debates about what and how much to publish thus shaped the constitution draft discussion in 1954. Print runs for booklets that discussed the constitution draft remained sizeable, though none reached the exuberant claim of millions of copies of the East China People's Press's booklets.[95] In July 1954, China Youth Press put out 900,000 copies of *An Introduction to Basic Constitutional Knowledge*. The Workers' Press followed in August with *An Introduction to Common Knowledge about the Constitution* at 135,000 copies, and in October North East Pictorial Press marketed a spin-off of the illustrated booklets called the *PRC Constitution Pictorial* at a mere 250,000 copies. Editors collated *Renmin ribao* editorials and commentaries and, in the case of Workers' Press and China Youth Press, pieces from the daily newspapers of the mass organizations with which they were affiliated. Such volumes were not necessarily published to provide readers with much new material. They returned to the tradition of the People's Press in seeking to provide handy compilations that would spare customers the work of collecting clippings.

Out of caution, most presses and publishers also did not publish their contributions right when the constitution draft was issued. Many publications appeared on bookshelves once the constitution discussion had been ongoing for several months. This led some cadres, such as one in Beijing, to complain that such materials could hardly be useful for the discussion if they were published much too late and, once finally published, if they lacked the concrete information needed to help with propaganda work.[96] How to produce and deliver materials on time all the while ensuring that the content was carefully checked continued to be a pressing question for publishers and publishing authorities.

Other problems that had surfaced between 1950 and 1953 remained. Although publishers had reduced print runs, critics continued to complain about the publishing "blindness" that regularly manifested during mass campaigns.[97] The print-run miscalculations surrounding the publication of the *Illustrated Marriage Law* also reverberated. In July 1954, when publishers were busy assembling materials on the new constitution, a letter to the editor in *Renmin ribao* reminded readers of the need to be frugal and reasonable in calculating print runs and to avoid repeating mistakes made during the Marriage Law campaign. The letter writer reported that the South-West People's Press had printed far too many copies of the *Illustrated Marriage Law* in 1952. Supply greatly exceeded demand and, according to the South-West branch of the Xinhua Bookstore, approximately half a million copies were left unsold, of which some 160,000 copies lingered in Xinhua Bookstore warehouses across the region. The issue with sales in this case was linked to campaign overlaps. When the "Three Antis" Campaign commenced, customers lost interest in readings about the Marriage Law, and backordered copies withered on the bookshelves. Then, months later, in an attempt to settle finances and compound losses, the press and the Xinhua Bookstore branch talked things over and decided that all merchandise would be shipped back from the stores to the regional main branch. In order to be able to ship everything in this way, and to prevent people involved in the shipment from picking up copies for free and re-selling them, the cover pages were to be torn off. This, however, meant that all these stocks would have to be destroyed once they reached the main branch.

The author of the letter seemed to be trying to intervene via *Renmin ribao* because he thought this was a "grave mistake." The bookstore had poorly prepared its print estimates, thus printing too many copies. Then the bookstore and the press did not consult carefully on what to do with the copies and instead just decided to destroy everything. The letter writer argued that prices should be lowered instead, or, with the help of local women's federation branches, the bookstore should consider presenting the remaining booklets as gifts to the masses, thereby ensuring that the books could fulfill their propaganda purpose as much as possible.[98] This was the route some local governments chose in the end, though not necessarily as a response to the reader's letter. As late as 1955, Hangzhou's municipal government handed out remaining copies of the booklet to district governments, which were to give them to newlywed couples as gifts once they had successfully registered their marriages.[99]

The general mechanics of publishing popular materials and the specific challenges of publishing materials for law propaganda determined how government and party could disseminate and implement laws. Not everything that was published was available to everyone, and those materials that were published were not necessarily state authorized just because they were published under a socialist government. It is important to remember that state attempts to coordinate and gain control over the publishing field and, more generally, the media coincided with the work to implement laws more systematically and to get the people to engage with laws. As the next two chapters illustrate, the fact that everything was happening at the same time posed additional challenges to carrying out effective law propaganda, which in itself was already a demanding task.

# PART II

PRACTICES: 1950–1962

# 3    What Is a Basic Spirit?

## The Marriage Law and the Model Legal Education Campaign

With its twenty-seven articles, the Marriage Law was meant to bring about a fundamental transformation in the configuration of family and marital life. The two articles that make up the law's "General Principles" (*yuanze*) summarize what this transformation should look like: Article 1 explains that "the feudal marriage system based on arbitrary and compulsory arrangements and the supremacy of man over woman, and in disregard of children, is abolished. The new democratic marriage system, which is based on free choice of partners, on monogamy, on equal rights for both sexes, and the protection of the lawful interests of women and children, is put into effect." Article 2 then states: "Bigamy, concubinage, child betrothal, interference in the remarriage of widows, and the exaction of money or gifts in connection with marriages, are prohibited."[1] Central government announcements painted a bleak picture of the "feudal marriage system" (*fengjian zhuyi hunyin zhidu*) as shaped by forced and arranged marriages, bigamy, polygamy, concubinage, abusive parents-in-law, family violence, mal-treated children and daughters-in-law, and forced child betrothals. Heralding a new era, the "New Democratic marriage system" (*xin minzhu zhuyi hunyin zhidu*) was to bring state protection, freedom to marry and divorce, gender equality, monogamy, happiness, harmony, and love.[2] As the Beijing municipal plan for cadre study of the law explained to its readers: the Marriage Law divides old and new marriage practices, and in doing so will help eradicate "old thinking," "old systems," and "old habits."[3]

The apparent simplicity of the language of the Marriage Law was deceptive. Ambiguous terms such as "happiness" and "harmony" made it difficult for people to know what the correct interpretation of the Marriage Law would look like. On paper, the framework of the new marriage system was broad enough to allow for different interpretations. Capitalist or bourgeois "reactionary" couples might lead lives that they considered happy and harmonious and that were therefore lawful (*hefa*) according to the Marriage Law. Party leaders, meanwhile, wanted people to interpret the Marriage Law more narrowly and within the confines of "Communist morality" and "social ethics." Read against the demands of Communist morality, simple marital happiness in line with the Marriage Law was not enough if the couple did not strive to lead a good socialist life dedicated to society, production, and the well-being of the country. Behavior of any kind, once it was labeled "feudal," could be linked to the feudal marriage system, which the Marriage Law declared unlawful (*bu hefa*). It followed that understanding and implementing the law involved more than knowing it by heart or being able to recite key passages. Implementation of the law through good political consciousness was the essence of the new marriage system. Operating within this system was, by association, lawful behavior.

This seemingly clear-cut division between old and new could be a problem for local party cadres, government officials, and activists who taught residents about the law. It could also be a problem for censors—the state's guardians of words and their meanings. And it could be a problem for cultural workers, including writers, artists, playwrights, and editors who worked for state, private, and joint state-private managed publishers, newspapers, theaters, and drama troupes. Educational materials assembled to explain the law within the old-versus-new binary had to help prospective audiences understand what the law meant beyond its generalizing articles and seemingly clear distinctions between old and new. Anyone who developed propaganda materials translated the law's words and categories into everyday stories to which they hoped audiences could relate. As Neil Diamant and Gail Hershatter have each demonstrated, personal and local circumstances ultimately determined how well this ideological framework of old and new marriage systems mapped onto the lives of the country's diverse population and how different people responded to it.[4] People's responses, in turn, were often contingent on the context in which they learned, and on the techniques used to teach them.

If having to make laws accessible and relatable within this at once rigid and vague framework was not already challenging enough, cultural workers also had to be careful not to accidentally *interpret* the law when all they were meant to do was to *explain* it. Reflecting on the production process of the *Illustrated Marriage Law*, the editors of East China People's Press told readers in a *Renmin ribao* article: "Popularizing government policies and laws is very serious work. One must adopt a very serious and cautious attitude. Even if it means explaining every single word or phrase, it all should have a certain basis, and under no circumstances should one add unauthorized supplementary explanations out of a desire to be concrete. Because publishers do not have the right to interpret laws."[5] Where to draw the line between explanation and interpretation, however, was a constant negotiation process between cultural workers and censors, rather than a matter of adhering to clear guidelines.

This chapter explores how the Marriage Law was taught, written about, performed, and learned during the campaign to thoroughly implement it in Beijing and Shanghai in spring 1953.[6] The campaign was an exceptional effort to teach one law to the general population. As the model legal education effort of the Mao period, it offers important insights into the rationale and logistics of teaching and learning laws under CCP rule.[7] In the context of this campaign, party cadres and government officials, municipal and district government bureaus and people's courts, cultural workers, and others considered in more detail than before how best to disseminate correct knowledge of the Marriage Law and how to make legal learning accessible through the use of mnemonic techniques and popular genres. I examine their public and internal discussions about how to create law propaganda and teach laws, and I trace how censors commented on materials. The diverse populations of these two cities responded in different ways to propaganda-based Marriage Law education, and I illustrate some of the responses that officials included in their formal reports. These different perspectives on the campaign suggest that most people who produced, controlled, and received Marriage Law education tried to make sense of socialist law. Often unknowingly, they also dealt with the state's problem of figuring out the role of the Marriage Law and of law more generally in a socialist society.

## Inhibitory Structures:
## The Paradox of Hierarchical Learning

When the central government decided to intensify the population's study of the Marriage Law with the help of campaign-style mass mobilization, local governments had to adapt their organizational structures. A national mass campaign brought much work for municipal governments and their departments. Campaign offices and bureaus were needed, work duties had to be assigned, education plans for the rest of the population were waiting to be drawn up and submitted, exhibitions required advance planning, propaganda materials had to be assembled, and study sessions needed to be scheduled.

Responding to the national Marriage Law Campaign Committee's instructions, most municipal and district governments began to set up their respective campaign committees and bureaus around early February 1953. Bureaus coordinated the daily work and held responsibility for implementing the committees' work plans.[8] In Beijing the campaign committee was led by the city's deputy mayor, Zhang Youyu, and included other officials involved in politico-legal work, such as Wang Feiran and Fan Jin. The Beijing campaign bureau was divided into four sections: a secretariat, an investigation and research group, a propaganda and education group, and a reception room (*qunzhong jiedai*) for the general public.[9] Over forty cadres were transferred from the Women's Federation, Propaganda Department, Bureau of Civil Affairs, procuratorate, Trade Union, and Youth League.[10] In both cities, the work units of specific industry sectors also had campaign offices— textiles, public utilities, construction, post and telecommunications, commerce, and transport.[11] Such structures were already in place in areas where investigation into the Marriage Law in late 1951 had been well organized and local governments could rename existing bureaus to reflect the aim of the new campaign. Following established patterns of CCP bureaucratic organization, control over the campaign was, officially, exercised vertically between different levels of government and horizontally between party and government offices.[12]

Campaign bureaus wrote up educational plans for the campaign that give some sense of its educational logic. The principal task of municipal campaign committees and district bureaus was to train high-level cadres first. Then the system cascaded downwards. High-level cadres were responsible for devising plans for the training of mid- and lower-level cadres in urban and suburban districts, factories, and work units. Besides educating the general population in basic knowledge of the Marriage Law, one of the purposes of the campaign was to continue party and government officials' general education in the country's main laws, following on from the Judicial Reform Movement. Even if they did not work full-time in the legal field, party officials and government personnel working at district, neighborhood, and street level often had to deal with legal questions. Next to being able to explain the Marriage Law to their residents, they had to be able to understand and put into practice the law's basic framework and principles.[13] All of this was to happen in three weeks so that educators would be ready by early March, the official national opening of the campaign.[14] In practice, preparations were delayed well into mid-March or sometimes later.

While official propaganda championed the revolutionary ideal of self-education, educational plans organized the dissemination of formalized knowledge from the top down. Top-down knowledge transmission reflected the mass line approach in which the party would educate the masses.[15] In practical terms, the central government also had to emphasize top-down education in order to try to achieve some cohesion in what people knew. Yet these educational plans disadvantaged those people and groups in local districts who needed the most education. Local cadres, officials, and activists were the ones to educate the most people and had the most responsibility for implementing the campaign at the grassroots, but they also received the least sustained legal training. This happened for two reasons. First, education plans presumed that those who were at the lower level of the education hierarchy had less need for more advanced theoretical contextualization of the law. Their seniors thought these people had a shorter attention span and could not be expected to learn as much as higher-level officials.[16] Second, the education program worked its way down from higher-level leadership to municipal and district government officials (including party cadres, trade union representatives, and women's representatives) and finally to state-employed report-givers, propagandists, and activists. By the time the final group was scheduled to receive education, there was often little time left because many district governments and work units were already well behind their campaign timetables. Seeking ad-hoc solutions to avoid further delays, many local governments chose to reduce training scheduled for grassroots operatives to a minimum.

The preparatory readings mirrored this top-down organizational hierarchy. The study plan of the Beijing Municipal Party Committee's Propaganda Department required that lower-level cadres read only the law, the propaganda outline of the campaign, and relevant directives. By contrast, it scheduled nine days of reading the law and associated directives for high-level cadres and dedicated another five days to teaching Communist morality. Mid-level cadres were permitted to skip some of the theoretical studies. They had to focus instead on detailed engagement with the full text of the Marriage Law, and they read other documents divided by party affiliation: party members studied the "Directive of Party Central on the Implementation of the Marriage Law." Non-party officials were given the "Directive of the Central People's Government Administrative Council on the Implementation of the Marriage Law."[17] They also had to read other directives, study the supplementary directive carefully, and work through volumes on love and Communist morality. This latter requirement reinforced the link between moral and legal dimensions that would become so crucial in Marriage Law propaganda. Deng Yingchao's "Study the Sublime Communist Morality of the People of the USSR"[18] was on the list, as was an essay on "the collective and the individual" published in the Soviet *Literary Magazine*.[19]

The training plan was more fragmented for propagandists and activists, who had the closest contact with residents and were in a position to exert influence over how laws were understood.[20] In Beijing's Qianmen District, the propaganda brigade consisted of dozens of activists who were specifically instructed in one propaganda technique to explain the law. Some were trained to discuss propaganda images; others narrated model stories, showed slide shows, or worked as amateur performers.[21] While such an approach ensured that activists had a clear portfolio and task, it also signaled that attaining a comprehensive understanding of laws required one to possess advanced knowledge and abilities and not merely good political consciousness—and it was for this reason that grassroots activists were limited to smaller, isolated tasks.

These educational plans chart the CCP's dilemma of knowledge transmission. With barely a month to prepare, however, local governments could not effectively respond to such gaps in training. Time available for preparations was cut further, moreover, when the central government suspended the campaign for seven days following Stalin's death. The city's residents had to organize and participate in national commemoration ceremonies and study Stalin's works in memoriam. Many work units further reduced the allotted days for cadres' training, which was originally between ten and fourteen days. In summary reports completed after the campaign, campaign committee branches often argued that they had been unable to devote time to learning about the law or to achieving a sufficient level of structure in their approach to training cadres, activists, and propagandists.[22] In some work units, such as the Shanghai No. 7 Cotton Mill, cadre training was limited to seven days, and ten days were left for general propaganda among the mill workers.[23] When, at the beginning of the general propaganda phase, the campaign committee of the Shanghai textile industry discovered that many mass organization members and propagandists had yet to receive any training, it told factories to introduce three-day crash courses relaying essential information about the law to participants, who were then sent out to impart their newly acquired legal knowledge. Meanwhile, those who had already acquired some understanding of the Marriage Law could make do with two days of supplementary training, to be carried out alongside campaign propaganda work.[24] Still, their education was patchy at best.[25] It was not uncommon for lower-level cadres to be in training for part of a day and then spend the other part propagating and explaining the law to others.[26] Cadres may then have been immersed in the material by the time they talked to people later in the day, but most could not explain the law comprehensively. Instead they proceeded bit by bit, as they learned about the law themselves, thus making misinterpretations and misunderstandings far more likely.[27]

By March, when the campaign month officially began, many cadres and activists were still waiting for their training and felt unsure about their responsibilities. In the avalanche of paperwork the campaign generated, reports about the shortcomings in preparatory work abounded.[28] Some summary reports, filed at the end of the campaign, likened it to a battle; the front had been too long and the time to fight it was too short for work to be truly successful.[29] Work units often had difficulties finding staff with knowledge of the Marriage Law who could be spared from other work. Some factories, such as the Shanghai Guangzhong Dyemaking Factory, reported that their campaign office was so poorly run that they restructured it in late March hoping to fulfill at least some of the propaganda targets.[30] All too often, office staff drifted off into personal chats with people who came by or offered solutions to marital and family problems. *Neibu cankao* reported more examples of this kind from other Chinese cities such as Wuhan and Kaifeng.[31]

The difficulties of organizing education made it more important that propaganda materials transmitted a coherent basic message about what the Marriage Law was and how it should be understood. The central government advocated selected educational and mnemonic techniques to simplify the learning process. For those cadres and residents who wanted to learn about the law, propaganda materials became important reference materials. Writings and images could be helpful additions or correctives to what they had learned in report meetings and discussions. Yet such materials were not a universal remedy that ensured that everyone learned and understood the Marriage Law in the same way. Propaganda materials could also add to people's confusion about what the law actually meant and what they were expected to do in response to having learned about it.

## Making Sense of the Marriage Law's Basic Spirit

The most important purpose of this mass campaign was to educate everyone in the "basic spirit" (*jiben jingshen*) of the Marriage Law. Party and government directives, propaganda materials, internal publications, and reports filed at the local level all talked about educating people in this "basic spirit." Focusing on the basic spirit, as the Shanghai Propaganda Department explained, would allow officials both to "mobilize" people and to "control" that they learned the law correctly.[32] Over time, the basic spirit became a convenient shorthand for that which people should know about the law, and an inconvenient impediment for anyone trying to pin down what the law meant.

The concept's simplicity could work well for propaganda purposes. Some documents explained that Articles 1, 2, 3, and 8 of the Marriage Law outlined the basic spirit. These were the articles that delineated the feudal marriage system and the New Democratic marriage system.[33] Arranged marriages, patriarchy, bigamy, concubinage, child betrothal, interference in the remarriage of widows, and bribes were all attributed to the feudal marriage system. The new marriage system stressed free choice of one's spouse, monogamy, gender equality, mutual love and support, harmonious families, and protection for women and children. To learn the dichotomy of the old and new marriage systems was to learn the basic spirit of the law.

There were different approaches to infusing the basic spirit into educational work during the campaign. The Beijing municipal government advised cadres to begin their reports and group discussions of the law based on Articles 1 and 2.[34] The South-Central region's Marriage Law Campaign Office recommended beginning with Article 8 and then branching out to Articles 1 and 2 and the basic spirit of the law. Report-givers could then discuss the entire law, if needed. The party cell preferred this approach because it claimed it prevented participants from learning only isolated elements of the law and legal vocabulary. If, for instance, in some meetings people only learned and discussed the slogan "harmonious families" (from Article 8), this could open up the door for some to argue they did not have to learn about the law, either because they were too young to have families or because they felt they already had harmonious families. The party cell also thought that this approach further forestalled the possibility that in marriages where the wife stayed at home and the husband worked, the couple could argue that their families were perfectly harmonious without the wife contributing to production.[35] Thousands of women across the country were housewives, and the basic spirit of the Marriage Law now suggested to them that the CCP's legal definition of harmonious families required more than love—it required both partners to contribute to the construction of a new society.

The basic spirit thus bound together law, morality, and people's consciousness. Propaganda work for the campaign, as we will see below, suggested to people that their private lives should conform to pre-determined frameworks of an ideal socialist marital and family life. It discouraged people from interpreting the stipulations of the Marriage Law to fit into their diverse individual lives. Behavior not explicitly prohibited by law could be criticized nonetheless. Propagandists and the authors of propaganda materials used the basic spirit to make sweeping claims about the manner in which the Marriage Law would help regulate society. By association with the unlawful old marriage system, any action or behavior associated with feudalism was no longer merely ideologically wrong but could be called unlawful.[36] Lawful behavior, meanwhile, was conflated with the moral category of good and the political category of correct behavior. This conflation was highlighted in the Beijing municipal government's campaign summary report, which explained that the city had focused on correcting people's viewpoints about the "good and bad, correct and wrong, lawful and unlawful."[37]

The basic spirit of the law also became a barometer for legal knowledge. Trying to make sense of how much people knew of the Marriage Law and how well they understood it, most reports classified people's legal knowledge as either correct, erroneous, or wavering in between and in need of more education. A person could either understand or fail to understand the spirit of the law. This approach conformed to Mao's theory of the mass line, with its advocacy of repeated rounds of learning and discussion in order to correct erroneous knowledge. Keeping within this logic, propaganda work for the Marriage Law would help to bring about change: from people not knowing the law's basic spirit to knowing it, and then from knowing it to understanding it and to fully living by the letter of the law.

The official demand that people should understand the Marriage Law's basic spirit therefore went beyond just knowing or supporting the law. During meetings, officials who only asked people "Is the Marriage Law good?" were criticized for failing to understand that this campaign was about more than getting people to voice approval. In turn, reports held up anyone in the audience who—when asked what they thought about the Marriage Law—responded plainly that "the Marriage Law is good," without being able to explain why or what the law actually said, as an example of a lack of understanding.[38] Conversely, understanding the Marriage Law also did not mean that all behavior in contravention of the law should automatically be subject to legal prosecution. In Beijing, the municipal Propaganda Department told officials to criticize anyone who thought that all legal problems, no matter how small, should be passed on to government authorities, anyone who argued that "the law should be followed more strictly," and anyone who thought that "any violations of the Marriage Law should be handled according to the law." All of these responses were "left mistakes" and showed that people had not understood the basic spirit of the Marriage Law, which put education and raising people's consciousness first.[39]

## The Basic Spirit in Practice

Propaganda materials handed out to cadres and activists were constructed along the binary of the basic spirit.[40] Mnemonic techniques helped to make this work. The simplified language of the law lent itself to memorization. Articles 1 and 2 could easily be juxtaposed, between the old and the new and right and wrong ideas and practices. The terms of the new marriage system were then set against colloquial slogans and popular proverbs to describe family life, now marshaled to represent the "feudal marriage system." These include the "three subjections and four virtues," "the husband sings and the wife follows," "parents determine marriage," "those who oblige are filial," and "exemplary chastity." Many of these slogans were associated with the Confucian, and now feudal, family system. The authoritative and homogenizing language of the law challenged the once-authoritative language of traditional customs.[41] The simple language of the law's general principles was further simplified into four-, five-, and six-character phrases, and thereby became a tool to delineate the scope of campaign discussions.

Cultural workers included abbreviated slogans taken from the full text of the Marriage Law in their stories, songs, rhymes, and images. The inclusion of these slogans on the pages of popular reading materials suggested to readers that propaganda materials authoritatively conveyed the law. Familiar propaganda techniques acquired a new legal dimension in the course of the campaign. Human-interest stories narrated the experiences of fictional characters or real people and invited audiences to find commonalities in their own lives and experiences. Songs, rhymes, and slogans encouraged people to memorize the law and embrace it emotionally. Three-character classics, four-character classics, five-character classics, and one-thousand character lessons, many of which were genres popular in elementary school education for decades and sometimes centuries before the Communist Party assumed power, rendered the text of the law and explanations into a familiar rhythmic pattern, making it easier for readers to memorize the law's basic content. The first two couplets of the *Marriage Law Seven-Character Song*, for instance, told readers: "The government promulgated the Marriage Law, [it] toppled feudal old marriages. Feudal marriages were unlawful, [they] sacrificed men's and women's happiness."[42]

Artists painted images to help people find and make sense of the basic spirit of the Marriage Law. Propaganda posters depicted happy revolutionary couples, dressed in plain rural clothes, walking hand-in-hand in front of an oversized copy of the Marriage Law opened at the pages of Article 1 and 2 of the "General Principles." Other pictures suggested how to understand the binary of lawful and unlawful behavior within the broader context of social ethics and Communist morality. One of the images in the *People's Thousand-Character Lesson*, for instance, contrasts two marriage ceremonies (fig. 3.2). The captions explain that the image on top represents a "lawful marriage" while the one on the bottom shows an "unlawful marriage." The "lawful marriage" is that of a couple with their backs turned toward the reader and looking at a cadre dressed in uniform who, below a portrait of Mao and the national flag, administers the marriage registration with a lecturing hand held high. To forestall doubts, on the backs of the bride and groom are printed the respective legal ages for women and men to marry: eighteen and twenty years old. The image of the "unlawful

Fig. 3.1. Yu Yunjie, "Freedom of Marriage, Happiness and Harmony," 1953. (Source: Landsberger Collection, International Institute of Social History [Amsterdam].)

marriage," illustrates a couple dressed in Republican attire, standing in front of a double happiness sign and a table at which the marriage ceremony is to be performed. Printed on the front of their bodies are their ages—clearly indicating that both are below the legal minimum age for marriage.

The Marriage Law did not include any rules about attire or decorations. The image tied the "lawful" behavior of meeting the legal

Fig. 3.2. "Article 8: Early Marriage Is Prohibited" from the *People's Thousand-Character Lesson: The Great Event of Marriage*, 1951. (Source: *People's Thousand-Character Lesson*, Shanghai: Yuanchang yinshuguan, 1951, p. 4.)

requirement of the minimum age for marriage to a person's external appearance, and linked law to political and moral expectations. To conform to sartorial, behavioral, and moral norms was to be lawful. That being said, images such as this could threaten anyone who did not know exactly how old they were and for whom a minimum age requirement could be a puzzling requirement or indeed a serious obstacle to marriage.

Another common image was that of the law as a material object bringing happiness and prosperity. The *Marriage Law Four-Character Classic* shows the Marriage Law as an oversized book floating in the air above a cheering crowd of rural and urban residents, against a background that is both industrial and agricultural (fig. 3.3). Artists borrowed from the visual repository of other propaganda campaigns; the first volume of Mao's *Selected Works* had been displayed as a larger-than-life book. The Marriage Law as an oversized book became reified as a symbol of a legal idea, bestowed onto people from the party on high, floating above "the masses."

Fig. 3.3. Cover page of the *Marriage Law Four-Character Classic*, 1951.
(Source: Shanghai: Zhenli shudian, 1951.)

## Writing about Models

If the basic spirit of the Marriage Law formed the ideological center-piece of the campaign, models were its primary mode of transmission. The party and government's emphasis on the basic spirit directed the search for models to typify the new and old marriage systems. Models, however, were not easily found or constructed. The experience of the editors at East China People's Press is indicative. In February 1953, *Renmin ribao* published the editors' recollections on preparing campaign materials to provide a model for other editors and authors to follow. According to their recollections, when they began to work on the *Illustrated Marriage Law*, they realized that it would not be possible to juxtapose "the People" and "enemies" in a discussion of all the articles of the Marriage Law because the division only applied to a few articles. Because the *Illustrated Regulations* had described how to identify and punish "enemies of the People," the editors and artists could exaggerate "the enemy" for added emphasis: "bad" elements wore sunglasses and bourgeois Western suits and hats, they smoked pipes, they were haggard and sickly. Members of the People, as well as party officials hunting the enemy, were healthy, robust, and tall men and women, clothed in simple and clean attire such as Sun Yatsen suits, workers' overalls, trousers, shirts, and simple dresses. Even the Agrarian Reform Law could be explained in terms of this dichotomy between "the People" as good and "landlords" as their enemies. As government directives insisted that the Marriage Law was mostly a matter among the People, the *Illustrated Marriage Law* had to first explain how feudal ideas were affecting Chinese people's marital and family lives, and then outline how the Marriage Law would address this. The Marriage Law also did not specify what would happen to those who broke the law, nor did it say what would happen to victims of feudal oppression once they were liberated. Because the Marriage Law was vague on these points, editors were unsure, for example, whether their booklet should help explain what pre-liberation foster daughters-in-law or remarried widows should do post-liberation.[43]

The editors decided to include one general explanatory image for each of the law's articles and a selection of specific personal model examples to discuss some of the most common problems in the law's implementation. They thought that specific examples would help them avoid generalizations. When the press submitted the draft for inspection, the regional and national cultural authorities suggested instead that any discussion of the Marriage Law should be developed on the basis of "socialist ideology" rather than individual case studies. Explanations should compare new and old marriage systems, and examples should, for instance, outline why the feudal marriage system was closely linked to feudalism in general. And so the editors rewrote the draft.

That the CCP saw models as one of the most important propaganda techniques for law dissemination was clear from the fact that even Mao Zedong took an interest in this topic. If the quantity of campaign records involving Mao in some way is an indication, Mao was barely concerned with the planning of the campaign. But he did spend a little time saying something about models. In mid-March he sent a telegram to Liu Jingfang, head of the national campaign committee, and instructed him to make extensive use of models. Upon reading issue no. 11 of the campaign committee office's internal briefings on the progress of the campaign, Mao had decided that examples of good and poor implementation of the law should be made available more widely with the help of "comrades at *Renmin ribao* and Xinhua News Agency."[44] The internal briefing had talked about two villages in Fengcheng County in Liaodong Province that had been selected as campaign trial areas.[45] Here, the method of comparing the old and new systems by way of personal stories in small groups and then as model stories in large village meetings had worked well to help villagers understand what the law was about and to encourage them to live "harmoniously." Four days later, *Renmin ribao* printed a feature story on the county's work.[46]

Even without Mao's intervention, propaganda authorities knew that they had to select models carefully. In 1951, educational materials had included plenty of negative examples of law implementation. By 1953, propaganda authorities wanted to emphasize mostly positive examples. Xinhua News Agency investigations and internal reports that detailed experiences of test sites for the campaign showed that models worked well, as long as these stories were carefully chosen and included plenty of examples of "happy marriages" (*meiman hunyin*).[47] As one report from Jiangxi Province explained: "This [using models] is the best method for the masses to educate themselves."[48]

In late January, Xinhua News Agency instructed reporters on what to look out for when they researched materials for stories that would be printed in the public (as opposed to internal) news. Reporters were told to avoid relationship problems, family fights (except those deemed feudal in nature), and "urban phenomena" such as bigamy. Xinhua News Agency wrote that these topics threatened to expose the grey areas of the law and could involve local officials in difficult conversations about how to dissolve bigamous relationships. Divorce, too, should be avoided, even if plenty of people were seeking divorces at the time. Stories should instead tell readers about couples who successfully reconciled. The agency listed different types of models: model cadres who had implemented the law well; couples who had successfully undergone struggles to achieve freedom of marriage; happy families and districts with happy families where production had increased; children who were the happy products of a free marriage; older couples and in-laws who had worked to change their thinking and render their families democratic and harmonious; model parents and grandparents who supported their children's quest for a free marriage; couples whose lives had greatly improved following mediation; and widows who had successfully struggled to remarry and now lived much happier and better lives. Negative examples were to be limited to those who actively interfered with the Marriage Law, and those who exhibited other "erroneous thinking" and behavior.[49]

Local campaign offices provided more specific guidelines to their own staff. In late March, the Shanghai municipal campaign office's propaganda group sent work units a detailed list of criteria for "models" to be selected for a major educational broadcast in early April. There were four different types. First, they were looking for new families built on gender equality, marriage freedom, mutual respect and love, active contributions to production, and progressive political thinking. Second, they sought out couples as well as pairs of mothers and daughters-in-law whose relations had improved as a result of Marriage Law propaganda. To qualify for this category, the personal stories had to show clearly how life was before learning about the law and how it changed immediately afterwards. The transformation should be clearly visible and based on a change in thinking; for example, the husband or the mother-in-law realizing that patriarchy or excessive desire to control others was not in line with the basic spirit of the law. Moreover, these models were supposed to be of average economic means in order to show that one did not have to be privileged to achieve change. Third, the propaganda section was looking for men and women who had struggled with the feudal marriage system and had "achieved a victory." Couples or individuals could only be included in the broadcast if they had found a solution to their problems without resorting to violence and—crucially—without eloping. Their stories should illustrate how thought reform, persuasion, and education taking place within people's daily lives and surroundings led to change. Moreover, the propaganda group only wanted examples of people who, at the time of the broadcast, could be reasonably defined as living in a free marriage and having a happy family life. Finally, the group wanted stories of propagandists or mass activists who had achieved evident successes, respected the law in their own lives, and in whom local residents trusted.[50]

Authenticity (*zhenshixing*) mattered to many propaganda officials. Reports had to be believable, and some cultural workers and local
officials could become too obsessed with making models interesting
and finding good stories. Xinhua News Agency cautioned reporters not
to exaggerate examples of happy and harmonious families excessively.
Models were not meant to be perfect; they were meant to be relatable,
in order to help people understand that learning the Marriage Law was
a matter of thought struggle among the People, not the kind of class
struggle they were familiar with from previous campaign experiences.[51]
The Shanghai municipal campaign office told news secretaries to be
careful when following leads for possible stories.[52] They were worried
because embellished personal stories circulated across town. In some
cases, writers felt that the true stories they witnessed did not make for
exciting reading. So they changed their stories or invented new ones. If
discovered, fake stories caused people to doubt all propaganda. Propaganda authorities were on the watch to ensure that the quality of publications met expectations.

Propaganda materials in support of the campaign were in good
supply; the problem was that many of the available readings had been
published by private, not state, publishers. Most people did not know
this. Often unaware of the alleged quality issues publishing authorities
complained about in their internal reports, or oblivious to their relevance, local library staff compiled catalogues and indexed available
materials, including newspaper and magazine reports, booklets, songbooks, and textbooks. Report-givers, cadres, and propagandists could
go to the library to get materials and prepare their reports.[53] Neighborhoods and work units opened their campaign work meetings with a
formal report explaining what the Marriage Law was all about and
using model examples.[54] Radio stations meanwhile invited models to
speak on their regular programs.[55]

Campaign committees placed report meetings and mass discussions of the law at the heart of the campaign.[56] Report meetings, which
entailed a report-giver explaining the basic spirit of the law and the
reasons why the law was important, were unexceptional. They could
be very unpopular, though, as men worried that their spouses would
"speak bitterness" against them, accusing them of physical violence
and maltreatment.[57] Mass discussions of real-life examples were even

more contested. People liked hearing about other people's experiences and struggles, but at the same time, topics on the Marriage Law lent themselves only too well to gossip, rumors, and interference in other people's lives.[58] Several residents admitted that they did not want to risk having certain details about themselves and their partners circulate publicly lest they would not be able to show their faces in that neighborhood again. During the previous two years, as Neil Diamant has discussed, many activists had used personal details revealed during discussions, making them seem scandalous in order to catch other people's attention in this way. This had been an especially prominent problem both in Shanghai and Beijing districts during the investigation into the enforcement of the Marriage Law that took place in late 1951 and early 1952, and it was still a problem in 1953. The central government could not prevent a new wave of such problems because its directives and supplementary directive either did not reach everyone on time, were not read, or were not taken seriously.

Although some residents worried that report meetings and public discussions could expose aspects of their family or marital lives they wanted to keep out of the public eye, many were less hesitant to participate in other types of propaganda activities. Propaganda picture discussions, story-telling sessions, blackboard reading classes, gatherings to listen to radio broadcasts, and theater performances successfully got people to pay attention to learning the law. These were activities for which district governments had trained activists. Photographs taken during the campaign showed young women activists in Shanghai, working as docents for local exhibitions. With wooden pointers in hand, they directed the attention of groups of a few dozen men and women to posters that explained the articles of the law in individual images, much like the *Illustrated Marriage Law*.[59] Docents were instructed to stay close to the materials and avoid inserting their own opinions, though this worked as often as not.[60] These types of lessons were popular. Compared to individual propaganda activities in neighborhoods or factories, moreover, campaign exhibitions offered a greater variety of propaganda materials to visitors, many of whom attended together with their work units.[61] A special Marriage Law–themed day with picture exhibitions and plays drew crowds to Beijing's Workers' Cultural Palace.[62] The city's Qianmen District also reported that picture discussions had brought many more people to meetings than before. Docents and report-givers would go to different alleys (*hutong*) to explain their pictures.[63] In one case, in Xiaoshun Hutong, the local residents made the report-giver stay on for the whole day, giving him drink and food and asking him more and more questions.[64]

Many of these activities were gendered, as we will see in the next section on plays and operas. Songs and dances gave local women the opportunity to combine activities they enjoyed with study and memorization of the language of the law.[65] Photos of picture discussions often showed groups of women workers engaging with the law, and officials emphasized that women had the most intensely emotional responses to their legal lessons, often writing that local women had cried when they finally "correctly" understood the Marriage Law. To promote such activities, for example, the Shanghai No. 9 Cotton Factory handed out hand-copied scripts for Marriage Law songs and shorter plays adapted from the Shanghai Film Studio and encouraged women especially to participate in staging performances.[66]

Municipal governments worried, however, about how local officials managed the campaign at the grassroots. In keeping with Zhou Enlai's February directive, they insisted that nobody should compel people to participate in propaganda during the campaign because this would go against the mass line "among the People." Writing several months after the campaign had concluded, the Beijing Party Committee explained that the general principle of letting the masses "come and go freely" had at first worried street-level and village grassroots cadres who thought that "if it's unchecked, who will come and listen?" Later, the report continued, many came to realize that "if people come but their hearts do not, then that is of no use."[67] In places where the voluntary approach worked, mass line propaganda could become a time-consuming activity as a consequence. When the Shanghai Municipal Propaganda Department wanted to have outdated People's Press Marriage Law posters removed from alleyways and factory walls, it told local officials to check if the posters had been hung up by residents living on the streets. If so, officials were not supposed to just take the posters down; instead, they were to help residents understand why these posters were no longer useful and encourage them to take them down themselves.[68]

While reports may have emphasized that people should be encouraged but not compelled to do anything, the practice of Marriage Law propaganda often appeared different. One common complaint was that cadres would go on lecturing about the Marriage Law, forgetting to tailor what they were saying to the audience they were speaking to, which simply bored people. The problem was so widespread that *Manhua yuebao* (Cartoon monthly) addressed it in a satirical cartoon about a couple's registration ceremony. The image shows the presiding cadre speaking at length to a room full of empty chairs. Except for the bride and groom, everyone else has fled the room, and the last person is just on their way out. The groom looks at his bride and tells her, "If I wasn't the groom, I'd leave as well."[69]

Personal experiences of disseminating the Marriage Law and of learning the law therefore varied significantly. The schematic approach may have divided "right" and "wrong," "good" and "bad" understandings of the basic spirit of the law, thus simplifying the work of campaign bureaus and unifying the experience of learning about the law across different parts of town. But this approach both helped and impeded understanding. Officials at the Beijing Municipal Propaganda Department complained that many of the residents they had spoken to were unable "to distinguish right from wrong" because they had not really understood the law's basic spirit.[70] At the same time, residents criticized cadres for being too simplistic in the way they discussed the laws. In Beijing, a few residents told local officials that one could not divide right and wrong in the way the new government was suggesting.[71]

A schematic approach to law dissemination, moreover, contributed to engendering similarly schematic responses. In both Beijing and Shanghai, local officials and residents repeatedly argued that because these urban centers were hardly feudal, the central directives were unsuitable to implementing the Marriage Law and would alienate the masses.[72] A *Neibu cankao* report on campaign advancements in the East China region, meanwhile, explained that the problem could colloquially be summed up as "the four fears and the three do not propagates." The three "do not propagates" referred to officials not propagating the law to those men who had a girl already, not propagating it to foster daughters-in-law, and not propagating it to unharmonious couples. The four "fears" were the fear of being delayed with core tasks, the fear of being disciplined for having done something wrong, the fear of trouble, and the fear of committing a mistake.[73]

## The Theatrics of Marriage and Law

Disseminating legal knowledge was a complicated task. At times it was also an unpopular activity. Yet drama and opera performances staged in support of the campaign were, together with films, among the truly popular components of state-mandated legal learning.[74] Performances, as Qianmen District officials explained, were what "the masses most liked to watch."[75] Drama and opera were not necessarily popular because of the legal information they imparted but because of the storylines into which legal information was infused. Campaign plans of neighborhoods and work units in both cities set aside two to three days for watching plays or films.[76] Plays were so popular that Xinhua News Agency journalists reported on cadres in Hebei Province who thought that having a few meetings, putting up some great colorful posters and some blackboards with the Marriage Law text, and then staging several plays that people enjoyed would be quite enough for a successful campaign and there would be no need for more extensive discussions.[77] Listings in local newspapers including Shanghai's *Xinwen ribao*, *Xinmin bao*, and *Jiefang ribao*, as well as *Beijing ribao*, were filled with the announcements of local theaters on their performances of famous operas about tragic romances, and plays about revolutionary love, couples' struggles, and families' new lives under CCP rule. Some of Qianmen's theaters sold several hundred tickets per performance, and sometimes many more people would come hoping for a ticket. Workers and residents as well as work unit theater groups put on plays for local residents.[78] Professional troupes traveled to more remote districts to give visiting performances to those who could not easily travel downtown. In this process, the stage became an essential space for legal education. Theatrical, operatic, and film performances enacted examples of "lawful" and "unlawful" lives far better than any picture or story could.

The central government had several reasons to promote plays and operas during the Marriage Law campaign.[79] These were traditionally popular forms of entertainment and had long also been used for educational purposes.[80] Drama scripts and opera scores were readily available material. Moreover, operas and dramas could reach audiences other genres could not. As Xia Yan, China's famous playwright who would become deputy Minister of Culture in 1954, explained, the problem was that Shanghai, much like other cities, had residents who would not read the newspapers, listen to radio broadcasts, watch spoken dramas, or go to see Soviet movies. Such genres were useless in trying to reform their thoughts. They loved Peking Opera, Hu Opera, Yue Opera, and the tabloids.[81]

Propaganda would have to respond to this challenge, and the implementation of the Marriage Law was especially well suited to working with theatrical material. Many familiar old operas were used to portray the "old marriage system," characterized by "feudal" life, tragic stories of love, and of families and marriages in an oppressive society. Traditional operas staged in support of the campaign seldom had a happy ending in order to ensure that audiences understood that life in the "old society" had not been happy. New revolutionary plays, by contrast, often showcased hardships that were eventually ended as a result of the law and the new marriage system. They focused on how struggles among families, local communities, and couples were resolved with the help of the Marriage Law. Such a sequence closely followed the narrative patterns David Apter and Tony Saich identify as exegetical bonding promoted by the CCP since its time at Yan'an.[82] Revolutionary plays presented idealized types and, as Haiyan Lee has written, "individuals who are embodiments of ideological categories, individuals without the refractoriness of individuality."[83] The theater stage allowed for the dichotomy of new and old systems to play out on several levels, from costume, make-up, and stage decorations to scripts, storylines, language, and acting. It was the place where audiences were confronted with interpretations of what it meant to be a hero, a heroine, or a villain.

When the Government Administrative Council called for renewed attention to Marriage Law implementation in late 1951, many of the PRC's leading writers and playwrights— including Guo Moruo, Zhou Yang, Tian Han, Lao She, Xia Yan, and Zhao Shuli—wielded their pens in support of the law. They composed new works, revised existing scripts, and suggested which old opera and drama storylines could be performed without revision. In his concluding speech to the First

National Congress on Theatrical Performances in autumn 1952, Zhou Yang, who was shortly thereafter appointed to the national committee for the Marriage Law campaign, then singled out several plays on the Marriage Law that he thought were of particular value to the masses.[84] The timing of the congress aided the implementation of the Marriage Law. Widely popularized, descriptions and photos of the performances staged at the congress provided guidance to dramatists and actors across the country during the campaign. Municipal and rural districts, counties, and villages also developed their own plays based on old tales or new model stories popular in the area. To help with this production work, the Shanghai Municipal Propaganda Department dispatched some of its cadres to take groups of writers to those parts of the municipality that it thought had implemented the Marriage Law well since 1950.[85]

The example of *Luohan Coins* illustrates the process of producing a play that was popular with both audiences and censors alike, and was soon known as "The Great Marriage Law Comedy."[86] Based on Zhao Shuli's story *Registration*, it was written to accompany the promulgation of the Marriage Law and was first published in the magazine *Shuoshuo changchang* (Recite and sing) in June 1950.[87] Set during the 1950 Lantern Festival, a month before the promulgation of the Marriage Law, the play tells the story of a young man, Li Xiaowang, and a young woman, Zhang Aiai, who fall in love and exchange Luohan coins as a token of their affection for each other. The village head and other villagers refuse to accept Li and Zhang's wish to marry. Zhang's mother discovers the coins in her daughter's bed and is reminded of her youth when she, too, exchanged coins with one man but was then forced to marry another. After several weeks, during which both mother and daughter resist the pressure of matchmakers, fellow villagers, and the village head, the Marriage Law is proclaimed and the village head is criticized and educated. The two lovers marry in a simple registration ceremony, and at the end of the play the cast sing "The Marriage Law, it has been passed, it has been passed, you men and women smile! From now on marriage must be free, it must be free, life will be good with much happiness!"[88]

The outward propaganda success of *Luohan Coins* was touted as an accomplishment resulting from the work of a team of authors who rewrote the play following the national congress. At the same time, internal reports showed that the making of *Luohan Coins* was closely linked to writers' anxiety about producing adequate work in the aftermath of the Thought Reform Campaign of late 1952. Conforming to the principle that "one person writes and several people revise," a collective revision team was formed consisting of Wen Mu, Xing Zhi, and Zong Hua, who all received additional advice from other team members. Reworked several times in the course of a month, the final draft was published in time for the Marriage Law campaign.[89] At the congress, Zhou Yang had been full of praise for the play, saying that it successfully depicted the victory of new marriages. Yet he had also mentioned that some passages felt unnatural and suggested that the authors had not spent enough time engaging directly with people in the countryside villages they sought to describe. Taking Zhou's criticisms seriously, the authors criticized themselves for writing too many formulaic and abstract sentences in the scene in which Zhang and Li register their marriage. This, so the report explained, was indeed because the authors had only experienced feudal weddings and could not convey to readers the emotions of a free marriage and registration. They could write about the feudal past, but they felt they had more difficulty describing the new present.[90] Given these shortcomings, the authors professed, at least in the context of this report, that people were justified in criticizing the play for its continued shortcomings, rather than for its few accomplishments. For audiences to feel moved by the law as it was performed on stage, it had to appear authentic.

If narrative authenticity came under political scrutiny, then so did styles of performance and choices of genre and representation. The play *Little Son-in-Law* tells the story of another young production activist, Yang Xiaocao, and the head of a local production team, Tian Xi'er, who are prevented from marrying because Yang's father has betrothed her to a twelve-year-old boy from a wealthy family. The miserable marriage is dissolved under the Marriage Law after Yang seeks the village cadre's help, pursues a divorce, and registers her new marriage with Tian.[91] The Ping Opera version of this storyline won prizes for best script and theatrical performance at the congress.[92] At the same time, newspaper articles criticized the Hu Opera version of the play, which had been performed in Shanghai before the congress. In the Ping Opera, Tian's mother is a loving woman and an active revolutionary who reforms herself following the Communist takeover. But the Hu Opera portrays her as an old, frail, angry woman, archetypical of what its directors thought was the classic feudal mother whom the Marriage Law had made unlawful. Articles in *Xinwen ribao* told troupes that performed this version that they had forgotten their rural roots and had become infected by the corrupted culture and tastes of petty urbanites.[93] Instead of focusing on the negative rural stereotype, they were supposed to celebrate peasants' daily life to urban residents and show how people in the countryside had successfully transformed their lives. Yet this complicated the work of writers and performers as they strove to illustrate the evil feudal marriage system in rural areas while at the same time glorifying rural life for urban audiences.

Such criticism could extend to the country's famous playwrights as well, as the example of Lao She's Marriage Law play *Liushujing* illustrates. The story is set in Liushujing Hutong in Beijing's Dongcheng District, from which its title is derived. The play centers on the twenty-year-old foster daughter-in-law Li Zhaodi, who was sold at age thirteen to the Wang family. Now widowed, Li wishes to marry her neighbor Zhou Qiang, but her in-laws try to prevent her from doing so and frequently mistreat her. When she attempts to drown herself in a well, the local cadre, the women's representative, and Zhou Qiang just manage to save her; finally, after a struggle session against her in-laws, she is free to register her marriage with Zhou Qiang.[94]

Performances of *Liushujing* were well attended, and amateur troupes often performed the popular play in Beijing's and Shanghai's alleys.[95] Audiences and critics, however, disagreed whether it contributed anything to Marriage Law education. They were also not in agreement on the question of whether Lao She presented and interpreted the law correctly. Tian Han, one of China's most prolific playwrights, thought that *Liushujing* "truly reflected the change between the new and old society."[96] Journalists in favor of the play argued that it best captured the plight or fortune of young couples, while also underscoring the need for local cadres and women's representatives to support people and actively help implement the law.[97] Readers' letters to the *Juben* editorial board, however, criticized that the play's final act, in which the in-laws are sentenced by a people's court, was much too harsh. Marriage Law implementation was meant to be about non-antagonistic education, and trials were to be the last recourse, only to be used in cases of clear criminal activity.[98] The *Juben* editorial board disagreed with this critical view, writing that the government had made clear that cases of severe maltreatment should be regarded as criminal offenses and tried in court. The board conceded that other aspects of the play might be misleading: the village head in the play failed to ask his district superiors for permission to hold a trial prior to the sentencing, and some of the words used during the trial were inappropriately harsh. It also admitted that Li Zhaodi was portrayed as too weak and in need of help from the government. Her character did not demonstrate the ideal that people would liberate themselves with the help of the law, instead of having the government come to their rescue.[99] They encouraged local drama troupes and publishers reissuing the play to revise these bits of the language.

If so-called new storylines often scripted scenarios of life under the Marriage Law, old operas advertised the new law by depicting how people had suffered under feudalism. One of the most popular operas of the early 1950s, *Liang Shanbo and Zhu Yingtai*, also became part of the Marriage Law campaign.[100] The opera was based on an oral legend brought to paper during the Tang dynasty. *Juben* magazine's editorial board issued a version of the story, which was then widely reprinted for the campaign.[101] In the story, a young woman, Zhu Yingtai, and a young man, Liang Shanbo, meet at a school where Zhu Yingtai has disguised herself as a man in order to be able to enjoy the education to which women were denied access at the time. They become insepara-ble, but after some time, Zhu has to return home to attend to her par-ents. Liang, unaware of who Zhu really is, comes to her home to see his friend, only to find that Zhu is a woman. Confucian morality prevents Liang from speaking to her directly, so he asks her father for her hand in marriage. But her father has already betrothed her to another man. Tormented by his grief, Liang returns home to work as a local magis-trate yet dies soon thereafter. On the day of her marriage, Zhu's carriage passes by Liang's grave. She stops the carriage, goes to the grave— which opens up in front of her—and joins her lover in death. After her act of devotion, two butterflies are seen circling around the grave before they finally fly away together in freedom.[102]

The play was a campaign hit. Local authorities estimated that between 1952 and 1953, the Yue Opera was staged 1,696 times in Shanghai and its suburban districts. Some 978,000 people watched these performances. The Beijing Opera version, though less popular, was staged 123 times, with more than 181,000 spectators.[103] But statistical success did not mean that there were no insecurities about how to interpret the play correctly in the context of learning about the Marriage Law. Some cultural workers worried that classic storylines of the intellectually gifted male and the virtuous female contradicted the message of Marriage Law education and its emphasis on gender equality.[104] The pair's transformation into butterflies, moreover, which Zhou Enlai had endorsed as a more optimistic ending to a tragic story, was an issue for some who felt that it supported superstitious beliefs in an afterlife. They were told that the butterflies were symbols of freedom, not icons of superstitious beliefs.[105]

Death and suicide were common themes in most old operas used for legal education, mirroring the popular and political concern with suicides and their drastic increase since the promulgation of the Marriage Law. The play *Rendezvous at Blue Bridge* recounts the legend of two lovers, Lan Ruilian and Wei Shengyuan.[106] Unable to marry because Lan has already been promised to another family, the two try to escape together but meet their tragic deaths at Blue Bridge when a flash flood kills Wei as he is waiting for Lan. Desperate at her loss, Lan jumps into the river to follow her lover in death. In addition to associating suicide with the pre-liberation years, the play also touches upon the tragic fates of foster daughters-in-law, and thus it met several requirements for prominent inclusion in the Marriage Law campaign.

But the play's thematic strength of connecting death to the "old society" was also its weakness. Cultural workers were unsure about some of the finer details of interpretation and the link between the play and the law. In a letter exchange printed in *Juben*, Ji Genyin and Zhang Peng, two cultural workers helping Qingdao Municipal Jinguang Theater Company revise the play, wrote to the editorial board about their difficulties with this work.[107] The two were desperate, having rewritten the play five times already, once after each of the company's performances. The main problem was the concluding scene in which Wei dies. When Ji and Zhang were revising the play, they came across the published minutes of a meeting that the Shandong Provincial Association of Writers had convened with cultural workers in Ji'nan to discuss the play.[108] Participants, the minutes recorded, had argued that the flash flood looked like a symbol of feudal oppression. Wei's death might therefore be interpreted to suggest that unexpected death would invariably result if one attempts to fight for freedom of marriage. This could intimidate people in the audience to the extent that they might not fight for implementation of the law. Instead, they suggested that Wei should commit suicide while waiting for Lan at the bridge because he doubts that she will come to the meeting point. This, they thought, would emphasize Wei's volition.

Ji and Zhang revised the play accordingly, but after that version had been performed a critic wrote in *Qingdao ribao* that this ending made Wei appear weak. This critic thought the ending was inappropriate because it did not show the true tragedy of feudal society. What, the two asked the *Juben* editorial board, was correct then? *Juben* editors eventually argued that Wei's sudden death was part of a role model story for the masses to resist the established norms of the old society and fight for freedom of marriage. Changing the ending would only diminish this story of heroism and love in the face of adversity, and emphasize the powerful hold that old customs still had over people. Audiences should not be intimidated but should feel encouraged to pursue their own acts of bravery in following the law, though it should be made clear that suicide was no longer necessary in New China.[109]

Plays brought emotion to the study of law. In Beijing's districts, officials reported that local madams (*taitai*) had cried watching neighborhood plays.[110] Many people went to see plays and operas during the campaign only because they wanted to be entertained.[111] Yet this did not necessarily matter because the emotional effects of the plays could, following the logic of propaganda work, help people raise their consciousness during the performance. More practically, if plenty of residents went to performances, propaganda officials could present this in statistics as self-education and precisely the sort of idealized voluntary learning that the directives had envisaged. For this to work, it was important that residents went to plays voluntarily. Any kind of compulsory allotment of tickets, as the Shanghai municipal campaign office wrote, was to be carefully avoided.[112]

## Taxonomic Mazes: Dealing with Errors of Fact and Interpretation

Throughout the campaign, censors and publishing officials worked to identify and correct "erroneous" understandings of the Marriage Law. In addition to organizing who could (or at least who should) publish on the Marriage Law, censors in the national, municipal, and regional propaganda and publishing offices also surveyed unpublished and published materials. They wrote up criticisms and went out to talk to publishers, editors, and writers about how to revise their materials. The General Publishing Administration and the Central Propaganda Department explained in regular notifications that careful supervision would produce good propaganda that told people clearly what the Marriage Law was and why it mattered.[113]

Even if censors were effective in spotting mistakes, at times they seem to have found it as difficult as local officials to establish clear distinctions between correct and erroneous explanations of the law. Already in the summer of 1952, officials at the General Publishing Administration became involved in a discussion about the Marriage Law serial comic *Li Fengjin*, published in November 1950 by the private Shanghai-based New Tide Press. The comic tells the story of a young woman's quest to divorce her abusive husband and seek protection under the Marriage Law. The comic book had been sold in bookstores for more than a year. In spring 1952, the cultural office of the Songjiang provincial people's government had spotted a problem in this pamphlet as part of a survey of privately published booklets. It notified the General Publishing Administration, and on 6 June 1952, the administration wrote to the Shanghai Municipal News and Publishing Office requesting that it stop sales everywhere in the city. The issue seemed simple: in the book, Li, having left her husband, cohabits with another man's family. Yet the Marriage Law prohibited cohabitation before marriage.

It seemed evident that the publishers had made the kind of mistake that called for stopping sales. The administration advised that the book could be sold again once the publishers had revised this bit of the narrative [114] Quickly, however, it reconsidered its initial verdict. The problem was more complex than initially thought. Cohabitation was indeed illegal, but cohabitation was but one of several legal issues described in the story that needed to be considered. Five days later, administration officials in Beijing wrote again to their Shanghai colleagues, advising them that if they had not already halted sales, they should not bother: "Although the booklet contains shortcomings," they reasoned, "it does not contain fundamental errors."[115] Li Fengjin's decision to cohabit could be excused as a consequence of the local cadre's illegal behavior: before cohabiting, Li Fengjin had asked the township head for a divorce in accordance with the Marriage Law, but he had refused. Since Li faced serious mistreatment at the hands of her husband if she now returned home, the administration argued, she really "could not but" cohabit with a person who could guarantee her safety. Li, they explained further, was not very bright and did not have a "higher level of understanding." Her low level of understanding meant that she did not see that she could have pursued her case further with district- and county-level people's governments before cohabiting. In the feudal environment in which she lived, she did what she thought best. The administration concluded that although Li may have violated the law, she had been forced to do so because her local cadre refused to enforce the Marriage Law. Seen in this way, her story had much educational value.[116]

Censors at times also disagreed over how to evaluate a publication and sent conflicting signals to publishers. In March 1953, the Central Propaganda Department, the General Publishing Administration, and regional propaganda departments all conducted investigations into propaganda work for the Marriage Law and uncovered a range of problems. In their discussions of the same faulty publications, censors judged the seriousness of these faults differently. Recall that in late March, as discussed in the previous chapter, the General Publishing Administration wrote that "very few" of the Marriage Law educational materials were "good," and "shortcomings and mistakes exist to different degrees."[117] Around the same time, the Central Propaganda Department reassured its readers in its internal *Xuanchuan tongxun* that most booklets about the Marriage Law were adequate, even though some contained mistakes that should be avoided in the future.[118] That being said, the department, too, sent mixed messages. The reassurance that the materials were adequate came one day after the department had also issued an internal memorandum to all cadres at provincial and municipal propaganda departments, reporters at the offices of *Renmin ribao*, Xinhua News Agency's main and regional branches, and broadcasting workers, explicitly criticizing a range of newspapers for failing to produce adequate reportage on the Marriage Law.[119]

The supplementary directive to the Marriage Law campaign that, as chapter 1 illustrates, created much confusion among local officials preparing for the campaign was also problematic for publishing and propaganda authorities. After the supplementary directive was issued, the East China Regional Propaganda Department criticized Shanghai's *Jiefang ribao* for printing an article about campaign test sites in Fujian Province that did not condemn obviously wrong practices, such as mass meetings and ad-hoc people's tribunals, to deal with those who had violated the Marriage Law. By that point, the newspaper editors knew about the supplementary directive because the Central Propaganda Department had informed regional governments of its content before it was officially published. The East China Marriage Law Campaign Committee had then phoned up the editorial board of *Jiefang ribao* and explained the upcoming policy reorientation. However, it was not passed down to all journalists, and the editors forgot to check the newspaper issue before it went to print.

In the larger scheme of things, such communication issues in newspapers and publishers were easier to address than were questions of the wording chosen to explain the Marriage Law and, subsequently, the ways it might be interpreted. The more authorities insisted on the principle that the campaign should rely on the people's own determination to learn and implement the law, the more they tried to control the language used to talk about it, and the more particular they became in terms of individual words. In a survey of newspaper reportage on the Marriage Law published between December 1952 and March 1953, the Central Propaganda Department noted, for example, that *Dongbei ribao* (North-East daily) had used an "inappropriate" formulation on 19 February 1953, when it wrote that "all powers should be concentrated toward destroying the feudal marriage system of arrangement (of marriages), coercion, and treating women as inferior to men." Its reasoning was that the word "destroy" (*cuihui*) might give readers the impression that old customs could be abolished in one month if only they tried hard enough.[120] *Yunnan ribao* (Yunnan daily), on 13 February, 1953, quoted a statement by the head of the Yunnan Marriage Law Committee: "This campaign is *basically* a matter among the people." This would have made sense since it allowed for cases of violations of the Marriage Law to fall outside the realm of "the People" and still form part of the campaign. And it was probably an accurate expression of what the committee's practical experiences had been so far. Yet officials in the Propaganda Department decided that the statement was incorrect. Following the wording of the supplementary directive, the law's implementation would be "purely" (*chunquan*) a matter among the People. Finally, *Shanxi ribao* wrongly explained the legal framework for cohabitation, a similar problem as in the case of the comic book *Li Fengjin*. *Shanxi ribao* had instructed cadres to prevent couples who had married before reaching the legal minimum age from cohabiting. Cadres should separate them, by force if necessary, until they were old enough to register their marriages. This, the department warned, was an example of "too strictly enforcing the Marriage Law" and was completely wrong. Even if they had married too early, couples should not be separated. Only then would people be willing to enforce the Marriage Law "consciously."[121] Similar cases were occurring elsewhere.[122]

To highlight mistakes that propaganda authorities should avoid, the Central Propaganda Department circulated examples it considered noteworthy. The problem was, as one article explained, that some books wrongly presented the basic spirit of the law. A 1953 booklet titled *Everybody Come Implement the Marriage Law* and published by Suiyuan People's Press, for instance, explained that "any violation of any article or section of the law, no matter who commits it, will be punished according to the circumstances." The author wanted to explain Article 26 of the Marriage Law, which stipulated: "Persons who violate this law will be punished according to the law." The Propaganda Department criticized that this explanation contravened the central directive, which stated that "cadres and masses who commit ordinary acts of interfering with freedom of marriage or acts of violating the Marriage Law that have not [produced] severe and disastrous results should be thoroughly exposed, criticized, and educated; as long as they determinedly correct the mistakes, there is no need to administer punishment."[123] The Shanghai private publisher Tongsu Wenhua Press, in its booklet *The New Democratic Marriage System*, stated that implementing free choice in marriage and abolishing all forced and "buy and sell" marriages would only be the start of the new marriage system because the more important part would be to allow people genuine freedom to divorce.[124] This contravened the regulations because it suggested that the government's main focus was on divorce and not on freedom of marriage. Beijing's publishing authorities had dealt with a similar problem in the case of Xinghua Bookstore's songbook *Singing the Marriage Law*. The book's author had confused the characters "must" (*xu*) and "should" (*ying*), telling readers that they "must" go to the people's courts to register their marriages, even though it was meant to be "should."[125] Despite the law's requirement that couples ought to register, registration was still limited, and thus linguistic caution was required to avoid sending people into a frenzy if they could not figure out where to register.

One of the more popular genres, the question-and-answer book, was among the types of material most often singled out for criticism because cultural workers repeatedly got both their questions and answers wrong. Northern Sichuan People's Press opened its *120 Questions on Marriage* with a question: "What is the basic spirit of the Marriage Law?" The answer explained that the law's most important principle was to abolish "patriarchy" and the notion that men stand at the center of society. The Propaganda Department decided that this was a misrepresentation of the law. It argued that the placement of this answer right at the beginning of the booklet gave the erroneous impression that the law was primarily about abolishing patriarchy. This fit only too well with popular misconceptions that the law was aimed against men. The Sichuan Provincial Propaganda Department was told to stop sales and revise the publication.[126]

At worst, publishing officials wondered whether authors "randomly" decided how to respond to a question. They thought that authors repeatedly failed to listen when they were told *not* to explain "complicated" questions relating to marriage.[127] Shanghai Puwen

Press, for example, printed a book titled *Marriage Law Study Questions and Answers* in which it asked questions such as, "If the woman commits adultery with another man and gets pregnant, and if she has the intention to kill her husband (and two people can testify to this), can they be granted a divorce?" Censors thought that this question was simply "baffling."[128] But as baffling as the question might have been, the Marriage Law did not provide a clear answer, and it seems the editors might have either felt that this was a question their readers might be interested in or would, at the very least, find entertaining.

Meanings of the law were negotiated in the work of censors and publishing officials. They became arbiters who, at least in parts, determined what the Marriage Law meant, and how party and government directives should be interpreted. Printed words and images could be hard to police once they were in circulation though. Once sold, volumes were not easily retrieved, even if their official publication and sale were halted. Mistaken interpretations circulated, often on the authoritative canvas of state-sponsored publications.

## Conclusion: From One Law to the Next

The Marriage Law campaign became a model for legal knowledge dissemination because it provided examples of what to do and what not to do when disseminating laws. Even if the campaign was beset with difficulties, writers, playwrights, artists, journalists, and editors successfully devised ways of talking about laws that folded much more closely into ideal images of socialist men and women, and socialist society more broadly. Meanwhile, censors gained practice identifying improper ways of talking about the Marriage Law. Over time, all of this made it more difficult to separate public talk about family and marital lives from the official language of the Marriage Law.[129] Within the directed public sphere of the 1950s, the language of the law strengthened its hold.[130] People could no longer find reassurance in any of the educational materials or in the discussions that any behavior that did not conform to the political interpretations of the basic spirit of the law—however that term was interpreted locally—would enjoy legal and political protection.

At the end of April 1953, the national campaign committee officially concluded the campaign and announced that Marriage Law learning would now become more regularized.[131] The national Marriage Law Bureau and local bureaus continued work with a reduced staff.[132] In July 1954, the bureau convened a general meeting, including the original members of the national committee, to debate how to best promote the law as part of the ongoing constitution discussion.[133] Since the constitution draft reaffirmed the validity of the Marriage Law, this seemed to be a good opportunity to remind people of the law. A year later, in 1955, at another bureau meeting, members discussed how to revive Marriage Law education as part of the upcoming Spring Festival celebrations and in anticipation of International Women's Day on 8 March.[134] By 1957, the Ministry of Internal Affairs reminded all provinces and municipalities about the importance of popularizing the Marriage Law and getting people to "abide by the law" (shoufa).[135] And during the socialist education movement of the early 1960s, too, the party cells of the Shanghai Municipal Bureau of Civil Affairs and the Shanghai Municipal People's High Court returned to the need to propagate and implement the Marriage Law because instances of "buy and sell marriages" and other so-called "feudal" practices had, to use the language of the report, "increased" across town since 1962 under the negative influence of "feudalist remnants" to an extent that worried party officials.[136] The regularization, at least in theory, of education work for the Marriage Law mirrored the continued engagement with legal learning during the remainder of the 1950s, as the next chapter illustrates.

Following the end of the Marriage Law campaign, legal lessons for the general population did not abate. By the early summer of 1953, the central government began to disseminate the Election Law, passed in March of that year, and prepared for discussion of the constitution draft months later. If talk about laws persisted, so did the problems of disseminating laws. Marriage Law education, as this chapter illustrates, had overwhelmed many residents who found it difficult to understand and adhere to the language of the law. Similar issues surfaced during the study of the Election Law, a law which contained many more specialist terms such as "political rights."[137]

Complaints from local residents and officials about the difficulty of having to study laws were as common during the dissemination of the

Election Law as they had been during the campaign for the Marriage Law. As many local officials actively participated in spreading word about the Election Law and the upcoming election as complained about being busy and resorted to the same makeshift techniques to get through this new chore.[138] Similarly, the language of the Election Law posed as much of a challenge as the language of the Marriage Law. From Shanghai's Putuo District, Xinhua News Agency journalists reported that they had come across groups of workers confounded by terms such as "election" and "political rights."[139] It may not have been the first time they heard about elections, but residents wondered what exactly elections would mean under Communist rule.[140] Cadres sometimes did not read the law properly and found it difficult to explain it in a way that made the election seem relevant to people's lives.[141] Where the Marriage Law campaign had eventually managed to draw out some interesting themes and model stories, the Election Law was particularly bland. Even in the publishing center of Shanghai, there was a shortage of popular propaganda materials to explain the Election Law. For lack of better ideas, local cadres once again mechanically read out the law, central directives, and newspaper editorials.[142]

Zooming out from the more specific questions about what worked and what did not work during the study of the Marriage Law and the Election Law, we can see that learning laws had by the end of 1953 become part of most urban residents' experience of politics in daily life; no matter whether they liked it or not, and no matter whether they paid much attention. Many of the most popular entertainment products, as we saw in the case of love dramas, were linked to law. They continued the dissemination of the Marriage Law after the campaign was over. The discussion of the state constitution draft in the following year, explored in the next chapter, then took legal learning for the broader population to a new level. It also amplified popular fears of what would happen to anyone who contravened laws.

# 4    Getting People to Abide by Law

## The Constitution Draft Discussion and Its Aftermath

The 1954 constitution draft discussion (*xianfa cao'an taolun*) was all about words, paper, and words on paper. In 1929, as the Nationalist government in Nanjing was busy working on a new Criminal Code, the political scientist Luo Longji wrote in his essay "On Human Rights": "It is unfortunately an irremovable fact that law is, in the end, only words on paper."[1] Twenty-five years later, Luo participated in the drafting of the PRC's first state constitution and thus in the CCP's attempt to put law on paper and publicize it as part of a national discussion. This discussion, as the Xinhua News Agency explained in an internal brief to its reporters in June 1954, would help people realize that the constitution was "absolutely not an ineffective law and an empty promise."[2] Newspaper reporters were told that the constitution represented the CCP's revolutionary achievements now fixed in law.[3] They were to remind their readers that these words on paper and their wide circulation were evidence that PRC law was among the superior kinds of law in the world because, like the law of China's socialist brethren, it made constitutional thought and language accessible and a weapon of the people.

To have a mass discussion of the constitution draft was to be revolutionary. Claiming for China the legacy of world constitutions borne out of the fervor of world revolution, Mao explained at the thirtieth session of the Government Administrative Council on 14 June 1954 that "the bourgeoisie, whether in Britain, France, or the United States, was revolutionary for a period, and it was during this period that the bourgeoisie started making constitutions."[4] The PRC, Mao announced, now revived this abandoned constitutional legacy.[5] Dictionaries published at the time explained that having a constitution draft discussion was a characteristic of socialism. The entry on *xianfa* [constitution] in the 1955 *Dictionary of New Terms* told readers that "socialist countries and people's democracies . . . usually carry out a national discussion."[6] Implicitly, these explanations forged a close link between democracy, access to laws, knowledge of laws, and people's ability and desire to abide by laws.

The ideal citizen, at least in 1954, was one who knew both his rights and his duties, who saw these not as separate but as linked, and above all who remembered that the most important duty—which would in turn guarantee availability of all rights—was to abide by the constitution and to remain loyal to the party and state that had created it. The correlation between rights and duties was central to the way that the constitution was explained. On paper, the constitution outlined the structure of the socialist state and announced—in its third section—an extensive catalogue of "fundamental rights and duties of citizens." Adapted from the 1936 Stalin constitution and other Eastern European constitutional documents and based on legal developments of the Republican period, these included political, economic, social, and cultural rights. Many had already been included in the 1949 Common Program.[7] In his report to the first National People's Congress on 15 September 1954, Liu Shaoqi, who was then vice-chairman of the Central People's Government, reinforced that both rights and duties were necessary: "In our country, the people's rights and duties are in complete harmony. No one has duties without enjoying rights, and no one enjoys rights without duties."[8]

Although influenced by the experience of the Soviet Union, China's constitution draft discussion was not merely a copy of the Soviet model; it merged imperial, Republican, and foreign legacies and influences with the CCP's own practical experiences of governing the country.[9] The idea for the discussion as a way to legitimize and popularize lawmaking owed much to the Soviet Union.[10] The mass line nature of the discussion process, and particularly the CCP's techniques to engage citizens in the study of law, also had roots reaching back at least to Sun Yatsen's program for the government to tutor people in the constitution so that they would become able citizens.[11] The call to citizens to abide by law, a central slogan of the discussion, was also reminiscent of the same demands the Qing and Republican states had made of their citizens. And in the short term, while propaganda authorities could make use of the materials and techniques developed during the dissemination of laws in earlier years, party and governments officials at all levels tried to avoid repeating mistakes made during Marriage Law and Election Law work.

The constitution discussion was the mass line in action. But it departed from the Marriage Law campaign in several ways. The discussion was not called a mass campaign, even though many of its components—such as study groups, report writing, top-down supervision mechanisms, and propaganda production—were similar to those found in earlier campaigns. Discarding the language of campaigning was no mere formality. Rather than educate people in the stipulations of a law that had already been promulgated, the national leadership now placed great rhetorical importance on people being part of the lawmaking process. A national discussion therefore served at least three purposes. First, it provided the Drafting Committee with revision suggestions. Second, it gave party and government authorities insight into popular understandings of the country's government and laws. Third, it symbolically involved citizens in the making of the state constitution and gave them shared ownership of the constitution as well as responsibility for abiding by its articles.

This chapter examines the discussion of the constitution draft, the promulgation of the constitution, and the way in which the constitution was used after 1954 to demand obedience to the law. The year 1954 saw the most intense law propaganda activities of the Mao Era, and the resultant paper trail reveals how the dissemination of legal knowledge was becoming more sophisticated and structured. The young CCP regime used the state constitution to solidify political structures and move the country symbolically from a country undergoing construction to a country with a formal legal framework.[12] For several years after 1954, whenever party and government officials carried out "law propaganda" (*fazhi xuanchuan*), they commonly referred back to the constitution's stipulation that everyone should abide by laws. Learning about the constitution, people approached the document with common sense and compared what they read and heard with what they had experienced. This challenged any attempt to create a cohesive narrative of law in the transition to socialism. Choosing to emphasize form over content, the regime focused its law propaganda on the general idea of having a constitution and the ritual of discussing it publicly. Propaganda officials, artists, and photographers turned the constitution document into a powerful symbol of government-directed legal knowledge. Form and ritual eclipsed legal particularities and words. And law propaganda became more important as a channel to mediate expectations of what law should and would do.

## Strength in Circulation Numbers: Publishing the Draft

The constitution draft discussion in June 1954 and the promulgation of the constitution in September of the same year were major media events. The "national phase" of the discussion began when the central government adopted the revised constitution draft on 14 June. It was made public the following day.[13] This was the second phase of the discussion. It followed extensive advance preparations over several months and a discussion of the "first draft" (*chugao*) among a more limited group of China's political, economic, and intellectual elite.[14] During the first phase, urban newspaper readers could keep up to date with these developments as newspapers printed daily snippets and articles with news of reportedly more than 8,000 people (a sleek figure continuously mentioned in coverage) who were participating in the discussion of this first draft.[15] In early June, this first phase then led over into the second phase and to the mass discussion. Much of the discussion of the draft was limited to urban and suburban areas, with over 150 million people participating.[16] Similar to the Marriage Law campaign of 1953, the second phase had two steps. Higher-level party cadres and party members were first trained on the copy of the "first draft." Next, they trained lower-level cadres and government bureaucrats, who then set out to explain the revised draft and gather responses from ordinary residents.[17]

In the first days after the draft was published, propaganda was at a high point. On 15 June, special broadcasts aired across the cities telling listeners about the upcoming discussion.[18] Hot off the press, broadsheets followed soon thereafter. All newspapers on 15 June carried the full text of the constitution draft, as per instructions of the Central Propaganda Department on 11 June.[19] Having been told that the new constitution draft was about to be promulgated in the day's newspapers, many people waited for the papers to arrive.[20] Copies sold quickly. In Beijing, several newspaper vendors in central districts sold all their copies. Within some single institutions, almost everyone purchased a copy of the newspaper that day. Of the 360 students at the middle school attached to Central Minorities College, for example, 330 bought a copy.[21] Newspaper sales figures across Beijing that day increased six-fold.[22] In Shanghai, too, several newspaper vendors sold out their copies early. Workers returned to their factories late that evening to read one of the subscription copies available there. Some made a special trip to local post offices hoping to get a copy after their vendors had sold out.[23] People who could not read asked family members or colleagues to read the text out loud, or they called on their local newspaper reader (*dubaoyuan*) to come help. Government reports especially highlighted that people had sought out newspaper reading officers. Usually it was the other way around, and officers had to summon people to read newspapers. Instead, hardly ever were they summoned, making this development all the more newsworthy in their opinion.[24]

Within a few days, the constitution draft became available as a thin paperback. Xinhua News Agency telegraphed the draft to printing plants on the night of 14 June, and plant workers put in night shifts to set matrices, print, and bind thousands of copies. Shanghai's Xinhua Press set dozens of matrices that messengers from other printing facilities then picked up. The press also printed 250,000 copies of the constitution by the afternoon of 17 June and immediately dispatched a first set of over 110,000 copies (fig. 4.1).[25] Newspapers and internal reports celebrated exuberant production figures and sales. Within a month, Xinhua Press announced that close to twelve million copies had been published, including more than 170,000 copies of the draft in Tibetan,

Fig. 4.1. "Workers at Shanghai Xinhua Printing Plant rush to print the PRC constitution draft in order to supply people with copies so that they can carry out the discussion," 1954. (Source: *Jiefang ribao* [Liberation daily], 20 June 1954, p. 5.)

Mongolian, Uyghur, and Korean.[26] Xinhua Bookstore's headquarters in Shanghai compiled statistics that showed that 187,000 copies were ordered within two days from bookstore branches across the city. Beijing's Xinhua Bookstore recorded major sales when, within a month, 740,000 copies of print materials that featured the constitution were sold. This included leading magazines such as *Zhongguo qingnian* (China youth) and *Xuexi* (Study).[27] It also included some 620,000 copies of the bound constitution draft.[28] *Renmin ribao* reported that a delivery of 1,000 copies sold within the hour at Beijing's Shijingshan Iron and Steelworks, a major industrial plant on the outskirts of the municipality.[29]

Wide distribution was essential to the draft discussion, to propaganda reporting on the draft discussion, and to the way history of the draft and of the final constitution was later recounted. In Shanghai, copies of the constitution draft retailed in all bookstores, at bookstalls, kiosks, and newsstands, reaching customers in neighborhoods and on street corners. Cinemas and theaters set up stalls that sold copies on consignment. Xinhua Bookstore sent salespeople to factories, offices, and army quarters and increased its mobile supply chains in the outer suburbs and the countryside.[30] Xinhua Bookstore branches designed window decorations to commemorate the draft and added to their celebratory decorations copies of the USSR and Eastern European constitutions, as well as copies of Mao Zedong's "On New Democracy" and "On the People's Democratic Dictatorship."[31] People were told that accessibility mattered most, even if they did not understand parts of the draft, could not read many of the characters, or (still) disagreed with some its contents. Local cadres proudly reported that they interviewed residents who, with a copy of the draft in hand, told them that "in the past, the reactionary cliques also had a constitution, but they would not let us see it."[32]

## Information Management: Anatomy
## of a Constitution Draft Discussion

While media exuberantly documented the dissemination of the draft, different party and government agencies organized the flow of public and internal information about the discussion. At the national level, the central Constitution Drafting Committee coordinated the national constitution discussion. The editorial group, one of several working groups of the committee, was the node compiling information. With a staff of over forty people, the twenty-five-year-old jurist Dong Chengmei, who had been transferred from his position at People's University, led the group.[33] It collated and processed summary reports sent to Beijing by all provincial and municipal constitution draft discussion committees that detailed people's revision suggestions and responses to the draft.

In May 1954, Party Central directed all local party committees to set up constitution draft discussion committees. Staffed by party and non-party members, these committees often included prominent figures.[34] Vice-mayor Zhang Youyu directed the Beijing Municipal Party Committee. Shanghai's mayor, Chen Yi, led the Shanghai committee.[35] The Beijing committee included legal experts such as Qian Duansheng, well-known intellectuals such as Liang Sicheng (Liang Qichao's son), distinguished writers such as Lao She, and several individuals who had already sat on the Marriage Law Campaign Committee and the Election Law Committee, including Fan Jin, Lei Jieqiong, and Zhang Dazhong, the deputy head of the Beijing Municipal Propaganda Department and editor-in-chief of the *Beijing ribao*.[36] Other members were transferred from the Propaganda Department, the Women's Federation, the Trade Union, the United Front Department, and the bureaus of the municipal government. Committee members then directed branches (*fenhui*) to conduct the discussion.[37] Beijing's and Shanghai's districts, suburbs, and people's committees each had a branch, as did public security, commerce, light and heavy industry, construction, military affairs, the Federation of Trade Unions, the arts, news and publishing, middle schools, universities, and religious circles.[38] Committees organized and scheduled reports on the constitution, printed and circulated information and discussion points, liaised with the cities' news and media outlets, scrutinized propaganda of all kinds, oversaw the coordination, training, and payment of report-givers and propagandists, and coordinated the collection of popular responses by reading through the reports of local branches.[39]

A draft discussion on this scale was unfamiliar territory for everyone. The propaganda logistics were more complex than in previous campaigns because propaganda activities were divided into two parts: one to accompany the national discussion of the revised draft starting in June 1954, and one to announce the final constitution once it was officially adopted in September 1954. Each of these drives, in turn, was divided into different phases. Accustomed to writing reports that reflected people's responses during mass campaigns, local officials now had to collect hundreds of revision suggestions and decide which ones to forward. This was a new task for them. In the end, though, the constitution draft discussion was better organized than the implementation of the Marriage Law. Calculating generously to ensure that there was sufficient time, the central government scheduled three months for the discussion, from mid-June through mid-August. The main branch of Xinhua News Agency meanwhile told its reporters that the work would most likely only take about two months.[40]

The population's legal learning process was extensively documented. Every few days, in addition to daily briefings, the Shanghai committee compiled an internal synthesis of branch reports and instructional materials for consultation[41] The Beijing committee also published a daily update, as well as regular work briefings and situation briefings every few days. Officials were given templates detailing how to keep notes and log revision suggestions. Reports had to document precisely people's responses first to sections, then to articles, and finally to the individual terms and words of the constitution. In doing so, it was important to distinguish between revision suggestions, misunderstandings, and plain criticisms. Representative responses and particularly egregious criticisms were to be highlighted and provided as quotations. The Shanghai Propaganda Department wanted its officials to record comments by people prominent in their community or work unit with names and work unit affiliations.[42] In Beijing, officials often included information about the class origin and party affiliation of the person who was being quoted, particularly if what he/she said was remarkably positive or negative. Both committees then sent reports to the national editorial group, with selections of responses and suggestions they considered important. From across the country, as Dong Chengmei recalls, reports were transmitted by long-distance phone calls, or were delivered by bus, train, or plane.[43] At the end of the constitution discussion, the editorial group compiled and published sixteen volumes of responses and suggestions volumes of responses and suggestions.[44]

Public and internal reports were carefully separated. In reports for a public audience, Xinhua News Agency asked reporters to emphasize that the discussion was a major "happy event" for everyone. They were to write about how people enthusiastically welcomed the draft, how they joyfully engaged with it and participated in the discussion. In other words, they were to write about the "happy atmosphere" they saw. Public reportage could narrate how the constitution was going to put into law the victorious achievements of the People under the leadership of the CCP and the proletariat. Articles were to explain why this was a "socialist kind of constitution," link it to socialist construction and transformation, and describe how the socialist system of ownership worked.[45] Xinhua News Agency told reporters to be careful, though. Every word and sentence was to conform to the spirit and the articles of the constitution draft. Under no circumstances were reporters to "chaotically" add words or sentences and freely interpret the draft.[46]

Negative news could only be reported in specific publications for internal circulation. In more certain terms than during the Marriage Law campaign, both Xinhua News Agency and the committees warned reporters, officials, report-givers, and propagandists not to report publicly on any controversies or disputes. Committees instructed their cadres that they should note any differences in opinion that crystallized during the discussion. The committees then decided how important these were and what to do about them.[47] Xinhua News Agency meanwhile told its journalists to send collected controversial opinions immediately to the main agency and to include observations about local officials' responses and the work of the committees. Cadres at the main agency decided which bits to include in *Neibu cankao* for further elite-level circulation. This work, Xinhua News Agency reminded its journalists, had to be done speedily and carefully.[48]

The demands were high, and the schedule intense. Much as in the Marriage Law campaign, the goal of making elite legal knowledge accessible to "the masses" became inverted in practice. Those considered to have the shortest attention span but the most to gain from the constitution received the least amount of education. To give structure to the discussion, the Beijing committee decided to train higher-level cadres based on three reports given by prominent party members: Zhang Youyu, Tian Jiaying (Mao's private secretary who had participated in the drafting of the constitution), and Yang Shu. Their reports focused first on the preamble and the "General Principles," second on the section "Structure of the State," and finally on citizens' rights and duties.[49] Cadres and report-givers then underwent training that was based on a report on the basic spirit and the most important content of the draft, one or two reports dedicated to an article-by-article discussion of the draft, and another report on how to propagate the draft to the masses.[50] Equipped with instructions, report-givers went out and conducted discussions first with cadres and workers, and then with "ordinary residents." Workers studied the draft during their political affairs lessons. Ordinary administrative cadres, activists, and "odd job personnel" who did not usually participate in theory study gathered for a "popular" report.[51] Three reports and two or three discussions were common, but it could be less, particularly in smaller work units where reports would take less than one and a half hours. In rural areas of the municipality, the discussion did not begin until July. Agricultural production cooperative personnel, state-owned farm workers, and farmers from collective farms received two or three reports. Everyone else would only receive one or two reports, as well as one discussion. Schools could design their own study plans, but teaching staff were to hear at least two reports and spend about twenty-seven hours in total reading and discussing documents, while students and school handymen only had to clock some twelve hours. Ordinary residents would receive two reports and spend no more than an hour discussing them, to account for their shorter attention spans.[52]

Beyond timetables and broad organizational structures, the plans were less clear about the content and educational methods. Xinhua News Agency saw the entire discussion as a major drive to strengthen the masses' patriotism and awareness to abide by laws so that they would voluntarily and loyally carry out their duties as citizens.[53] Yet no unified national instructional guidelines told the committees how to study and discuss the draft. The Beijing committee advised going section-by-section and article-by-article.[54] The Shanghai committee recommended this technique as well, but it did not want cadres to focus too much on each individual article because this might bore people and cause them to stop listening. Instead, it suggested comparing old and new ways of life and relating them to the constitution. To make the constitution seem more relevant and practical, committees in both cities encouraged participants to see the constitution in the context of daily life. Workers might talk about their concerns and their new rights, while capitalists and those working in businesses could talk about ownership issues. This, however, did not mean that discussions should focus solely on a few areas of concern to individual groups— that would put too much emphasis on individual interests and too little emphasis on the constitution as a document of the people at large. It did not suffice, the Shanghai committee argued, to target discussion points to specific audiences. In the case of groups made up only of women workers, for example, limiting the discussion to constitutional provisions for women and families risked that women would know little about the constitution overall.[55] The committee also thought that certain questions, such as "What is the basic content of the constitution?" were no good. In some factories, cadres had opened with this question and then spent a long time answering it and discussing complex legal points while local workers were at a loss to understand. "Why draft a constitution" or "What is the difference between the laws of the old and new society?" were much better because they encouraged talk about concrete examples.[56]

## Classifying Responses

The draft discussion created a class-based classification of legal knowledge. In their reports, officials captured what residents said about laws and how they responded to learning laws in one moment.[57] They did not trace sustained engagement with constitutional ideas. Discussion reports, moreover, reveal which answers report-writers, as state agents, selected and how their choices reinforced the premise that class consciousness determined legal knowledge. Report-writers associated topics with social groups and class labels. Sections listing capitalists' responses focused on property, ownership, and the role of the national bourgeoisie. Workers' responses generally centered on labor rights and ownership. In sections on students and intellectuals, report-writers included comments on freedom of speech and the press, and the right to education. Although the committees advised discussing the constitution draft holistically, cadres leading the discussion groups often directed the conversation toward specific topics that they deemed relevant to certain classes. As a result, the draft discussion became a public and internal confirmation of social and political identities, helping to reaffirm and link to law the classifications promoted by previous mass campaigns, including "capitalists," "intellectuals," "students," "workers," and "peasants."[58]

Within this class-based taxonomy of legal knowledge, report-writers emphasized binaries of "correct" and "erroneous" understanding, rather than complexities in legal learning and understanding. Correct class consciousness would facilitate correct legal knowledge. Residents, meanwhile, responded in many different ways. Many took a serious interest in the constitution draft. Workers at a Shanghai writing pen manufacturer commented that because the constitution draft was going to be the country's basic law and a major event, not understanding it was not an option.[59] Comments recorded in reports often also demonstrated complex layers of individual legal knowledge conditioned by their local environments and personal trajectories rather than by national legal and political narratives and categories. Many residents compared what they were learning about the new draft with what they knew about constitutions and laws in general. This could be an advantage. An older worker from a railway engine repair workshop in Beijing commented, "Our constitution is discussed by the people, revised by the people, passed by the people's congress, and obeyed by the people; this really is the first people's constitution since ancient times."[60]

It could also be a disadvantage if people thought the constitution draft was neither as new nor as much of a revolutionary rupture as it claimed to be. A Xinhua News Agency reporter writing from the city of Harbin in Heilongjiang Province noted a comment by one man who thought that there was really little difference between the Great Qing Code and the PRC constitution. Ultimately, life was about working, making a living, and having enough to eat.[61] In Beijing's Fengtai District a tax office cadre, labeled clearly as having formerly been affiliated with the Guomindang, asked, "What about the constitution draft is different from the old law? As I see it they're about the same."[62] Having studied law before liberation, a non-party cadre working at a Beijing post office branch explained that "our constitution is the realization of Sun Yat-sen's Principle of the People's Rights and Democracy."[63] He thought the draft put in place Sun's political rights of election, recall, initiative, and referendum and that the right to work and rest was part of the realization of Sun's Principle of the People's Livelihood. Moreover, as he explained to his colleagues at the post office, the draft laid down the separation of the State Council, the people's courts, and the procuratorate as separate "systems" (*xitong*). Yet this contravened the official line that all these institutions were closely tied together under the leadership of the people's democratic dictatorship. Because his colleagues had no legal training, they felt they could not do much except disagree.[64]

In some cases, the fact that certain concepts were included in the draft and thus associated with legal validity and legal force drew people's attention where they might previously not have been interested.

What, some asked, was the difference between people and citizens?[65] This was an important question because the constitution referred both to the People and to citizens. At the same time, as many people in both Beijing and Shanghai had experienced firsthand, not everyone was part of the People. Now it was unclear to them how the legal concept of citizenship compared with the political concept of the People. Some questions, moreover, touched upon legal problems that were not at all unique to China. If women were citizens like men, for instance, then why would they need to be specially mentioned in Articles 86 and 96 and given added protection?[66] With the many impressions of attacks on counterrevolutionaries still fresh in people's memories, intellectuals wondered how freedom of speech fit in with the Regulations for the Punishment of Counterrevolutionaries. Reports mentioned that people working in broadcasting stations commented on the concepts of freedom of speech and freedom of the press and said they knew full well that they could not "talk counterrevolutionary talk" or issue "counter-revolutionary publications."[67] What exactly constituted "counterrevo-lutionary" activities, beyond the broadsheet explanation provided in the 1951 regulations, was subject to political shifts. Many people knew this because they had only just partaken in or witnessed the Campaign to Suppress Counterrevolutionaries.

Although they often lived in separate social and political worlds, local report-givers and legal experts could at times mull over similar constitutional questions, with the difference that the spatial and temporal setup of group draft discussions put local report-givers under pressure to find immediate answers. Most residents found it difficult to figure out where to draw the line between the constitution as a foundational document of a general nature and the constitution as a collection of individual articles that might affect their lives. The language of "rights and duties" could be as worrying as it could be enthralling.[68] It made sense to expect that the right to work meant that local people's representatives would be responsible for finding jobs for unemployed residents.[69] Others wondered why certain rights should be included in the constitution, particularly since it was clear that they most likely would never be able to enjoy them. An older middle-school student, later labeled a "backward element," asked whether he could take a large flag and go protest in front of the central government's offices, or perhaps print some reactionary leaflets instead, as a demonstration of free speech.[70] In Dongdan District, participants told their report-giver that all those stipulations laid out in the constitution draft sounded nice, but they were not sure they would ever be able to get holidays as provided for in Articles 92 and 93 of the constitution draft.[71] Depending on the official penning of the report, such comments were framed as criticisms of the regime or as a desire for laws to be practicable.

Responses also demonstrated that mass legal education since 1950 had left an imprint on many residents who had internalized the propaganda line that they should take laws seriously and avoid violating the law. Unwittingly, their reactions mirrored some of the ambiguities about law already present in internal government discussions on how to explain laws and how to make sense of them. It seemed reasonable to many that, once promulgated, the constitution would be a further element in fighting "violations of law." But the general nature of the constitutional provisions was poorly suited to defining violations in these binary terms. That was not necessarily a deterrent at that moment; the 1951 regulations had also been vague. The constitution, once passed, was going to part of the people's democratic dictatorship, and it was logical to identify its dictatorial and democratic components. One resident in Beijing's Qianmen District explained that the constitution was a "law" (*fa*) and that it would therefore also "restrict" (*xian*) bad elements in society. A "capitalist" from Xidan District thought that "the constitution is a great law to control the people."[72] "Restrict" was a homophone of the first character in the word for "constitution," and this fit in neatly with earlier talk about the role of law in the suppression of non-People.[73]

If the constitution was another step in the fight against violations of the law, then it made sense to be prepared. The Beijing Municipal Bureau of Education noted that many residents they talked to thought that "you should study the constitution well because if you do not study it well then you may have to face the force of the law." Worse, some told each other that if they did not study the law then they were bound to commit mistakes and violate the constitution somehow.[74] Everything would now be done "according to law."[75] This, as women workers in Shanghai's Yimiao District explained, applied in particular to men, who were—they thought—far more prone to committing crimes.[76] Some prepared for the likelihood of violating the law in some way. Two people labeled as capitalists in Beijing's Qianmen District made a bet to see who would violate which one of the articles first.[77]

Many people therefore did not think that laws were meaningless; they were afraid of laws. If the phrase "abiding by law" had in the past most frequently been used in communicating to those on the margins of the People, it was now used in propaganda for all. Of particular note was the mention of having to not only abide by laws but also to respect social ethics in Article 100 of the draft: "Citizens of the People's Republic of China must abide by the constitution and the law, uphold discipline and work, keep public order, and respect social ethics."[78] The Beijing Municipal Party Committee soon found that the mention of social ethics in the constitution was a problem because it combined legal demands (*falü yaoqiu*) and moral demands (*daode shang de yaoqiu*). Giving reports, some cadres told people that "from now on, when there is a meeting you cannot be late because if you are late you will have not respected social ethics, and that is a violation of the law." Consequently, study of the constitution was "not like cultural study; if you do not study well then you violate the law."[79] Studying the constitution seemed to be the only safety net to avoid committing mistakes, if there was one at all. Many residents responded strongly to this warning. More talk about how everyone should receive "education to abide by laws" had propelled many people to see all behavior as possibly contravening the law. In Beijing, this interpretation spiraled out of control. In multiple versions of a major work report, the Beijing draft discussion committee warned everyone not to attach random "labels" (*maozi*). Across the city, following lessons to learn to abide by laws (*shoufa jiaoyu*) that extensively covered the constitution, people had labeled individuals as those who "violated the constitution" if they exhibited undesirable behaviors such as failing to queue for the tram, eating seeds in the meeting hall, or arriving to work late or leaving early.[80]

Another common concern was the question of how the constitution as a law aligned with other policies and theoretical teachings of Marxism-Leninism-Mao Zedong Thought. Xinhua News Agency reporters were instructed to write that the constitution developed from the 1949 Common Program. It solidified the achievements made under the Common Program, and it also laid out all the advancements that the Chinese people would and should strive to achieve.[81] Citing Stalin's comment that the constitution should be a document of what is "now" rather than what will come in the future, people in Chongqing suggested in discussions that the constitution was not really a constitution in the strict sense of the word, but rather a "program." Many of its articles contained programs for future reform rather than achievements already made. To them, the draft was not a legal document enshrining in law the legal expectations of the status quo, as they felt it ought to be.[82] However, Mao had said in his speech "On the Draft of the Constitution of the People's Republic of China," that precisely this flexibility was the hallmark of China's advanced socialist constitution. Socialism made laws not only simple but also flexible. Xinhua News Agency picked up on Mao's statement and explained that the constitution was a "socialist kind of constitution," which meant that it wrote into law the socialist construction and transformation of the country and its current systems of ownership, but that it also had to allow for future changes; otherwise it would stifle the transition to true socialism.[83] Reporters writing from Wuhan and Kunming noted that the people they had observed were often quite worried about the relationship between studying theory and studying the constitution draft. Could the study of laws and the study of Marxism-Leninism-Mao Zedong Thought contradict each other? Some of the ways in which reporters explained the constitution seemed to suggest this.[84]

Local officials had some leeway in deciding whether a person's response was just "erroneous" or "heinous." Residents who patently questioned the populist claim of the constitution draft, who thought it was little more than "empty words" to be enjoyed only by people working for the party and government, or who doubted the intentions of its drafters could be severely criticized. Xinhua News Agency's reminders to its reporters that the constitution was not merely a piece of paper or an "empty promise," and its instructions to ensure that their reports reflected this, suggest that this sort of response was not uncommon. Reactionary talk included public mention of the fact that the United States, too, had a version of a State Council and the Guomindang also had a constitution.[85] People who made such comments were quickly labeled "class enemies." Reports were at pains to highlight that these class enemies were not party members (even though plenty of party members also made such comments) and that they did not come from good class origins.[86] "Reactionary talk" of this kind, moreover, was particularly worrying because it aligned with outside criticisms published by the Nationalist Central News Agency on Taiwan, which attacked the promises of the PRC constitution and asked how anyone could trust a document in the face of clear evidence of oppression, persecutions, refusal of legal trials, state price-fixing, mandatory state purchases of grain, and the stripping of ownership rights.[87]

Taken together, the discussion reports indicate that most people were trying to make sense of the draft and what its stipulations might mean for their lives. What seemed like a familiar exercise of hearing about or reading a text and discussing it as part of a mass education drive was so much more difficult now because it was a comprehensive law. The discussion took the Communist project of simplifying law to its logical conclusion, involving ordinary people in the making of law, even if some of this involvement was only symbolic. It meant, though, that fundamental epistemological challenges of constitutionalism were placed at the doorsteps of residents and cadres. People with little if any experience with laws, no legal training, and limited ability to make sense of the simplified legal language now faced abstract questions and problems of law implementation. What was law, what was a constitution, and what force did it have? How did general, abstract legal principles relate to one's everyday life? How they responded to these questions may have been a reflection of their personal circumstances at that moment. But reports interpreted responses as expressions of political consciousness and class status.

## Dealing with Legalese

Among its many purposes, the constitution was meant to prove that a socialist state could have effective laws without excessive legalese. The constitution's creators, editors, jurists, and discussion committee members repeatedly wrote that accessibility was one of the constitution's distinguishing features.[88] Dong Chengmei later recalled how Mao insisted on using the more colloquial "and" (he) over its more formal equivalent (yu) common in written and literary Chinese. Mao argued that China's famous May Fourth writer Lu Xun, whom he greatly admired, had after all also not used the formal character much.[89] Although the more formal term seemed more appropriate for a state law, Mao defied rules of style.[90] It was a seemingly small tweak, but it sent a clear message that the language of the law should be the colloquial language of everyday life. Lü Shuxiang, one of the two well-known authors of the 1951 *Lectures on Grammar and Rhetoric*, which outlined a comprehensive reform to purify the Chinese language and make it fit for use in a socialist society, advised on matters of language during the drafting of the constitution.[91] And the country's language reformers praised the constitution as the country's first constitution ever to be "written using the easily understandable language of people today."[92]

While sending a strong political message that legal language should be democratized, simplification often added an additional layer of difficulty for anyone who wanted unambiguous explanations of what the constitution actually meant. In Beijing, a person labeled a capitalist thought it would be best to learn parts of the constitution and especially Article 10 by heart, to avoid making any mistakes.[93] A report in *Neibu cankao* notes that participants at a discussion session with capitalists and representatives of democratic parties in Changsha requested "a detailed manual in order to avoid violating the law because one has insufficiently grasped its 'spirit.'" They did not want to contravene the constitution accidentally, or be blamed for breaking the law, only because they were not clear on how they were meant to understand it.[94] Those who had observed and understood the CCP's manipulation of language now looked for reassurance and concrete guidelines that told them what to do—what was right, and what was wrong. So-called capitalists and members of the national bourgeoisie, whom the CCP had for years admonished to "abide by law," wanted as many precise instructions as possible telling them how to behave.

Their requests for detailed instructions were probably not fulfilled, but they had identified a major shortcoming in the published literature on the constitution and a structural problem in the CCP's dissemination of legal knowledge. In an environment that suggested a stark distinction between correct and incorrect understandings of the law, the absence of authoritative explanations that clearly delineated which interpretations were correct was striking. Party officials who participated in drafting the constitution had discussed a similar problem, without finding a solution. Shortly after the constitution draft was opened for discussion, Mao called his secretary, Tian Jiaying, and Dong Cheng-mei to the CCP's summer resort in Beidaihe to task them with writing for publication a set of interpretations of the constitution's articles. Dong and Tian, together with Chen Boda's two secretaries, Shi Jing-tang and Yao Luo, as well as Tian Jiaying's secretary, began work im-mediately. When half of the draft was completed, Dong and Tian gave it to Mao, who wanted his office to publish and distribute it to the members and alternate members of the Central Committee. Dong and Tian, however, worried that if at any point questions were to arise about how to interpret the constitution, it might no longer be clear whether they should be answered according to the articles of the con-stitution or according to these explanations. Another problem was that the constitution draft stipulated that the power to interpret the constitution rested with the National People's Congress and its Standing Committee. Publishing such a volume would contravene the constitution draft and set a problematic example. Persuaded, Mao abandoned the project.[95]

The anecdote suggests that Mao and the party leadership were not necessarily trying to be non-committal about interpretations. They were trying to uphold the appearance of constitution-based demo-cratic procedures, at least at that moment. Had the drafting committee issued a publication explaining what the articles actually meant, this would have come with an authoritative stamp of approval suggesting that these were reliable interpretations rendered by those at the center of political power. While that might have been an accurate portrayal of the power balance among the central leadership, emphasizing party dominance over the National People's Congress, it would have contra-vened the show of united front democracy that the constitution was meant to bolster.

Without such a publication, the work of explaining laws was trans-ferred to local governments, party propaganda officials, and people conducting the discussion in the two cities. They had to determine correct and incorrect explanations. Throughout the discussion and once the constitution was promulgated in September 1954, propa-ganda officials corrected and directed how the constitution's words and formulations were used, not only in discussions but particularly also in the media-based propaganda intended to explain and promote the draft.[96] There was a substantial quantity of materials to check. Xinhua News Agency had stipulated that of all newspaper articles published at the beginning and the end of the period of discussion, one-third of them were to be dedicated to the draft. During the rest of the campaign, one-fourth of all articles were to cover the draft.[97] And propaganda authorities found many articles that they thought contained mistakes, were misleading, or incomplete.

Censors spent much time pointing out basic errors and omissions that appeared repeatedly in media reportage. In August 1954, the Central Propaganda Department criticized several newspapers for forgetting to mention the Common Program in their reportage. As a result, they had failed to explain that many of the rights the constitution draft bestowed on citizens had long been "won" since the establishment of the PRC: lacking precise discussion, the department worried that readers might think that rights would only exist once the constitution was promulgated, thus jeopardizing how people viewed the early years of CCP rule. When speaking and writing about the draft, moreover, many officials called the constitution draft a constitution. Involuntarily, they were suggesting that this was the finalized law.[98] Newspaper reporters made the opposite mistake, some writing that people should "abide by the constitution draft."[99] Propaganda officials worried that readers would pay no attention to the actual constitution once promulgated. Worse, they might mistakenly continue to refer to copies of the draft. Meanwhile, Shanghai's *Jiefang ribao* made a different but equally problematic statement when one of its reporters wrote that China was working towards 'state/national socialism' instead of 'socialism.' The *Jiefang ribao* journalist might have been trying to emphasize the national scope of socialism, but it could be interpreted as linking the CCP to Nazi Germany. This had to trouble officials, not least because CCP propaganda posters at the time were attacking Chiang Kaishek's Republic of China on Taiwan as fascist.

Censors searched equally carefully for the kind of wrong explanations of the constitution that could have severe political and legal implications. Several Shanghai newspapers had written that "everyone has the right to work, the right to rest, and the right to receive an education," even though the constitution stated that only citizens would be able to enjoy these rights.[101] Confused by the statement that eighteen years was now the age for reaching adulthood, some journalists thought that this meant that people could vote if they were in their eighteenth year of age, rather than already eighteen. Discussants were instructed to explain that a person had to have "fulfilled eighteen years of age" in order to be eligible.[102] Several Youth League newspapers mistakenly asserted then that only adults would enjoy the full rights and duties of citizens. They were telling their young readers that they did not have citizenship rights. Worried, the Central Propaganda Department pointed out that, on the contrary, this only applied to the right to vote and to the right to stand for elections, not to all rights. Journalists, they wrote, would have known this if they had carefully read Article 86 of the constitution.[103]

In general, propaganda materials had a hard time explaining correctly how the law defined crucial issues such as ownership, socialism, and political rights. The Shanghai Municipal Propaganda Department had come across discussions that changed the meaning of Article 7, which read: "The co-operative sector of the economy is either socialist, when collectively owned by the working masses, or semi-socialist, when in part collectively owned by the working masses." The problem was that the phrase "in part collectively owned by the working masses" was sometimes turned into "collectively owned by parts of the working masses."[104] This completely changed the meaning of the sentence. Outside of Shanghai, the provincial newspaper *Jilin ribao* had explained that "state ownership and collective ownership are socialist ownership and semi-socialist ownership," only to be criticized publicly by the Central Propaganda Department for using an entirely incorrect formulation because collective ownership did not equal semi-socialist ownership.[105] *Liaoxi ribao* wrote that "the constitution wants to determine the relations between person and person and between class and class," but this was wrong, the department explained, because the constitution intended to abolish the exploiting classes and the practice of exploitation of one class by another.[106]

Wishing to prevent such problems entirely, propaganda officials in Shanghai sometimes took a practical approach and decided to delete key components of the constitution draft from the list of topics for discussion. This was the case with the term "political rights" (*zhengzhi quanli*), which was central to understanding Article 19: "The state deprives feudal landlords and bureaucrat-capitalists of political rights for a specific period of time according to the law."[107] Because several report-givers and discussion leaders wrote that the term "political rights" was "unclear," and the constitution draft also did not offer a conclusive explanation, the Shanghai propaganda officials advised avoiding the term entirely. In doing so, the officials ironically contradicted some of their own earlier criticism of newspapers: that while there were plenty of articles endorsing the constitution draft, too few actually dared to address questions of ideology.

Newspaper reportage, as these examples show, was under regular scrutiny. Even when Shanghai journalists working for major newspapers such as *Xinwen ribao*, *Laodong bao* (Labor daily), *Wenhui bao*, and *Xinmin bao* made no actual mistakes, propaganda authorities sometimes considered their work wanting. The municipal Propaganda Department surveyed the city's newspapers between 16 and 25 June 1954 and found fault with all of them for focusing mostly on the rights granted by the draft, not on citizens' duties.[108] Department officials argued that several of the articles the newspapers published or the manuscripts they submitted for scrutiny were too limited in scope. Articles written for workers seemed to mention only the right to work and the right to rest, and those written for capitalists focused on the constitution's provisions to protect ownership rights. Articles written for people working in education, literature, science, and the arts talked mainly about the way in which the constitution provided for a basic right to education and protected artistic, literary, and scientific creations.[109] Finally, articles written for young people focused on education and the possibility of personal and professional development. Yet these pieces did not say enough about the role of the CCP, of workers, and of the people's democratic dictatorship. Without such discussion, department officials wrote, readers would not be able to grasp the political frameworks within which the constitution draft and all the rights described therein were situated.

The Shanghai Municipal Propaganda Department therefore took a different stance from that of the Central Propaganda Department in Beijing, which had advised that newspapers should help explain the

Fig. 4.2. "People's representatives and women workers in Putuo District ardently discuss the great joyous event of the promulgation of the constitution draft," 1954. (Source: *Laodong bao* [Labor daily], 16 June 1954, p. 1.)

constitution to their target readership by focusing on those articles that would be of interest to them.[110] The Central Propaganda Department's approach was consistent with the general organizational principle that individual newspapers should cater to specific readerships, whereas the Shanghai department seemingly thought that it was safer for all newspapers to report fairly comprehensively on the general facets of the constitution draft in order to ensure cohesion across the citywide discussion.[111]

Not everything that propaganda departments criticized, however, related to legal explanations. They also policed images. Shanghai's censors especially disapproved of the *Laodong bao* cover image on 16 June, the day after the constitution draft was promulgated. The image showed a woman in Putuo District discussing the constitution with other workers (fig. 4.2). Department officials had decided that the woman looked unhappy, as if she were denouncing someone. They complained that the image failed to focus on the happy atmosphere during legal learning and might affect how readers responded to the entire discussion. Officials went to talk to someone at the newspaper and were told that the photographer had staged the image. *Laodong bao*'s editorial board then missed this and the cover went to print. Whether or not this was true, it was a convenient explanation for the woman's facial expression.[112]

## A Cult for the Constitution

To steer the constitution discussion, propaganda authorities scrutinized publications at the level of individual words and their meanings. Harmonizing everyone's personal legal interpretations with official interpretations of the constitution was not realistic, however. Trying to divert attention away from detailed questions of interpretation, they emphasized instead that people should celebrate the constitution as a material object given to them by the CCP. Propaganda—as the Xinhua News Agency wrote in its instructions—was supposed to chronicle the "happy atmosphere" of these celebrations.

But what did propaganda about a "happy atmosphere" mean, precisely, and what role, if any, did it play in the process of legal learning? Constitutional propaganda was in full swing by August and into late September, in time for the promulgation of the constitution, the fifth anniversary of the founding of the PRC, and the first National People's Congress. The Ministry of Justice was closely involved with propaganda preparations, and on 18 June 1954, a few days after the draft was made public, ministry officials met with leading figures from the arts and literature world to discuss how to advance propaganda on the constitution and judicial propaganda in general.[113] Wei Wenbo (1905–87), the Vice-minister of Justice, explained that everyone should coordinate propaganda work better, and those working in propaganda and those working in law should keep in regular contact. Judicial workers and artists had to communicate better to promote "patriotic education to abide by law" (*aiguo shoufa jiaoyu*). The Ministry of Justice would provide more materials to artists and authors, and this would "help art and literature workers advance in their creations."[114]

Municipal governments turned the streets of downtown Shanghai and Beijing into spaces for celebrating the constitution draft, as a

*Renmin ribao* reporter described in August.[115] Gilded golden characters on large red banners towered above most of the city's thirty-five cinemas and seventy-eight theaters, celebrating the draft as a national achievement. Public storytellers were narrating stories about how the Chinese people under the leadership of the CCP had successfully struggled to achieve this victory. The city's residents could take their pick of constitution-inspired entertainment from a selection of short plays, musical dialogues, and slide shows. Mobile theater troupes visited factory workers on the outskirts of the city and gave performances in workers' palaces and around the neighborhoods. These were generally short dramatic pieces full of the promise that the constitution and the general line would continue aiding China's people on the road toward achieving ever better lives under socialism. Artists had drawn close to one hundred different propaganda posters and serial comics. The East China People's Press, once again actively involved, designed some five different high-quality color posters, of which reportedly more than 400,000 copies were dispatched across town. Some of these posters contained basic explanations of the constitution's articles, but most focused less on textual content and instead featured images of people ardently welcoming the constitution. The Shanghai Municipal People's Library and the Shanghai Library organized exhibitions of reference materials to aid people with reading the draft. The eleven reading rooms of the People's Library set up special exhibition rooms as well, and readers could borrow copies of the draft. When the August heat subsided, residents went out to the cultural centers or to parks and watched free slide shows.[116]

Propaganda workers told stories of how people enjoyed their newly enshrined freedoms, constrained as they might have been in practice. People were depicted reading the draft freely and enthusiastically. Holding and reading the book of law became a common trope for constitution propaganda. When the constitution draft was first issued, newspapers and magazines showed workers, farmers, teachers, students, youth, cadres, and members of the nationalities pouring over the constitution draft in newspapers.[117] Sometimes they were photographed reading alone. More often, they were shown as groups of people huddled together, around one or two people holding a copy of a newspaper.

Fig. 4.3. "People across the country enthusiastically endorse the
PRC constitution draft," 1954. (Source: *Xinwen ribao* [News daily],
27 June 1954, p. 3.)

These images worked in multiple ways. At one level, there were
people reading and coming together to read. At another, people reading
the paper would see other people reading the paper. Taken together, the
message conveyed that in the new socialist society, people read the constitution draft, read about the constitution draft, and read about people
reading the constitution draft. For those who might not have been able
to read, they could see others looking at the draft and the papers, just

Fig. 4.4. Gu Pu, "The People's Great
Joyous Event," 1954. (Source: *Man-
hua yuebao* [Cartoon monthly],
August 1954, cover page.)

as they themselves did. One issue of *Xinwen ribao* featured an entire
page filled exclusively with images of this kind (fig. 4.3).

Propaganda authorities searched for a point of unity that could be
effectively communicated across the country. Images emphasized common exegetical bonding and acquisition of legal knowledge through
group reading and discussion.[118] Publicity focused less on getting
people to learn detailed content and more on using the constitution
draft and its carefully selected slogans as symbols to champion national
unity, people's sovereignty, and the road of transition to socialism—
together with the general line and the first five-year plan. Authors, editors, and artists made extensive use of the technique, already explored
on a smaller scale during the Marriage Law campaign, to highlight the
book and images of the book as the material manifestation of the CCP's
constitutional idea.

The symbol of the constitution manifested in the form of a book
reified PRC law as a whole and suggested that everyone would flock
toward the book of law. A cartoon by Gu Pu, one of the artists who had
drawn images for the *Illustrated Marriage Law* in 1952, depicts this idea
against a bright red background on the cover page of the August 1954

issue of *Manhua yuebao* (fig. 4.4). Among the cheering crowd, there are men and women cadres clad in blue Mao suits and caps, urban workers in overalls, nurses, officials on the way to conduct topographical surveys, construction workers with tools in hand, farmers holding bundled crops, and urban residents in suits and pretty skirts. A female cadre, a child with a young pioneer scarf, and an old woman with her white hair knotted in a bun surround and cheer the larger-than-life constitution draft book while saying things like, "The ideals of our martyrs have been realized," or "[we] deeply thank the motherland for protecting us." Members of China's ethnic nationalities are dancing and proclaiming that "the constitution is a sun that will not fade," while an air force pilot flying above the draft pledges to safeguard the people's rights.

The symbol of the larger-than-life book was also meant to instill in people a new sense of national identity and patriotism. These ideals were then set in a framework of international socialist brotherhood. To make the link clear to audiences, the constitutions of the Soviet Union and Eastern European socialist countries were made visible as part of the material culture of constitutionalism that emerged in Beijing and Shanghai during these months. The municipal Bureau of Culture commissioned prints of the Soviet constitution and had cadres and activists arrange displays of these brightly colored images close to the Sino-Soviet Friendship Building and the exhibition halls on Huaihai Middle Road in Luwan District and on Changshou Road in Putuo District.[119]

Propaganda condemning the "heinous propaganda" of "imperialist" countries also made use of the book trope. Mocking the GMD, *Manhua yuebao* reprinted an image drawn in 1946 to criticize the GMD constitution adopted that year. Showing a visibly malnourished man having to read the constitution upside down, hanging from a rope with his feet tied (fig 4.5), the caricature is titled "hanging upside down" (*daoxuan*). The cartoonist was playing with words because the term for hanging upside down also means to be in dire straits. In addition, the magazine reprinted a Soviet cartoon that depicted the US constitution as a black book, with a dollar sign printed on the front and shady creatures emerging from its pages. Ku Klux Klan members, capitalists with top hat and cigars, and lurking bandits with knives in hand guard the pages, on which are sarcastically written "democracy," "individual freedoms," and "freedom of speech" (fig. 4.6).

Fig. 4.5. Mai Guo, "Hanging Upside Down," 1954. (Source: *Manhua yuebao* [Cartoon monthly], August 1954.)

Once the newly assembled National People's Congress adopted the constitution on 20 September 1954, people were expected to endorse the document and fulfill their constitutional duty to abide by its articles. Propaganda idealized the constitution as an organic whole, no longer lingering over questions of language and specific provisions. Publicly, constitutional knowledge was truncated to knowledge of the fact that China had a constitution, that citizens enjoyed legal rights and had a duty to abide by the law, and that the democratic process by which the constitution had been conceived set China apart from its enemies and from less-advantaged countries. He Lüting, director of the Shanghai Conservatory, composed a refrain for his song "Praise the Constitution" that gave melody to this baseline of constitutional knowledge: "We praise the constitution, we endorse the constitution, we resolutely defend the constitution, the People's own constitution!"[120]

Newspapers printed stories and photos of the constitution as an object. Xinhua News Agency circulated a photograph by Zhang Ruihua that showed people dancing under a banner welcoming the constitution at Beijing's Tian'anmen Square.[121] Large-scale "constitution models" (*xianfa moxing*) were particularly popular. Shanghai's *Xinwen ribao* reported on local parades in factories where "good news announcement troupes" had taken to the streets with homemade posters and constitution models.[122] *Guangming ribao* showed students at

Fig. 4.6. Aibulaomofu, "The Hideous Nature of the US Constitution," 1954. (Source: *Manhua yuebao* [Cartoon monthly], August 1954.)

Beijing Institute of Politics and Law preparing a large book model with the slogan "All power to the people."[123] Across the country, people paraded constitution models. And on 1 October 1954, a model of the constitution book, several meters high, was driven past the visitors' podium in front of the Forbidden Palace at Tian'anmen to celebrate National Day and the five-year anniversary of the PRC (fig. 4.7).[124]

Abstract legal ideas thus turned into concrete material form. Together with the discussion and images of people reading, the constitution was popularized as an idea materialized by the CCP. Having a tangible constitution was as important as reading it.[125] In late October, *Renmin ribao* reported that in total 12,500,000 copies had been printed.[126] Selected popular comments on the constitution also emphasized the significance of accessibility. Factory workers in Shanghai's Penglai District happily told a reporter that they were actually illiterate but had still bought copies as a memento to commemorate the occasion.[127] One woman told members of the Beijing Municipal Propaganda Department that she planned to save the copy of the day's paper as a memorabilia and pass it on to the next generation.[128] Some

Fig. 4.7. Constitution model,
Tian'anmen, 1 October 1954.
(Source: *Renmin huabao* [People's
pictorial], no. 10, October 1954,
pp. 2-3.)

bought the newspaper because they wanted a copy of the photo of Mao
Zedong displayed on the front page of all papers that day.[129]

## The Importance of Abiding by Law

The constitution remained a popular propaganda symbol after 1954—
so much so that, in late 1955, the Ministry of Culture felt compelled to
remind municipal people's committees and cultural bureaus that they
should check the widespread practice of embellishing items of everyday use by printing articles from the constitution on them. Producers
were not supposed to use any parts of the constitution, leader portraits, the national flag, the national emblem, or parts of the "Internationale" on diaries, in advertisements, on wrapping paper, or on other
products. Keeping a close eye on the production of these items would
help "avoid mistakes."[130] Things were not quite so serious, though.
Products in storage or already on sale could remain until stocks were
depleted, if there was nothing "reactionary" on them. Diary printing
shops wanting to add or retain some educational text, such as articles
from the constitution, would have to run this by their local party
committee.[131]

The constitution continued to play a symbolic role in other ways as well. Based on Article 100 of the constitution, the demands to "abide by the constitution" and to "abide by law" also became political slogans. Just before the national discussion of the draft constitution, at the sixth national meeting on public security in early June 1954, Dong Biwu (1886–1975), as chairman of the Central Politics and Law Commission, had called for the need to foster among the masses a sense of having to "abide by law." Enemies, he argued, would be given an easy point of attack if the masses did not abide by laws. It was crucial to raise the masses' "legal consciousness" (*falü yishi*) and to see legal consciousness as closely linked to, but not conflated with, political consciousness.[132] In October 1954, the jurist Yang Yuqing further explained that "we certainly must ardently love and abide by the people's own laws."[133] Yang argued that it had been acceptable and necessary to not abide by laws during the period prior to liberation when laws had been instruments of oppression by the ruling classes. Things were different now, however. Most visibly manifested in the new constitution, the new laws were clearly the laws of the People. It was time, Yang argued, for people to change their attitudes and behavior and embrace the laws as their own. Nobody, he wrote, should think that "now that we have gained political power, we do not need laws, or we can [choose to] not abide by our own laws."[134]

Newspapers and magazines also continued to print articles explaining why it was important to abide by laws. In mid-November 1954, for example, a *Renmin ribao* editorial called for "strengthening law abidance education." Because not everyone had so far understood the new society and many still pined after aspects of the old society, the editorial reasoned, many people were prone to committing violations of law. Anyone who believed that the law dealt only with enemies was completely wrong.[135] The editorial cautioned that not only could the People violate the law, they could also be punished for it, as Mao had warned years earlier. People also had the duty to defend the law, and in order to do so they needed to know it. Not knowing the law would give others a loophole to misuse the law. Popular how-to books echoed this argument and explained why it was important that everyone pay attention to laws. In the popular booklet *Talking about Abiding by Law*

(Tantan shoufa) published by the Popular Readings Press in October 1955, the author Sun Guohua advised his readers that "earnestly abiding by laws is of great importance to raising people's socialist thinking and morality and to establishing a new social atmosphere." Education to abide by laws would raise people's "knowledge of the revolutionary legal system."[136]

Local government and party officials continued to be among the groups that were particularly advised to study the constitution. Yet their legal lessons could take on a different perspective, one that focused on aligning CCP rule with law-abiding behavior. Public security workers and local police officers had been among the groups most worried during the constitution draft discussion. Many had been concerned that widely disseminating such an extensive catalogue of citizens' rights would make their work and life much more difficult. They feared that residents would use the constitution to protest and question public security work. After the discussion concluded, many cadres still thought teaching people the constitution was asking for trouble (mafan).

To many local public security officials, in particular, it remained unclear how to harmonize party directives and constitutional demands. In a directive issued in January 1955 and circulated in the internal magazine Gongan jianshe, the Ministry of Public Security tried to address this question and assuage cadres' worries. The ministry explained that the constitution regulated what was lawful and should be enforced, and what was unlawful and should be prohibited.[137] Many public security workers, it wrote, still had "not understood the significance and use of the constitution and law." They were stuck in "old ways," and too often they thought that since things had worked just fine before the constitution was promulgated, one might as well avoid trouble for a bit longer and continue without implementing the constitution and laws.[138] But, as the ministry reminded its readers, this was not an acceptable way of thinking. Orderly and law-abiding public security workers understood the constitution and laws and knew how to comport themselves. Crucially, they also knew when to deal with matters according to internal party procedures. Because the constitution and the country's laws could only be properly implemented with adequate party leadership and oversight, internal party procedures would take precedence over laws.[139] This, the directive explained, would give public security officials the flexibility to deal with "special circumstances," loosely defined. It would, the ministry added, not diminish the significance of the constitution and laws; it would help ensure that the constitution and laws were implemented even better.[140] Public security workers had to know the constitution and laws in order to know how to navigate this fine line.

Several weeks later, *Gongan jianshe* reported on how public security workers in different districts and cities had studied and implemented the directive.[141] Readers learned that Qingdao municipal cadres now had a new understanding of what it meant to abide by laws. The magazine cited one local public security official who explained: "Although I studied the constitution in the past, I had not yet understood the constitution's essence. I always thought that the constitution punishes bad people, and I put myself outside of the law. Now I understand that the only way to get the support of the broad masses is to abide by the constitution and correctly enforce the constitution and laws."[142] But this theoretical realization often did not translate in daily work. *Gongan jianshe* continued to regularly uncover instances of local cadres abusing their powers, tyrannizing residents in their neighborhoods, raping local women, or making "corrupt" deals.[143]

In the months between the promulgation of the constitution in autumn 1954 and the beginning of the Hundred Flowers Movement in 1956, the Ministry of Justice and legal experts worked to construct a stronger socialist legal system. Multiple drafts of a new Civil Code and Criminal Code were composed, while a regularized legal system was in the making.[144] Public security, the procuratorate, and the people's courts were to work closely together in delivering justice to people and in producing law propaganda and public security propaganda, though reports show that frictions between the three abounded at the local level.[145]

Things swiftly changed in 1957 when law propaganda and calls to abide by laws became a source of conflict in what became the Anti-Rightist Movement. Pointing to provisions made in the constitution, intellectuals such as Luo Longji, with whom this chapter began, publicly called on the CCP to live up to the guarantees it had made in its laws, to establish a proper legal system, and finally to enact all necessary legal codes and work toward actual judicial independence. By the end of 1957, Luo and others were attacked as "rightists."[146] Already in

January 1957, countering such calls for more legal reform, Mao had explained at a meeting of party committee secretaries of provinces, municipalities, and autonomous regions: "We definitely want to abide by law, we definitely want to eliminate counterrevolutionaries, we definitely want certain success. Abiding by law is to abide by socialist law, so abiding by law cannot destroy the legal system."[147]

Controversies unfolded over questions of what it would mean to abide by laws and which laws to abide by. In April 1957, *Renmin ribao* printed a scathing accusation against those who had called for more legal reforms of "using" talk about laws to "smear" the revolutionary system. According to the article, critics of the current legal system had said that there was "no law" because there was either "no law to rely on" or because existing laws could not be relied upon. How, the article asked, could anyone argue that there was no law? The PRC had passed more than 4,000 laws, regulations, and decisions between 1949 and 1954, it reasoned. Domestic and international audiences had sung the praises of PRC laws. The real problem, the piece continued, was that rightist critics felt that a "people's law" (*renmin fazhi*) was the wrong kind of law, and they looked down on it with hostility. The article accused them of doubting the laws that were already in existence; and of criticizing the government and the party for "violating law" (*weifa*) and "violating the constitution" (*wei xianfa*). Moreover, the article continued, they blatantly disregarded the fact that both the central government and the party had underlined the importance of abiding by laws. After all, every time a new major law had been passed, it was propagated and implemented so that all people would become involved. All of this, the article reasoned, was "something that has never before been done in the history of our country and in any capitalist country." Acccording to the article, so-called rightists were pretending to protect the law but were really only hypocritically "upholding the constitution." In doing so, they portrayed their true bourgeois inclinations.[148]

Raising awareness of its law propaganda work was part of the CCP's attack on rightists. Articles in national newspapers argued that the simple fact that public security offices and people's courts had continued law propaganda work showed the state's commitment to law. Li Daguang, writing in *Renmin ribao*, told readers in March 1957 that "many areas" across the country were conducting law propaganda to educate people and help them better understand laws.[149] Organized by courts, judges and local judicial workers were sent to factories, enterprises, schools, and mass organizations to talk to workers and residents about laws. In Jiangsu, Li explained, some eighty counties had become involved, organizing over 1,200 talks with some 568,000 people in attendance. Court officials wrote texts for news coverage, radio broadcasts, and small volumes of popular readings. Some cities organized judicial work exhibitions with posters that showed ordinary citizens engaged in mediation. Hubei, Jiangxi, and Hebei Provinces all participated as well. Li concluded that all of these activities had helped to "raise people's knowledge of the law."[150]

If the central government used law dissemination to prove the party's superiority, it also continued to use it to try and maintain order among its rank and file and within the population. As its fifth point of action, the 1957 public security propaganda work plan included the need to make everyone more aware that the socialist legal system was important and that things should be done "according to the law" in any kind of struggle. Public security workers should "model behavior of abiding by laws."[151] A report by the CCP Liaoning Provincial Party Committee meanwhile explained that, on the one hand, people were dissatisfied with their local government, and this was something that needed to be taken seriously. On the other hand, people's political education was poor, and this needed to be improved through political learning, study of the constitution, and a better understanding of Communist morality.[152] Also in August 1957, the Ministry of Internal Affairs sent a letter to provinces and municipalities instructing them to set up Marriage Law study sessions again and work toward "strengthening the legal system." Studying the Marriage Law, the letter argued, would be a good method to "pay attention to legal system thought education" and to "foster the custom of abiding by law." It, too, exhorted cadres to strive to be "models of abiding by laws."[153] By April 1958, *Gongan jianshe* reprinted a speech by Liu Binglin (1909–82), head of the Political and Legal Affairs Commission of Shandong Province, who had told an audience composed of heads of the province's municipal people's courts and public security bureaus to "vigorously launch law propaganda" and to take it "to every township, to every commune, to every street, and to every village."[154]

While law propaganda was intensifying locally, the party leadership slowly dismantled judicial bureaucracies at the national level. Newspapers and magazines had repeatedly, sometimes implicitly, attacked the Ministry of Justice in the preceding months. In January 1958 *Renmin ribao* alleged that the Law Press had commissioned poor-quality publications, mismanaged the editorial and revision process, and defrauded government funds. The press had been established in 1954 in response to a lack of professionalization in law publishing and placed under the ministry's supervision. *Renmin ribao* now accused legal experts who had written for the press, often in addition to their regular duties, of being shoddy "after-hours authors" who only wrote for the money yet did not actually submit drafts worth the paper on which they were printed.[155] Tellingly, the criticism concluded: "the problems at the Law Press are so serious, the Ministry of Justice, which directly leads this press, cannot not have known this." In 1959, the Ministry of Justice was shut down.

After the Anti-Rightist Movement concluded and the Ministry of Justice was closed, law propaganda remained a task of public security and legal work at local courts, partly because it could contain many different kinds of educational content.[156] Party and government could interpret some of the ambiguous language of laws as it suited their purpose, and law propaganda became a tool that officials could use to assert state authority when needed. In Beijing's Chaoyang District, during the years of shortages following the Great Leap Forward, the local public security office used "education to be law-abiding" as a way to try to protect grain and food provisions from theft and pillaging. They encouraged communes in the district to find those who had committed "small" and "large" crimes of this kind, and people in the communes strengthened security work, including instituting nighttime surveillance of kitchens and grain storehouses. As a result, *Gongan jianshe* reported, one commune alone had managed to solve or uncover useful clues in eleven cases.[157] Law propaganda, in cases such as these, focused both on those who had committed crimes and those who were merely trying to make do under difficult conditions.

Even more than during the early 1950s, official discussions of law-abiding behavior during the early 1960s turned the term into a synonym for obedience to party-state authority. The importance of being law-abiding applied to both good people and bad people. In May and June 1961, articles in *Renmin gongan* (People's public security) called on public security workers to "raise consciousness to abide by policy, law, and observe discipline," reminding readers that good people could easily commit mistakes and that bad people were likely to commit crimes.[158] The danger, as another editorial outlined, was significant in both cases, though good people who committed errors usually did so because they did not understand laws. These people, the editorial reasoned, failed to see that the country's laws were the reflection of party policies and the sum of the party's experiences in the struggle and dictatorship against enemies.[159]

Law propaganda work therefore continued in many places, but it could be difficult to carry out. A report from Heilongjiang Province listed a range of different things that had gone wrong in propaganda work conducted by local courts in the province. Internal trial information and party directives had been printed for public circulation, for example. And some local courts had, against the directive of the Supreme People's Court, conducted so-called traveling judgments. These involved local judicial staff and a judge carrying out the same trial and pronouncing the same verdict again and again, each time in a different locality. Yet in one case, at the end of several installments of the same judgment, the defendant had asked whether counting all the different individual judgments together meant he would have to go to jail for over a hundred years.[160] Meanwhile, in June 1962, several months after the 7,000 cadres conference during which Mao took a step back in national politics, Hebei Province was featured on the front page of *Renmin gongan* with a contribution on how Luotian County's public security office had taken up law propaganda education by conducting public trials, issuing new printed materials explaining laws and producing radio broadcasts. Aiming to improve "legal standpoints" (*fazhi guannian*), the county even went so far as to call these efforts a "legal propaganda campaign" (*fazhi xuanchuan yundong*). The editors seemed skeptical, though. They invited readers' comments and criticisms on this piece, and there was little follow-up on the story in the following issues.[161]

## Conclusion: How to Deal with Lawlessness

The national discussion on the constitution draft in 1954 was the apogee of law propaganda while Mao was alive. It left a lasting impression and a repository of techniques for propaganda and public security workers to talk about laws. It also left a host of problems in its wake. Widespread talk of laws had created a range of expectations, disappointments, and understandings that were not easily influenced even as the official goals of law propaganda changed. By the late 1950s and throughout the early 1960s, whenever the media used terms such as "law propaganda" (*fazhi xuanchuan*) and "legal education" (*fazhi jiaoyu*) it often signaled moments in which party and government officials, be they local or national, were trying to control actions they deemed wrong. Particularly in the aftermath of the Great Leap Forward and during the Socialist Education Campaign, advocacy for law propaganda reflected officials' anxieties about how to influence residents' behavior. At times, it seemed that many local officials, who had worried about changes that the new constitution and laws would bring, had come to realize that some reference to laws could be useful.

The early years of the Cultural Revolution spelled an end to mass legal education. As the rift between the CCP and the Soviet Union worsened following Khrushchev's call for de-Stalinization, the concept of "socialist legality" and the idea of a regularized socialist legal system became associated with Soviet governance. Under Khrushchev there had been a public turn to socialist legality. Khrushchev had "promised to revive the Party and to 'create an atmosphere of intolerance toward violations of the law.'"[162] In 1966 Mao had called for people to smash "public security, the procuratorate, and the legal sector" (*gong-jian-fa.*)[163] Local courts were dismantled and replaced by mass struggle sessions and mob justice.[164]

Denunciations of laws bolstered revolutionary claims. On 31 January 1967 *Renmin ribao* published a short article with the provocative title, "In Praise of Lawlessness" ("Wufa wutian zan").[165] Xin Wu, the author of the article, passionately attacked "bourgeois law" (*zichan jieji falü*) and "bourgeois lawfulness" (*zichan jieji youfa youtian*) and associated it closely with the activities of "capitalist-roaders." Xin argued that rather than adhering to laws that were instruments of class oppression, the Chinese people should wage a revolution against the established legal system and the cloaking control of the bourgeoisie. Lawlessness against bourgeois law would bring about the destruction of bourgeois lawfulness, eventually clearing the way for socialist laws and lawfulness (*youfa youtian*). Xin echoed Mao's argument made in early 1957 that abiding by laws meant abiding by socialist laws. The article also replicated the arguments of legal reformers during the early 1950s who had called for violating bourgeois law as a matter of principle and as a matter of building a socialist legal system. For Xin, however, socialist laws and socialist legality advocated during the 1950s were the new bourgeois laws.

The article contributed to setting a powerful framework for the analysis of law during the Mao Era and after 1978. Its wording also drew the attention of readers outside of China when a translation was printed in the influential *Survey of China Mainland Press*.[166] A call to lawlessness mirrored the lawless practices of the early Cultural Revolution. Courts that had been disbanded in the late 1960s only slowly returned to work during the early 1970s. The extreme violence during this time has been well documented in scholarship on the Cultural Revolution.[167] But I propose to distinguish lawlessness in people's daily lives from the official trajectory of the term "lawlessness" in political discourse. Already during the late 1960s, media repeatedly spoke of lawlessness, but the quantity of media reports that dealt with the term does not seem to have been extraordinary for the time. After the Cultural Revolution was officially concluded, however, the term rapidly became shorthand for a party-sponsored historical narrative of the recent past and for a new normative framework. Lawlessness served at least three functions: first, as an analytical category for Mao Era historiography; second, as a national concept within which to frame the collective past of China's citizenry for the purpose of contemporary politics; and third, as a term used by individuals to contextualize and describe personal memories. Lawlessness, as the next chapter illustrates, became a condition for the party to stage the return of law propaganda during the late 1970s.

# PART III

REVIVALS: 1970–1989

# 5  Constitutional Dilemmas

## Reworking Law Propaganda for a New Socialist Era

The CCP regime's rediscovery of law propaganda during the late 1970s and 1980s signaled at once a break and continuity with the three decades since the founding of the PRC. As the CCP emphasized, the number of laws passed marked a departure from the years under Mao.[1] Yet many of the methods used to disseminate legal knowledge were adapted from the 1950s. Law propaganda still aimed to change people's consciousness, but the CCP now wanted people to develop a specific "legal consciousness" in order to participate in the party-state's quest to transform Chinese society through laws. Raising people's legal consciousness, party leaders argued, would help build and maintain "socialist democracy" (*shehui zhuyi minzhu*).[2]

Law propaganda became a common feature of the urban landscapes of post-Mao Beijing and Shanghai. Newspapers and magazines printed article after article that explained laws. Bookstores stocked shelves with legal self-help books. Authors wrote educational crime fiction, and magazines serialized stories about citizens' quests for justice.[3] As more people acquired television sets, the central broadcasting services and local stations developed TV series that explained to viewers what laws meant and why it was important to abide by them. Audiences were encouraged to write to editorial offices with legal questions and concerns. Editors selected the most common, pressing, or noteworthy contributions and had them reprinted in regular legal advice columns or discussed on air.

Besides helping to shape a new legal and political future for Chinese socialism, laws were also supposed to help break with and then reorder the recent past.[4] During the late 1970s and early 1980s, following the formal end of the Cultural Revolution, official and unofficial accounts increasingly used the term "lawlessness" to describe the violence, the breakdown of the legal system, and the chaos of the years between 1966 and 1976. Official media reports and documents soon referred to the decade as "ten years of turmoil" (*shinian dongluan*). As the Cultural Revolution became a lawless period in the historical narrative, law propaganda became a technique to rescue China's population from its lawless past.[5] Advocates of law propaganda claimed that people had to learn laws because the Cultural Revolution had destroyed the legal developments of the 1950s. How, they asked, could people know anything about law after their minds had been thoroughly corrupted by the events of these ten years? How could younger generations, who had not witnessed the 1950s and had grown up during those years of turmoil, know anything about the importance of stability through law? Moreover, party leaders, as Suzanne Weigelin-Schwiedrzik argues, started to frame everyone—both ordinary citizens and local cadres—who had lived through the Cultural Revolution as complicit.[6] Universal complicity in the events and violence of the Cultural Revolution was supposed to prevent complex and individual public engagements with personal memories of suffering and persecution. If everyone had been complicit, then everyone needed to learn laws to avoid breaking the law in the future. The CCP's calls to mass legal education had a powerful new rationale.

What should law propaganda in this "new period" (*xin shiqi*) look like, and how could popular legal knowledge serve a new vision of reformed CCP rule? By the late 1970s, in line with the call to "seek truth from facts," the party leadership explained that law propaganda would build on people's practical experiences.[7] Different from the 1950s, law propaganda now focused on furthering knowledge of the socialist legal system (*shehui zhuyi fazhi*) as a whole, with its composite parts of individual laws and the constitution. Party leaders who supported the expansion of law propaganda did so for different reasons. Some saw it as a useful tool for crime prevention and government control. Others thought that state authorities could hold citizens who knew laws accountable and that citizens could, in turn, hold state authorities accountable. Law propaganda promised not only to create new legal knowledge but also to correct and homogenize what the population already knew about laws. If the CCP had told people during the 1950s that they should learn laws to liberate themselves, it now urged them to learn laws in order to live their lives in safety.

Law propaganda continued to be an instrument to influence citizens as well as a method to empower and mobilize them, in support of law and in support of the socialist state, though these goals could be mutually exclusive for some. In the ideal world of its creators, law propaganda would help to perfect the socialist man and woman.[8] This is not to say that everyone was comfortable with the task of teaching and learning laws. Many government officials remained skeptical, and many doubted just how effective control via law would be. Law propaganda could damage party authority when implementation was slow or people thought that laws were nothing more than another attempt by the party to assert its power on paper. Still, because it had value to different groups of people who otherwise disagreed over other aspects of legal reform, law propaganda assumed a presence in the everyday lives of Chinese citizens even as party-state politics oscillated between economic and political reforms, on the one hand, and repeated attempts to fight spiritual pollution, bourgeois liberalization, and to advocate socialist morality, on the other.[9]

Contestations about what laws meant and what purpose they served during the 1970s and early 1980s are the subject of this chapter. Lacking comparative sources for Beijing, the chapter focuses on available archival documents from Shanghai to trace how law propaganda developed in the context of the changing constitutions of the 1970s, waves of new legislation after 1978 including a new Criminal Law, and continuous discussions over what made for good propaganda, and why. From the aborted 1970 state constitution draft to the 1975, 1978, and finally 1982 constitution, local governments repeatedly made urban residents read, discuss, and comment on constitutions and other laws.[10] Three of these constitutions were short-lived. The legal lessons they imparted were not.

## Aborted Beginnings:
## The 1970 Constitution Discussion

The PRC's decade of new constitutions began in the summer of 1970. On 20 July, Party Central sent out *Zhongfa* no. 53 to municipalities, provinces, and autonomous regions across the country announcing the upcoming discussion of how to revise a new state constitution draft.[11] On 9 September, *Zhongfa* no. 56 announced the mass discussion of the revised constitution draft.[12] The directives informed revolutionary committees that this mass discussion and study period should help revise the constitution to be "popular and easy to understand, memorable for everyone, convenient to use" (*tongsu yidong, renren nengji, bianyu yunyong*). Following the discussion, the party leadership planned to ratify the new constitution at the fourth National People's Congress.[13]

Because the state constitution draft became part of an elite conflict involving Mao Zedong and his then closest comrade-in-arms Lin Biao, the draft was not promulgated and the fourth National People's Congress did not convene until 1975.[14] People in Shanghai's districts, however, knew none of this at the time. They heard about, read, and discussed the draft between August and September 1970 thinking that a revision of the 1954 constitution would soon come into force and that this would bring a respite from the revolutionary upheavals of the preceding years. Although a limited group of party cadres discussed the first draft in August, only the second and revised draft version was open for public discussion. When municipal offices received this draft on 15 September, they informed work units that same night. By the next day, officials had read the draft out aloud in many public places, and—reports made sure to note—propagandists had even taken the time to visit the sick and retired in their homes.[15]

Revolutionary fervor and a new state constitution were not mutually exclusive. If a limited amount of text made a law more accessible, then the mere thirty articles of this new draft were promising. More articles, a report explained, were neither necessary nor would they be indicative of a better or more thorough law.[16] One department store worker summed up a common sentiment that the concise thirty articles truly protected the working people's (*laodong renmin*) rights (*quanli*), and this was all that was needed.[17] The constitution seemed to be the "concrete realization" of China's and the world's revolutionary struggles and of the brilliance of Mao Zedong Thought.[18]

What exactly to include in a slim constitution was less clear. Members of one Mao Zedong Thought Study Group for the Discussion of the Constitution Revision that was attached to the municipal First Office of Commerce debated whether the constitution really needed a preamble. Similar to the 1954 constitution, the 1970 draft was divided into a preamble and a main body of articles. The preamble recounted the "rise" of the Chinese people, the role of the CCP, and the significance of the PRC and Mao Zedong Thought. Group members wondered whether the preamble and the section on "General Principles" could be merged.[19] In the end they decided to advocate for a preamble in their report. Convinced that the pre-eminence of Mao Zedong Thought was an "objective reality" (*keguan cunzai*), they argued that the articles of a law could not codify objective realities. Besides, a separate preamble narrating revolutionary China's history would ensure that the constitution remained easy to understand (*tongsu yidong*).[20]

Cadres in the group supported a distinction between what could be written into legal articles and what could not, but they did not think that the country required more legal structures to implement these articles. Debating whether some of the legal institutions—such as the procuratorate—that had been dismantled in previous years should be restored, most argued that citizens could report on whether departments, officials, and other citizens "abided by laws." They could also sue others if necessary.[21] That made more formal structures unnecessary. Some formal structures seemed to be missing though, as a department store branch secretary indicated when he noted that the draft did not mention how delegates to the National People's Congress were to be elected.[22] This omission must have been puzzling given that people expected the fourth congress to take place very soon. The right to go on strike, moreover, sparked some controversy; and opinions diverged on whether to enshrine it in law. One group argued that the right to strike had been a "weapon" against oppressors before the PRC was established. Enshrining it into law now would make it a weapon "against ourselves." Others thought it was a necessary tool to prevent a renewed rise of capitalism and to "combat and prevent revisionism."[23]

As in 1954, the draft discussion became a mirror of people's concerns about how the constitution might affect their lives. The draft legislated the principle of "from each according to his ability, to each according to his work." This principle and its counterpart, "from each according to his ability, to each according to his needs," which was associated with the realization of communism and a truly equal society, had been repeatedly and fervently debated in earlier years.[24] Upholding the principle of "to each according to his work," Article 9 of the draft now stated: "He who does not labor, neither shall he eat." Shanghai residents argued that this simply could not be implemented in practice. In different study groups, participants thought that it was only realistic in the countryside, not in the city. Shanghai was a large town, where plenty of people had either quit their jobs or were retired, or could not work. What would they eat? This system also seemed unfair given that so many people were still receiving very different wages. Daily realities mapped poorly onto some of the claims of the constitution draft.[25]

Article 9 of the draft also promised that the state would safeguard people's ownership rights to labor wages, savings, housing, and a livelihood. This affirmation of ownership looked like a serious change of political course in the aftermath of the widespread search of homes and confiscation of property (*chaojia*) that had been part of the early Cultural Revolution. It led one older worker to wonder whether the housing that he owned and that he had been forced to rent out to others could now be returned to him.[26] The work units directed by the Office of Commerce "ardently" (*relie*) discussed whether Article 9 meant that they would have to return objects and money confiscated from capitalist homes in previous years. Cleverly, they suggested to change the original wording of "the state protects citizens' rights of ownership to labor wages, savings, housing and other means of livelihood" to "the state protects civic labor's rights of ownership to wages." This could be accomplished by shifting one grammatical particle to the front, thus changing the noun "citizens" into the adjective "civic" and ensuring that the rights did not extend to those who had been denounced during the Cultural Revolution. They reasoned that this phrasing would ensure that confiscated property did not have to be returned.[27] One shop clerk, classified in the report as being from a bourgeois family background, wondered what would happen to the savings of those who had died.[28] Many people in the study groups took the constitution seriously, and they pondered its consequences.

These reports tell us little, though, about how officials conducting the study sessions felt. Many might have been rather anxious given the kinds of topics residents raised. Similar to the 1950s, report writers continued to label some comments and "tendencies" (*dongxiang*) as erroneous. These were generally comments that revealed, on purpose or accidentally, the inconsistencies of CCP rhetoric and policy over time. A party member working in the organization group of a medical herbs company wondered why the draft described Mao Zedong Thought as the moving force in the country's history. How, he asked, could this be possible given that Mao Zedong Thought had only been around for a few decades while the laboring people had a much longer history? When discussing the statement that Mao was "the leader of the dictatorship of the proletariat," a cadre in the leadership group of a hardware shop suggested that this was misleading as Mao had not been at the top of the CCP when it was first founded. Other members of the group agreed, but the report classified this as wrong.[29] Having stumbled over the statement that China had made a great contribution to mankind, meanwhile, one person asked "Has the revolution been exported successfully?"[30]

It would be an exaggeration to argue that China's population at large was immersed in legal learning in the summer of 1970. Many Shanghai residents were not involved. The draft soon disappeared from public discourse, the fourth National People's Congress was postponed indefinitely, and then Lin Biao fell from grace. Yet the draft did not disappear as quickly from people's memories as it was erased from the official chronology of political events. Many residents who had discussed this draft would remember it during the other constitution draft discussions that followed over the next twelve years.[31]

## A Week's Work: The 1978 Constitution

The 1970 draft became the basis for the 1975 constitution. The 1975 state constitution once more enshrined in law people's duty to abide by the constitution and laws, and to support the leadership of the Chinese

Communist Party. Closely associated with the "Gang of Four's" last few years in power, the 1975 constitution provided for what it called the freedom to speak out freely, air views fully, hold great debates, write big-character posters, and the right to strike. Hailed as socialist and democratic, party newspapers presented these freedoms and rights as infinitely superior to the legal systems of other socialist countries, particularly the revisionist Soviet Union. In late 1976, only a few months after Mao had died, *Renmin ribao* published a scathing attack on what would become the 1977 Brezhnev constitution. It criticized that "Brezhnev has several times howled that 'the legal basis of the state and social life should be strengthened' and has declared that 'strengthening the legal system is not only the task of state organs.' Party organizations, the trade union, and the Communist Youth League also have a duty to work hard toward safeguarding the strictest obedience to the law and to improve the legal education of the working masses."[32] *Renmin ribao* took issue with the call for the "strictest obedience to the law" that the constitution demanded and argued that—different from the rights granted to PRC citizens in the 1975 constitution—it expected only obedience without participation, gave more legal powers to the police, and expanded the definition of counterrevolutionaries to include anyone resisting state authority.

Public pronouncements of Chinese revolutionary legal superiority disappeared as the CCP began to build a legal regime that resembled the very same Soviet model that *Renmin ribao* had denounced. Much as in the Soviet Union and European socialist countries at the time, law and law propaganda were reinstated as instruments designed to stabilize party rule. In 1977, a few months after the *Renmin ribao* article was published, the party policy magazine *Hongqi* (Red flag) exhorted readers to "strengthen the socialist legal system."[33] This transition of words and then actions began with the campaign to denounce the "Gang of Four."[34] Directives blamed the Gang of Four for the destruction of the legal system. In the internal "Propaganda Outline on Strengthening the Revolutionary Legal System and Rectifying Social and Public Order," the office of the Shanghai Municipal Party Committee explained: "Strengthening the revolutionary legal system was a consistent instruction of our Great Leader Chairman Mao, and the 'Gang of Four' was the ringleader in destroying the revolutionary legal system."[35] Invoking official language from the 1950s, the mention of the "revolutionary legal system" signaled that the party leadership was positioning the legal system as one of the organizational victims of the Cultural Revolution that had to be resurrected.[36] In writing that Mao had consistently called for a strong revolutionary legal system, the outline disregarded Mao's attacks on the legal system. It was a way of focusing instead on Mao's earlier statements that laws would be necessary in order to uphold the people's democratic dictatorship.

The promulgation of another state constitution in March 1978 brought back campaign-style law propaganda. In mid-May 1978, the central government announced plans for municipal and county people's governments to organize a "propaganda week" (*xuanchuan zhou*) to disseminate information about the new constitution and the party's "general task for the new period" (*xin shiqi de zong renwu*), which enshrined the "Four Modernizations" in agriculture, industry, national defense, and science and technology.[37] Because the central government feared that too much propaganda and mass mobilization would overburden citizens and remind them of the recent Campaign to Criticize Lin Biao and Confucius, it decided on a propaganda "week" that would last seven to ten days and then spill over into regularized propaganda work.[38] A few days before the week was announced, a lead editorial in *Renmin ribao* called on readers to "study the new constitution, propagate the new constitution, abide by the new constitution." It referenced Article 56 of the constitution, which specified that citizens had a duty to "abide by the constitution and laws."[39] Bringing back the familiar language of 1950s law propaganda, the citizens' duty to "study the new constitution, propagate the new constitution, abide by the new constitution" soon became the third on a list of fifteen slogans ranked in order of priority that was sent out to districts for use on wall posters and blackboards.[40]

The week was meant to signal that mobilization was possible without the excesses people associated with the past "ten years of turmoil." Local governments therefore had to pay attention to how they coordinated activities. Several months earlier, in January 1978, the revolutionary committee of the Shanghai Municipal Bureau of Education had brought members of the Public Security Bureau, the

municipal High People's Court, and the municipal Bureau of Education to the downtown Ruijin Theater to talk about their experiences
conducting socialist legal education and political thought work with
lower-level cadres and students.[41] The propaganda week was then officially inaugurated with a carefully choreographed ceremony on the
afternoon of 27 May that was broadcast on public television.[42] District
governments, as well as street-level and neighborhood committees,
arranged for hundreds of TV sets to be set up as "watching stations"
(shoukandian) across districts and in work units.[43] Sitting in front of
TVs, people watched as the week was officially announced and participants broke out in song and performed "The East Is Red," the popular tune from the Cultural Revolution model opera.[44]

Propaganda brigades set out having been instructed to focus on
three specific parts of the constitution: the preamble, the general principles, and the rights and duties of citizens. Cadres were to set good
examples of abiding by laws, and to lead the masses to abide by laws
"of their own initiative."[45] Schools and colleges used study time to read
editorials and hold seminars about the "general task" and the constitution. Anyone frequenting workers' palaces, youth palaces, cultural centers, libraries, science and technology points, museums, or public parks
came across large banners, slide shows, picture exhibitions, and posters with the approved slogans. In a progress summary, the municipal
Propaganda Department reported that districts established 159 propaganda points, sent out 1,669 cultural brigades, mobilized 38,000
propagandists, and staged 1,800 performances, which some 2,760,000
people in total attended. Propaganda cars and small brigades went into
alleyways and onto construction sites; activists stood at prominent
spots in bus and train stations, visited shops, hotels, and hospital
wards, and patrolled commercial centers.[46]

Publishers and neighborhood groups resorted to familiar propaganda genres to help popularize the constitution. In some districts,
such as Huangpu, retired workers performed plays. Some of the plays
they wrote themselves, such as one imaginatively titled "Four Wives
Study the Constitution."[47] The Shanghai People's Arts Press brought to
the market some 150,000 copies of a newly edited booklet of Illustrated
Explanations of the PRC Constitution, which explained the new constitution using one to two images and some basic explanatory text per

Fig. 5.1. "Article 45" from *Illustrated Explanations of the PRC Constitution.*
Article 45 of the 1978 constitution states: "Citizens enjoy freedom of speech,
correspondence, the press, assembly, association, procession, demonstration,
and the freedom to strike, and have the right to 'speak out freely, air their views
fully, hold great debates, and write big-character posters.'" (Source: *Zhonghua
renmin gongheguo xianfa tujie*, Shanghai renmin meishu chubanshe, 1978, p. 74.)

each article. This was the same format the East China People's Press—
the precursor to the Shanghai People's Arts Press—had introduced in
1951 with its *Illustrated Regulations,* and it had already been replicated
in 1975 for the short-lived constitution.[48] The 1978 leaflet outlined citizens' rights to air their views and write big-character posters, but it
illustrated clearly that this was meant to happen as part of orderly public reading and discussion, guided by an able local official. To air views
was to support the smashing of the "Gang of Four," as the image included on the wall of big-character posters suggested (fig. 5.1). Often
based on these publications, middle school students drew propaganda
illustrations that they supplied to cultural palaces, cinemas, and shops
where the images were put out as window dressing.[49]

The party met its goal to limit propaganda to one week and to
make it a comprehensive experience. Seemingly content with some of

the work its cadres had carried out, the municipal party committee quoted residents who had said, "We heard the lecture in our work unit, when we went back to the lane house we looked at an exhibition, when we walked along the road we saw people spreading propaganda, and even on the bus we listened to propaganda and were educated."[50] The comment could be interpreted as an expression of either approval or disapproval. Some residents were tired of being inundated with the same message everywhere they went. Moreover, not everything worked as well as officials wanted it to, especially when it came to educating people about the constitution. Many work units involved had not actually spent as much time talking about the constitution as they had spent explaining the "general task." Thinking that the constitution was hardly as important as the political "general task," some had not mentioned it at all.[51] People voiced their insecurities and doubts about the ongoing political changes and economic developments to propagandists and local public security officials. Several people, a report noted, complained that it really was not clear why they should have this propaganda week. Cadres at times even decided to talk about things other than the constitution or the "general task" because giving the same "empty talk" again and again bored them.[52]

The 1978 propaganda week was the last phase of mass mobilization for legal learning that was clearly labeled a "propaganda campaign" (xuanchuan yundong). The term was seldom used during the 1980s, partly to create further rhetorical distance from the turbulent mass campaigns of the Mao Era.[53] The experience meanwhile showed that the idea of having a one-week campaign—designed not to "disturb" production and to avoid excessive propaganda—brought other unanticipated challenges. Despite numbering in the thousands, there had not been enough propaganda teams to cover the entire city in only ten days. Teams were unprepared to do what felt like several weeks of work in only one week. Some residents were left disappointed, commenting that this propaganda week could hardly match the activities and intensity of the propaganda campaigns of the 1950s.[54]

Issues both trivial and practical also affected the extent to which propaganda could be conducted: campaign plans, for example, said nothing about what to do in poor weather. As it happened, it rained on several of the days that week, and propagandists had made no contingency plans. Trying to salvage the campaign as much as possible, a few performance troupes and propaganda brigades braved the rain and marched out. One lone worker was featured in several reports because he had performed a song about the "general task" and the constitution in the pouring rain—not minding, the reporter thought worth mentioning, his drenched white worker's shirt.[55] More commonly, however, activists who manned propaganda points in neighborhoods and on the streets packed up their things when it started to rain and only returned once the weather improved.[56] All things considered, law propaganda did not seem terribly urgent.

## Making Laws to Disseminate Laws

Law propaganda's main purpose was to explain and elicit support for the country's "democracy and legal system" (*minzhu yu fazhi*). The phrase "democracy and legal system" became a core formulation of the late 1970s and early 1980s: it made one of its first prominent appearances on the front page of *Renmin ribao* in mid-July 1978, a few months before Deng Xiaoping took over power from Hua Guofeng. Opening with the familiar refrain that Lin Biao and the "Gang of Four" had been the "most ferocious enemies" of the "socialist legal system," the editorial argued that the country would need to construct a new socialist legal system in the aftermath of the arrest of the "Gang of Four." Reactionary elements had to be punished and the interests of the people and their democratic rights required protection. Socialist democracy, the editorial reasoned, was impossible without a socialist legal system. Mutually dependent, democracy and the legal system had to be based on three imperatives: "Everyone must abide by laws. The masses must abide by laws. Cadres must abide by laws."[57]

There were few laws to abide by, however, and the socialist legal system was still fragmentary. Law propaganda had to walk a fine line between educating people in laws that were already available on paper and calling attention to shortcomings in the laws. Though it permitted talk about these shortcomings, the CCP worried that too much of it, particularly outside of specialist circles, might encourage people to find too many faults with the ruling regime or, as propaganda authorities repeatedly reminded each other, give criminals a chance to exploit legal loopholes and claim that their actions could hardly be crimes since there was, as yet, no law that said so. Too much popular legal learning would expose systemic weaknesses and would lead to even more talk of the need for discipline and order.

Both the shortcomings of the nascent legal system and also the potential power of mass legal education became evident in late 1978 in Beijing and Shanghai (as well as in other cities) when residents took up their constitutional right to voice their opinions through letters, big-character posters, and unofficial magazines. Many residents wanted to see the socialist "democracy and legal system" in action. They were doing what the propaganda week in May 1978 had told them they were entitled to do. Beijing residents wrote letters and commentaries about the need for better law implementation, a freer press, and fair treatment of victims of the Cultural Revolution, and they attached these letters to the Democracy Wall in Xidan District where people widely read them. In Shanghai, university students and other residents put up similar comments on university notice boards.[58] At first, party leaders around Deng Xiaoping supported them, proclaiming their contributions a sign of democracy at work.[59] In November 1978, the CCP also rehabilitated victims of the 1976 Tiananmen Incident and called for the re-examination and revision of "unjust, false, and wrong cases" (*yuan jia cuo an*). This decision ignited local engagement with cases from the Cultural Revolution and even earlier, including verdicts from the Anti-Rightist Movement.[60] Actively using legal language, people petitioned for their own cases or the cases of their family members to be re-opened. Many called on local and higher-level government officials to do right by laws and justice, increasingly also writing up their experiences and posting them on the wall at Xidan.[61] Laws and legal language, as Daniel Leese has shown, were finding willing audiences and immediate practical applications, often leaving local party officials overwhelmed and on the defensive.[62]

As information about laws and rights circulated, this mobilized people to make use of laws. In response, state authorities soon desired more control over the legal information in circulation and more oversight over people's use of laws. The first arrests of Democracy Wall activists were carried out in March 1979. In early September 1979, the central government passed several new laws and the Shanghai Municipal Propaganda Department began to coordinate another wave of "democracy and legal system" propaganda activities.[63] Citizens sat down to learn about the "seven laws" (*qi fa*), including the Joint Venture Law, the Organic Laws for People's Congresses and Local Governments, the Organic Law for People's Courts, the Organic Law for People's Procuracy, the Election Law, the Criminal Law, and the Criminal Procedure Law. In 1980, after a second Marriage Law came into force, the "seven laws" became "eight laws."[64] Because many of these laws were not really relevant to most residents, propaganda focused on the Criminal Law, the Criminal Procedures Law, and the Marriage Law.

Trying to guide propaganda better than in previous years, the Central Propaganda Department issued an internal outline explaining how to "strengthen socialist democracy and the legal system, struggle for our country to become a socialist modernized powerful country."[65] Extending to twenty-four pages, the document made clear that the CCP determined what the slogan "socialist democracy and legal system" meant. Law propaganda had to communicate much more clearly that the party was essential to socialist democracy, economic development, and the creation of a legal system in support of these goals. To ensure that people understood this, engagement with the new laws was to be the "most focused, systematic propagation of the legal system since the founding of the country."[66] In no uncertain terms, the outline reinforced that laws were instruments to maintain order. Learning laws, by extension, was an essential part of citizens' civic duty and daily life. Department officials worried, though, that having laws only on the books left too much room for interpretation. Once laws had been passed, the department warned, one "cannot let them be formalities or decoration or have them be transformed into ineffective rules, one must resolutely implement them."[67]

The question remained how to do this exactly. People's "legal outlook," a term already used during the 1952 Judicial Reform Movement and after, had to be strengthened. Propaganda would have to generate faith in and respect for the law. The outline explained that the lasting effects of the reign of the "Gang of Four" were to blame for the recent protests at Xidan and elsewhere and for people's "erroneous beliefs" about what kinds of social and political changes were needed. Whoever thought that "law has no use and that you can do with or without laws" had to be educated to know better. So did those who thought that strengthening the legal system would allow them to do as they pleased. Exposed to proper legal education, the outline concluded, good citizens would voluntarily see the merits of the socialist legal system and begin to abide by laws. Only education could ensure law and order and prevent violations of law and discipline. Without spelling it out clearly, the outline suggested that any interpretations of the slogan "democracy and legal system" that contravened the interpretative hegemony of the CCP could be deemed counterrevolutionary thought or criminal behavior.

To make law propaganda work in this "new period," party officials had to revisit some of its basic premises. During the 1950s, the binary between People and non-People in the context of the people's democratic dictatorship had determined what kind of legal education different parts of the population required. Even if the line between who belonged to the People and who did not was extremely fluid over time, the basic premise largely remained: party policy saw those categorized as People as less likely to commit crimes. Members of the People who committed crimes were cast as exceptions, or their labels were changed to illustrate that they had always been non-People. The full force of laws, meanwhile, would have to be used constantly to deal with non-People. During the late 1950s and into the mid-1970s, the CCP adapted this lexicon. The dictatorship of the proletariat replaced the people's democratic dictatorship, and the catalogue of non-People was vastly expanded.[68] Starting in the late 1970s, CCP leadership then carried out "semantic surgery" on this political lexicon.[69] Propaganda materials deemphasized class struggle and increasingly indicated that almost all of China's population was part of the political group of the People and the legal group of citizens.[70] The concepts of People and citizens soon overlapped in practice.[71]

This profound semantic change had immediate consequences for the way law propaganda could be presented and conducted. If everyone was part of the People, it followed that the People committed the majority of crimes.[72] And if the People at large were now more in danger of committing crimes, it was the CCP's responsibility to educate them as widely as possible in order to try and prevent crimes. This gave added emphasis to the need to learn the new Criminal Law that came into force in January 1980.[73] One of the Criminal Law's articles was especially confusing for ordinary people at the time. Article 102 stipulated that counterrevolutionary acts would include any activity carried out to resist or sabotage the implementation of state laws, as well as any activity aimed at inciting the overthrow of the dictatorship of the proletariat and the socialist system.[74] As a result, many of the protesters at Xidan were labeled "subversive elements."[75] Many local residents, however, could not easily make sense of the logic that fellow residents who had gone out and made use of their constitutional rights were now subversive elements. Moreover, were not party committees revising verdicts of exactly this kind where people had, often only because of minor actions, been accused of counterrevolutionary activities and sentenced to years in jail? Semantic surgery had left semantic wounds.

Party leaders tried to deal with these semantic wounds in different ways. Widely circulating in newspapers and magazines at the time, a new official formulation explained that to "know the law, abide by the law, enforce the law" would "establish a good atmosphere within society of respecting discipline and abiding by the law," and "realize order across the country."[76] In a discussion about law propaganda with news work units in Beijing in late June 1979, Peng Zhen meanwhile explained that the CCP enabled and protected democracy with discipline and a strong legal system. Once laws were made, he explained, "you have to handle things according to law, and enforcement of laws must be strict."[77] He told his audience that he had heard some citizens comment that only China had a people's democratic dictatorship and that any dictatorship was anathema to laws. Defensively, he replied: "There are some who say that none of the world's laws are written in this way. So what? We write our own laws!"[78]

The party-state's attempt to gain hegemony over key terms was manifested in the media landscape. In August 1979, in another move to assume authority over the meaning of "democracy and legal system," the flagship magazine *Minzhu yu fazhi* (Democracy and legal system) took up publication from Shanghai. Built on the basis of the former *Faxue* journal, and renamed with the consent and support of the Propaganda Department, the magazine was initially run by an editorial team of academics from Shanghai. After the central government decided to reinforce law propaganda, the Shanghai Municipal Party Committee wanted to adapt the magazine to have a broader mass appeal. *Minzhu yu fazhi* was supposed to explain laws to specialists and lay people alike, and was to be widely available at magazine stalls and bookstores.[79] After some discord among the original and new editors, the magazine's editorship was expanded to a group of five editors, some of whom were legal experts and some of whom were propaganda experts.[80] Subscriptions to the magazine increased, going from the first print run of 20,000 copies to more than 60,000 copies by late 1980, with a further increase anticipated for 1981.

*Zhongguo fazhi bao* (China legal daily, later renamed Legal daily) also took up publication in 1980, announcing that it would "disseminate laws and policies, report on the achievements in legal construction, answer the masses' legal questions, propagate the constitution, laws, and decrees, exchange experiences in politics and law work, spread legal knowledge and theory."[81] Magazines and newspapers soon began to feature "legal knowledge inquiries" columns on a regular basis, and films portraying model trials illustrated how the reformed legal system assisted and protected citizens.[82] The task of such publications, as the Shanghai Propaganda Department reminded propaganda workers in October 1979, was to explain to people that law propaganda would ensure that freedom and discipline went hand in hand, and this was only possible if both democracy and centralism, in the form of democratic centralism, was preserved.[83] A few months later, also in the pages of *Minzhu yu fazhi*, the well-known cartoonist Shen Tongheng suggestively depicted this need for ordinary people and cadres alike not to focus only on democracy (the left side of the book) or centralism (the right side of the book), but to read the two together (fig. 5.2).

More funds were also invested into exhibitions that opened spaces for visitors to explore the country's turn to law.[84] One exhibition on "socialist democracy and legal system education," for instance, invited visitors to peruse educational materials, analyze case reports, examine photos, and investigate confiscated evidence on display. Visitors could compare the "Great Laws" of the 1950s with laws promulgated after 1978. "Legal knowledge inquiries" rooms gave people an opportunity

Fig. 5.2. Shen Tongheng, "Each Takes What He Needs," 1980. (Source: *Minzhu yu fazhi* [Democracy and legal system], no. 6, June 1980, back cover.)

to ask questions. Municipal and district governments used these exhibitions to narrate the end of the Cultural Revolution. Unintentionally, however, they suggested continuities. Only a few years earlier, at the height of the Cultural Revolution, people had visited exhibitions that exposed counterrevolutionary elements and displayed confiscated property as evidence of "black" activities.[85] Now visitors examined the confiscated evidence of legally convicted criminals. In the spaces where larger-than-life propaganda images and statues of the *Selected Works of Mao Zedong* and the *Little Red Book* had adorned Cultural Revolution exhibits, visitors could study images of people learning laws and a twenty-foot replica of the state constitution, cushioned in red velvet, encircled by potted trees, and framed by flags. The symbolic resemblance was striking. On the covers of paperback books explaining the constitution, oversized law booklets, enveloped in rays of sun, floated above the heads of cheering crowds. In visual terms, the constitution once again assumed a position in the pantheon of CCP symbolism.

## Linking Crime and Legal Knowledge

Late 1970s law propaganda fused legal knowledge and crime prevention. In the autumn of 1979, Shanghai's cadres and propagandists began to study and prepare for the implementation of the Criminal Law and Criminal Procedure Law. City police, court workers, and staff at East China Politics and Law College helped train lower-level cadres and sent out investigation teams to find out how law enforcement was proceeding in districts, and what people knew of the new laws. In October, test sites including the Penglai residential area of Nanshi District, Wuning Middle School, Jiading Chengdong Commune, and Shanghai Diesel Oil Machine Factory learned about the two laws.[86] At major conventions held in the stadium and cultural arena and broadcast on television, municipal party officials announced and discussed the texts. In factories, shops, and commercial centers, people were told to read the laws in their study time. They were given lessons in which docents explained the new laws using illustrations (fig. 5.3a), some of which had been drawn by the pupils of Wuning Middle School (fig. 5.3b).

Despite extensive preparations, however, the government's emphasis on the need to study laws still seemed odd to many people, local state officials and ordinary residents alike. Aware of this problem, the Shanghai Municipal Party Committee put much pressure on its cadres when it reminded them in mid-October that everybody was now paying attention to "whether or not we can firmly implement these two laws."[87] Propaganda workers were expected to implement the laws properly. Only if they managed to do so could the country develop, strengthen production, and achieve "stability and unity." The directive warned:

> Within the party little attention was paid to constructing and perfecting a socialist legal system since liberation, and instead negating laws, slighting laws, having party usurp government, words usurp laws, and not relying on laws where there are laws, all of this has become a habit for many comrades who think that it does not matter whether there are laws or not, who feel that law is tedious, think that government policy is law, and think that you don't need laws if you have policies.[88]

If these problems were not solved, the committee wrote, "then the country's laws will be difficult to implement and enforce, and the people will not trust our party." Every work unit was instructed to talk about four issues: (1) the significance of strengthening socialist democracy and the legal system, (2) the basic content of the Criminal Law, (3)

Fig. 5.3. "Shanghai vigorously launches legal system propaganda and education," 1979. (Source: *Minzhu yu fazhi* [Democracy and legal system], no. 5, December 1979, inside cover.)

the basic content of the Criminal Procedure Law, and (4) the importance of respecting the law, abiding by the law, defending the law, and struggling against all violations of the law and criminal behavior.[89]

In order to raise support for public security organs, the large-scale and multi-week law propaganda activities were, on the one hand, a response to the swift rise in petty crime, sexual crime, and other kinds of crime that had marked the late 1970s, and, on the other hand, they were also a tool to kindle residents' fears of crime and desire for a strong state response. Connected to anti-crime campaigns, laws appeared to be primarily punitive instruments rather than regulatory rules. Propaganda materials suggested that anyone who did not know the laws was more likely to violate them and be re-educated or punished.[90] Changes on the streets and in everyday life reinforced this appearance. Trade unions set up worker disciplinary patrols that inspected residential areas. Local police officers patrolled the streets day and night. Residents discussed how law propaganda would help return public order to society, transform youth who had violated the law, manage activities that violated the law, and ensure that public security work was done well.[91] Investigating carefully the family life of someone who had committed a crime, and understanding the reasons that had led him or her to do so, became part of the process of dealing with anyone deemed to have committed a crime.

Law propaganda tied in with youth morality education. Municipal officials focused on young people—a group the CCP determined to be most in need of education because they had grown up during the chaos of the Cultural Revolution and therefore lacked discipline and legal consciousness. At the municipal level, propaganda officials wrote candidly about seemingly all-pervasive youth crime, from petty theft and drug possession, to violence and homicide. Propaganda officials thought that educating these youths would only work if legal education was combined with "morality education" and "discipline education." Immorality was likened to germs, and illegal behavior to the illness that would result if germs were allowed to spread.[92] In response, primary and middle schools added law classes to the curriculum, and the media praised the advantages of self-examinations, self-criticisms, and group criticisms as part of learning about law, morality, and discipline. The Shanghai Light Industry Bureau reported that its morality competition month included lessons on abiding by laws; it also reported that some units had organized "politeness weeks" (*limao zhou*) and "talking heart-to-heart weeks" (*tanxin zhou*) next to regular law propaganda work to better account for the specific needs of youth.[93]

In other parts of the country, similar activities were underway, and the pages of *Zhongguo fazhi bao* were full of examples. A party branch cadre in Hunan, for example, reported how a school in the province's Hanshou County had had enormous difficulties with "illegal behavior" and "unhealthy thoughts." Teachers decided to have a common legal knowledge learning session once a week in every class. They also added legal knowledge to the political theory exams at the end of the year, and it made up for 30 percent of the exam. Students had responded well to this, the author claimed, with some coming forward to confess petty crimes, making self-criticisms in front of their class and thus gaining rehabilitation. So successful was this kind of an education, the article boasted, that when the student found as little as three yuan on the street he handed it to his teacher rather than keeping it for himself.[94] Such an approach seemed promising for other attempts to re-educate those youths who "opposed bureaucracy," who wanted democracy without centralization, who did not want "discipline and law," and who "incited anarchism, bourgeois liberalism, and extreme individualism."[95]

Conducting good propaganda work was not easy, though. Internal discussions often reported that mid- and higher-level cadres spent far too much time lecturing citizens, many of whom had received only basic schooling and had expressed little interest in hearing about legal theory and jurisprudence. Lengthy reports about how to understand laws in the larger context of socialist construction were lost on them. They found the reports tedious, boring, and pointless, and would simply stop listening. Yet propaganda outlines explicitly excluded from open discussion those topics that people would have found more interesting—controversial legal questions or personal stories. These topics, the Shanghai Propaganda Department explained, were supposed to be limited to academic or party circles. This left cadres with little effective official material.[96]

Propaganda and cultural authorities considered carefully how to get people to engage more with official legal learning. Public trials seemed to offer one solution to enliven propaganda. Public trials had been common during the 1950s, but not later, when authorities preferred sentencing rallies that took place outside of courtrooms instead.[97] The 1978 constitution introduced a new provision that all trials should be open to the public. Endorsing this provision, Li Zhun, vice-president of the Supreme People's Court, called public trials "a classroom for law propaganda."[98] Shanghai's public security offices and people's courts selected cases that they thought were educational—often showcasing common incidents of petty theft or vandalism—and then filmed these for television audiences, bringing a human face to law both in the courtroom and at home on people's TV screens. Such education was, as one directive put it, both "concrete and symbolic."[99]

Still, officials wanted to play it as safe as possible and tried to control what was said in trials, when and how it was said, and what was done. Cadres felt they had to rehearse before going public. It was widely known that trial participants coordinated the trial before they appeared in public. Trials were now also supposed to include a defense, which did not make matters easier. The Shanghai Party Committee worried about this and wrote in its municipal *Xuanchuan tongxun* that trials should not seem too prepared or rehearsed. It wanted lawyers to give a genuine, not a false, defense.[100] Residents were not happy with cadres' attempts to keep trial performances in check, though. In Qingpu County and Nanshi District, the Propaganda Department reported that onlookers thought the defense was much too "formulaic."[101] With everything rehearsed in advance, the defense stood little chance to build up a proper case. Those arguing for the defense would often simply concur with the prosecution. In the end, people found it hard to tell the defense apart from the prosecution. To some it appeared that all parties were all saying the same thing. Lawyers who received defense assignments proceeded cautiously, worried that anything they said could be taken as a sign of their personal positions. They did not want to take any risk. In many instances, the defense argued that whatever crime had been committed had been due to the bad influence of Lin Biao and the "Gang of Four." Asked to comment afterwards on the trials they had observed, residents thought such a defense was pointless. After all, they said, everything could be connected to the bad influence of Lin Biao and the "Gang of Four" and, if that was the case, then anyone could be a lawyer.[102] Workers at Shanghai's Yuyuan Bazaar expressed the opinion that "in other countries, lawyers plead on behalf of the defendant; because they are connected by money, reputation, or family, they can do their utmost to plead the case. In China, because the lawyer has no vital interest in the defendant, not wanting to offend the government he will not do his utmost on behalf of the defendant."[103] Even if the defense adequately defended the accused and made a good case for his innocence, the presiding judge would often nonetheless render a prearranged verdict. Such presiding judges, propaganda officials criticized, simply "parroted a text" they had already prepared. Public trials seemed a charade, with audiences going away feeling that the defense really was "only there for propaganda purposes."[104]

Shanghai's officials and propagandists were torn between the demands of party superiors and propaganda guidelines, on the one hand, and the reality of their workplace, on the other. Some expressed discomfort with being asked to conduct law propaganda. It was obviously an unfamiliar task, but more importantly they did not think it was possible to explain laws to people as one had previously explained party directives.[105] They logged in their reports that residents were bewildered by the campaign, thought it would not work, or had concluded that this was yet another political fashion of the day that would soon pass. Cadres, too, may have thought it likely that law propaganda was merely a brief political phase and that the regime's commitment to clamping down on crime would be short-lived.[106]

The trial of Wei Jingsheng, who had been one of the most outspoken participants in the Democracy Wall Movement, began in October 1979 and complicated the CCP's attempt to teach local residents clear legal lessons. Reported in the media, the trial was used as a national example of why local dissemination of laws was important. Propagandists had been instructed to link the national case of Wei Jingsheng with local cases of petty crime. When in December residents in Shanghai studied the Criminal Law, however, they could not see the connection between street crime and the leaking of military information. Wei had been arrested and tried on charges of passing state secrets to a foreigner. To many residents, that seemed a reasonable cause for arrest. Still, some were confused and used the occasion to ask their local propagandists some pertinent questions: why had Wei only been charged now, given that the felony of supplying military evidence had happened months earlier? They also wanted to know why the people who gave him the state secrets that he then divulged had not been charged.[107] Conversations about the Democracy Wall ensued that local cadres found difficult to navigate. Some cadres complained in their reports that some of the people they talked to only wanted democracy but did not want state centralization, while some others only wanted freedom and thought discipline was pointless. This does not mean that everyone was against the Criminal Law. On the contrary, most people were supportive. A few people in their responses voiced their concern that the Criminal Law was much too lenient and unspecific, and they feared that criminals could make use of loopholes in the law to get away with crimes.[108]

Trying to tie education in abstract laws to concrete examples, legal learning encouraged questions for which many propagandists felt unprepared, having to fall back on standard propaganda slogans that residents then waved off. Circumventing any discussion of these responses, and why people had raised them, many internal reports instead determined that propagandists required better training. Ordinary people, too, were seen as confused because they had not been educated well enough. In early January 1980, the Shanghai Municipal Propaganda Department wrote that it had not spent enough time developing a clear plan for how to propagate laws. The notion that "in legal system propaganda you just have to publicize and publicize [the law] and that'll do" was insufficient to address the mounting problems with crime, especially youth crime. "You cannot just propagate the legal system for the sake of propagating the legal system," the department wrote; instead, "legal system propaganda must be combined with present struggles," including issues of morality, the need to propagate the Four Cardinal Principles, the Four Modernizations, and the continued denunciation of the "criminal behavior" of Lin Biao and the "Gang of Four."[109] Little of this advice had much practical resonance with cadres' everyday work. The formulaic language of party directives was becoming more abstract, while cadres faced concrete problems. The department meanwhile told them to avoid "on the one hand carrying out legal system propaganda, and on the other hand letting criminal activities run rampant." If they failed, then "the propaganda results cannot possibly be any good." In the end, the report concluded, "this is an issue of outlook that needs to be resolved. Namely, is it the Communist Party that is afraid of bad people? Or are bad people afraid of the Communist Party?"[110]

Law propaganda work thus presented local officials with a range of dilemmas. One internal report on "thought trends" concluded that public security officials often avoided having to seize local officials who had committed crimes until they absolutely could not avoid it anymore without incriminating themselves. Explaining the laws widely, moreover, meant that offenders often knew their rights. Illustrations of the Criminal Law made it clear to readers that public security officials were not permitted to detain anyone illegally, or mistreat prisoners (fig. 5.4). If, as was repeatedly the case, the offender was himself a state official, however, he knew that if he were caught and detained public security would have to let him go eventually, or else he could stir up a ruckus. People were still often detained for longer periods than the law called for, but officials complained that having laws that stipulated a certain

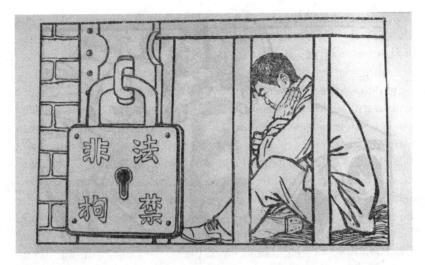

Fig. 5.4. Article 143 of the 1979 Criminal Law states: "The unlawful detention of another person, or the use of other means unlawfully to deprive another of his freedom of the person, is strictly prohibited." Translation from "The Criminal Law of the People's Republic of China," *Journal of Criminal Law and Criminology* 73, no. 1 (Spring 1982): 138-70. (Source: Shanghai renmin meishu chubanshe, ed., *Zhonghua renmin gongheguo xingfa tujie* [Illustrated explanations of the PRC Criminal Law], Shanghai: Shanghai renmin meishu chubanshe, 1979, p. 72.)

number of days for detention made their work all the more difficult, especially when offenders knew the laws. It also seemed to make public security work less successful, something that officers had difficulty appreciating as a merit of the law.[111] Propaganda work focused on explaining how knowing laws would create security, but for public security workers—as had been the case in 1954 and thereafter—legal knowledge also nurtured insecurity.

## Yet Another Constitution?

The first wave of mass legal education following Mao's death was book-ended by two constitution discussions, in 1978 and 1982. Between these two discussions, legal learning largely centered on law and order, on punitive laws, procedural regulations, and crime—mostly juvenile and economic crimes. There was one notable exception. In September 1980, the central government promulgated a revised Marriage Law. Starting in January 1981, residents studied and discussed legal questions surrounding marriage, love, and divorce.[112] Shortly thereafter, the Marriage Law study was eclipsed by another new constitution. Because the 1978 constitution did not mention the Four Modernizations, reform-minded party officials considered it outdated. Deng Xiaoping, in a conversation with guests from Japan, explained that the fundamental question was what kind of socialism people wanted and whether people "want to have a socialist country with an advanced democracy and modernized civilization."[113] If so, then China needed a new state constitution that, as a report by the Shanghai municipal government promised, would offer "long-term stability."[114] Steps toward a new state constitution were not unilaterally supported, though, with the occasional report noting that some people had asked, "Do we really need a new constitution?"[115]

Promulgating a new state constitution became one of several symbolic steps the central leadership took in 1981 and 1982 to break with the recent past. It stood next to the 1981 "Resolution on Certain Questions in the History of our Party since the Founding of the People's Republic of China" and followed the nationally televised trial of the "Gang of Four."[116] Official pronouncements discussed the constitution as a manifestation of the country's development away from Cultural Revolution "lawlessness" and used the resolution and the constitution, with its long historical preamble, as tools to rewrite recent history from the Opium Wars to the present with, as residents soon pointed out, selected omissions.[117]

As before, local propaganda departments began to get ready months before the draft was published.[118] In 1981, the Central Propaganda Department's annual key points for propaganda work instructed provincial and municipal departments to focus on preparing for the constitution revision and to concentrate on promoting socialist democracy and the legal system; this was in addition to conducting propaganda and education about economic reforms, the party resolution, and the eightieth anniversary of the founding of the party.[119] On 28 April 1982, the new constitution draft was adopted. Article 53 of the new constitution stipulated that "Citizens of the People's Republic of China must abide by the Constitution and other laws."[120] In the same year, the central propaganda key points for 1982 named the "strengthening of legal system propaganda and education to respect discipline and obey the law" as a key goal to work toward "reforming the social atmosphere."[121]

The draft was opened for four months of countrywide, structured discussion, with a first internal discussion phase including selected cadres, model workers, and activists.[122] During the second, public phase of the discussion, officials were given several tasks. They were asked to gather responses to three questions: Should the constitution be expanded? Should it be shortened? And should specific changes be made? They were also told to explain to people that this new constitution was good because it eliminated "leftist" mistakes and because it combined all the good parts of the previous three state constitutions.[123] The party committee instructed them to tell residents that the constitution was the only way to administer the lives and affairs of one billion people, and that the public discussion was a sign that all citizens directly participated in administering the country.[124] Residents whom officials knew would want to ask specific questions that would only distract from discussion of important issues were supposed to be discouraged from speaking. Splitting hairs, the Central Propaganda Department reasoned, was unnecessary and only led to excessive engagement with individual questions that were not of concern to a foundational law such as the constitution.[125]

If reading the new constitution draft was the next major step in the national program of legal learning, it also became a barometer to evaluate how laws had been learned so far. One of the main challenges was to make clear why yet another constitution was necessary. While guidelines had instructed officials to encourage residents to compare the 1978 and 1982 constitutions, officials found that people often did so without being prompted. Many made sense of this new draft by comparing it with what they recalled from the last constitution discussion in 1978 and even earlier discussions. In reports, the sections on positive responses to the constitution often noted that residents were generally supportive of this constitution because it was more detailed and substantial than the previous two versions. With 138 articles, it exceeded the 106, 30, and 60 articles of the 1954, 1975, and 1978 drafts respectively. This fact, far from a mere quantitative issue, was repeatedly mentioned in propaganda materials, and many reports portrayed it as a testament to the democratic nature of the new draft.[126] Such positive comments of course contrasted with positive comments that officials noted down in 1970, 1975 and 1978, when people had lauded the constitution's brevity. In 1982, too, quite a few residents deemed 138 articles excessive; the new version was, they complained, "too long" and had "too many articles and too many words," which made it "difficult to remember."[127] China's lawmakers, however, no longer considered extreme brevity a virtue. They thought it was a risk.

More than just comparison, learning about the new draft became an exercise in criticizing the old draft. Discussion groups were asked to comment on why the existing constitution was inadequate for the needs of a much-transformed state and society.[128] As one resident commented, in a remark that must have pleased officials because it fell nicely in line with the central party leadership's main message, the new draft no longer contained "left" formulations and slogans.[129] Responses highlighted that people thought it befitting of this new society that the section on "citizens' rights and duties" had been moved up and was featured in the second section of the draft. One member of a Shanghai work unit discussion group saw this as a sign that personal rights would now count more than they had during the Cultural Revolution. The 1978 constitution had brought in some personal freedoms, he said, but it clearly was not enough. No longer would laws "exist in name but be dead in practice." Nor, he felt, could anyone in power easily search homes, confiscate property, or force people to struggle against others.[130]

Some topics generated heated group debates and lengthy comments in written reports. The freedom to strike, a topic already debated in 1970 that had been included in the 1975 and 1978 constitutions, no longer appeared in the 1982 draft.[131] At the municipal Bureau of Meters, Instruments, and Telecommunications Industry, a meeting with workers ended up with two factions split over the question of whether the constitution should grant the freedom to strike and whether this should be enshrined in law.[132] Mirroring reports from other work units that called such a right a "left" mistake, some thought getting rid of it was a good idea. One worker from an open-hearth furnace repair workshop commented: "I've been at this factory for more than thirty years and have never seen workers strike. In their hearts, workers all understand that to strike will create losses for the country, so what advantage does that have for workers?"[133] More pragmatically, some thought they would not be allowed to make use of this right, so it had no place in the constitution.[134]

By contrast, cadres at the Yaming Lightbulb Factory contended that the right to strike might be crucial if someone worked in a factory where "bureaucratism" was particularly severe and cadres violated law and discipline. Without this right on paper, how would they be able to voice opposition and insist that this was their constitutional right for which they could not be penalized? This argument made sense, particularly when linked with law propaganda's call for people to identify economic crimes and call out cadres and factory owners if they detected cases of "violations of law and discipline." With no constitutional protection, where was the reassurance on paper that workers would not be worse off if they legitimately protested poor conditions? Cadres at the Shanghai Municipal Finance and Trade Office phrased the issue more succinctly when they asked why the right to strike, with its vital importance to maintaining socialist democracy, had been taken out while significantly less useful rights such as the right to travel and protest, both of which they thought few people could ever make use of, remained in the constitution.[135] Meanwhile, arguing that the right to strike would endanger the well-being of the collective, *Xuanchuan tongxun*, Shanghai's internal party magazine on propaganda work, explained to its readers why the right to strike should not be included: "If the workers at Shijingshan Electrical Power Plant suddenly strike, the whole of Beijing city will go pitch-black; if coal and gas workers at coking plants strike, there will be no natural gas, there will be no food to eat; if railway and aviation workers strike, what kind of result will that bring?"[136] Aware of the possible transnational significance of arguing against the constitutional right to strike, the editors hastened to add that these were "not considerations because of the lessons of the Polish strikes."[137] It was simply that such a right did not belong in a constitution. The mere mention of the events in Poland, however, suggested to readers that the connection mattered nonetheless.

One of the major challenges of law propaganda by this point was therefore how to give an impression of consistent legal development since 1978 while at the same time legitimizing the government's demands for people to learn, unlearn, and re-learn legal stipulations as they changed over time, sometimes in quick succession. We can see this in discussions about whether the country now really needed a state chairman. In 1970, Lin Biao, then not yet fallen from favor, had strongly advocated for such a position, while others including Kang Sheng and Zhang Chunqiao were against the proposal. Mao himself was not in favor, though he seems to have used the discussions surrounding the position to play party leaders against each other.[138] The discussion subsided when the draft was shelved. Now, the creation of a state chairmanship re-appeared in the draft. To many this seemed odd. Some reports made sure to include mention of any positive comment about this change, sometimes vaguely stating that many people had said this was "a good thing." But the historical irony of including this new position was not lost on many. In a Shanghai iron and steel factory, the factory's party committee noted that workers expressed strong doubts about the need for a state chairman, particularly since Mao himself had been so adamant not to include one in a previous constitution.[139] Would this, some asked, not contradict the call for simpler state structures?[140] Employees at the Bureau of Meters, Instruments and Telecommunications Industry were as divided on this issue as they were on the right to strike. "Most people," the report elaborated, had commented that they thought there should be a "comrade of noble character and prestige leading the country."[141] But "some" thought the state chairmanship position was in the constitution in order to "create a job to accommodate someone" even if it really was not needed. It looked like party leaders were playing tricks at the top level, moving positions to and fro, though people also thought it would not make much difference to the masses either way.[142]

Throughout the discussion, residents asked probing questions that showed their personal investment in these legal texts. As in earlier constitution discussions, some were honest and told their representatives that they did not think the constitution should stipulate freedoms of publication, assembly, travel, and protest. They reasoned that citizens were not going to be able to do any of this in practice anyhow, even if they had the rights on paper. There was no need to add them.[143] This line of thinking also applied to the statement that "everyone is equal before the law." Some people did not think this was achievable and wanted it removed from the draft. Power and privilege, one report noted, would always trump law; statements such as these were a reminder for the CCP that many people were simply comparing what they saw on paper to what they saw in their everyday lives, and all too often these impressions did not match.[144] For some residents, these doubts were compounded by the fact that the constitution preamble made no mention of the Cultural Revolution. If the preamble placed such an emphasis on Chinese people's struggles throughout history, some argued, then this "painful" period of history should be included. Mentioning the Cultural Revolution in the country's fundamental law would surely be a lesson to everyone to avoid repeating history, and this was after all one of the main rationales behind the CCP's call for new laws and legal learning.[145] At the very least, as one man commented, one could add "a sentence or two" on the Cultural Revolution.[146]

Judging by the responses collated in these reports, the regime had a long road ahead before it could convince people that law mattered beyond the politics of symbolism. Having so many different constitutions in such quick succession created doubts and cynicism. "Yet another constitution!" was one of the most commonly recorded reactions. Reluctance to engage in-depth with the text or even take it seriously was another. It seemed entirely reasonable to presume that if there were another leadership change, a new constitution might follow before too long; extensive learning would then be a waste of time. After all, as one comrade noted, "whatever they want to protect, they will protect; whatever they want to drop, they will drop." In one work unit, people wisely commented that "propaganda in the newspapers and magazines says that law is greater than power, but in real life power is greater than law. Because if you have power then you can write laws and change laws, regulations, and decrees."[147]

Indeed, as some commented, far from being a sign of regime strength and reliability, a new constitution implied a lack of stability and continuity in the country. The government did not want people to say such things publicly, and these comments were filed under the heading of "exposed thinking" or "confused thinking" at the end of reports.[148] Yet, the number of people who commented along these lines was not insignificant. Many work units forwarded comments about the instability of China's constitutional order and the fact that other countries, such as the United States, had not revised their constitutions so frequently and therefore seemed much more stable.[149] The PRC government may have, by then, actively promoted cautious engagement with other countries' legal systems, but this came at a price to the legitimacy of their own legal reforms. People who said such things were compelled to write self-criticisms, but in the process they had at least made their point.[150]

If the 1982 constitution was meant to bolster CCP rule, it had the opposite effect in many cases as people decided, as one report termed it, to "wait and see." People often tried to avoid joining the discussion. Familiar excuses resurfaced: people said they had too much work already or argued that the party leadership was capable of figuring this out on its own. Some thought it would make little difference whether there was a constitution or not, as long as they lived their lives honestly, took a wage, had enough to eat, and did not do anything illegal. It did not occur to them that "not doing anything illegal" was not enough.[151] They had not understood that, as the Central Propaganda Department's outline wrote, every citizen had a duty to learn the constitution in order to abide by it.[152] Instead, as a reporter writing about the discussion among labor models, leading cadres, and experienced workers in one of Shanghai's steel companies explained, many residents were not terribly interested in the promulgation of the draft constitution because they had long lost their trust in laws.[153] It would take much work and time to change this: local governments would have to try and "reach every household" to explain the constitution "article-by-article."[154]

## Enlightenment for Those Blind to the Law

The years between 1978 and the mid-1980s saw the development of new modes of talking about legal learning and new ways of using the media to persuade people that learning laws was a good thing. Law dissemination returned to the Leninist model of "cultural revolution." In Lenin's view, as Elizabeth Perry writes, "a cultural revolution was conceived as a mass education initiative directed toward the needs of industrial modernization."[155] Techniques for teaching laws developed during the late 1970s and early 1980s emphasized top-down guided

细 读 新 宪 法 (年画)     南运生 姬国强 作

Fig. 5.5. "Carefully reading the new constitution (*nianhua*)," 1982. Illustration by Nan Yunsheng and Ji Guoqiang. (Source: *Zhongguo fazhi bao* [China legal daily], 24 December 1982, p. 4.)

study as a way of encouraging voluntary legal learning and conscious-ness building. While focusing on the need for people to study laws, both in groups and individually, educational plans downplayed the significance of individual interpretations of laws. The ideal outcome of good law propaganda was the emergence of the new legally literate socialist man and woman: they would be healthy, disciplined, law-abiding, and patriotic. If that ideal was difficult to achieve, then at least socialist men and women should not be "blind to the law" (*fameng*). Blindness to the law, as *Renmin ribao* cautioned, was now a much larger problem even than illiteracy. It was also dangerous because it could be used as a retrospective excuse for a crime already committed, and this was unacceptable.[156]

Propaganda materials ceaselessly stressed that legal knowledge was the first, essential step to personal safety. Families that knew and abided by laws, images suggested, could enjoy a prosperous life pro-tected by the watchful eye of the state. On 24 December 1982, the same month the constitution was promulgated, an image in *Zhongguo fazhi bao* (fig. 5.5) depicted a young mother reading the constitution with a

Fig. 5.6. "She has come to understand a person's worth," 1985. (Source: *Falü yu shenghuo* [Law and life], no. 8, August 1985, back cover.)

well-nourished baby on her lap. Sitting at a large wooden table, the mother reads the constitution surrounded by the amenities of modern urban socialist living; there is a thermos bottle with fashionable print, a television set in the background, and the woman herself is wearing a stylish sweater. The room is simple but comfortable and well-furnished.

Propaganda images also suggested that a strong and reliable government that could help prevent crime and keep order was impossible without CCP leadership. Laws assured security, structured daily life, and put behind bars criminals who endangered this homely safety. In the first half of the 1980s, newspapers specifically dedicated to laws regularly printed images of this kind, and so did other daily broadsheets.[157] Celebrating new laws and especially the new constitution, pictorials told stories about how ordinary citizens implemented laws in their daily lives. Whereas 1950s law propaganda had depicted strong women and men fighting the enemy and exposing counterrevolutionaries with the help of public security forces, images now suggested that the new men and women were strong but also vulnerable. Surrounded by the overwhelming environment of the anonymous urban

Fig. 5.7. "The child hopes for the return of a good father, the wife waits for a good husband, society gains a useful new man." 1985. (Source: *Falü yu shenghuo* [Law and life], no. 2, February 1985, back cover.)

metropolis, they wielded the law as a weapon. But they needed laws even more for their personal protection and safety, as the image of a lonely woman in a modern high-rise apartment in Beijing's concrete jungle at nighttime suggests (fig. 5.6). With the help of law enforcement, conversely, people and especially men could become, as another image in *Falü yu shenghuo* told readers, good husbands, good fathers, and useful "new men" laboring for the socialist society they lived in (fig. 5.7).

Artists made women and children the main theme of many images, often as protagonists of picture stories about how law and state authorities had come to the citizens' rescue. Women and children were the country's vulnerable future that needed to be protected from harm. They were also symbolic for the family and the private sphere, which the CCP claimed would be enabled and kept safe by state public security.[158] In the CCP's socialist state, public security protected people's private lives and allowed them to live free from existential fear. Law propaganda thus united fear and comfort. It was meant to be deeply discomforting and worrying, depicting possible dangers lurking every-where in citizens' daily lives. Yet propaganda materials at the same time comforted and reassured, promising citizens that learning and abiding by laws, and trusting the party that made and guarded laws, was a simple way of dealing with everyday complexities and threats.

Promoting such images, the CCP became part of a larger global moment of government discourses about crime, youth crime, crime prevention, criminal justice, laws, and the state. In Western Europe, governments told citizens to be more vigilant, reinforced police sys-tems, and debated how best to keep the population safe under the looming threat of domestic and international terrorism. Digital profil-ing of crimes and criminals promised governments a future in which crimes could not only be efficiently reconstructed but altogether pre-vented.[159] In Eastern European countries and in the Soviet Union, state authorities not only talked up the role of the party in preventing crime but argued forcefully that citizens had a responsibility to acquire knowledge of the law in order to support the state in its benevolent work. If they lived law-abiding lives, they would enjoy order and stabil-ity supported by state security.[160]

For people to truly endorse laws, law propaganda had to touch them emotionally. Unlike science fiction and espionage novels, serial-ization of exciting crime stories, and tales of police investigative work, however, law propaganda about public security victories, vulnerable families, and homes secured by local party officials gripped fewer people. Law and order, as well as crime, were the most popular themes. As Jeffrey Kinkley argues, authors, editors, publishers, and propa-ganda officials enthusiastically endorsed such literature, giving it the official label "legal system literature" (*fazhi wenxue*).[161] Police officers and authors collaborated in writing stories for publication and setting up writers-in-residence programs.[162] Public security bureaus, munici-pal and provincial justice bureaus, and provincial governments set up their own law publications one by one, many making profits from high print runs that sold well.[163] Eight provinces—Fujian, Guangxi, Hebei, Hubei, Jiangxi, Qinghai, Shandong, and Ningxia—established their own legal dailies around the time of the 1982 constitution study campaign. Jilin, Yunnan, and Anhui Provinces followed suit in 1983. There were also a few municipal legal dailies—in Dalian, Tianjin, and

Wuhan. By 1985, every province had its own law publications. Pulp magazines, printed quickly and filled with exciting gory stories about crimes, soon challenged the primacy of officially approved publications.[164] There was a market for crime stories, and plenty of people sought their share.

Not all materials that successfully popularized laws were therefore good law propaganda. Behind the public face of open print media, party officials tried to explain in articles written for internal publications why some stories were a problem, how such problems might be avoided, and which legal information was fit for public consumption. In late April 1982, a week before the draft constitution was issued for public discussion, *Xuanchuan dongtai* printed a long article written by officials at the Shanghai Municipal Propaganda Department in which they reported on the attempts of a newspaper review group organized by the Jing'an District Propaganda Bureau to deal with local law propaganda.[165]

Jing'an officials had observed many significant improvements in the popularization of laws. Materials were richer and more diverse than they had been before, and publications featured laws more prominently than in the past. Nonetheless, the group thought that many people had a negative impression of laws because law propaganda had honed in on crime prevention and was designed to intimidate audiences. Another problem, they argued, was that publications with plenty of stories about gory crimes dangerously pandered to readers, particularly those readers who already had an "unhealthy mentality."

Stories describing cases of homicide and sexual crime, usually in lurid detail, had caught the attention of readers as well as government authorities. Group members were concerned that concrete depictions of crimes, criminal methods, and the process of solving cases might disturb some readers and incite others. One crime story in a magazine that the report did not disclose but that was titled "Shadow in the X-Ray Room" included details of how a young woman had visited a doctor and had been sexually assaulted. The details are not given in the report, but the group felt that the story had been so vivid in its description of what happened at the doctor's office that anyone reading it might easily reconstruct the events. They feared that the story might "teach" mentally disturbed readers to do similar "mischief."[166] Details of the crime committed might also scare young women and keep them from seeing a doctor when they needed medical attention. Many magazines, the report explained, treated actual crime stories like fictional detective stories, aiming to please audiences with the suspenseful language of following leads, looking for traces of a crime, and reporting of abnormal conditions of an injury. They wrote about degenerate people, but they did not explain why they had degenerated.[167] That was not proper law propaganda. Such articles barely mentioned why it was important for people to be educated in laws. Although education and explanation ought to have been the center of attention in these pieces, the Jing'an officials criticized that the majority of journalists at best dedicated only "a few characters" to these educational efforts.

As the Jing'an group saw it, journalists had failed to abide by the new constitution. They had failed to adhere to propaganda specifications and had allowed people to "air their own views," something that the 1978 constitution had still permitted but the 1982 did not mention. In the case of reportage on the new Marriage Law, for example, some publications wrote in favor of the freedom to divorce, while others fervently argued against hasty divorces.[168] The group found this troubling. In the society these propaganda officials seemed to envisage, publications were to abstain from any reportage that might confuse readers. Readers needed clear moral imperatives about what to do. To this the group added that there should be no open discussion about whether laws were complete or not. Such matters were subjects for internal discussion, not public debate.[169] One newspaper had printed readers' letters that discussed whether seducing one's underage biological daughter was a criminal offense. The laws at the time were not conclusive about this issue, even if the moral answer was obvious. The group thought the issue was an important one, but not one that should be mentioned in public as long as the judicial field had not yet issued a clear decision on the matter. Making it public, they feared, would only give "bad elements" an opportunity to exploit a loophole in the current law. Moreover, reporting on a court case before a definitive and positive verdict had been pronounced could suggest to readers that "good does not overcome evil."

The Jing'an report hints at the ideational vacuum in which some publishing authorities wanted law propaganda to take place. Law propaganda was supposed to concentrate on "positive education" to increase people's confidence, frighten criminals, and compel them to repent and reform. Good topics for readers included stories about competent judicial officers who enforced the law strictly, who were courageous, and who engaged with practical life. Readers would learn that they could rely on their judicial and public security cadres. Publications might consider having guest authors who had traveled abroad to examine foreign legal systems write up their impressions to show readers why the socialist legal system was superior to that of capitalist countries. Papers should, however, avoid writing stories about abuses of power, for example police misusing their office or heads of people's courts sexually assaulting female litigants. Stories about assaults on women in particular should be avoided. All of this could again be exposed internally, but not publicly. Reporters were further told to emphasize that youth should "respect discipline and abide by the law."[170] Having experienced so many contradictions in their study, work, and family life during the "ten years of turmoil," youth needed proper guidance now. Only then would they be able to struggle against criminal behavior and avoid feeling dejected. To get all of this right, editors and reporters should study the laws more thoroughly.[171] If they failed to follow the directives, journalists could be accused of seeking profit over fulfilling their moral duty—an old accusation that echoed discussions from the early 1950s about private publishers, as well as claims during the Cultural Revolution that profit rather than politics was "in command."

## Conclusion: On the Institutionalization Path

With some effort, party-state authorities revived the state-sponsored circulation of legal knowledge during the late 1970s. But legal knowledge often did not circulate in ways propaganda officials deemed suitable. By the early 1980s, many propagandists had given people the impression that the party and the government were either out of touch with the developments in popular culture that surrounded them, unable to adapt, or too stoical in the belief that these were but deviations. A growing diversity of materials about laws was desirable, for it meant that legal information was quickly spreading and people were reading about laws. Yet the more diverse the materials became, the more they threatened to shed critical light on the failures of laws and the more difficult it was to supervise their content. Advocates of law propaganda were convinced that the solution to this problem was to strive for better techniques and more popularization of law, not less. As the following chapter shows, this led them to devise and implement the first national five-year plan for the popularization of law in late 1985.

# 6    A New Type of Five-Year Plan

## Institutionalizing "Common Legal Knowledge"

Announced in late 1985 and implemented between 1986 and 1990, the first five-year plan for the popularization of common legal knowledge turned legal learning into a regularized technique of CCP governance. It was another channel through which the party and the government permeated everyday life in Beijing and Shanghai, at some moments more visibly than at others. Tying together many of the different law propaganda techniques developed since 1978, the plan set out a state-sanctioned lexicon for talking about law and, often unsuccessfully, tried to curtail talk that did not conform to this lexicon. Even when not explicitly mentioned, the constitution's demand that citizens had not only the right to enjoy laws but also a duty to abide by them reverberated in all law propaganda activities. Constant official talk about laws, whether or not it was effective in creating more obedience to the law, reinforced the message that laws and the regime were closely linked. At the same time, corruption was rampant, and many local cadres' obedience to laws seemed questionable if not downright nonexistent. Law propaganda, and the greater attention to the popularization of common legal knowledge that the five-year plan enabled, gave the central government a chance to argue that despite everything that was going wrong, their intentions, as expressed on paper in laws and repeated in all media across the country, were good.

The plan helped to institutionalize and bureaucratize the popularization of "common legal knowledge" (*falü changshi*), as this chapter shows. Law dissemination gained the same official recognition science

dissemination enjoyed. Special bureaus dedicated to law popularization in local governments soon followed, mirroring the institutionalization that science dissemination had undergone during the early
1950s. Laws were declared "scientific" (*kexuede*).[1] Social scientists, psy-
chologists, and legal experts developed new methods to teach people
laws in the most scientific way. Legal consciousness would be raised,
but in an objective and quantifiable manner. New media, including television and high-gloss magazines, and new technologies, including
computers, were to serve the cause.

Challenges to this clean vision of law propaganda were manifold.
No matter how hard propaganda departments tried to create exciting
new programs, shows, or events to disseminate laws, they kept encoun-
tering the same problem: stories about crime sold copy, but the less
crime was involved the less interesting most laws became. Local officials might just be able to get residents in work units and neighborhoods involved in a discussion of laws. But they had a much harder
time with the cities' young people, who preferred to read glossy magazines and exciting novels sold by commercial publishers, watch TV
shows that were not about laws, or listen to their own music on por-
table cassette players. With the competition of privately published
popular books and fiction, it had already been difficult in the 1950s
to convince the cities' residents to bother about law outside of the
party's established communication channels such as newspaper reading groups or study sessions. Now, in the mid-1980s, the economic
policies of "reform and opening" had led to so much commercial
media diversification that it became even more difficult to circulate a
cohesive story about law and the post–Cultural Revolution CCP. The
central government responded to these challenges in at least three
ways: it prioritized the quantity of law propaganda and dominated
urban public spaces, emphasized rote learning and the dangers of not
knowing laws, and kept working to find better ways to make laws
worth studying.

The ironies of the link between laws, the dissemination of legal
knowledge, claims to the "scientific" and "objective" nature of laws, calls
for obedience to the law, and the continued power of the CCP regime
were not lost on some of the cultural workers who were creating law

Fig. 6.1. Fan Shijie, "The Remedy," 1986. (Source: *Zhongguo fazhi bao*
[China legal daily], 12 March 1986, p. 3.)

propaganda at the time. Take the example of Fan Shijie's cartoon "The
Remedy" (*wanjiu*), published in *Zhongguo fazhi bao* in the spring of
1986 (fig. 6.1). In Fan's cartoon, the patient is someone who has lost his
way or has deviated from the correct path. The doctor is about to
administer an oversized injection of "legal system education" (*fazhi
jiaoyu*). Fan's cartoon can be read in different ways. It can be taken as
a reaffirmation that legal learning and knowledge of the law injected
into citizens, especially those who have gone astray, will come to the
remedy of all. Betterment can be achieved through the acquisition of
ever-greater quantities of legal knowledge. Or maybe the cartoon is
suggesting that in a socialist society that heralded scientific rationality,
all those who deviate from the correct path can be straightforwardly
fixed with education. With one needle per person, much like a vac-
cination or an antidote, legal knowledge can set the body politic of
socialist China right. Fan's cartoon played on local practices of rote

legal learning, increasingly popular among advocates of law propaganda and in Chinese education in general. Fan left it up to his readers
to decide just how desirable such a remedy really was.

The cartoon encapsulated some of the dilemmas and contradictions inherent in the government's increasingly fervent calls to disseminate legal knowledge. Theoretical debates about law propaganda were
one part, practical implementation another. Examining the enforcement and effects of law, particularly after 1989, political and social
scientists have illustrated how individuals and groups claimed rights
once they were aware of laws and rights. They also demonstrated
that many local officials, overwhelmed, worried, and at times panicked
about the legal demands people made on them, tried actively to deter
and obstruct popular legal education even though it was mandated by
the central government.[2]

Based on what we know about some of the effects of legal knowledge and how people used laws to defend their interests, this chapter
takes a step back to reveal how party and government conceptualized,
carried out, and strengthened law propaganda as part of the five-year
plan. It asks how people learned about laws, and how modes of education shaped popular legal understanding. For some people, legal
knowledge became an instrument to take legal action; others acquired
some legal understanding without ever seeking legal redress. If their
trajectories diverge in the application of law, many converge in the story
of *how* people learned.

## Legal Consciousness Quantified

From the CCP's proclamation that laws were scientific it followed that
people's engagement with laws could be objectively quantified, qualified, classified, and understood as "legal consciousness." In the early
1950s, theorists and those involved in law propaganda did not conceive
of popular learning as an avenue toward a separate "legal consciousness" (*fazhi yishi*). Knowledge of laws was part of political study and
socialist consciousness-raising. In the mid-1980s, the media began to
speak of legal consciousness as an analytical category in its own right.
Yet this was a difficult category to deal with. Terms such as law

propaganda and legal education denoted activities carried out by state authorities, while legal consciousness was both the ephemeral goal and a state of mind that propaganda and education sought to influence.

Contemporary media and academic works written about post-Mao legal reforms have tended to speak of a "rise of legal consciousness."[3] Mary Gallagher criticizes this expression because the acquisition of legal consciousness is a more complex process than the one-directional term "rise" suggests.[4] In China, the expression was widely popularized during the 1980s. Social scientific surveys and research into people's attitudes spoke of a rising legal consciousness, suggesting that legal learning would develop first from not knowing laws to knowing laws, and next to being able to abide by them. Legal knowledge became testable, tangible, and material.

Discussions located within legal consciousness a separate category of "constitutional consciousness." As one article in *Xiandai faxue* (Contemporary jurisprudence) remarked: "Constitutional consciousness is the complex of people's constitutional thinking, outlook, knowledge, and mentality," and that in turn was a component of legal consciousness that encompassed people's knowledge, mentality, and thinking about law in general.[5] Because the constitution was the most important "fundamental law," how people understood the constitution had potential bearings on how they understood other laws and the legal system as a whole.[6] This was the premise of a survey conducted in March 1985 by a research team at the Chinese Academy of Social Sciences under the leadership of Yan Xiansheng. Using questionnaires distributed across selected Beijing districts, Yan and his team tried to establish how public discussions of the 1982 constitution and later calls to study the constitution had helped ordinary urban citizens develop constitutional consciousness.[7] Published in the same year in which the central leadership decided to inaugurate a five-year plan for the popularization of law, the survey garnered much attention. If only by association, Yan's statistics and interpretations legitimized the necessity of such a plan. Assembled by researchers from one of China's foremost policy institutes, the survey gave the government an indication of what selected urban residents knew. It helped to determine which specific aspects of constitutional consciousness they should target in the popularization of law.[8]

Divided into four sections, the questionnaire asked twenty-two questions to probe people's basic understanding of the constitution, their views on citizens' basic rights and duties, on the election process, and on the application and protection of the constitution. For two weeks in March 1985, Yan and his team distributed 450 copies of this questionnaire to fourteen different work units in five municipal districts. Research was supported by the Beijing Municipal Bureau of Civil Affairs, the Haidian District People's Committee, the Haidian District Bureau of Justice, the IT center of Beijing University, and other work units. In selecting participants, Yan was careful to include the official spectrum of China's socialist citizenry: workers, peasants, military personnel, teachers, party and government cadres, scientific research personnel, university and middle school students, and local residents. Most participants represented not only the urban but also the educated workforce, many with close links to the party through their work units or professions.[9] Intentionally or not, the survey also focused on districts that were already more established centers of legal learning. The report did not mention that by 1985, Haidian District had emerged as a model district repeatedly praised by the municipal government for its law propaganda work.

The responses detailed in the survey and Yan's interpretations of his findings contributed to the available information about people's constitutional knowledge, but they revealed even more about the manner in which people felt they could talk about constitutional knowledge. Asked whether they had read the 1982 constitution, 47 people (11.7 percent) stated that they had systematically read it, 143 people (36.2 percent) had looked through it once, 62 people (15.7 percent) had leafed through it, 61 individuals (15.5 percent) had read parts, 71 people (18 percent) admitted they had not read it, and two chose not to answer the question. A following question asked about the position of the constitution. Most respondents (68.6 percent) replied correctly that the constitution was above all other laws. Yan thought the 14.9 percent of respondents who answered that it was on par with the Criminal Law had probably been confused by the recent propaganda efforts to promote these two codes. There was also some confusion about the question, "Who controls the country?" About 40 percent of respondents thought it was the National People's Congress, while another 40 percent thought it was "the people" (*renmin*), and almost 10 percent presumed that it was Party Central.[10]

Questions on citizens' rights, as defined by the constitution, prompted more noteworthy responses. Participants may have found it difficult to answer these questions if they felt that they had to find a balance between their own opinions and what they were willing to admit publicly. Asked whether they thought constitutional provisions were authentic, 132 people (33.3 percent) responded that citizens' rights were completely authentic and could be enjoyed. The majority, 194 people (49.1 percent), stated more carefully that most rights could be enjoyed and realized. Only 26 respondents (6.6 percent) thought most rights could not be realized, and a rather sizeable 39 people (9.9 percent) stated they were "unclear" about the question.[11] Similarly, when asked how they understood freedom of speech, only 40 people (10.1 percent) said that this was the ability to say whatever one thinks. The great majority—240 people (60.8 percent)—carefully stated that this was something one could enjoy if it did not violate the law, while 55 people (13.9 percent) believed that these rights would not be protected in real life, 13 people (3.3 percent) thought the rights had no relation to their lives, and 31 people (7.8 percent) were unclear about the question.[12] Compared to other questions, where only one or two people did not reply, here eight people chose not to respond to the question, not even taking the option of stating that they did not understand it. Finally, asked to evaluate how well they thought the constitution could be implemented in the future, 269 people (68.1 percent) thought that if people worked hard it could be implemented. Only 4 people (1 percent) believed it could not be implemented, while 77 people (19.5 percent) thought parts could be implemented and 15 people (3.8 percent) were doubtful. When asked what they thought about the statement, "Some people have said 'The constitution is good, but I fear it is unrealistic,'" 47 respondents (11.9 percent) said they "completely agreed," 134 people (33.9 percent) did not agree, 183 people (46.3 percent) conceded that these people had a point, and, tellingly, 26 people (6.6 percent) said they felt unclear about what the question was asking.[13]

Comparing the percentages listed with Yan's interpretation of the figures highlights gradations in how the numbers could be read. The statistics on the question of who had read the constitution and to what degree they had engaged with it show that the great majority of people had not systematically read the constitution despite the discussion. Yan evaluated this more positively and argued that the majority of people had paid some kind of attention to the constitution. Because he did not reflect on compulsory reading sessions or work unit contexts in which respondents would likely have come across the constitution, he judged that 79 percent had read the constitution and that education and law propaganda had therefore had a "definitive effect" (*yiding xiaoguo*). Concluding that citizens required more guidance to understand the relation of legal knowledge to their "political, economic, and social life," Yan conceded, though, that a *partial* reading of the constitution might affect legal consciousness, and he recommended that more time be spent on popularizing a *comprehensive* understanding of all articles.[14] This conclusion alone, together with a statistical sliver of a particular segment of the urban population's psyche, suggested a rationale for further long-term law propaganda. Meanwhile, because the article provided both Yan's interpretation and the survey results, readers could draw their own conclusions.

## Origins of the First Five-Year Plan

Yan's survey was a reflection of its time. In the autumn of 1984, the Shanghai municipal government had begun to host citywide activities to popularize laws among its residents.[15] Following the model of the 1978 constitution propaganda week, Beijing's municipal government, too, organized a law propaganda week in 1983 and in 1984, and these were widely reported on in *Zhongguo fazhi bao* and other magazines. The 1984 week concluded with the first Democracy and Legal System Work Conference, held at the end of December. These propaganda activities were part of the CCP's attempt to curb what it called "spiritual pollution" and excessive "bourgeois liberalization."[16] Personal continuities, moreover, were important in facilitating law propaganda. In Beijing, for example, Wang Feiran and Fan Jin, who had partaken in the Judicial Reform Movement and had also been members of the Beijing Marriage Law Campaign Committee and the Constitution Draft Discussion Committee, were once again involved. They, as well as prolific and now rehabilitated party members such as Peng Zhen, were part of a group of party leaders who firmly believed in the need for a strong socialist political system and strong laws that people knew and abided by. More practically, they helped devise educational plans and a theoretical foundation to combat "blindness to the law."

A series of work conferences held in the course of 1985 signaled that the central government was about to change how law propaganda was conducted across the country. By the end of the year, the "Five-Year Plan for the Basic Popularization of Legal Knowledge to All Citizens" was formally circulated in a joint notification by Party Central and the State Council, and issued as *Zhongfa* no. 23.[17] But it was not in Beijing, and not at the center of political power, that the decision to intensify law popularization was made. It was in Benxi, in Liaoning Province, a city known for its steel production, iron manufacturing, and mining. There, in June 1984, a national work meeting to discuss law propaganda took place, with leading figures, including Minister of Justice Zou Yu (b. 1920), present.[18]

In the years after law popularization became a national policy, the Benxi municipal party committee and government tried to promote the memory of its city as the origin of the country's five-year law popularization plan. This plan, it explained, had been a result of Benxi officials' own advanced experiences in conducting law propaganda among its residents.[19] Policy decisions in China have often been accompanied by stories explaining how decision-makers came to make a particular choice, or adopt a particular policy, that then went on to influence the country's development. In 2012, a reporter writing for *Liaoning fazhi bao* (Liaoning legal daily) recorded one such story about a certain Mr. Yang and a donkey in Benxi in 2012. One day in 1981, the report explained, Yang, a young man, decided that he wanted to eat donkey meat, a delicacy that few people could afford. Another family had a donkey, so he took a knife and secretly cut out several chunks of flesh from the donkey's backside. At home, he made them into dumplings and enjoyed a bowlful. Shortly thereafter, because he had infringed on another person's property, the Public Security Bureau arrested Yang. It asked him why he had done such a cruel thing, and whether he knew that he had broken the law. Yang, readers are told, shouted that he was being treated unjustly, that he had not killed anyone or committed some other major crime, and that he could not understand why eating meat should be a crime.[20] Sun Yanfang, head of the Benxi Municipal Bureau of Justice, heard about this case and, the reporter tells us, was saddened by it. In an industrial city such as Benxi, where the standard of living was rising, Yang's case showed that there were still many people who followed the principle of "a life for a life." Sun ordered an investigation to establish how much people actually knew about laws and presented the findings to the municipal party committee. The story of Yang and the donkey reportedly moved the committee members as well, prompting the decision that the city's residents needed to be educated and that Benxi needed a new approach to the popularization of law.[21]

The Benxi narrative became a national law propaganda model. In interviews that circulated through internal party propaganda work periodicals, in *Falü yu shenghuo* (Law and life) and other public magazines, the Benxi Party Committee assistant secretary, Li Zhida, presented Benxi's technique as simple, noteworthy, and, above all, new.[22] Education, he said, should not begin with ordinary people—it should begin with cadres, and then spread outward from cadres toward all citizens. Laws, Li explained, were useless if cadres were unable to follow them, either because they did not know them or because they did not care.[23]

Little about Benxi's approach was new. It was the method that had structured 1950s law dissemination. Benxi's leadership either did not remember this legacy or chose to frame its work as new for added emphasis. Its point of comparison was legal education work in the late 1970s and early 1980s, which they thought had been too singularly focused on reforming young people and teaching them about laws, particularly the Criminal Law. Without attention to cadre training now, it argued, all other law popularization efforts would be futile.[24] The education of cadres had to come first, and then the education of the young—only in this way would everyone benefit.[25] As Zou Yu, then Minister of Justice, recorded later, this system worked so well that when he briefly talked to an old woman of about eighty or more years of age during a visit to Benxi in 1983 and asked her whether she knew what the constitution was, the woman answered: "I know, the constitution is the mother, other laws are the sons, [and the] mother is bigger than the sons."[26] Interpreting the woman's words as a success for recent law propaganda, he did not mention the possibility that given her age, she might have reiterated law propaganda she had already encountered during the 1954 constitution discussion, when she would have already been in her fifties.

Benxi's story of Mr. Yang and the donkey was not unusual; it would have been one out of hundreds of cases of theft and pillaging that were logged across China during the early 1980s.[27] To readers of *Liaoning fazhi bao* in 2012 it might have sounded cruel and strange, and the fact that Yang would not have known that stealing meat was illegal might have seemed hard to fathom. This was not so during the early 1980s. If this was indeed how the story transpired, Sun Yanfang may well have selected Yang's case from many similar incidents and used it to underline his point. Uncontrolled pillaging recalled memories of famine during the Great Leap Forward and after, as well as memories of public security failings during the Cultural Revolution. Yang's story worked because it was so common, because it could be linked easily to calls for stricter law enforcement, and because it presented the young Mr. Yang, uneducated as he was, as a person whose future could be salvaged if only he learned about laws. Zou Yu, too, emphasized this idea of betterment through legal education in his recollections when he wrote that, during his Benxi visit, he had attended a law propaganda lesson and had asked one of the workers in the factory why he thought learning laws was useful. The worker responded that there had been fewer instances of things going missing from his factory workshop after people had received legal education. Now that they knew that taking things was stealing and unlawful behavior, many had even brought things back to the workshop.[28]

Once the 1984 national work meeting to discuss law propaganda in Benxi concluded, the Central Propaganda Department commenced preparations for the five-year plan. On 2 December, when the country's national propaganda department directors met in Beijing, the head of the Central Propaganda Department, Deng Liqun, informed them that one of the tasks of propaganda authorities was to strengthen law propaganda.[29] The department was keen to improve law propaganda work in newspapers and magazines. A notification by the Central Propaganda Department and the Central Politics and Law Commission in

March 1985 criticized newspapers and magazines for what they called "truthful reportage" and for the sloppy way in which they reported on court cases.[30] The media had recently reported on a corruption and bribery case in Wuxi city, Jiangsu Province, filed against Sun Yonggen. The department thought that it had turned what was a clear case of bribery into a story about a rags-to-riches self-made man who had rendered outstanding service to society, thus making the court's guilty verdict seem questionable. Law propaganda, the department contended, would have to do better.

As in the cases of crime stories that the Jing'an propaganda group had worked on, the central propaganda authorities, too, thought that reportage sometimes just superficially chased good stories and wrote sensational reports. These publications reported on cases with outstanding verdicts, which caused much "ideological confusion" when the final verdict then did not align with the media's earlier prognoses. Officials thought that this could only erode people's trust in the law, as well as in the reliability of reportage. Media reportage should report on a case from different angles but should never fail to report facts "truthfully" and "accurately," and should never lose sight of what was educationally significant about a case.[31] A reporter unsure of the full details of a case or unaware of the final verdict should refrain from reporting or speculating. Moreover, under no circumstances were reporters to use public opinion to exert pressure on the judicial system—a practice that, as Benjamin Liebman has shown, was quite common.[32] Reporters unhappy with a verdict could voice their criticism internally, but propaganda authorities did not want them to undermine the legitimacy of a judge's decision in publicly circulating news media. Mistaken reportage was to be corrected immediately. Anyone who purposefully and maliciously put out wrong information should be reported to his superiors.[33]

In June 1985, the department and the Ministry of Justice organized a large meeting in Beijing to discuss law propaganda work. *Falü yu shenghuo* later told its readers that this had been the largest meeting on popular legal education since the founding of the PRC.[34] Closer involvement of the Central Propaganda Department in law work tethered propaganda officials across the country more closely to law propaganda work. Many of them had, until then, been focused more on directing propaganda to advocate discipline and morality. Even if officials were still skeptical about popularizing laws, plenty of laws had been passed with the goal of regulating life under CCP rule, and the regime wanted propaganda officials to come up with a more coordinated approach to law propaganda. Also in June 1985, *Xuanchuan dongtai* announced that law popularization was to be a major project that would, together with scientific thinking and socialist morality, profoundly change the "face of the country and of society."[35] Already a widespread practice, law propaganda now had to be turned into a regular, systematized, and institutionalized practice.[36] The result of the meeting in Beijing was the creation of a work summary for a period of "approximately five years" during which law would be popularized. Peng Zhen, who had for years promoted law propaganda, made clear that "if we want to do things according to the law, then we cannot do without propaganda work."[37] The five-year plan, as *Falü yu shenghuo* noted in its summary of Deng Liqun's presentation at the meeting, would "give the law to one billion people."[38] By the end of 1985, the period of "approximately five years" had been renamed a five-year plan.[39] As the official yearbook for 1985 announced, the year was "an opportune moment" to begin the plan.[40]

What did the five-year plan entail? Following the Benxi model, the first year was to focus mostly on educating cadres and young people.[41] By 1987, in the second year, propaganda activities would then include all citizens. A central directive—*Zhongfa* no. 20 issued in October 1985—argued that youth, "the hope and future of our country," would need help "to strengthen thoughts, morals, discipline, and legal system education."[42] Continuing the familiar argument that youth were a troubled group, the directive argued that cadres and youth broke laws because "they do not know the laws."[43] Permitting provinces and municipalities to decide how to carry out propaganda and how to examine legal knowledge, the five-year plan suggested that anyone who had successfully completed their legal learning could be given a certificate of completion, or their names could be posted on notices on local blackboards. Ideally, education in the law was to begin, as *Liaoning xuanchuan dongtai* (Liaoning propaganda trends) contended, when a person was still a baby.[44]

Two shifts in policy language marked the changed policy for law propaganda. First, the plan was given an official name and formulation:

the "popularization of law" (*pufa*). The plan's architects correlated the popularization of law and the popularization of science (*kepu*), illustrating that they thought learning law and learning science could work in similar ways. Since the 1950s, the verb "popularize" (*puji*) had commonly been used in the context of popularization of scientific knowledge. But it was seldom used for law. Because laws were now scientific, they could be understood and lived by if people handled matters scientifically and objectively.[45] Zou Yu noted in a speech in February 1986 at a meeting of work units that had conducted the first tests of law popularization across the country, that PRC laws were developed on the basis of past practice and experience. As long as people linked laws to their everyday lives, they would come to understand the logic of PRC laws and why they were necessary. "Law," Zou reminded his audience, "is not a tool to control the masses, but instead a weapon in the hands of the masses to safeguard their own legal rights."[46]

Second, the formulation spoke of common knowledge (*changshi*), rather than knowledge (*zhishi*). This was an important distinction. Zou Yu recalled that when he approached Peng Zhen to talk about the possibility of a five-year plan, Peng was skeptical, doubting that it would be possible to convey actual legal knowledge to the entire population. Zou explained that this plan would focus on common knowledge. Knowledge and common knowledge were two different things, he said. Common knowledge meant giving a basic (*jiben*), not comprehensive, education in law to everyone. Basic education, moreover, would be restricted to the most fundamental laws, including the constitution, the Criminal Law, and the Civil Law. This Peng agreed to.[47]

Although the term "common knowledge" had been popular throughout the Mao Era, it had not been frequently used for law dissemination. By contrast, during the Republican period publishers and newspapers had widely advertised common legal knowledge for everyday use. Common legal knowledge during the 1930s and 1940s, for example, included anything from matters of family law to criminal provisions. Now the CCP officially reconnected common knowledge and law dissemination. Dictionaries reflected and canonized this language shift. The 1986 *Newly Edited Newspaper Readers' Handbook*, for example, featured a section titled "common legal knowledge" and explained that the term referred to the need for people to understand a basic set of laws in order to be law-abiding citizens.[48]

Reference to common legal knowledge indicated a regularization (*jingchanghua*) of law dissemination. This aligned with the government's rhetorical, though not practical, departure from campaigns as a method of governance.[49] Zou Yu, Peng Zhen, and others such as Deng Liqun carefully avoided associating the popularization of law with the Maoist campaign legacy. Legal learning, the way individuals such as Peng Zhen, Deng Liqun, and Zou Yu understood it, was presented as a safety net to prevent the return of Maoist mobilization and to curb the excesses of economic reform.[50] *Zhongguo fazhi bao* meanwhile cautioned readers not to conduct law popularization in campaign style or accidentally speak of campaigns, because this would be a serious impediment to long-term legal learning.[51]

## Creating a Narrative of Law Propaganda: District Gazetteers

Even as it broke with the Cultural Revolution decade, law propaganda as a socialist activity required some legitimizing socialist past. Over the years, the 1981 resolution influenced local governments to rediscover historical precedents to law propaganda in the 1950s, now officially the "golden age" of CCP rule. Published by each city district, local gazetteers (*difangzhi*) have since retold China's legal history and legal accomplishments.[52] Beijing and Shanghai district gazetteers demonstrate how different districts have wanted to remember their support of law propaganda and their willingness to embrace the new five-year plan. Gazetteers also give a glimpse into districts' different activities to institutionalize law propaganda once it became clear that it would gain the same status as science dissemination.

Gazetteers all emphasized that districts in Beijing and Shanghai had already worked toward establishing an infrastructure for law propaganda between 1981 and 1985. After the Ministry of Justice took up work again in July 1979, it oversaw parts of the criminal justice system, the education of cadres, and law propaganda work.[53] Municipal and district justice bureaus opened in March and April 1981 as part of a national extension of the Ministry of Justice into municipalities, provinces, and districts. Local bureaus organized law propaganda work in their localities, and assisted with training judicial cadres and administering courts. Public security branches, the state procuratorate, people's courts, mass organizations, and propaganda departments had conducted most propaganda up until then. The propaganda sections of the justice bureaus took on some of their work and became a central node for law propaganda coordination. They provided advice and support to report-givers and propagandists and oversaw the production of educational materials at the local level.

Districts in both Beijing and Shanghai highlighted in their gazetteers how proactive they had been in setting up structures for law popularization. Several district cadres in the country's political capital seemed determined to be law propaganda pioneers. Beijing's Haidian District, home to universities, colleges, and research institutes, opened a section of its justice bureau devoted to law propaganda. District officials coordinated the local production of study materials based on national templates but specifically catering to the needs of district residents. Street-level offices, communes, factories, and schools all received copies. By May 1982, the district had twelve large law propaganda stands. That same year, 170,000 visitors were recorded at an image exhibition, while by 1983, 179 law propagandists had concluded their training and were ready to conduct work. In April 1983, the district organized a week of activities to study the constitution. This came a month before the entire Beijing municipality held a "legal system propaganda week."[54] During this time, more than 200,000 copies of different laws were sent to lower-level work units. Officials hung up posters explaining the constitution, the Marriage Law, and the Criminal Law in parks, at markets, and in other public spaces. The authors of the gazetteer report estimated that about 500,000 people would have looked at these posters while they were displayed. So promising was the Haidian District government's work that China Central Television came twice to film a documentary.[55]

Other districts were not far behind. By 1985, Fengtai District had trained 3,567 legal instructors, report-givers, and propagandists equipped with special "law popularization identity cards."[56] Identification cards resembled those that activists and propagandists had received in the

1950s to mark them as being—on paper—trained and often examined in a particular type of propaganda and ready to educate the masses. Xicheng District installed special law propaganda window displays at Beihai Park, in the zoo, and at the newly opened Chegongzhuang subway station.[57] When the five-year plan began, Xicheng had 212 report-givers, while Chaoyang District reported 198 propagandists as well as several other staff able to help with law propaganda. In Chaoyang, in the few years before 1985, statistics listed a total of 387 talks about law, 15 different street-level legal advice events (including open door advice centers for people with legal questions), 90,000 pages of local propaganda materials, and a total of 500 days of itinerant exhibitions.[58] In Dongcheng District, meanwhile, officials noted that they had circulated a total of some 246,000 pages of materials since the justice bureau began work. There were also 278 propaganda boards filled with information, in addition to thirteen different plays and films drawing in some 100,000 viewers.[59] Dongcheng had started in 1981 with a staff of 19 people. By 1985 it had trained 1,700 cadres at all levels, handing out over 2,000 booklets in the process. During the five-year plan, district officials claimed to have dealt with some 30,000 questions from residents. Xuanwu District trained 3,158 people to give law propaganda education, with some 50 different kinds of propaganda materials assembled and written at the district level—a high number for any district and certainly not in line with the mantra to avoid excessive variety in favor of more accuracy and control.[60] People in the district were ordering many of these materials via subscription and watching videotapes jointly produced by the district law popularization office, the Beijing Municipal Bureau of Justice, and the Beijing Municipal Bureau of Culture. Xuanwu District rivaled Haidian District for its progress and speed in law propaganda, as it later claimed to have completed its work for the five-year plan in two years.[61]

Gazetteers of Shanghai's municipal district told a similar story that was focused on numbers and activities rather than results. The city had several "advanced" units whose cadres had been particularly successful, by national comparison, in their law propaganda work. Jing'an District's Justice Bureau handled the popularization of law from 1981 on.[62] During the propaganda week of early June 1983, Jing'an was reported to have set up twenty-one propaganda points, and to have distributed over 3,100 posters and cartoons, as well as some 16,000 pieces of other kinds of propaganda.[63] Luwan District claimed to have set up an extensive law propaganda network with sixty-eight offices below the district level. Wallpapers and blackboards contained news snippets from national law propaganda publications to make these accessible to people who did not subscribe or have direct access via their work units.[64] Xuhui District also reached some 80,000 people with its hundreds of materials and, following the Beijing example, held a "legal system propaganda month" in June 1983. Here, some 299 images were plastered across the district, and 955 blackboards became nodes of law propaganda. Eleven public trials were staged to bring law propaganda closer to the people. In preparation for the five-year plan, the municipal justice bureau named Xuhui an "advanced team" in 1985. Putuo District judicial officials, meanwhile, sent out a propaganda bus to the busiest commercial streets to give people a chance to pick up a bit of legal education while they were going about their daily errands.[65] Jing'an District, with its lively street culture, also had a propaganda bus that chauffeured performance artists to different public law propaganda stands to perform brief pieces.[66] In Putuo, moreover, about 667 individuals were trained to become law propaganda teachers. Eventually, the Putuo bureau would be voted one of the nation's most advanced law popularization bureaus. Across the city, "propaganda days," "propaganda weeks," and "propaganda months" became a common feature. So did legal counsel points, which often consisted of little more than a few people who had some experience working with laws (usually trained law propaganda workers or, more frequently as time went on, lawyers) setting up at a table with some chairs and then talking to anyone who came by about their specific legal questions.[67]

## Constructing Propaganda Networks

Gazetteers which compiled the statistics of propaganda work, give a sense of the scale and speed at which law propaganda activities were institutionalized across central districts of both cities. Yet they gloss over the many problems of law propaganda. The media landscape in both cities had diversified fast in the late 1970s and early 1980s. Commercial publications, as well as unofficial and mimeographed publications circulating outside of official channels, were often more attractive to audiences that demanded greater variety.[68] State publishers, too, now had to publish for a profit and could no longer rely on mandatory subscriptions as work units were no longer allowed to subscribe to all available papers but instead had to make selections.[69] Media therefore had to try to please consumers and censors with law propaganda products—a challenge that was not easily met. Seeking to compete on the market, and benefiting from the closure of many private magazines during the fight against "spiritual pollution," the Ministry of Public Security, for example, set up its own publisher that commissioned crime stories. As Jeffrey Kinkley shows, these stories were supposed to provide good examples of law propaganda, but they also pleased readers with "awful crimes and suspense."[70] Trying to attract new readers with promises of reliable legal information and advice, meanwhile, state newspapers such as the newly published *Beijing fazhi bao* (Beijing legal daily) advertised: "Do you want to learn legal knowledge? Do you want to obtain legal support? Do you want to use laws to safeguard your personal lawful rights and interests? Please subscribe to *Beijing fazhi bao*."[71]

Party leaders envisioned an ideal type of engagement with law: the patriotic law-abiding socialist citizen who would want to spend his or her free time learning laws to showcase this patriotism. Yet most people did not think law was an exciting subject to read about, unless it was part of criminal and detective stories. There was little leisure in perusing information about what people were permitted or forbidden to do in their daily lives. As the statistics noted in gazetteers suggest, district governments tried to develop propaganda networks that would infuse legal information into people's everyday lives, thus making newspapers and magazines but one of the ways in which citizens came into contact with laws. Artists were commissioned to draw images that mapped out the physical spaces for these propaganda networks, as in Shen Tiancheng's image "Springtime for the Popularization of Legal Knowledge" (fig. 6.2), published in the magazine *Minzhu yu fazhi huabao* (Democracy and legal system pictorial).

In the upper left corner of the image there is a legal knowledge contest underway on the second floor of a lane house. On the first floor of the building, a female teacher explains laws to her pupils. On the

Fig. 6.2. Shen Tiancheng, "Springtime for the Popularization of Legal Knowledge," 1986. (Source: *Minzhu yu fazhi huabao* [Democracy and legal system pictorial], 6 February 1986, p. 2.)

ground floor, a local official hands out residential identity cards. Outside of the building, marked by a large red sign with the words "legal counsel," is a table where people advise residents on questions of law. A female schoolteacher talks to a mother and her son, telling them that "from today, school and family will work together more"; and behind the long table where legal counselors are working, a male teacher gives a book to a schoolboy and tells him that he should "study diligently." In front of the legal counsel table, a man pushing a bike with books strapped onto the back tells a local cadre that he is just on his way to the reform school to deliver books. To their left, a man bows his head in deference as a policeman admonishes him: "do not intensify conflicts." The two men stand behind a "hall of glory" with large portraits of three model citizens who have excelled in their work of keeping public order. Balloons in hand, people walk over a bridge in the foreground while looking at the images. On the left side of the bridge, a man with a loud-speaker tells passers-by to "carry your backpacks in front of you" to prevent theft. Affixed to the bridge, which leads over "Civilization Street," are six big-character posters reminding drivers to "pay attention to traffic safety." In the middle of the street a policeman directs buses, mopeds, and bicycles in an orderly manner. The inscription on the side of the bus reads, "five years to popularize legal knowledge." Just behind the bridge, people are reading the wallboards of a mobile picture exhibition on the importance of abiding by traffic rules. In the building behind them, plenty of different law propaganda activities are underway. The little bookshop to the left of the building advertises *Minzhu yu fazhi* and *Minzhu yu fazhi huabao* magazines, while behind the shop a woman in a red sweater gives a presentation on "law propaganda." On the first floor of the building, both rooms are full of people intently perusing a "national exhibition on striking hard against criminal offenses." On the second floor, people are watching a TV show about laws, while in a small room above, three generations of family members are engrossed in a large red book on "legal knowledge."

Shen modeled his image on the central leadership's 1978 call for a "springtime for science," which had been part of the implementation of the "Four Modernizations."[72] The image of legal learning in downtown Shanghai claimed a space for law and legal knowledge in every aspect of citizens' lives: from private to public spheres, in school and at rest, on the road and at home, while talking with neighbors or with the local police, and in their leisure time as well as at work. The idealized world painted in this image rarely mirrored the daily lives of residents. Still, provincial and municipal internal bulletins with guidelines on propaganda work spent much time trying to explain to grassroots propaganda officials how to construct such propaganda networks and why new types of media, such as television, were crucial.

*Liaoning xuanchuan dongtai* told readers that Cai Cheng (1927–2009), soon to be the Minister of Justice, had advised that varied and colorful law propaganda should be the top priority for magazines and pictorials.[73] The Zhejiang Provincial Propaganda Department counseled readers of its *Xuanchuan tongxun* that law popularization required special efforts using "all ways and forms" to succeed.[74]

In line with the five-year plan, provincial newspapers, magazines, broadcasting, and TV stations were all directed to set up new law popularization columns, regularizing the more sporadic law propaganda work of previous years.[75] Propaganda workers went out to investigate which kinds of materials the people in their districts especially enjoyed. Novels, plays, and serial comics continued to be important. Television shows about laws, feature films, popular science films, newsreels, and film serializations could all be helpful, both when broadcast live and when supplied as cassettes and videotapes to local work units. Propaganda officials also hired more artists and tried to coordinate the political training of local drama troupes.[76]

Comparing law propaganda materials published during the early 1980s with materials issued a few years later, it is evident that cultural workers creating law propaganda on behalf of state authorities had tried to diversify. Materials were more colorful and glossy, with more personal stories, and they worked across genres, using the same storyline in illustrations, photo stories, and short stories to create a more comprehensive experience for the reader. Competition was a concern for magazines, as was the desire to make publications attractive to potential customers and to sell copy. Demands for diversification drove the editorial board of *Minzhu yu fazhi* magazine to bring *Minzhu yu fazhi huabao* to the market. It quickly became a popular magazine, with copies printed in Shanghai, Tianjin, and Wuhan, and offering an airmail service. In its first few months, the pictorial featured plenty of cartoons, serial comics (*lianhuanhua*), and caricatures, with fairly little text overall. Despite its name, however, it soon began to look less like a pictorial, as images gave way to more and more text. Images, even with captions, were still much more difficult to control, and their interpretations were more fluid than those of textual genres.

Other magazines such as *Falü yu shenghuo*, issued by the Ministry of Justice and the Law Press starting in late 1984, tried to keep up with trends. Addressing a readership beyond police, public security, and legal workers, *Falü yu shenghuo* tried to attract readers with photo stories, novel serializations, and columns with names like "Neighborhood and Alley Discussions," "Ask a Lawyer," "The Lawyer's Page," "The History of Law," "A Window into Foreign Law," and—perhaps less enticing to many though clearly in line with the expectations of the five-year plan—"Life, Morality, Law."[77]

Law propaganda was one element in larger discussions about how to control media and encourage "healthy" cultural production.[78] Party cadres wary of market and media liberalization feared that society was becoming too unruly. Now more involved in law propaganda work, the Central Propaganda Department worried in particular about media coverage of laws and legal cases. In March 1986, Li Maoguan evaluated the quality of law propaganda in the intra-party journal *Lilun jiaoliu* (Theory exchange) and concluded that even more law propaganda was needed in order for the quality to improve. Li wrote: "Law propaganda has not yet become a regular enough practice, it is not systematic enough, and not yet broad enough in its reportage. Some reporting is untruthful, inaccurate, and poorly affects practical work; sometimes (it) focuses excessively on uncovering a dark side and giving incomplete explanations, and then the effects on society are not good."[79] He thought propagandists needed to better differentiate crimes from actions that were not crimes. Journalists should be able to "cite the articles of the law and use legal language in propaganda to respond to legal questions." Some papers, Li thought, used too many examples or stirred people's emotions too much, making it difficult to tamp down the message. There were too many "socially unhealthy small volumes and magazines" available on the open publications market. Citing investigation into Beijing's booksellers in the districts of Dongcheng, Chongwen, Xuanwu, and the Northern Suburbs, he noted that among ninety-four different kinds of magazines, many had far too explicit content. Although they attracted readers, Li warned that they distorted the legal situation and were unbalanced. Internal reports and thought pieces regularly lamented the difficulty of controlling the message. In a similar vein, provincial propaganda departments reminded local officials to support proper reportage, ensure that contents remained diverse and addressed a broad readership, and report matters truthfully.[80]

Effective censorship, however, required an understanding of when to intervene. Jiangsu Province's *Xuanchuan tongxun*, for instance, cautioned its readers not to be too quick in deciding what to censor. One article lectured readers, "There are two sides to all things in this world, and literary and artistic products are no exception. When commenting on a work, a program, or a TV drama, you cannot say that everything is good if one is good, you cannot blindly send manuscripts to the press, but you should also not demand perfection, or (say that) if one is not good then all are no good; we want to avoid the appearance of this kind of one-sidedness . . . and of being in a rush."[81] The work of censors remained in all but the most obvious cases difficult, volatile, and circumstantial.

Reportage and media reports about laws were a constant potential source of problems. Propaganda authorities wanted much reportage and often called on media outlets to produce more. Yet, at the same time, officials were constantly concerned that they had to keep checks on publishers, authors, artists, playwrights, and film directors. Wrong styles of reportage, issues of fact and timing, and problems of interpretation could all limit the value of law propaganda pieces. In the worst scenario drawn by propaganda officials, as one article in Zhejiang's *Xuanchuan tongxun* discussed, specific law propaganda products could have the exact opposite effect to the one intended by encouraging wrong interpretations or convincing audiences that the law gave them rights or stipulated provisions that it did not.[82] Concealed behind such comments was a problem that had already vexed propaganda officials during the early 1950s: how might they use law propaganda to prevent people from reading and interpreting laws on their own, in ways that were deemed politically wrong?

## "Legal Fevers": New Media to Mobilize the Masses

China's cultural workers and propaganda authorities were not alone in having to deal with the question of how to make legal learning both educational and entertaining. In the GDR, for instance, party officials advocated the "popular scientific" approach.[83] This approach called for a careful balance between objective, accessible, educational, and entertaining information.[84] In China and the GDR the tested tools of law propaganda, such as discussion meetings and newspaper editorials, appeared outdated. As in East Berlin, Beijing and Shanghai's district governments and magazine and newspaper editorial boards tried hard to open up interactive study possibilities that went beyond group work and that could also be used to raise the profile of law propaganda activities in print publications, on radio broadcasts, or on television.

Legal knowledge contests met these requirements. Shen's image "Springtime for the Popularization of Legal Knowledge" had included a small legal knowledge contest on the second floor of a Shanghai lane house. Contests also took place on a much larger scale and, starting in 1985, quickly became an essential propaganda activity for all districts. Beijing's Dongcheng District reported that it organized sixty-two legal knowledge contests with some 135,000 participants in the second half of the 1980s.[85] It is difficult to establish whether such numbers are accurate. Even if we presume that the numbers were exaggerated, the attendance figures were probably still high. Other districts tried to keep up. Beijing's Xuanwu District reported a total of 693 contests, some of which were smaller events in work units or neighborhoods while others were organized district-wide.[86] In Shanghai, Wujing Chemical Plant was credited with initiating a city-wide trend for legal knowledge contests.[87] Work units continued to set the trend, and in March 1986, the Shanghai Municipal Bureau of Justice and the Shanghai Television Station awarded the Shanghai Municipal Office of Light Industry first prize for its performance in a legal knowledge contest that month.[88] There were soon larger events, such as a legal contest held in March 1987 in Xuhui District's Shanghai Sports Stadium, with some sixty-eight work units and several hundred people competing.[89]

Knowledge contests of all kinds were a media fashion during the 1980s. In May 1986, *Xinwen jizhe* (Journalist monthly) in Shanghai replied to a reader named Tan Lijing who had written a letter to the editor with the suggestive question, "Why do audiences warmly welcome 'knowledge contests'"? Noting that the local Shanghai TV station was showing a great deal of different knowledge contests, Tan wondered about their actual educational value. Such a question clearly provided ample ground for editors to give a lengthy explanation

legitimizing why contests were useful. Knowledge contests, readers
were told, were not only extremely popular among viewers, but they
also brought real people into the studios, making TV broadcasts so
much more lively and interesting for both participants and audiences.
There were drama contests, archaeology contests, after-hours comparisons of TV program hosts, home hygiene knowledge contests, consumer knowledge contests, legal knowledge contests, and so on. In
many cases, TV stations would team up with local or national magazines. Shanghai TV, for instance, co-hosted with *Xiaofei bao* (Consumer report). "Knowledge is power!" the magazine told its readers,
and contests could make knowledge acquisition easy and fun.[90]

Contests did indeed act as a catalyst for people to acquire legal
knowledge. And while contests could be entertaining, they also encouraged contestants to take pride in knowing laws. Propaganda authorities moreover considered contests useful because they required
contestants to have a broad knowledge of laws. Answers were multiple-
choice based, or required repetition of keywords and set phrases
from legal texts. Contests suggested that laws were one-dimensional,
with a solution to every question, when in fact they were not. This one-
dimensional approach tallied well with the way propaganda outlines
seemed to conceptualize law—as something to be learned, understood,
and then applied.

The trend of legal knowledge contests went countrywide with a
major national contest organized by the *Minzhu yu fazhi* editorial
board. Slightly more than a year before the five-year plan, in late
1984, the board announced a "Legal System Knowledge Study Contest." Readers across the country were asked to respond to 217 questions. Before publication, the magazine had all questions scrutinized
by a team of legal experts and advanced law students. Some were
multiple-choice questions, some were "yes" or "no" questions, and
some asked for longer written answers. After the 31 January deadline,
the magazine's Shanghai office had received 304,700 responses.[91]
According to the magazine's own account, roughly 27 percent of the
contestants worked on the "frontline" of political-legal work, as
clerks, public security officers, law teachers, and so forth. The others
were lay people interested in the study of law. More than testing

memory, questions were designed to encourage contestants to go out and study legal education materials, engage with the law, and find the right answers.

The magazine's editors expressed surprise at the number of submissions and the high level of participation. A "legal fever," as one article put it, had broken out among the masses.[92] The presumption evident in all discussions of this contest was that people voluntarily participated. It was entirely possible that work units compelled their staff to participate; this was something that would not have been discussed in the magazine's pages, presuming that the editors knew about it in the first place. A storyboard with photos of people from across the country enthusiastically preparing for the contest suggested as much—it showed cadres in the Shanghai Municipal People's Procuratorate comparing questions to materials in *Minzhu yu fazhi* back issues, comrades in the Cangzhou public security branch office in Hebei Province poring over books in a small library room, women from a textile mill in Xinjiang's Shehezi city talking to each other about the questions while studying law popularization leaflets, and young women from Shanghai University filling in the answer sheets. Photographers, it seems, had been on site around the country to document the first-ever nationwide legal knowledge contest.[93] Such photo stories and high submission numbers were needed to legitimize the usefulness of the contest. Editors interpreted the high participation rate to "vividly illustrate that the popularization of legal knowledge has already become a conscious demand of the broad citizenry."[94]

Technological advances and scientific modernity made the contest possible, something the editors did not fail to bring to readers' attention. Contest submissions were evaluated in a multi-step process involving human readers and the newest computer technology, thus drawing a parallel between the scientific nature of laws and the science-based technology that now evaluated the accuracy of participants' legal knowledge. A team of Shanghai judicial staff first scrutinized all 304,700 submissions to determine which qualified and which should be excluded because they were incomplete or incorrectly completed. Then, scientific workers at East China Computer Technology Research Institute ran all valid submissions through their newest computers. The computers identified and processed the submission sheets, which the magazine had pre-printed and circulated in the issue with the contest questions. With the computers' help, the workers at the research institute could then generate a list of winners.

In its March issue, the magazine announced these winners. Twelve people won a first prize, and twenty-four won a second prize. Fifty people were awarded a third prize, and a thousand individuals received commemorative prizes. Shanghai name-brand firms sponsored all 1,086 prizes. Learning laws and submitting a successful entry for the contest came with material benefits. In a festive ceremony to celebrate the successful submissions, contestants who won the first prize were given a Red Lantern label 2L1410 radio and cassette recorder which boasted the newest technology and featured four loudspeakers, four wavebands, and frequency modulation. The second- and third-prize winners received a slightly less fancy radio and cassette recorder with two speakers and one speaker, respectively. Commemorative prize winners were given a Hero 329 model quality iridium-topped fountain pen from the famous Shanghai Hero Foundation Pen Manufacturer.[95] Because of the popular appeal of the contest, the magazine's editorial board decided also to reward those who had not won prizes. Participants were informed that they could receive a commemorative badge if they sent a letter to the Shanghai office and included a stamped and addressed envelope.

Participation statistics and the description of how submissions were processed drove home the contest's mass appeal. But the contest held even more propaganda value in its aftermath. Personal stories of how selected contestants learned about their success opened the magazine's April issue.[96] They gave readers human-interest stories that were popular among broad readerships of magazines generally, not merely *Minzhu yu fazhi*. From the list of first-prize winners one contestant's name stood out: Fan Xiaolan was the only winner who did not work in the judicial and public security apparatus or in the party-state apparatus and the only winner with no apparent higher schooling. One of the few female first-prize winners, Fan was an ordinary worker in Wuxi City's No. 2 Wool-Spinning and Dyeing Factory.

Because she was a woman and not highly educated, Fan's success in the contest made for an excellent human-interest piece that fulfilled all the requirements of a Mao Era model story. He Wannan, the author of the article, presented Fan Xiaolan's participation in the contest as an extraordinary story born out of the ordinariness of everyday life in a post-Cultural Revolution urban factory. Thirty-one *sui*, thirty years old in Western counting, Fan had only completed a junior middle school education. To notify her of her successful participation in the contest, the magazine editorial board sent a telegram to her work unit, which simply read: "Fan Xiaolan has won a first prize in the Legal Knowledge Study Contest. Quickly send two half-body photos. The *Minzhu yu fazhi* Editorial Board."[97] When her workshop leader handed her the telegram and asked what it was all about, she was completely taken by surprise. We are told that Fan's co-workers and her boss could hardly believe that she could have won a first prize in anything.

Readers soon learned why Fan, an unlikely winner, could be successful. It was, as might have been expected, an achievement born out of self-motivation and self-discipline, but also one resulting from a supportive family. Years before the contest her father-in-law, a former shipyard worker, had been influential in Fan's decision to learn much more about the law. He had lost part of his privately owned home during the Cultural Revolution. This meant that he and his family lived in a tiny room, with little space for his son and daughter-in-law. After the end of the Cultural Revolution, having read a copy of the 1978 constitution and learned that citizens' legal property should be protected, he set out to regain what was rightfully his. He spent two years writing to, petitioning, and then suing those he felt were responsible for the loss of his property. Eventually the property he had lost was returned to him, and other people started looking to him for legal advice on how to regain property that had been seized during the Cultural Revolution. Inspired by his story, Fan Xiaolan herself became interested in the law during the early 1980s and, so the article's author proudly informed readers, was quickly an ardent subscriber to *Minzhu yu fazhi*. In middle school she excelled at one-minute legal knowledge competitions in the classroom. Soon, she and her family had become "law fans."[98] She owned a Xinhua Bookstore subscription, which gave her access to the newest law propaganda materials hot off the press. Her home was filled with laws and books explaining the Criminal Law, Marriage Law, Inheritance Law, and Civil Law.[99]

Fan Xiaolan, as a prize winner, would contribute to changing the destiny of her work unit at large. Her story therefore made her a representative not merely of individual improvement, but also of social change at large. The factory in which she worked was renowned for its criminal elements and for its poor transition out of revolutionary turmoil. The article described the work unit and its workers as "Blind to the law, ah, tragically blind to the law!"[100] Following a municipal survey of criminal activity in Wuxi's factories, in which the No. 2 Wool-Spinning and Dyeing Factory performed poorly, the factory leadership set out to raise its workers' legal consciousness. Trips to legal knowledge exhibitions, more political study of the law, and regular information columns on factory grounds gave everyone plenty of opportunities to learn and self-improve. With Fan's dedication to her work unit, so He Wannan told readers, they all would soon leave the realm of those blind to the law.

The editorial board of *Minzhu yu fazhi* decided to continue these contests and organized a second one at the end of 1985.[101] Anyone interested in reading all the questions and answers from the first contest could find these in a freshly published booklet. The second contest allowed for many more winners: in total there would be 300 winners and 5,000 commemorative prizes. The format worked well for the magazine and brought new readers to a publication that had, before 1985, struggled to keep up with a publishing field undergoing decisive shifts in readership and readers' demands. Because they emphasized rote learning over critical thinking, yet still actively involved people in legal learning, contests exemplified the ideal legally informed citizen. He or she was studious, dedicated, and supportive of the future vision defined by Party Central, and at the same time able to recognize and reject any violations of the law committed by local party and government cadres that jeopardized this vision.

Contests remained popular, and they were also useful from a law propaganda perspective.[102] In 1987, *Guangming ribao* and the national Trade Union organized a legal knowledge contest for workers, involving a reported thirty million people across the country. Zhang Youyu handed the one hundred first-prize winners their awards and certificates in a national ceremony held in the Great Hall of the People in Beijing.[103] A few years later, following the violent quelling of protests in both Beijing and Shanghai in spring 1989, districts used contests as part of "constitution propaganda" weeks and events designed to use legal knowledge as way of pacifying society in the aftermath of the national protests. In December 1989 alone, Shanghai's Xuhui District organized fifty-five constitutional knowledge competitions with more than seven hundred participants.[104]

## Conclusion: Silent Brothers-in-Law

Despite the continuous call for people to learn laws of their own volition, legal knowledge contests demonstrated that voluntary learning had to be accompanied by didacticism and top-down structured teaching. Winning a contest involved not only factual knowledge, but also the ability to use legal language and formulations correctly. A winner had to be the kind of citizen who would represent the ideal legal learning story—one of acquisition of standardized legal language and knowledge of how to understand and use this language.

Official formulations, once party propaganda authorities approved them, glued together law propaganda and appeared on blackboards, in the press, and on radio and television. Formulations emphasized that people should "learn law, understand law, enforce law" (*xue fa, dong fa, zhi fa*),[105] that cadres and ordinary people alike should "respect discipline, abide by laws" (*zun ji shou fa*), and that "laws must be followed, law implementation must be strict, violations of law must be punished."[106] Despite this extraordinary effort at standardization and simplification, legal language was perhaps even more difficult to control than any other kind of official terminology. The ideal legally-informed citizen was at once a political asset and a potential problem. He or she was a person who might help maintain order—or who might reveal the weaknesses of the government and party and know how to frame them in the officially endorsed language of law and morality. The CCP's claim to scientific laws enabled and yet complicated law propaganda work.

By the mid-1980s, China was one of many socialist countries that actively conducted law propaganda. In the course of the late 1970s and 1980s, law propaganda had become a common solution to the dilemmas of socialist rule globally. That the legal systems of the PRC and the Soviet Union seemed more similar than the media were allowed to admit during the early 1980s was already clear to people during the 1982 constitution discussion. One factory worker, for example, had asked what exactly was the difference between the PRC proclaiming that all power belonged to the people, on the one hand, and the Soviet Union's all-people's state, on the other.[107] The worker could not know that people in the Soviet Union and the GDR were asking similar questions about the structure of the state and the role that laws played.[108] No matter whether it was the PRC, the Soviet Union, the GDR, Poland, Hungary, or other socialist regimes, they all felt compelled to justify continued one-party rule as both necessary and logical. At the same time, party leaders struggled to explain why the state continued to control people while promising that eventually the state would become obsolete. In this context, the socialist state as the guarantor and enabler of laws that made possible safety, happiness, and prosperity was not merely a trope commonly found in Chinese newspapers and magazines but an element of a larger perception management campaign for socialism internationally.[109]

In the socialist bloc, law and law propaganda were part of the Cold War systemic competition.[110] Challenged by Western countries for their lack of rule of law and for being "unlawful" dictatorships, socialist countries were on the defensive by the 1970s, trying hard to prove their legitimate claims to sovereignty and national rule.[111] Western liberal jurisprudence during this time argued that rule of law, political freedoms, human rights, and independent judiciaries were hallmarks of a liberal democracy.[112] They called for laws to be as independent of state interference as possible. In contrast, socialist countries argued that Western jurisprudence furthered bourgeois interests and that socialist jurisprudence guaranteed social and economic rights and accessible legislation for all.[113] Socialist laws required a strong party and government to ensure that laws served ordinary people and protected more than bourgeois interests. Similar to the CCP, the regimes in Eastern Europe and the Soviet Union argued that the only way to guarantee that laws were in the interest of the people was for laws to be responsive, simple, and under the constant control of the party-state. Law propaganda was needed to help socialist citizens see that laws existed because the socialist state passed them, and rights existed because of the Communist Party, not independent of it. Survival of the party, so the logic went, guaranteed the existence of rights.[114]

As in China, the two ideals of the "law-abiding citizen" and "legal consciousness" frequently appeared in the propaganda and internal discussions of many socialist countries. In 1970, Leonid Brezhnev issued a directive outlining measures to improve workers' knowledge of the law.[115] A good legal understanding would raise work discipline, productivity, and the quality of economic products. Brezhnev emphasized that promoting a "law-abiding" population would also give each citizen a feeling of legal security and state protection under the law. This was only possible if citizens were able to identify and abide by laws in their everyday lives.[116] In 1975, law propaganda and the molding of "law-abiding citizens" was the topic of a special meeting convened in Budapest at which ministers and deputy ministers of justice of the Soviet Union, GDR, Hungary, Romania, Bulgaria, Poland, Cuba, the Democratic Republic of Vietnam, and the People's Republic of Mongolia participated.[117] The GDR in particular argued for comprehensive law propaganda, by which it meant law propaganda not only for individual laws but for all laws. The GDR's minister of justice told his colleagues in Budapest: "We are aware that it can no longer suffice to limit legal education and law propaganda to a few areas of law or to certain fora. In the development of state consciousness and legal consciousness we have achieved good results wherever all forms, means, and methods of politico-ideological work were harmoniously aligned with each other and were employed according to political tasks."[118] In the same year, the newly published GDR *Dictionary on the Socialist State* (Wörterbuch zum Sozialistischen Staat) defined "law propaganda" as a distinct category within propaganda:

> Law propaganda is the systematic dissemination and thorough explanation of legal principles and concrete legal norms, which gives workers insights into the GDR's legal order and speaks to their emotions, so that they consciously receive socialist law. Law propaganda is a specific aspect

of Marxist-Leninist propaganda and an integral component of socialist human leadership. The Marxist-Leninist party attributes great importance to it.[119]

The desire to "speak to people's emotions" linked Chinese law propaganda work with other international socialist projects of the kind. Commentary on learning laws and dictionary entries such as the above showed the central importance of emotional engagement and active participation in living the law. As in China, an enormous amount of time and effort was redirected to garner support for laws. In the Soviet Union, the Komsomol, High Court, Ministry of Internal Affairs, State Procuratorate, Ministry of Culture, Ministry of People's Education, the law institutes, radio, television, and other media organizations all cooperated to produce law propaganda.[120] A magazine called *Man and Law* was published with a print run of three million copies per issue. In Poland, the weekly magazine *Law and Life* circulated widely, and there were numerous cooperative ventures between the party and state media to create popular programs about law.[121] Polish state authorities organized national symposia on civic legal consciousness.[122] Hungary and Mongolia focused on legal education in schools, universities, and vocational schools.[123] In East Germany the department of law propaganda at the Ministry of Justice collaborated with writers, artists, and broadcasters to develop radio programs, periodicals, and television shows.[124] On Radio GDR, people could listen to programs titled "Elements of a Crime" ("Tatbestand") or "Your Law / Your Right" ("Dein Recht").[125] State TV channels broadcast informational programs about marriage and family law such as "She and He and 1,000 Questions" ("Sie und Er und 1000 Fragen") or about questions of criminal, civil, family, and labor law in "The State Prosecutor Speaks" ("Der Staatsanwalt hat das Wort").[126] In 1985, the CCP regime could pursue its five-year plan for the popularization of law in the knowledge that law propaganda was an established mode of governance with a record of maintaining socialist rule internationally—at least until 1989 when this legal and political system began to unravel in Europe.

# Conclusion

## A History of Legal Dilemmas

As a policy, the popularization of legal knowledge developed at different moments in the history of the PRC, though this was by no means a linear development of any kind. Many different people were involved in teaching laws, making sense of laws, and developing propaganda materials. Throughout parts of the four decades analyzed here, people coped with a legal lexicon in constant political motion. Some of the terms in this lexicon were familiar yet meant new things. Some of the terms were entirely unfamiliar, even if CCP officials had been at pains to find terms they thought everyone would understand. People, moreover, contended with dichotomies of "correct" and "erroneous" on paper that did not necessarily map onto their everyday lives. And, no matter whether they worked for state authorities or not, people repeatedly had to deal with official demands to abide by laws even as the meanings of laws seemed to change over time and depending on who was speaking on behalf of "the state." Party and government authorities, meanwhile, sought out ways to cast what people actually knew about laws within more carefully outlined frameworks of CCP ideology, policy, and Communist morality. Legal knowledge was made to fit political categories, some of which were newly devised and not suited to the complex manner in which people across the country actually understood laws.

The story of this book ends in the late 1980s because the year 1989 was an important turning point for socialist law, in China and internationally. Only a few years earlier, in the mid-1980s, law propaganda was still all the government rage in the socialist world. In 1985, cosmopolitan socialist travelers could have picked up copies of a Polish *Law and Life* magazine in Warsaw or they would have come across discussions of law on the radio in Budapest, law cartoons in Sofia, or the TV shows *Police Alert 110* ("Polizeiruf 110") in East Berlin and *Man and the Law* ("Chelovek i zakon") in Moscow. Chinese citizens may not have known this at first, but when they perused law propaganda pamphlets, read about law in the pages of *Zhongguo fazhi bao*, *Minzhu yu fazhi*, or *Falu yu shenghuo*, visited law exhibitions across the country, or walked past propaganda notice boards in their work units, they came across similar explanations for why they should study law as people in East Berlin, Warsaw, Moscow, Budapest, and Sofia. For most of the 1980s, then, the socialist legal world appeared stable to many domestic and foreign observers alike. Law in these socialist countries had advanced structurally and theoretically in ways that suggested it would remain an international legal vision of some import for years to come.[1] Socialist countries, be they the Soviet Union, China, or the German Democratic Republic, were actively involved in the United Nations, participated in international legal discussions, wrote elaborate legal codes, and were establishing new legal systems to allow citizens more options for legal redress. They were also repressive regimes with extra-legal forms of punishment, prison and reform through labor camps, and advanced forms of citizen surveillance, all of which had become a core component of their rule.

To the shock and surprise of many, this legal world unexpectedly unraveled in the early 1990s. Yet some of its legacies survive today, particularly in China. Let us return briefly to the year 1989, to trace the expected and unanticipated roles law dissemination played in China and in East Germany, the two countries that would come to define the "global moment" of 1989.[2] The famous suppression of protests in China in the spring was followed by the fall of the Berlin Wall in the autumn, and then the slow collapse of the socialist bloc in the wake of the dissolution of the GDR. Behind the curtains of these momentous events, the year also spelled the end to a series of conversations that Chinese legal experts, government officials, and party leaders had been developing with their socialist counterparts since the mid-1980s. In some of their conversations, recorded in East German documents, party leaders in China had remarked that their early explorations of Western legal systems showed clearly that in certain respects Western law was a poor fit for socialist China's needs. Laws that defined the party-state's relation to its citizens, the role of citizens, state security, and prison systems, for example, could all benefit more from talks with socialist legal colleagues.[3] Conversations also included questions of how to conduct good law propaganda. In April 1989, Wan Li, Chairman of the National People's Congress Standing Committee, mentioned that he was impressed with the GDR's ability to maintain political stability. Procurator-General of the Supreme People's Court Liu Fuzhi, worried about the upcoming anniversary of the May Fourth protests, emphasized that he was prepared to uphold the law and to use force to secure political stability and the protection of China's laws.[4] As late as 22 May, the Minister of Justice, Cai Cheng, visited East Berlin for talks about a legal aid agreement in civil and criminal matters.[5] The talks could not be concluded until later because, as the GDR conversation minutes mention, "The Minister had not received the necessary authorization in time because of the most recent events in the PRC."[6]

In the course of the year, the GDR and PRC Communist regimes became brothers-in-law in unanticipated ways. Both countries faced a wave of popular protests that brought together a broad group of intellectuals, students, workers, and local party-state members in seemingly unlikely unions, calling for their socialist governments to live up to the promises enshrined in their countries' fundamental laws.[7] Many of those who joined the protests in China were neither looking for substantial political change nor to depose the socialist system; they were asking party leaders to address the social inequalities resulting from the recent economic reforms.[8] What happened in China then had a bearing on the way East German protesters understood their protests, as they linked their own activities to those of the protesters suppressed in China. Some East German citizens admonished their government for even considering any cooperation with a regime such as that in China, referencing in particular the legal agreements East Germany and China were seeking to conclude. The West German newspaper *Die Welt*, for instance, reported in late September 1989: "In East Berlin opposition forces are climbing onto the rooftops in the Prenzlauer Berg. With whistles, pot hitting, and rattling water pots they are demonstrating against the 'lawless law enforcement agreement' between the GDR and China."[9] While the Chinese government declared martial law and violently suppressed the protests, the GDR government chose not to declare martial law, and the protests resulted in the opening of the borders and the beginning of a process that would lead to German reunification and the end of socialist rule in East Germany.

Protesters challenged the regimes using the language of law, and the regimes responded to protesters using the language of the law. In China, protests were framed as the activities of a few counterrevolutionary elements who were failing to obey laws. In late May 1989, with the protests at Tian'anmen Square ongoing, Peng Zhen spoke at a forum of the non-party deputy committee heads of the seventh National People's Congress Standing Committee. Peng explained that the protesting students "are not familiar or not very familiar with the law" and he warned that it was essential to use the constitution and law to unify thinking in order to avoid a repetition of the "chaos" of the Cultural Revolution, with all of its "lawlessness."[10] Bourgeois liberalization was a "violation of law." An individual's constitutional rights, expressed in Article 35, to freedom of travel and demonstration should not be wantonly interpreted outside the context of the constitution's Article 51, which stipulated that "Citizens of the People's Republic of China, in exercising their freedoms and rights, may not infringe upon the interests of the State, of society, or of the collective, or upon the lawful freedoms and rights of other citizens." This was, he explained, an example of people who spoke of the legal system, but who themselves "trampled" over the constitution and laws.[11]

Party-state officials in China and East Germany were challenged on the terms they themselves had taught their citizens. Protesters and officials both claimed the authority to interpret the law "correctly" and argued that they were abiding by laws. Abiding by the law had always been a multivalent term, and the protests as well as the official responses sharply mirrored this ambiguity. I do not mean to argue that law propaganda led to the protests or that learning about the laws during the 1980s led all people to protest for their rights in 1989 and then led to the tragic clampdown on the protests. But in seeking to understand the role that knowledge of the constitution and belief in the constitution may have played during these events, we need to account for state-directed activities in the systematic popularization of legal knowledge, at least as of the mid-1980s.

Globally, the PRC remained one of a few countries with a Communist party-state after the fall of European socialism. Although the 1990s saw the continuation of the CCP's broad engagement with laws in non-socialist countries, it also continued some of the legacy of what had once been a wider socialist vision for law dissemination. In spring 1991, the government regime announced a second five-year plan for law popularization. If the first five-year plan had been designed as an ointment to treat the scars left by the Cultural Revolution, the second five-year plan tried to lead Chinese society swiftly away from the fateful events of spring 1989.

## The Laws of PRC History

Studies of laws in China since 1949 have often remarked that laws existed on paper but their implementation was irregular or non-existent. Indeed, throughout these decades it was common for laws to be honored only in the breach, and for several years during the early Cultural Revolution the entire legal system came to a grinding halt. This book does not question these findings. I suggest instead that adding to the focus on lawmaking and the practical application of laws, the perspective of their study and dissemination reveals some of the social and cultural processes by which laws were formalized as an instrument of party-state power, albeit a difficult one to command. This history has important implications for how we make sense of what people knew about laws and what they did with this knowledge. It suggests new perspectives on the history of laws as they were applied, ignored, contested, debated, and otherwise engaged with.

Following the establishment of the PRC in 1949, party and government worked to make laws more accessible. It transferred much formal legal responsibility to non-professionals with little if any expertise in laws. And it tried to give state authorities more influence over people's legal interpretations. Taken together, these three changes led, first, to wide and active dissemination of laws and, second, to ever more anxious officials in the central government who determined that if laws had to be disseminated, then they wanted to ensure that laws were understood "correctly." The dilemma of CCP rule was simple and yet difficult to solve: the desire for more control over how people understood laws meant that information about laws would have to be widely disseminated. Wide dissemination, however, gave more people than ever before a chance to engage with laws and to judge the practical application of laws against the CCP's promises. To make sense of this dilemma, this book has examined how the CCP regime was involved in shaping what people heard, read, and saw about laws, rather than what people actually knew about laws. People did not solely learn about laws from state sources, to be sure. Law propaganda was one of many ways in which people encountered laws. Hearsay, gossip, and personal experiences played at least as important a role. However, bringing state educational efforts back into the mix of how we study popular legal knowledge helps to understand how and why laws have mattered at different times in the history of modern China.

I have taken two approaches to examining law propaganda. First, I traced the popularization of laws across the 1978 divide that separates the Mao period from the years following Mao's death. Looking at the longue durée of law dissemination highlights developments over time that would have been difficult to see otherwise: the reconfiguration of consciousness, the return of similar educational techniques, and the return of common problems of how to create "correct" propaganda to explain laws. But there were also noticeable changes: the scientific turn of laws, the increasingly top-down didactic approach to law propaganda, the changing role of class in learning about laws, and the move to expand the catalogue of laws that citizens should be aware of. Above all, this long-term approach to law propaganda reveals that despite long periods in which there was less or no systematic dissemination of law, for example during the late 1960s and the first half of the 1970s, the developments of the early 1950s left an important legacy that the CCP regime assumed after 1978. It shows the dissemination of laws during the early 1950s to be at once a useful repository of past experiences for post-1978 party rule, and a deeply problematic past in which laws, knowledge of laws, and class struggle were linked in a way that no longer suits the current historical narrative of socialist China's path toward the rule of law.

Second, I examined the popularization of laws as a practice that was both Chinese and transnational. The concept that laws should be made widely accessible and easy to learn can be found in the Qing period and earlier. It developed fully during the early twentieth century when international civil law influences on Chinese law from Germany, Switzerland, Japan, and the Soviet Union also transformed how intellectuals and politicians conceptualized the demand that citizens should know the law. Popularizing laws the way the CCP did was neither a clear Soviet import nor was it uniquely Chinese, though the Chinese government after 1949 was unusual—at least for a while—in the extent to which it mobilized people for legal learning.

The methods and practices of law popularization thus mirrored the diversity of agents involved, including government officials, politicians, legal experts, and especially cultural workers and propaganda authorities. Of course, government officials, politicians, and legal experts are standard protagonists of legal history. Other protagonists, in particular cultural workers, propaganda officials, and propaganda workers, also shaped PRC legal history. Cultural production's role in mediating ideas about laws during the imperial and Republican periods has been explored extensively. Yet so far the break at 1949 implicitly suggests that any cultural products on laws thereafter were unified and fairly uncontested, though they were neither. I have tried to describe the diverse role of cultural workers in the cultural history of law during the Mao period and beyond. Cultural production was perhaps the most contested field of law dissemination in the PRC, often simply because cultural workers had exactly the same problems trying to make sense of laws as did the "ordinary citizens" at the grassroots level whose opinions the historian of socialist China seeks to discover.

Bringing cultural workers into the history of PRC law propaganda highlights the need to account for the transmission process of legal knowledge and the role of the media. The media were a crucial link between formal lawmaking, on the one hand, and people and their responses, on the other. Questioning the channels by which information about law was disseminated, the modes and nodes of communication, and the techniques of collecting people's responses are all methods that help to connect lawmaking and popular responses. It shows that the close involvement of the "propaganda apparatus" in the dissemination of law is part of the "revolutionary legal tradition" in China today.[12]

Giving space to the perspective of propaganda authorities and cultural workers further helps to avoid writing the history of legal knowledge dissemination along what Stephen Kotkin has called the "single axis of repression and enthusiasm."[13] The dissemination of law often caused great anxiety and even terrorized people. This is a crucial part of the story. Yet a focus on enthusiasm and repression risks losing sight of how extraordinary the CCP regime's attempt to disseminate individual laws in such an intense way was for almost all residents in Beijing and Shanghai who were involved, no matter whether they were government officials or party officials, cadres, workers or intellectuals, men or women, young or old. It sometimes confused people and sometimes made them anxious, hopeful, or fearful; it both pleased and annoyed them at different times and for different reasons. How they responded had as much to do with their personal circumstances as with their opinion of the CCP regime.

If the axis of repression and enthusiasm is a poor analytical fit for law dissemination, then so is the axis of success and failure. A history of law dissemination cannot determine what successful legal knowledge dissemination would even look like. Would law dissemination have failed if someone jaywalked? Or could it be classified as a success if the person who jaywalked did so but later regretted it, knowing that they had broken the law? To emphasize Mary Gallagher's point, legal consciousness does not rise or fall.[14] It is not possible to determine whether law dissemination failed or succeeded. It depends entirely on perspective. To echo Luo Liang's point about propaganda, one man's law dissemination success is another's failure.[15] At the same time, it is instructive to historicize the axis of success and failure, as this provides a valuable lens into how party-state officials perceived law dissemination. The CCP constantly searched for categories that could help to define success or failure in legal learning as it searched for "correct" and "erroneous" explanations, knowledge, behavior, and consciousness. This search for clear-cut categories shaped the history of law dissemination throughout the period covered in this book.

## Socialist Characteristics?

Explicitly and implicitly, this book has explored how the methods of and approach to law propaganda in Communist China compared with the dissemination of laws during the Republican and imperial periods, on the one hand, and with law propaganda as practiced in other socialist countries, on the other. Was there anything particularly "socialist" or "Chinese" about the CCP party-state's approach to popularizing law? The chapters in this book only provide fragmentary answers, but these may be indicative for future research on China's legal history after 1949.

Party and government, propaganda authorities, local officials, and ordinary citizens alike called law propaganda "socialist." For this reason I have used the term as well. Party cadres, political scientists, and jurists, especially those who advocated and helped devise law propaganda, sought to distinguish what they were doing from non-socialist countries. They claimed that the dissemination of accessible legal knowledge in this way was unique to socialism. To them, socialist citizens could enjoy this advantage because the socialist state bestowed rights onto citizens and took the time to help them learn laws. According to the people who designed and conducted law propaganda, and even to many of its recipients, it was and remains a socialist practice.

Beyond this subjective perspective, it is more difficult to explain what—if anything—made law dissemination in China socialist. Disseminating laws per se was certainly not a socialist or authoritarian practice. Compared to the early modern and medieval ages, modern states globally have been more active in making laws systematically accessible to their polities.[16] After World War II, European liberal-democratic countries and the United States, for example, launched efforts to disseminate laws. They seemingly followed in the footsteps of Thomas Hobbes, who had argued that the state had to make laws accessible to people if it expected people to inform themselves of their civic duties and abide by laws.[17] Liberal-democratic countries published laws, made leaflets and copies of laws available to citizens in public libraries, included some of them in school books for civic education, taught children and adults about laws ranging from traffic rules to the constitution, and championed the sanctity of the rule of law and the importance of abiding by laws in general. In post-war Western liberal-democratic states, moreover, the private entertainment sector promoted popular legal learning, largely but certainly not always independent of state interference. Legal self-help guides sold well in Europe and the United States, and the entertainment sector made a fortune from popular TV programs and films about people going to court, law enforcement, and "law and order."[18] In its early form, this was the system that civic education in China during the Republican period replicated to some extent when it demanded obedience to the law, included basic legal knowledge in textbooks and civic educational materials, but also allowed a growing commercial publishing industry to assume a large share of the task of explaining laws to a diverse and fragmented polity.[19]

Liberal-democratic states, however, had to be much more careful about how they involved themselves in citizens' legal learning. Neither post-war West Germany, nor the United Kingdom, nor the United States, for example, developed anything comparable to Communist China's law propaganda sector. To do so would have challenged one of the basic premises of the "rule of law": that politics should be independent of and supervised by laws. Making laws accessible through civic education and written materials was acceptable, but there were continuous debates about where the limits to state involvement should be. At least in theory, government authorities should not interfere excessively in citizens' decisions about how and when they learned about laws. We can trace changing ideas about how much state involvement is necessary, desirable, and permissible, in the history of civic education in different countries and over time, both in textbooks and by following the enthusiasm and unease of different governments to assume the task of informing citizens about laws.

As the party of the People, the CCP, by contrast, understood it to be its task to actively and visibly structure the dissemination of laws and educate people. The story of state-directed law dissemination in the PRC as told in the chapters of this book thus emphasizes five connected aspects that make law propaganda in China between 1949 and 1989 noteworthy: the explicit connection of law and politics, the levels of engagement expected, the techniques by which legal learning was conducted and encouraged, the spaces designated for learning, and the role of the state in devising the techniques of learning and in permeating the spaces of engagement with laws. Socialist law propaganda was designed to create and fortify the link between state, law, and citizens. Party-state authorities did not merely claim to protect laws and rights; they claimed that these rights would only be possible for as long as the socialist state was in place to protect them. Learning laws in China after 1949 thus involved much more than simply knowing the content of laws. To learn, know, and understand laws was a process of building political consciousness and a sign of loyalty to the socialist state that was presented as the embodiment of the People. Whenever the CCP regime decided to emphasize the importance of laws, abiding by laws could be read as a sign of loyalty and correct consciousness. Behavior felt to be wanting by anyone in power, at the grassroots or nationally, by contrast, could be read as a violation of the constitution and a sign of poor consciousness. This dichotomy opened a grey area for state power that still exists today.

## The Legal Legacy of the Mao Period in Contemporary China

The CCP has maintained law propaganda as a key element of socialist democracy, announcing its seventh five-year plan in 2016.[20] After the initial difficulties of the 1980s, the media adapted and diversified their law propaganda offerings. Daily TV shows such as *Legal Report* (*Jinri shuofa*) now give viewers a thirty-minute update on legal developments and stories. Online games and cartoons for learning laws are supposed to make study fun. A plethora of newspapers and periodicals with legal information and a battery of legal advice and self-help books try to provide reliable information about what laws are, what they mean, and how they should be employed.[21] Many of these media products have become quite engaging, and as Stockmann and Gallagher note, they are "satisfying and attractive to an average reader."[22]

The basic educational premise of law propaganda in China today shares many similarities with its Mao Era and early Reform Era precursors. The government continues to take a strong interest in the kind of legal knowledge its citizens acquire and how they use it, though it wavers between stronger and weaker efforts at the popularization of law at different moments. On 4 December 2014, for example, the People's Republic of China celebrated "constitution day" to commemorate the promulgation of the 1982 constitution and the sixtieth anniversary of the 1954 constitution. Much state-sponsored publicity promoted study of the constitution and, once again, citizens' duty to abide by the constitution. Xinhua News Agency published an image titled "Everyone Abides by Laws," which depicted the constitution as a thick red book safely hatched out of an egg that is gently held by a woman's hands. Photographs circulated on the Internet showing school pupils parading a larger-than-life cardboard constitution book and professing their determination to abide by state laws and the constitution. These images suggest that no matter how contested constitutionalism remains today, people should remember that the constitution as a material manifestation continues to be something to hold, protect, and cherish.[23]

If state-sanctioned legal knowledge dissemination has continued to be a strong presence in people's lives, law, justice, crime, and morality, too, have remained exceedingly popular topics. Cultural producers, be they commercial, state, official, unofficial, or something that defies all these clear-cut categories, continue to play a crucial role mitigating what people see, hear, learn, and know about laws. The clash between laws on paper, laws in application, and moral questions of right and wrong manifests in talks everywhere—from news and social media to books and films— about the way the state and the legal system handle legal disputes, accidents, homicides, corruption, and so on. Already in 1992, only a few years after the protests in 1989 and two years into the second five-year plan for the popularization of laws, Zhang Yimou's film *The Story of Qiu Ju* (*Qiu Ju da guan si*) famously questioned the relation between law, justice, the individual, and the collective over time. Qiu Ju, a woman willing to fight for justice for her family, takes her claim all the way to the higher courts, where she is ultimately faced with the dilemma that the person from whom she claims justice in the end comes through in unexpected ways. The law eventually acts on behalf of Qiu Ju, and the man she accused is arrested. Although things are made right by the requirements of the written law, however, Qiu Ju does not feel justice is served because in the end she has decided that she would rather he not be arrested. Her feeling of what is right and wrong is situational, while the law in that moment is not.

Seeing law propaganda not solely as a post-1978 invention suggests that tensions between law propaganda, enforcement of laws, social morality, and people's concepts of justice developed not only as a result of market liberalization or the breakdown of a Maoist order. They are anchored more deeply in the basic premises of socialist governance. This raises new questions, which this book cannot answer. How do law propaganda and ideas of justice overlap? What were some of the long-term social effects of law propaganda for individuals and families across the diverse regions of China and across different historical periods? Perceptions of justice are as complex and fragmented as patterns of identification, but taking law seriously as one factor that shaped Chinese socialism since 1949 can open up new perspectives on the history of how law dissemination mattered to different people, in different places, and at different times, and how it shaped what they understood socialism to be or not to be over time.

In contemporary China, meanwhile, the call to "abide by laws" remains omnipresent. To abide by laws is to be patriotic. In Beijing's and Shanghai's streets and alleyways, cardboard signs stuck in flower-pots, on patches of grass on sidewalks, or on the outer walls of residential compounds and houses remind passers-by to be civilized (*wenming*), abide by laws, and pay attention to the rule of law (*fazhi*). On public transport and at stations, posters and short movies instruct passengers in orderly and law-abiding behavior. In bookstores, the sections on law offer customers a range of legal self-help books, little red pocket-sized books that contain the full text of different laws, and other educational materials. Many people read and buy them. Many people ridicule them. Most have become accustomed to this kind of legal information as part of their daily lives. No matter how individuals engage with law propaganda, its continued presence is a reminder of a legal dilemma that the Chinese government is still grappling with today.

# Notes

## Introduction

1  NBCK, no. 171, 31 July 1954, 522.
2  The historiography of the Mao period is too expansive to cite here. Recent book-length studies that have been widely discussed include, for example: Brown, *City Versus Countryside*; Brown and Johnson, *Maoism at the Grassroots*; Brown and Pickowicz, *Dilemmas of Victory*; Eyferth, *Eating Rice from Bamboo Roots*; Hershatter, *The Gender of Memory*; Leese, *Mao Cult*; MacFarquhar and Schoenhals, *Mao's Last Revolution*; Perry, *Anyuan*; Schoenhals, *Spying for the People*; Walder, *China under Mao*; and Zheng Wang, *Finding Women in the State*. Most studies examining the early 1950s mention the PRC's major laws, and many also talk about drives to implement these laws. Few, however, see this kind of legal-knowledge dissemination as pertinent to understanding the Mao period more generally. The legal history of this period is often dealt with at more or less length in studies on contemporary PRC law, e.g., Lubman, *Bird in a Cage*; Peerenboom, *China's Long March toward Rule of Law*; and Potter, *From Leninist Discipline to Socialist Legalism*.
3  A comprehensive Civil Code and Criminal Code existed in multiple drafts but never came into force. See Potter, *From Leninist Discipline to Socialist Legalism*, 71.
4  Following Schoenhals, I translate *renmin* as the People (with a capital "P"). The term does not refer to ordinary people in general, but rather to the political category of "the People" within CCP discourse. I will use the term non-People for anyone who was designated as not part of the People, including reactionaries, enemies, the landlord classes, and the bureaucrat-bourgeoisie. (Schoenhals, "Demonising Discourse," 466). The relevance of this distinction to law dissemination is explained in the section on "Law and the Socialist State" in this introduction.
5  For a historical account of the Mao Era built entirely on the concept of "lawlessness" see Ladany, *Law and Legality in China*. For a criticism of this approach see

Zhang Ning, "Political Origins of Death Penalty Exceptionalism." The prevalence of "lawlessness" as a paradigm in studies of Soviet law is addressed in Burbank, "Lenin and the Law."

6  The irony that dissemination of legal knowledge results in people knowing more about law and using this knowledge to contend with state authority has been noted for contemporary China in Alford, "Double-edged Swords Cut Both Ways."

7  I have adopted the phrasing of law as product and practice from Van der Burg, *The Dynamics of Law and Morality*, 21–22.

8  The pluralist legal order of Qing China is discussed in Cassel, *Grounds of Judgment*; Li Chen, *Chinese Law in Imperial Eyes*; Svarverud, *International Law as World Order in Late Imperial China*; and Ruskola, *Legal Orientalism*.

9  Xu Xiaoqun, *Trial of Modernity*, 25–83. See also Philip C. C. Huang, *Code, Custom and Legal Practice in China*, 49–69; and Xu Xiaoqun, "The Fate of Judicial Independence in Republican China."

10  For a Chinese overview of China's legal history see Zhang and Han Yanlong, *Zhongguo geming fazhishi* [A history of China's revolutionary legal system].

11  For example, Bernhardt, *Women and Property in China*; Philip C. C. Huang, *Code, Custom, and Legal Practice in China*; Sommer, *Sex, Law, and Society in Late Imperial China*; Sommer, *Polyandry and Wife-Selling in Qing Dynasty China*; Kuo, *Intolerable Cruelty*; and Zelin, *The Merchants of Zigong*.

12  See, for instance, Kung-Chuan Hsiao, *Rural China*, 185–92; and You Chenjun, *Falü zhishi de wenzi chuanbo* [The written dissemination of legal knowledge].

13  Kung-Chuan Hsiao, *Rural China*, 185–92; de Bary, *Asian Values and Human Rights*, 65–86.

14  Zurndorfer, "Contracts, Property and Litigation," 92.

15  How print materials were used to deal with laws or to study laws is discussed in Bryna Goodman, "'Law Is One Thing'"; and Zarrow, *Educating China*. Culp, *Articulating Citizenship*; and Reed, *Gutenberg in Shanghai*, have illustrated the role of publishing houses in the state's plans for civic education.

16  Kinkley, *Chinese Justice, the Fiction*, 14. Peter Zarrow points out that at the turn of the century Yan Fu, for example, argued against spreading too much knowledge of the law because he feared that this would lead people to find legal loopholes. See Zarrow, *After Empire*, 144–45.

17  For examples of the historiography that traces how people acquired legal knowledge and then used it to file claims, appeal their cases, and seek recourse in the law or, conversely, avoid the law during the imperial and Republican periods, see You Chenjun, *Falü zhishi de wenzi chuanbo*; Zhao Ma, *Runaway Wives*; Kuo, *Intolerable Cruelty*; Lean, *Public Passions*; Ocko, "I'll Take It All the Way to Beijing"; Ransmeier, *Sold People*; and Sommer, *Polyandry and Wife-Selling*.

18  Melissa Macauley, *Social Power and Legal Culture*; on private legal specialists see Li Chen, "Legal Specialists and Judicial Administration"; and Li Chen, "Regulating Private Legal Specialists."

19  Wu Yanhong, "The Community of Legal Experts"; Li Chen, "Zhishi de liliang" [Power of knowledge].

20  Wan, "Court Case Ballads"; Hegel and Carlitz, *Writing and the Law*; Waley-Cohen,

"Politics and the Supernatural in Mid-Qing Legal Culture"; Wu Yanhong, "To Teach and to Entertain."

21  Conner, "Legal Education during the Republican Period"; Tiffert, "The Chinese Judge"; Xu Xiaoqun, *Trial of Modernity*.

22  Lean, *Public Passions*; Bryna Goodman, "'Law Is One Thing.'"

23  Chen and Zelin, "Rethinking Chinese Law and History," 4.

24  In this regard, the CCP regime took a similar approach to Nazi Germany where party authorities also pushed people to dedicate themselves to the laws and emotionally connect with them. See Ecke, "Der Film 'Jud Süß,'" 275.

25  A focus on the dilemmas of socialist rule underlies most of the historiography of the PRC. Some of the book-length studies that have traced these dilemmas include Brown and Pickowicz, *Dilemmas of Victory*; Brown, *City versus Countryside*; Cheek, *Propaganda and Culture in Mao's China*; DeMare, *Mao's Cultural Army*; Dillon, *Radical Inequalities*, 118–91; James Gao, *The Communist Takeover of Hangzhou*; Gross, *Farewell to the God of Plague*, 43–82; Hershatter, *The Gender of Memory*; Perry, *Anyuan*, 153–204; and Smith, *Thought Reform and China's Dangerous Classes*.

26  On the difficulties of legal transition see Tiffert, "An Irresistible Inheritance"; and Tiffert, "Judging Revolution" (unpublished PhD diss., University of California, 2015, cited with the author's permission). For an overview of the group of people who contributed to PRC laws during the 1950s and had studied abroad in earlier decades, see Hao Tiechuan, "Zhongguo jindai faxue liuxuesheng yu fazhi jindaihua" [Modern China's law students who studied abroad and the modernization of the legal system]; and Hao Tiechuan, "Zhongguo jindai faxue liuxuesheng yu xin Zhongguo chuqi da fazhi jianshe" [Modern China's law students who studied abroad and the construction of the legal system in the early years of New China].

27  Burbank, "Lenin and the Law"; Pashukanis, "Lenin and the Problems of Law."

28  Potter, *From Leninist Discipline to Socialist Legalism*, 64–69; Schoenhals, "Demonising Discourse."

29  For a study of this concept of betterment of the criminal through education in the first half of the twentieth century see Kiely, *The Compelling Ideal*.

30  Cohen, "The Party and the Courts"; Strauss, "Morality, Coercion and State Building," 52–54; Mühlhahn, *Criminal Justice in China*, 186–87.

31  Lenin himself had seen "courts as an education weapon of discipline"; see Pashukanis, "Lenin and the Problems of Law." For Lenin, "terror was a means to educate and was a part of law"; see Burbank, "Lenin and the Law," 44. The reality of this practice in China was heavy backlogs and administrative delays. See Tiffert, "An Irresistible Inheritance"; and Cohen, "The Party and the Courts."

32  Studies on the Marriage Law include Croll, *Feminism and Socialism in China*; Croll, *The Politics of Marriage in Contemporary China*; Davin, *Woman-Work*; Diamant, *Revolutionizing the Family*; Diamant, "Re-Examining the Impact"; Glosser, *Chinese Visions of Family*, 167–95; Hershatter, *The Gender of Memory*; Huang Chuanhui, *Tianxia hunyin* [Chinese marriage]; Kay Ann Johnson, *Women, the Family*; Meijer, *Marriage Law and Policy*; Stacey, *Patriarchy and*

*Socialist Revolution in China*; Zheng Wang, *Finding Women in the State*; and Wolf, *Revolution Postponed*. For an overview of other Chinese-language studies of the Marriage Law see Zhu Hongxia, "Xin Zhongguo chengli liushinian lai de hunyinfa yanjiu" [Marriage law research in the sixty years since the founding of New China]; Li Honghe, "Xin Zhongguo chengli chuqi guanche 'hunyinfa' yundong zhong de shehui wenti ji qi jiejue—yi Henan wei zhongxin de lishi kaocha" [Social problems in the implementation of the Marriage Law in Henan Province in the early days of New China and their solution]; and Zhang and Mo, "Xin Zhongguo diyibu 'hunyinfa' xuanchuan yu guanche hunyinfa yundong shulun" [A discussion of the propaganda and implementation campaign of New China's first "Marriage Law"].

33  Most famously, Hinton, *Fanshen*. See also Luo Pinghan, *Tudi gaige yundong shi* [A history of the Land Reform Campaign].

34  Yang Kuisong, "Reconsidering the Campaign to Suppress Counterrevolutionaries"; Strauss, "Paternalist Terror."

35  Zhang Jishun, "Creating 'Masters of the Country'"; Zhang Jishun, *Yuanqu de dushi* [A city displayed], 83–132; Hill, "Voting as a Rite."

36  Cohen, "China's Changing Constitution"; Han Dayuan, *1954 nian xianfa yu xin Zhongguo xianzheng* [The 1954 constitution and New China's constitutionalism]; Li Huayu, "The Political Stalinization of China"; Tiffert, "Epistrophy"; Zhang and Han, *1954 nian xianfa yanjiu* [Research on the 1954 constitution]; Diamant and Feng, "The PRC's First National Critique."

37  This was not the way all legal experts working in the Chinese government (many of whom were not CCP members) saw law, but it was the way propaganda explained laws. For a more discerning study of different legal ideas during the 1950s see Tiffert, "Judging Revolution."

38  Patricia Thornton has traced the role of norms in Chinese state-making in Thornton, *Disciplining the State*, 1–21.

39  Throughout the 1950s and into the 1980s, state documents insisted on what Susan Trevaskes has called the "educative and creative potential of law . . . to create a new 'socialist man'"; see Trevaskes, "Propaganda Work in Chinese Courts," 6.

40  This aspect is briefly mentioned in Victor Li, "The Role of Law in Communist China," 74–80. On the role of morality and normative appeals in regime consolidation see Strauss, "Morality, Coercion, and State Building."

41  Incorporating this language into one's vocabulary became a process akin to "speaking Bolshevik." See Kotkin, *Magnetic Mountain*, 237. "Speaking Bolshevik," however, could be creative in ways unanticipated by those who designed law dissemination. See, for example, Diamant and Feng, "The PRC's First National Critique"; Diamant, *Revolutionizing the Family*; and Zhang Jishun, "Creating 'Masters of the Country.'"

42  Brown and Johnson, "Introduction," in *Maoism at the Grassroots*, 3. On the state-society binary see Perry, "Trends in the Study of Chinese Politics."

43  Schneewind, *Community Schools and the State*, 2.

44  The role of propaganda as educational and a tool to transform the socialist person is discussed in Cheek, "Redefining Propaganda." Pre-1949 GMD practices

of transformation through education are discussed in Fitzgerald, *Awakening China*. I am grateful to Tim Cheek for his advice on this section.

45 Given the centrality of propaganda to CCP ideology and governance, there is a broad field of scholarship on the subject. Julian Chang, "The Mechanics of State Propaganda"; Johnson, "Beneath the Propaganda State"; and Volland, "The Control of the Media," all outline the structure of the "propaganda apparatus" and its internal workings. My study uses the English term "propaganda" to represent the term *xuanchuan* used by the Chinese government at the time. *Xuanchuan* can be translated as propaganda, publicity, or dissemination. As this study shows, law propaganda functioned in all three ways, and they cannot be clearly separated from each other. Rather than changing everything people knew, propaganda, as Aminda Smith has argued for CCP education work in general, was designed to "to elicit voluntary and informed support by providing an interpretive framework through which people could see the 'facts' and 'truths' they already knew in a fresh light" (Smith, *Thought Reform and China's Dangerous Classes*, 99). As Timothy Cheek argues, propaganda should be understood as an attempt "to propagate what one believes to be true" ("Redefining Propaganda," 53). For an institutional and biographical study of propaganda production, see Cheek, *Propaganda and Culture*. For further helpful discussions of the term and practice of "propaganda" and possible analytical pitfalls see Kushner, *The Thought War*, 4; and Mittler, *A Continuous Revolution?*, 3–32. As Luo Liang reminds us, "One man's propaganda is another's declaration of faith or even anthem of freedom." See Liang Luo, *The Avant-garde and the Popular*, 15. For a critical examination of propaganda frameworks in global comparison, see Schoenhals, "The Global War on Terrorism."

46 On the question of how laws are made in the process of writing and why this is a crucial component of the process of lawmaking see the conversation in Unger, "Priorities of Law."

47 Scott, *Seeing Like a State*, 2–7, 72–73.

48 Scott, *Seeing Like a State*; Diamant, "Making Love 'Legible' in China."

49 The work of cultural workers and their engagement with state authorities is traced in Hung, *Mao's New World*.

50 Matthew Johnson, "Beneath the Propaganda State," 207.

51 The term "perception management" is taken from Schoenhals, "Demonising Discourse," 478. The role of official "formulations" as the language of the state that is determined by CCP policy and that shapes how people can and cannot speak in public is discussed in Schoenhals, *Doing Things with Words*; and Schoenhals, "Talk about a Revolution."

52 Eyferth, *Eating Rice from Bamboo Roots*.

53 On the politics of language and the language of politics see, in addition to the works cited above, Link, *An Anatomy of Chinese*, 234–348.

54 Havel, "The Power of the Powerless."

55 Representative studies that offer an assessment of how to understand PRC laws especially in comparison to the US legal tradition include Cohen, *The Criminal Process*; Lubman, *Bird in a Cage*; Peerenboom, *China's Long March toward*

*Law*; Alford, "Law, Law, What Law?"; Alford, "Double-edged Swords Cut Both Ways"; and Alford, "Zhu Qiwu."

56  Seymour, *China*, 99. On the "legal education campaign" of the 1980s see also Exner, "Die Verbreitung der Gesetzeskenntnis unter den Bürgern der VR China."

57  Seymour, *China*, 81–83.

58  On constitution discussions in the Soviet Union during and after Stalin's reign see Nathans, "Soviet Rights-Talk in the Post-Mao Era," 171–73; and Getty, "State and Society under Stalin."

59  Mazower, *Governing the World*; Hoffmann, "Introduction"; Weitz, "Self-determination," 489–96. Jürgen Habermas argues that the juridification ("Verrechtlichung") of the world, which he sees as a global post-war process, belongs to the key criteria of modernity. See Habemas, *Theorie des kommunikativen Handelns*, 522ff.

60  Alford, "Double-edged Swords Cut Both Ways," 46 and 62; Liebman, "Watchdog or Demagogue?"; Leng, *Justice in Communist China*.

61  Steinmetz, "New Perspectives," 46.

62  For a careful analysis of the 1989 protests in the context of modern Chinese history, see Wasserstrom and Perry, *Popular Protest and Political Culture*.

63  Elizabeth Perry argues against an "overly simplistic understanding of the sources of support for the contemporary Communist state." See Perry, *Anyuan*, 291. On the different meanings of law in contemporary China see the essays in Diamant, Lubman, and O'Brien, eds., *Engaging the Law in China*. Kevin O'Brien and Lianjiang Li have uncovered the complex ways people make use of legal knowledge to claim rights; see O'Brien and Li, *Rightful Resistance*.

64  Cohen, "China's Changing Constitution," 832. On freedoms in Chinese history see Kirby (ed.), *Realms of Freedom*.

65  On legal education see Conner, "Legal Education during the Republican Period," and Conner, "Lawyers and the Legal Profession." On legal professionalism see Xu Xiaoqun, *Chinese Professionals*; idem, *Trial of Modernity*; and Qian Qinfa, *Haipai da lüshi* [Famous Shanghai lawyers]. See also Asen, *Death in Beijing*, for a study of the development of legal forensics in China, and Zhao Ma, *Runaway Wives*, for a social history of law in Beijing.

66  On the category of "closed"/internal sources see Hsiao and Cheek, "Open and Closed Media," 76–88; and Schoenhals, "Elite Information in China."

67  For recent historical studies that work extensively with such internal materials see, for example, Diamant and Feng, "The PRC's First National Critique"; Leese, *Mao Cult*; and Schoenhals, *Spying for the People*.

68  Hershatter, *The Gender of Memory*, 4 and 26–27.

# Chapter 1

1  Tiffert, "An Irresistible Inheritance," 85; Xiong, "Feichu 'liufa quanshu' de yuanyou ji yingxiang" [The reasons and impact of the abrogation of the "Complete Book of Six Codes"], 10–13.

2  "The Common Program of the Chinese People's Political Consultative Con-
ference, 1949," 1–20. The transition is also discussed in Tiffert, "An Irresistible
Inheritance," 85; Tiffert, "Judging Revolution"; and Cong, "'Ma Xiwu's Way of
Judging,'" 29–52.

3  RMRB, 18 June 1949, 1. New Democracy, as Mao had outlined in his 1940 speech
"On New Democracy," was to be an intermediary developmental stage in
China's history as it progressed from being a "semi-colonial" and "semi-feudal"
to a "socialist" country. See Mao, "On New Democracy," January 1940, 342.

4  Tiffert, "An Irresistible Inheritance," 85.

5  Schmalzer, The People's Peking Man, 114.

6  For a discussion of this problem in Lenin's writings, see Burbank, "Lenin and
the Law." In the case of Mao Zedong Thought, party leaders and government
ministers working on laws constantly referred to many of Mao's canonical
speeches and key party texts, but these did not go into much detail when it
came to laws.

7  Bryna Goodman, "'Law Is One Thing,'" 151. Learning about laws was part of the
wider field of Republican popular education that began to develop in the late
Qing. Representative studies of Republican education and popular education
include Bailey, Reform the People; Culp, Articulating Citizenship; Judge, Print
and Politics; and Zarrow, Educating China. The years leading up to the 1911
revolution are discussed in Bastid, Educational Reform in Early Twentieth-
Century China.

8  Bergère, Sun Yat-sen, 378–82.

9  Zarrow, Educating China, 59, 104–5, 131.

10 Bryna Goodman examines some of these publications, including Hu and
Huang's Susong changshi [Basic knowledge about lawsuits], to illustrate vernac-
ular understandings of judicial procedure in the 1920s. See Goodman, "'Law Is
One Thing,'" 151–52.

11 Publications on parts of the Civil Code that contributed to general legal education include, for instance, Wang Bo, Qinshufa ABC [Family law ABC, 1931];
Wang Bo, Jichengfa ABC [Inheritance law ABC, 1930]; and Zhu Caizhen, Falüxue ABC [Jurisprudence ABC, 1929] by the same Shanghai World Publishing
Company. For other family law–related publications see Gao Deming, Jiating
falü changshi [Common legal knowledge for the family].

12 Sigrid Schmalzer has termed this process the "class politics of knowledge"; see
The People's Peking Man, 9.

13 Li Yizhen, Hunyinfa yu hunyin wenti [Marriage law and marriage problems].

14 Conner, "Lawyers and the Legal Profession," 215–48; Tiffert, "An Irresistible
Inheritance"; Xu Xiaoqun, Chinese Professionals and the Republican State; Xu
Xiaoqun, Trials of Modernity.

15 Xu Xiaoqun, Trials of Modernity, 84–92.

16 Lean, Public Passions, illustrates the competing demands made on the judiciary and the legal system when the topic of a trial challenged law on the books
and ideas about morality and propriety. For evidence of cases tried at the local
level and the complications involved see, for instance, Xu Xiaoqun, Trials of

*Modernity,* part 4; Philip C. C. Huang, *Chinese Civil Justice: Past and Present*; Kuo, *Intolerable Cruelty*; and Tran, *Concubines in Court.*

17 Cong, "'Ma Xiwu's Way of Judging,'" 32–33.

18 *Women of China* was renamed *Women of New China* (Xin Zhongguo funü) after 1949. See Zheng Wang, *Finding Women in the State*, 78–111. The other group members were Shuai Mengqi (1897–1987), the "girl commander" and "red amazon" Kang Keqing (1912–92) who was also Zhu De's wife, and Wang Ruofei's widow, Li Peizhi (1904–94). Biographies of these women are included in Xiao Hong Lee, *Biographical Dictionary of Chinese Women*. For a biography of Wang Ruqi see Xiong Xianjue, "Lüshi zhidu de tuohuangjue Wang Ruqi" [Wang Ruqi, a pioneer of the lawyer system], 458–64.

19 Edwards, *Gender, Politics, and Democracy*, discusses the vitae of many of these women before they reached the Communist base areas.

20 Huang Chuanhui, *Tianxia hunyin*, 45–49.

21 "Non-technical language" in Communist Chinese law is discussed in van de Valk, "Previous Chinese Legal Language," 617; and Finkelstein, "The Language of Communist Chinese Criminal Law." For the wartime genesis of some technical terms in marriage regulations see Cong, "From 'Freedom of Marriage' to 'Self-Determined Marriage.'" The making of the 1950 Marriage Law was the subject of a historical debate in China. One side argued that Chen Shaoyu (Wang Ming), the man with whom Mao Zedong competed for power, wrote the law. The other side argued that the group of women mentioned in this chapter wrote it. For the initial article that stirred the controversy see "Mao Zedong assigned Wang Ming to draft the Marriage Law," RMRB (Overseas edition), 24 August 2001. Luo Qiong replied in RMRB (Overseas edition), 22 October 2001, reprinted in Huang Chuanhui, *Tianxia hunyin*, 15ff. A short version of Luo Qiong's recollections of writing the Marriage Law is published in "Zasui fengjian hunyin jiasuo de zhongyao falü—hui di yi bu hunyinfa dansheng qianhou" [An important law to smash the shackles of feudal marriage to bits—remembering the birth of the first Marriage Law], RMRB, 3 May 1990. Part of Huang's findings and interviews with Luo were published in the Shanghai Municipal Archives magazine *Dang'an chunqiu*, no. 12 (2006). An early article arguing for Wang Ming's role is Wu Yuenong, "Wang Ming yu xin Zhongguo di yi bu 'hunyinfa'" [Wang Ming and New China's first Marriage Law]. The controversy is discussed in Altehenger, "Simplified Legal Knowledge in the Early PRC," 344–46; and Zheng Wang, *Finding Women in the State*, 13–14 and 267–68n23.

22 Cong includes a quotation from a High Court judge in the Shaan-Gan-Ning Border Region who, in the context of a freedom of marriage discussion, stated that "a freedom of law is not really a freedom." See "From 'Freedom of Marriage' to 'Self-Determined Marriage,'" 205.

23 "The Common Program of the Chinese People's Political Consultative Conference," 1949.

24 Zhonggong zhongyang wenxian yanjiu shi, *Mao Zedong nianpu (1949–1976)* [Chronicle of the life of Mao Zedong (1949–1976)], vol. 1, 158–59. *Guomin* was

among the most controversial political terms of the early 1950s. For a study of the different uses of the terms *guomin*, *renmin*, and *gongmin* (citizen) in the early 1950s, particularly the way these political labels incited fear and even led some to commit suicide out of a fear of persecution, see Feng Xiaocai, "Shenfen dingyi yu shehui fanying" [Determining identity and societal responses] (unpublished paper, cited with the author's permission).

25  Mao, "On the People's Democratic Dictatorship," June 1949, vol. 4, 419.

26  The number of "non-People" categories increased three-fold until the Cultural Revolution. For a detailed discussion see Schoenhals, "Demonising Discourse," 467; and Smith, *Thought Reform and China's Dangerous Classes*, 2.

27  Potter, *From Leninist Discipline to Socialist Legalism*, 64.

28  Yang was a historian who had taught at the Yan'an Party School and a contemporary of Wang Ming on the Legal System Committee. Yang shortly thereafter took up a position in the Central Propaganda Department in Beijing. See Yang Shaoxuan, "Zhongguo falü bianqian shilüe yu xin faxue guan" [A brief history of changes in Chinese law and the new view on jurisprudence], 12–16. Yang's biographical information is found in Zhonggong dangshi renwu yanjiuhui, *Zhonggong dangshi renwu zhuan* [Biographies of personalities in Communist Party history], 210.

29  Lin and Tang, *Dubao cidian* [Newspaper readers' dictionary], 192.

30  Mao, "Some Questions Concerning Methods of Leadership," 1 June 1943, 119. The mass line and its implications for thought reform work are discussed in Smith, *Thought Reform and China's Dangerous Classes*, 98–99.

31  Wang Feiran, "Youguan hunyinfa de wenti" [On the question of the Marriage Law], 16–17. The article was a transcript of a broadcast disseminated by the Central People's Broadcasting Station on 25 April 1950.

32  For another well-known theoretical discussion of "self-education" see Mao, "Be a True Revolutionary," 23 June 1950, 37–40.

33  Schoenhals, *Spying for the People*, explains that the term *tewu* is difficult to translate because it was formally meant to refer to "operatives of hostile intelligence services" but in practice came to denote "anyone suspected of maintaining links with perceived external enemies of the PRC," 2n7. Scholarship on mass campaigns is vast and includes noted works such as Yang Kuisong, "Reconsidering the Campaign to Suppress Counterrevolutionaries"; Strauss, "Paternalist Terror"; Strauss, "Morality, Coercion and State Building"; Cell, *Revolution at Work*; and Bennett, *Yundong*.

34  Shi Qiubo, ed., *Shanghai sifa xingzheng zhi* [Shanghai judicial administration gazetteer], 219.

35  As of 1953, the slogan was often associated with Mao's 1953 intra-party directive on combating "bureaucratism, commandism, and violations of law and discipline," which initiated the "New Three-Anti Campaign" (*xin sanfan*). This intra-party directive, dated 5 January 1953, is discussed in Zhonggong zhongyang wenxian yanjiu shi, *Mao Zedong nianpu (1949–1976)* [Chronicle of the life of Mao Zedong (1949–1976)], vol. 2, 3–5. On the New Three-Anti Campaign see also Smith, *Thought Reform and China's Dangerous Classes*, 143–44.

36  Chen Bei'ou, *Renmin xuexi cidian* [People's study dictionary], entry on *falü* [law], 223.

37  Teiwes, *Politics and Purges in China*, 29–32.

38  Officials in local police stations chronicled the "mood" of residents in "social intelligence" reports that included information collected by "social eyes and ears" (*shehui ermu*) working on behalf of local police offices; see Schoenhals, *Spying for the People*, 51.

39  On public security and police work in the PRC see Dutton, *Policing Chinese Politics*. On surveillance work see Schoenhals, *Spying for the People*.

40  See, for example, James Gao, *The Communist Takeover of Hangzhou*, 108–12; and Mühlhahn, *Criminal Justice in China*, 264–65.

41  Speaking bitterness as a technique to shape and incentivize revolutionary emotions is discussed in Yu Liu, "Maoist Discourse."

42  Yang Kuisong, "Reconsidering the Campaign to Suppress Counterrevolutionaries"; Schoenhals, "Reactions to Executions in Beijing (1951)"; Strauss, "Paternalist Terror," 85–87; Strauss, "Morality, Coercion and State Building," 52–54.

43  The campaign was initially based on the Double Ten Directive, published on 10 October 1950. Strauss, "Paternalist Terror," 82–83; and Zhang Ning, "Political Origins of Death Penalty Exceptionalism," 122.

44  Even in prisons, as Jan Kiely writes, "legal regulations and procedural codes . . . were typically unknown by those detained and unfamiliar to those who detained them." See Kiely, *The Compelling Ideal*, 275; and Dikötter, *Crime, Punishment, and the Prison in Modern China*. On thought work in prisons see Kiely, *The Compelling Ideal*, 288; and Perry, "Studying Chinese Politics."

45  Schoenhals, "Reactions to Executions in Beijing (1951)," 12.

46  Ibid.

47  Ibid., 15.

48  Ibid.

49  Julia Strauss writes that in Shanghai following the "first city-wide wave of mass arrests and executions in late April . . . government cadres came to focus on the seriousness of the campaign." See "Paternalist Terror," 87.

50  Diamant, *Revolutionizing the Family*, provides numerous examples of this practice. These public performances, moreover, could go wrong. Gail Hershatter writes of a case where the female plaintiff had to be escorted off the stage for her own protection and people attacked the judge's car because they were furious about the female plaintiff's impertinence to ask for a divorce. See Hershatter, *The Gender of Memory*, 109–10.

51  RMRB, 8 March 1952.

52  Glosser, *Chinese Visions of Family and State*, 180–82. The link between land reform and the Marriage Law consequently led some visitors to believe that the Marriage Law was irrelevant to their lives since they were urban residents.

53  The definition of "intellectuals" was very broad, encompassing teachers and others with some middle school training and above. It also included unemployed intellectuals as a group. See U, "The Making of Chinese Intellectuals"; and Smith, *Thought Reform and China's Dangerous Classes*.

54  "Xuexi gongtong gangling, xuexi Mao Zedong sixiang" [Study the Common Program, study Mao Zedong Thought], 1–4; "Gongtong gangling shi woguo xianshi de genben dafa" [The Common Program is our country's current fundamental great law], 1–2; "You xitongde xuexi Mao Zedong sixiang lai jinyibu gaizao sixiang" [Systematically study Mao Zedong Thought to further reform thinking], 8–12.

55  On the United Front in the early PRC see van Slyke, *Enemies and Friends*, 208–53.

56  Zhonggong zhongyang wenxian yanjiu shi, *Mao Zedong nianpu (1949–1976)*, vol. 1, 594.

57  Tiffert, "Epistrophy," 65–66.

58  Shi Liang, "Zhongyang renmin zhengfu sifabu buzhang Shi Liang guanyu chedi gaizao he zhengdun guojia renmin fayuan de baogao" [Central People's Government Minister of Justice Shi Liang's report on thoroughly transforming and rectifying the country's people's courts]. Statistics compiled by the regional offices claimed that in Tianjin, cadres with old legal outlooks made up 16 percent of the staff at all people's courts, while in Beijing more than 25 percent had been employed in the city's courts before 1949; cf. Zhonggong zhongyang huabeiju bangongting, "Huabei ju guanyu sifa gaige yundong xiang zhongyang de baogao" [North China office report to Party Central on the Judicial Reform Movement], 823–25. See also BMA 2-5-58.

59  Shi Liang, "Zhongyang renmin zhengfu sifabu buzhang Shi Liang guanyu chedi gaizao he zhengdun guojia renmin fayuan de baogao."

60  "Cong falü de jieji xing tan suqing jiufa guandian" [Discussing the elimination of old legal outlooks on the basis of the class character of law], 3–5.

61  Zhongyang zhengfa jiguan sifa gaige bangongshi, *Sifa gaige yu sifa jianshe cankao wenjian* [Reference documents on judicial reform and judicial construction].

62  BMA 2-20-314, 027–28.

63  The movement also had profound consequences for the make-up of the PRC judiciary. For a detailed discussion of the Judicial Reform Movement and its implications for the judiciary in Beijing and nationally see Tiffert, "Judging Revolution."

64  Xie Juezai, "Yao xuexi falü yu xuanchuan falü" [One should study law and propagate law], 9.

65  "Cong falü de jieji xing tan suqing jiu fa guandian," 3–5; "Chedi suqing jiu fa guandian he jiu sifa zuofeng" [Thoroughly eliminate old legal outlooks and old styles of judicial work], 35–38.

66  NBCK, 17 September 1952, 295.

67  Ibid. 295.

68  Ibid.

69  For the details of who was dismissed in Beijing and on what grounds, see Tiffert, "Judging Revolution."

70  Zhang Min, "Shilun 1952 nian sifa gaige yundong" [On the judicial movement in 1952], 57.

71  BMA 2-4-37, 020.

72  "Huabei xingzheng weiyuanhui dangzu guanyu sifa gaige yundong xiang hua-
    beiju de baogao" [North China regional administrative committee party group
    report to the North China Office on the Judicial Reform Movement], 458.
73  Ibid.
74  BMA 2-4-37, 001–8.
75  BMA 27-2-59, 003.
76  "Huabei xingzheng weiyuanhui dangzu guanyu sifa gaige yundong xiang hua-
    beiju de baogao."
77  SMA B92-2-77, 001. See also SMA B92-2-77, 003.
78  BMA 2-4-37, 007.
79  Ibid., 018.
80  Tiffert, "Judging Revolution."
81  BMA 2-4-37, 012–18.
82  Zhonggong zhongyang huabeiju bangongting, "Huabeiju guanyu sifa gaige
    yundong xiang zhongyang de baogao," 823. Shanxi Province reported more
    than 3,600 meetings with some 40,000 re-examined cases, of which 27,000
    were cases that ordinary citizens had brought to the attention of those carrying
    out judicial reform. See "Huabei xingzheng weiyuanhui dangzu guanyu sifa
    gaige yundong xiang huabeiju de baogao."
83  Kay Ann Johnson, *Women, the Family, and Peasant Revolution*, 99–101.
84  All the women listed here feature in Louise Edwards's discussion of political
    women in Nationalist and wartime China; see Edwards, *Gender, Politics, and
    Democracy*.
85  Zheng Wang, *Finding Women in the State*, especially part 1.
86  "Zhonggong zhongyang guanyu qingzhu 'wu yi' laodongjie de kouhao" [Party
    Central on the slogans to celebrate "May 1st" Labor Day].
87  Deng's 1951 speech is recorded in BMA 1-6-442, 033–41. Deng had, however, already
    pointed out much of this in her speech on 14 May 1950 explaining the Marriage
    Law; see Deng Yingchao, "Guanyu 'Zhonghua renmin gongheguo hunyinfa' de
    baogao" [Report on the "PRC Marriage Law"].
88  BMA 1-6-442, 038. That the initial implementation of the Marriage Law after
    1950 led to a spike in suicides and homicides has been both well documented
    and extensively discussed in all the literature on the Marriage Law. See Kay
    Ann Johnson, *Women, the Family, and Peasant Revolution*, 127–46.
89  BMA 1-6-442, 041.
90  The Central Propaganda Department's internal periodical *Xuanchuan tong-
    xun*, for example, informed all propaganda workers in August 1952 that despite
    the 1951 directive to investigate the implementation of the Marriage Law, many
    areas failed to pay proper attention. Within a few months, or at the latest by early
    1952, the Three- and Five-Anti Campaigns occupied cadres' time, and they had
    lost sight of the law's implementation or they linked the Marriage Law to other
    campaigns. See Xuanchuan tongxun bianjibu, "Xuanchuan gongzuozhe zhuyi"
    [For the attention of propaganda workers].
91  BMA 1-6-753, 057–58.

92   Implementation problems were widely reported in the daily papers and in internal reports. See, for instance, NBCK, no. 186, 12 October 1951, 26–27; NBCK, no. 242, 28 December 1951, 133–34; and NBCK, no. 159, 15 July 1952, 169–72. See also BMA 196-2-470 for a central directive of the Ministry of Internal Affairs and the Ministry of Justice on the overlap with other campaigns, including the Three-Anti Campaign. These reports, as Diamant has shown, tallied with what was being reported in internal government communications and investigation reports in Shanghai, Beijing, and Yunnan Provinces. See Diamant, *Revolutionizing the Family*, chaps. 2 and 3; Croll, *Feminism and Socialism in China*; Croll, *The Politics of Marriage in Contemporary China*; Davin, *Woman-Work*.

93   Diamant, *Revolutionizing the Family*, e.g., 79–97, 215.

94   The pattern described in this paragraph was also noted as a problem for the law's implementation and interpretation by Meijer, *Marriage Law and Policy*, 79–82.

95   "Zhonggong zhongyang guanyu guanche hunyinfa de zhishi" [Party Central directive on implementing the Marriage Law], 461–66.

96   "Zhonggong zhongyang guanyu guanche hunyinfa de zhishi."

97   Ibid.; Zhonggong zhongyang wenxian yanjiu shi, *Mao Zedong nianpu (1949–1976)*, vol. 1, 627.

98   RMRB, 10 January 1953, 1.

99   Committee members included Deng Yingchao, Shi Liang, Yang Zhihua, and also Lei Jieqiong, professor of sociology at Beijing Institute of Politics and Law, who had helped draft the Organic Laws and who was one of the editors of *Xin jianshe* magazine. The Vice-minister of Internal Affairs, Wu Xinyu, sat on the committee, as did the Vice-minister of Public Security, Xu Zirong. Hu Yaobang, chairman of the Youth League, was involved, as was Lai Ruoyu, secretary of the All-China Federation of Trade Unions, who brought in the third mass organization next to the Women's Federation and the Youth League. Liang Xi, chair of the All-China Association for the Dissemination of Scientific and Technical Knowledge, was experienced in the popularization of science and brought this knowledge to the popularization of law. Li Chang, the vice-chairman of the Commission for the Elimination of Illiteracy, brought expertise in dealing with the challenge of explaining difficult political content as part of literacy education. Leading cadres from national media were present: Deng Tuo, deputy managing editor of *Renmin ribao* and a member of the Central Propaganda Department; Wang Yunsheng, editor-in-chief of the newspaper *Dagong bao*; Shao Zonghan, Central Propaganda Department member and editor-in-chief of *Guangming ribao*, China's national daily on all cultural matters; and Zhou Yang, Vice-minister of Culture. For a full list see RMRB, 10 January 1953, 1.

100   *Zhongguo dangdai mingrenlu* [Who's who in contemporary China], 208.

101   Occasional references to this briefing can be found in edited collections such as Zhonggong zhongyang wenxian yanjiu shi, *Mao Zedong nianpu (1949–1976)*, vol. 2, 58, where it chronicles how Mao read and commented on one of the briefings. These references, however, give little information about the Marriage

Law campaign or about what Mao actually contributed, and seem to largely serve as a symbolic statement that Mao was involved in some way. I have not been able to access the actual briefings.

102 RMRB, 2 February 1953, 1.

103 Ibid.

104 On this different emphasis of the campaign see also Kay Ann Johnson, *Women, the Family, and Peasant Revolution*, 142–46.

105 Mao's intra-party directive to "combat bureaucracy, commandism, and violations of law and discipline," 5 January 1953, is discussed in Zhonggong zhongyang wenxian yanjiu shi, *Mao Zedong nianpu (1949–1976)*, vol. 2, 3–5.

106 NBCK, no. 26, 2 February 1953, 12.

107 People's Publishing House, *Hunyinfa jianghua* [Introduction to the Marriage Law], 1.

108 NBCK, no. 34, 11 February 1953, 171.

109 NBCK, no. 26, 2 February 1953, 12, and NBCK, no. 58, 14 March 1953, 365.

110 NBCK, no. 26, 2 February 1953, 12.

111 It is difficult to show that reports provoked policy changes at the national level, though in this case available documents suggest such a connection. On this problem see Schoenhals, "Elite Information," 65–71.

112 RMRB, 19 February 1953, 1. Kay Ann Johnson notes the change in rhetoric and the significance of the supplementary directive. See Johnson, *Women, the Family, and Peasant Revolution*, 142–44. She infers from these public notices in RMRB what had happened, and I have tried to correlate her information with information from internal sources.

113 RMRB, 19 February 1953, 1.

114 Zhongyang guanche hunyinfa yundong weiyuanhui, "Guanche hunyinfa xuanchuan tigang" [Implement the Marriage Law propaganda outline], 12–22; see also RMRB, 25 February 1953, 1.

115 Zhongyang guanche hunyinfa yundong weiyuanhui, "Guanche hunyinfa xuanchuan tigang."

116 Adjusting campaign policy, in general, was difficult. The CCP leadership had had to deal with this problem during the Campaign to Suppress Counterrevolutionaries; see Strauss, "Paternalist Terror," 89–90.

117 NBCK, no. 42, 24 February 1953, 348.

118 Ibid.

119 NBCK, no. 64, 21 March 1953, 526.

120 NBCK, no. 58, 14 March 1953, 363.

121 Ibid.

122 Ibid., 365.

123 Ibid., 363.

124 BMA 38-1-81, 001 to 017, 002.

125 NBCK, no. 58, 14 March 1953, 367.

126 Ibid., 362.

127 NBCK, no. 48, 4 March 1953, 60.

128 NBCK, no. 58, 14 March 1953, 369.

129  NBCK, no. 48, 4 March 1953, 60.
130  NBCK, no. 58, 14 March 1953, 365.
131  NBCK, no. 42, 24 February 1953, 349.
132  NBCK, no. 40, 21 February 1953, 302.
133  NBCK, no. 58, 14 March 1953, 365.
134  BMA 1-6-753, 061.
135  NBCK, no. 48, 4 March 1953, 60.
136  Ibid.
137  NBCK, no. 58, 14 March 1953, 364.
138  German Federal Archives BArch, SAPMO, DY31/1117.

# Chapter 2

1  The coordination between party newspapers and party policy dates back to the CCP's time in Yan'an during the late 1930s and early 1940s; see Stranahan, *Molding the Medium*.

2  E.g., RMRB, 16 April 1950, 1; RMRB, 30 June 1950, 2.

3  I translate *tongsu* as "popular" in the sense that it was aimed at a broad audience of different educational levels. The term can also denote that something was well liked and enjoyed, and this is certainly how the CCP wanted its popular materials to be understood. But accessibility was the primary criteria for something to be *tongsu*. Liang Luo has discussed the different meanings of the "popular" in twentieth-century China; see *The Avant-garde and the Popular in Modern China*, 13–14.

4  The term "publishing authorities" suggests a monolithic entity in control of the national publishing industry. No unit within the PRC state exerted such control, even though the Central Propaganda Department, the General Publishing Administration, and the Ministry of Culture, as well as regional offices, exerted a great deal of power over the publishing process. I have tried to disaggregate the term "publishing authorities" whenever possible. In some documents, the General Publishing Administration or the Central Propaganda Department, however, use aggregate terms to refer to national publishing activities, and in these cases I have adopted these terms.

5  The promises of "New Democracy" gave private publishers a limited degree of protection from excessive state interference during the early 1950s. The general transformation of the publishing industry after 1949 is discussed in Zhu Jinping, *Zhongguo gongchandang dui siying chubanye de gaizao, 1949–1956* [The CCP's transformation of the private publishing industry, 1949–1956]; Zhou Wu, "Cong quanguoxing dao difanghua" [From national to localization]; Volland, "The Control of the Media," 227–86; Volland, "Cultural Entrepreneurship in the Twilight"; Du, "Shanghaiing the Press Gang"; and Culp, "Culture Work."

6  Chen and Zelin, "Rethinking Chinese Law," 10.

7  Ting Zhang, "Marketing Legal Information," 232.

8  Official copies were often treated as objects to be venerated rather than used in

the daily administration of legal matters; see Ting Zhang, "Marketing Legal Information," 234–35.

9 Chen and Zelin, "Rethinking Chinese Law," 8. See also Ting Zhang, "Marketing Legal Information."

10 Ting Zhang, "Marketing Legal Information," 244.

11 Li Chen, "Regulating Private Legal Specialists," 254.

12 Shanghai emerged as China's center of publishing toward the end of the nineteenth century. For a discussion of Shanghai as the center of print capitalism see Reed, *Gutenberg in Shanghai*. Rudolf Wagner traces the formation of the newspaper in China to *Shenbao*, which was published from Shanghai; see "The *Shenbao* in Crisis," and Wagner, "Shenbaoguan zaoqi de shuji chuban" [The early publishing activities of the Shenbaoguan], 169–78. Home to China's leading publishers by the early twentieth century, Shanghai soon turned into a key location for the production of textbooks, many of which supported civic education during the Republican period; see Culp, *Articulating Citizenship*.

13 The role of newspapers and sensationalist reportage surrounding high-profile court cases is discussed in Lean, *Pubic Passions*.

14 The General Publishing Administration, part of the central government, was responsible for the guidance of the national publishing industry. It was attached to the state rather than the party structure, and it received instructions both from the central government and from the CCP Central Propaganda Department. All private and state-owned publishers, presses, and distributors had to submit to the administration regular reports and work plans that were subject to examination and revision. For an explanation of the government's publishing authorities see SMA B1-1-1864, 008, which provides a chart dated 18 October 1949. See also SMA B1-1-1862, 011–12. For an English overview see Alan Liu, *Communications and National Integration in Communist China*, 46.

15 New laws were published in compendia such as *Renmin shouce* (People's handbook), issued annually with updates about policy documents, government personnel, party-state structures, and other basic information about the state of the country. These types of volumes were encyclopedic reference works with general information about the organization and governance of the People's Republic. The People's Handbook Editorial Committee at *Dagong bao* (L'Impartial) annually updated its handbook for publication; in the first years after 1949 there were also a few other handbooks, but these stopped publication soon thereafter; see for example Guangming ribao she bianjisuo, *Dubao shouce* [Handbook for reading newspapers].

16 Reprints of the Marriage Law and the Election Law were issued across the country, and print runs amounted to several million copies. On efforts to arrange for sufficient print runs see Chen Kehan's letters dated between 25 March and 23 April and collected in Chen Kehan, "Chen Kehan jiancha Huadong, Zhongnan chuban gongzuo zhi youguan bumen ji fuzeren de xin" [Chen Kehan's letters to relevant departments and leading cadres on the investigation into publishing work in East China and South-Central China], 138–70. See especially

the letter of 18 April 1953 that Chen Kehan wrote to Hu Yuzhi, Huang Luofang, Mao Dun, Jin Canran, and Hua Yingshen (p. 160).

17   The establishment of the People's Press is outlined in Renmin chubanshe, *Renmin chubanshe 50 nian dashiji*. [The People's Publishing House, a chronicle of fifty years].

18   For important volumes such as those on national laws, paper size and content were decided by Beijing. Once the central government released the document to the General Publishing Administration, it went straight to the administration's editing and screening office, which then assembled the "one-volume edition" or a similar format. This was printed in Beijing. In the meantime, the Xinhua Bookstore passed on, via telegram or express letter, the title of the volume, the names of the editors, and the table of contents, so that regional branches could prepare to print using the blueprint produced in Beijing. See Hu Yuzhi, "Hu Yuzhi ni gedi chuban zhengfu wenjian de fangzhen yu banfa gao jiao chuban zongshu bangongting banli de xin" [Hu Yuzhi's letter on the draft for the guiding principles and regulations on publishing government documents, transmitted to the General Publishing Administration's office for processing], 159–61. Chen Kehan addresses the issue of deliveries and timing on his investigative trip to East China and South-Central China in "Chen Kehan jiancha Huadong" [Chen Kehan's letters to relevant departments and leading cadres on the investigation into publishing work in East China and South-Central China].

19   For a detailed overview of legal materials and genres see Hsia, "Chinese Legal Publications," 20–83.

20   Examples of people's court status reports can be found on the website "Social History of China, 1949–1976," http://projekt.ht.lu.se/rereso/sources/peoples-court-status-reports/ [last accessed: 1 September 2017]. The Ministry of Public Security ran internal bulletins at different levels of access restriction. See Schoenhals, *Spying for the People*.

21   I take this definition of popular readings from "Chuban zongshu dangzu xiaozu guanyu chengli tongsu duwu chubanshe de qingshi baogao" [Report and request for instructions by the small group of the General Publishing Administration party group on establishing a popular readings press], 476; also "Zhongyang xuanchuanbu guanyu chengli tongsu duwu chubanshe de jueding" [Central Propaganda Department decision on establishing a popular readings press], 165–66. In 1951, the Shanghai Municipal Government issued an explanation of publication classifications outlining the categories for publishing houses, distributors, and bookshops. These were different from the categories used in libraries; cf. SMA B1-1-1944, 011. See also SMA B1-2-3591, 011. Popularity, following the mass line principle, was engineered from above. Success depended on the reading in question. Such volumes could then become popular, in the sense that people enjoyed reading them, but those were specific cases. The label "popular" was applied well before authorities could establish readers' actual responses.

22   "Lu Dingyi zai zhonngxuanbu tongsu baokan tushu chuban huiyi shang de zongjie baogao" [Lu Dingyi's summary report at the Central Propaganda Department's meeting on popular newspaper, magazine, and book publishing], 132.

23  Ibid., 134–35.
24  Ibid., 135.
25  "Wei tigao chubanwu de zhiliang er fendou" [Struggle to raise the quality of publications], 219.
26  Materials used for the popularization of science are discussed in Schmalzer, *The People's Peking Man.*
27  "Zhongyang xuanchuanbu guanyu muqian chuban gongzuo de zhishi" [Central Propaganda Department directive on current publishing work], 58–61.
28  "Wei tigao chubanwu de zhiliang er fendou," 225. For an overview of the General Publishing Administration, its creation, work portfolio, and changing structure in the first years after 1949 see Volland, "The Control of the Media," 258–89.
29  Culp, "Culture Work."
30  "Wei tigao chubanwu de zhiliang er fendou."
31  Ye provided more statistics: 28 percent of all words printed were in private publishers' products; also, 17 percent of the total publishing volume and 21 percent of paper used nationally were from private publishers. See "Wei tigao chubanwu de zhiliang er fendou," 237.
32  On publishers' role in reproducing serial comics (*lianhuanhua*) see Hung, *Mao's New World,* 155–81; Seifert, *Bildergeschichten für Chinas Massen;* and Volland, "Cultural Entrepreneurship." For examples of adaption of existing publisher portfolios see Culp, "Culture Work." Some of the three-character classics of the early PRC are discussed in Mittler, *A Continuous Revolution?,* 156–84.
33  "Zhongyang xuanchuanbu guanyu muqian chuban gongzuo de zhishi," 58–61.
34  Volland, "The Control of the Media." The 1952 regulations on publishing required publishers and bookstores to send to the government a copy of anything they published at the same time as they delivered their goods to the bookstores. However, discussions in 1954 show that this was often not done, even once the regulations were published; see "Chuban zongshu guanyu xianzhi siying feifa chuban tushu de tongbao" [General Publishing Administration circular on restricting private businesses' illegal publication of books], 339–41.
35  Hu Yingxi, *Hunyinfa sanzijing* [Marriage Law three-character classic].
36  Miao Peishi, *Hunyin ziyou ge* [Freedom of marriage song].
37  *Renmin qianzike: Hunyin dashi* [People's thousand-character lesson: The great event of marriage].
38  Huadong renmin chubanshe, ed., *Hunyinfa tujie tongsuben* [The Marriage Law: Illustrated popular explanations]; and Huadong renmin chubanshe, *Zhonghua renmin gongheguo chengzhi fangeming tiaoli: Tujie tongsuben* [The Regulations of the People's Republic of China for the Punishment of Counterrevolutionaries: Illustrated popular explanations].
39  RMRB, 8 December 1951, 3; and "'Zhonghua renmin gongheguo chengzhi fangeming tiaoli tujie tongsuben': Shanghai 500 wan ren, du le 62 wan ce" ["Illustrated Regulations of the People's Republic of China for the Punishment of Counterrevolutionaries": Shanghai's five million people read 620,000 copies].
40  RMRB, 8 December 1951, 3.
41  Ibid.

42 This number of a first print run of nine million copies followed by more reprints is continuously repeated in internal conversations about publishing work. See Hu Yuzhi, "Chuban gongzuo wei guangda renmin qunzhong fuwu" [Publishing work serves the broad masses of the people], 228–32. Hu gives a print run of 11,500,000 copies for the *Illustrated Marriage Law* and a print run of 10,680,000 copies for the *Illustrated Regulations*. The print run is also discussed in Zhu Jinping, *Zhongguo gongchandang dui siying chubanye de gaizao, 1949–1956*, 126. The highest print runs in literary publishing, including the most popular novels translated from Russian such as *The Story of Zoya and Shura*, went up to a million copies; see Volland, "Translating the Socialist State," 63ff.

43 RMRB, 8 December 1951, 3.

44 "Di yi jie quanguo chuban huiyi yilai Xinhua shudian de gongzuo" [Xinhua Bookstore's work since the first national meeting on publishing], 281–305. This report used the booklet as an example of publishing for mass campaigns more generally.

45 "Zhonghua renmin gongheguo chengzhi fangeming tiaoli tujie tongsuben."

46 "Di yi jie quanguo chuban huiyi yilai Xinhua shudian de gongzuo," 283.

47 Ibid., 287.

48 Ibid.

49 "Zhonggong zhongyang xuanchuanbu guanyu chuban gongzuo xiang zhonggong zhongyang de baogao ji Mao Zedong de pishi" [Central Propaganda Department report to Party Central on publishing work and Mao Zedong's memo], 349–53.

50 For a discussion of the making of the Little Red Book and its print run see Leese, "A Single Spark," 23.

51 Hu Yuzhi, "Chuban gongzuo wei guangda renmin qunzhong fuwu," 229. Moreover, in October 1951, the Central Propaganda Department was still confident that the volume might even reach a print run of 20 million; see "Zhonggong zhongyang xuanchuanbu guanyu chuban gongzuo xiang zhonggong zhongyang de baogao ji Mao Zedong de pishi," 350.

52 RMRB, 1 February 1953, 3.

53 "Chuban zongshu guanyu jianjue jiuzheng shukan faxing gongzuo zhong qiangpo tanpai cuowu de zhishi" [General Publishing Administration directive on resolutely correcting the mistake of forced allotments in book and periodical distribution], 1–5. The issue was extensively discussed in "Chuban zongshu guanyu chubu jiancha qiangpo tanpai shukan de baogao" [Report of the General Publishing Administration on the first investigations into forced allotments of books and periodicals], 8; and "Xinhua shudian zongdian chubu jiancha qiangpo tanpai shukan qingkuang de baogao" [New China Bookstore main branch report on the first investigations into the situation of forced allotments of books and periodicals], 9–15.

54 NBCK, 22 May 1953, 329–31. Adding emphasis to its reports, the General Publishing Administration wrote of a crying child being forced to buy a book; see "Chuban zongshu guanyu jianjue jiuzheng shukan faxing gongzuo zhong qiangpo tanpai cuowu de zhishi," 1.

55  "Zhonghua renmin gongheguo chengzhi fangeming tiaoli tujie tongsuben."
56  "Chuban zongshu guanyu jianjue jiuzheng shukan faxing gongzuo zhong qiangpo tanpai cuowu de zhishi," 3.
57  "Zhonghua renmin gongheguo chengzhi fangeming tiaoli tujie tongsuben."
58  "Chuban zongshu guanyu jianjue jiuzheng shukan faxing gongzuo zhong qiangpo tanpai cuowu de zhishi," 2.
59  "Xinhua shudian zongdian chubu jiancha qiangpo tanpai shukan qingkuang de baogao," 10–11.
60  "Chuban zongshu guanyu chubu jiancha qiangpo tanpai shukan de baogao," 8.
61  "Guanyu xuanchuan hunyinfa de chubanwu de youxie quedian" [On some shortcomings in publications propagating the Marriage Law], 401–4, 402.
62  "Zhengwuyuan banfa 'qikan dengji zanxing banfa,' 'guanli shukan chubanye yinshuaye faxingye zanxing tiaoli' ji pizhun 'guowai yinshuapin jinkou zanxing banfa,' de mingling" [Government Administrative Council order on the promulgation of the "Provisional Regulations on the Registration of Periodicals," the "Provisional Regulations on the Administration of Book and Periodical Publishing, the Printing Industry, and the Distribution Trade," and the ratification of the "Provisional Regulations on the Import of Foreign Print Products"], 172. The original regulations are reprinted in "Guanli shukan chubanye yinshuaye faxingye zanxing" [Provisional regulations on the administration of book and periodical publishing, the printing industry, and the distribution trades], 433–35.
63  "Guanli shukan chubanye yinshuaye faxingye zanxing," 434.
64  "Chuban zongshu bangongting guanyu zai baoshang deng fanyin Jiefangshe, Xinhua shudian shuji qishi de tongzhi" [Notification from the office of the General Publishing Administration on giving notice on reprinting *Liberation Daily*'s news agency and New China Bookstore's books in newspapers], 1–2. See also Volland, "The Control of the Media," 255.
65  BMA 8-2-699.
66  Volland, "The Control of the Media," 254–55.
67  SMA A22-2-143, 004.
68  BMA 8-2-699.
69  SMA A22-1-92, 002.
70  SMA A22-1-92, 004.
71  BMA 8-2-699.
72  SMA A47-1-160, 002; SMA A47-1-161, 049.
73  "Chuban zongshu dangzu xiaozu guanyu chengli tongsu duwu chubanshe de qingshi baogao," 474.
74  Ibid., 475.
75  Ibid.
76  The CCP's publishing and propaganda work in Yan'an and its relevance for the post-1949 era is discussed in Julian Chang, "The Mechanics of State Propaganda"; and Volland, "The Control of the Media," especially chaps. 2 and 3.
77  Zhongyang xuanchuanbu, "Tongsu shuji de xuyao he chuban qingkuang" [The publishing situation and demand for popular works], in "Chuban zongshu dangzu xiaozu guanyu chengli tongsu duwu chubanshe de qingshi baogao," 483.

78 Editors were responsible for the production of publications according to party-state policy. The role of editors and the editor responsibility system are discussed in Volland, "The Control of the Media," chap. 4; and Zhongyang xuanchuanbu, "Tongsu shuji de xuyao he chuban qingkuang," 483–84.

79 This problem and the local implementation of thought reform in Hangzhou is discussed in James Gao, *The Communist Takeover of Hangzhou*, 152. On the history of thought reform in the PRC see also Smith, *Thought Reform and China's Dangerous Classes*; and Goldman, *Literary Dissent in Communist China*, 87–157.

80 NBCK, 10 October 1952, 104–7.

81 My observations are based on a survey of RMRB, GMRB, XWRB, and *Beijing ribao* (Beijing daily).

82 The original reader's letter, however, was not included. RMRB, 1 April 1953, 2.

83 "Chen Kehan jiancha Huadong, Zhongnan chuban gongzuo zhi youguan bumen ji fuzeren de xin," 168.

84 This issue had already been mentioned in reports; see "Zhongyang xuanchuanbu guanyu muqian chuban gongzuo de zhishi," 58–61.

85 Chen Kehan, "Chuban zongshu dangzu guanyu xiuding 1953 nian gongzuo jihua zhi zhongyang de baodao" [General Publishing Administration party group report to Party Central on revising the 1953 work plan], 25.

86 Chen Kehan, "Guanyu xiuding 1953 nian jihua de yijian" [Suggestions on revising the 1953 plan], 202.

87 Ibid.

88 "Chen Kehan jiancha Huadong, Zhongnan chuban gongzuo zhi youguan bumen ji fuzeren de xin," 159–60.

89 BMA 8-2-469, 007–8. See also BMA 8-2-469, 001–2.

90 Ibid., 011–12.

91 Zhongyang xuanchuanbu, "Tongsu shuji de xuyao he chuban qingkuang."

92 "Zhongyang xuanchuanbu guanyu chengli tongsu duwu chubanshe de jueding" [Central Propaganda Department decision on establishing a popular readings press], 487–88. The new press would henceforth publish all popular materials pertinent to central government policies, directives, decrees, and laws.

93 "Chuban zongshu dangzu xiaozu guanyu chengli tongsu duwu chubanshe de qingshi baogao," 477.

94 "Chuban zongshu guanyu siying zazhishe, chubanshe bu de fabiao he chuban jieyi xianfa cao'an de wenzi de tongzhi" [General Publishing Administration notification on private magazines and publishers not being permitted to issue or publish interpretations of the words in the constitution draft], 301.

95 See SMA A6-2-25, 112–14, for a directive on using articles and newspaper essays in publications and "small people's books" for the constitution draft discussion.

96 BMA 1-6-957, 013; Chen Kehan continued to deal with the problems of timing, longevity of books (compared to newspapers), and quality control; see Chen Kehan, "Guanyu chubanshe gongzuo de mouxie wenti" [On a few problems in publishing work], 318–28.

97 Complaints about wasteful print runs were occasionally published in magazines. For a prominent and outspoken article that discusses overfilled storages,

excessive quantities of campaign materials, and their short lifespan, see Li Yi, "Buyao mangmu chuban shuji" [Do not blindly publish books], 1.

98  RMRB, 31 July 1954.

99  HMA, J127-2-7, 079–82.

# Chapter 3

1  The full translation of the law is rendered in Kay Ann Johnson, *Women, the Family, and Peasant Revolution in China*, 235–39, from which I have taken the translations of the two articles.

2  BMA 196-2-473.

3  BMA 1-12-128, 001.

4  Neil Diamant has illustrated the local dynamics and diverse responses to learning about the Marriage Law in his book *Revolutionizing the Family* and in his article "Re-Examining the Impact of the 1950 Marriage Law." Diamant explains that "[p]art of the problem was that officials without much authority or legitimacy were enforcing a law with an unfamiliar language and a very vague ideological agenda." See *Revolutionizing the Family*, 67. Hershatter's interviews with rural women meanwhile have illustrated that many young women felt empowered by the new law and found ways to make use of it; see Hershatter, *The Gender of Memory*, 108–16.

5  RMRB, 1 February 1953, 3.

6  Past studies have noted the wealth of propaganda materials produced for this campaign, but few have systematically examined the contents and variety. Notable exceptions to this are Davin, *Woman-Work*; Glosser, *Chinese Visions of Family and State*, 174–95, which focuses on a selection of Marriage Law pamphlets; and Meijer, *Marriage Law and Policy*, which gives a detailed analysis of newspaper reportage during the campaign.

7  The Marriage Law campaign became one of the most famous mass campaigns of the early PRC. Within months scholars across the world had begun to examine the law, leading Teemu Ruskola to speculate that "perhaps there has never been written so much about any marriage law in the world as that of the People's Republic of China." See Ruskola, "Law, Sexual Morality and Gender Equality," 2531–65.

8  BMA 1-5-105, 002.

9  Ibid., 004-5. On the structure of the campaign in Beijing see also the campaign summary report in BMA 1-6-753, 055.

10  BMA 1-6-753, 055.

11  SMA A47-1-161, 044.

12  The structure of the state during the 1950s is discussed in Schurmann, *Ideology and Organization in Communist China*, 188–92. On the organization of trade union branches in urban work units see Bray, *Social Space and Governance in Urban China*, 101–6. These branches were responsible for workers' welfare as well as for organizing political campaigns within the unit.

13  Family and marital disputes were commonly mediated at the local level, for

example. Mediation was part of the state's civil litigation system and knowledge of the law was necessary. For a study of mediation procedures in the PRC see Philip C. C. Huang, *Chinese Civil Justice: Past and Present.*

14  SMA A47-1-161, 033–040.

15  Schmalzer has discussed a similar problem in the dissemination of scientific knowledge that proceeded from the top, thus in practice contradicting the CCP's claim of mass-based education; see *The People's Peking Man,* 57 and 113–18.

16  "Zhonggong zhongyang guanyu guanche hunyinfa de zhishi."

17  BMA 1-12-128, 001–2.

18  Published also as an article in *Xin zhongguo funü,* no. 11, 1952.

19  BMA 1-12-128, 001–2.

20  Anyone with the right class background could become an activist, and so could those who did not possess the right class background but wished to try and redeem themselves by doing activist work. District governments, local police stations, and work units also recruited mass organization activists, as well as propagandists and report-givers, from the Youth League, the Trade Union, and the Women's Federation. As Leese notes, "The distinguishing of activists had been one of the main instruments of the CCP to secure a stratum of like-minded successors who both provided information on local conditions, and helped in taking over responsibilities from the chronically understaffed party secretaries." See Leese, *Mao Cult,* 103.

21  BMA 38-1-81, 003.

22  SMA A47-2-365, 183-84 and SMA A47-2-365, 130–31. Trade Union cadre Yang Zhihua argued for carefully calibrating time spent on activities such as Marriage Law study so that this would not affect other essential industrial work needed for the "reconstruction" of the country. See "Zhongyang dui quanzong dangzu guanyu zai gongkuang qiye zhong xuanchuan guanche hunyinfa yundong de baogao de pishi" [Party Central memorandum on the Trade Union party group's report regarding propaganda for Campaign to Implement the Marriage Law in industry, factories, and enterprises], 541–42.

23  SMA A47-1-161, 036.

24  SMA A47-2-365, 011.

25  Ibid. Scant understanding of the law was also a problem reported in, for example, Shanxi Province: see NBCK, no. 64, 21 March 1953, 524. In Hebei Province, propagandists wondered how they could possibly fill seven or eight days with education to residents since they themselves had only received five full days of education. NBCK, no. 69, 27 March 1953, 668.

26  SMA A47-2-365, 023–26.

27  SMA A59-1-302, 077–82.

28  For a detailed analysis of reports from different districts in Beijing and Shanghai see Diamant, *Revolutionizing the Family,* especially chaps. 1 and 2.

29  SMA A47-1-161, 039. The militarization of language in the political campaigns of the early 1950s is discussed in Dutton, *Policing Chinese Politics,* 411–12.

30  SMA A47-1-161, 077–79.

31  In Kaifeng, Henan Province, the campaign committee's office only had one and

a half cadres—one reporter (*tongxunyuan*) and one person from the Bureau of Civil Affairs who was there part-time. See NBCK, no. 59, 16 March 1953, 397. In Wuhan, Xinhua journalists reported that cadres staffing Marriage Law campaign offices were clueless and would send anyone with questions to the next-higher campaign office. See NBCK, no. 58, 14 March 1953, 367.

32  SMA A22-1-92, 001–5.

33  Article 8: "Husband and wife are in duty bound to love, respect, assist, and look after each other, to live in harmony, to engage in productive work, to care for their children, and to strive jointly for the welfare of the family and for the construction of the new society." Adapted from Kay Ann Johnson, *Women, the Family, and Peasant Revolution*, 236.

34  BMA 1-12-128, 001–2.

35  "Zhongnan qu guanche hunyinfa shidian xuanchuan gongzuo jingyan" [Propaganda work experiences of the Marriage Law implementation pilot tests in the South-Central region], 544–45.

36  Timothy Cheek has made this argument also in the context of Deng Tuo's reading of the Common Program. See Cheek, *Propaganda and Culture in Mao's China*, 137.

37  BMA 1-6-753, 042.

38  BMA 1-5-105, 004–5.

39  Ibid., 004–5.

40  See BMA 196-2-473 for an example of "Marriage Law Propaganda Reference Material" built on the division of old and new marriage systems.

41  Propaganda, by intention, left little space for regional diversity, nor did it account for the fact that certain customs, now decried as feudal, had never been practiced in some areas or that certain "innovations" the CCP claimed for the Marriage Law, such as permission to let widows remarry, were not new in other regions. I base my analysis here on a range of different propaganda materials issued before and during the campaign. These include Zhongnan minzhu fulian chouweihui, ed., *Hunyin wenti wenda* [Marriage Law questions and answers]; Sha Lin, *Hunyinfa sizijing* [Marriage Law four-character classics]; Huadong renmin chubanshe, *Hunyinfa tujie tongsuben* [Marriage Law: Illustrated popular explanations]; *Tantan hunyinfa* [Talking about the Marriage Law]; Shi and Ge, *Hunyinfa tongsu jianghua* [Popular introduction to the Marriage Law]; Shu Bo, *Dajia lai shixing hunyinfa* [Everyone come help implement the Marriage Law]; Liang Yongkai, *Hunyinfa qizige* [Marriage Law seven-character song]; Huadong wenhuabu yishu shiye guanlichu, *Hunyinfa gequ ji* [Anthology of Marriage Law songs]; Lu Qi, *Hunyin yao zizhu* [Marriage should be self-determined].

42  Liang Yongkai, *Hunyinfa qizige*, 1.

43  RMRB, 1 February 1953, 3.

44  Mao Zedong, "Zhongshi dianxing baodao" [Pay attention to model reports], 15 March 1953, 520. Also see Zhonggong zhongyang yanjiu shi, *Mao Zedong nianpu (1949–1976)*, vol. 2, 58.

45  Liaodong Province was merged into Liaoning and Jilin Provinces in 1954.

46  RMRB, 19 March 1953, 3.

47  NBCK, no. 40, 21 February 1953, 305–6.
48  NBCK, no. 44, 26 February 1953, 405.
49  "Guanyu guanche hunyinfa yundong yue de baodao tishi" [Briefing on the Campaign to Implement the Marriage Law month], 347–51.
50  SMA A47-2-365, 001–2.
51  "Guanyu guanche hunyinfa yundong yue de baodao tishi," 349.
52  SMA A47-2-365, 004.
53  Examples of such catalogues (which were structured very differently and often hand-written) include Shandong sheng tushuguan, ed., *Guanche hunyinfa yundong cankao tushu mulu* [Catalogue of reference readings on the Campaign to Implement the Marriage Law], 10 March 1953; Qingdao renmin tushuguan, ed., *Guanche hunyinfa cankao ziliao suoyin* [Index to reference material for the implementation of the Marriage Law], 25 March 1953; Tianjin shi renmin tushuguan, ed., *Guanche hunyinfa youguan ziliao suoyin* [Index to relevant materials for implementation of the Marriage Law], 10 March 1953; Huabei tushuguan, ed., *Guanche hunyinfa yundong cankao ziliao mulu suoyin* [Index and catalogue to reference materials on Campaign to Implement the Marriage Law], 25 February 1953; Shanghai shi Hongying tushuguan, ed., *Guanche hunyinfa yundong qikan cankao ziliao suoyin* [Index to periodical reference materials on the Campaign to Implement the Marriage Law], 8 March 1953.
54  BMA 38-1-81, 003. See SMA A47-1-161, 080 for a good example of a daily breakdown of Marriage Law activities. There were usually one or two such report meetings in urban areas; see BMA 1-5-105, 010–14. The report also explains that areas outside the urban core had fewer reports.
55  RMRB, 23 March 1953.
56  BMA 38-1-81, 011–12, and BMA 1-6-753, 039–52; see also BMA 1-12-128, 003–9.
57  These complaints can be found among the archival documents; see for example SMA A47-2-365, 097–98. They have been extensively explored in Diamant, *Revolutionizing the Family*; and Diamant, "Re-Examining the Impact of the 1950 Marriage Law."
58  For a plethora of examples of people's diverse responses to mass meetings see Diamant, *Revolutionizing the Family*; and Diamant, "Re-Examining the Impact of the 1950 Marriage Law."
59  SMA H1-11-3-054; SMA H11-11-3-055; SMA H1-11-3-058.
60  BMA 1-6-753, 052.
61  SMA A22-2-143, 004–5. These exhibitions had also taken place in 1951; see SMA C31-2-60, 001–2. The Shanghai Marriage Law exhibition included images from the *Illustrated Marriage Law*. Marriage Law exhibitions also took place in some city districts, such as Gaoqiao District; see SMA A71-2-915, 115–19.
62  RMRB, 23 March 1953, 1.
63  BMA 38-1-81, 013.
64  Ibid.
65  Hershatter writes that "Singing . . . was one of the means by which women were integrated into public space" and that it linked "the formal message imparted

in political meetings to the work of daily life." See Hershatter, *The Gender of Memory*, 103.

66  SMA A47-2-364, 017–27.

67  BMA 1-5-105, 013.

68  SMA A59-1-298, 108.

69  *Manhua yuebao*, 1 December 1951, no. 19.

70  BMA 1-12-128, 004.

71  Ibid.

72  NBCK, no. 58, 14 March 1953, 366; and BMA 1-12-128, 004.

73  This was a play on the "three subjections and four virtues," a slogan now denounced as a symbol of women's subjugation. NBCK, no. 58, 14 March 1953, 366.

74  Internal statistics compiled by the Shanghai Municipal Government confirm that the Marriage Law campaign was among the campaigns to make the most extensive use of drama and opera between 1950 and 1953. See SMA B172-4-209, 032.

75  BMA 38-1-81, 012.

76  SMA A47-1-161, 080.

77  NBCK, no. 69, 27 March 1953, 667.

78  BMA 38-1-81, 012.

79  On plays for the Marriage Law campaign see Zheng Wang, *Finding Women in the State*, 184–85, and Xiaoping Cong, *Marriage, Law, and Gender in Revolutionary China*.

80  Most people had enjoyed local dramas and operas long before the Communist authorities took over. People flocked to the stages in peacetime to enjoy leisurely entertainment. During wartime, theatrical and operatic worlds helped people cope with political transitions, material shortages, and suffering. Storylines could rally audiences to the cause. Using drama and opera for political education was anything but novel—Republican and imperial governments had already been doing this well before the CCP came to power. Neither was it a modern propaganda technique. Storylines of operas and especially dramas had for centuries contained political messages—be they implicitly hinted at or explicitly spelled out. On theater reform and performances in the early PRC and in modern Chinese history see Jiang, *Women Playing Men*; DeMare, *Mao's Cultural Army*; McDougall and Clark, *Popular Chinese Literature and Performing Arts*; and Johnson, Nathan, and Rawski, *Popular Culture in Late Imperial China*. The power of operas and dramas lay in their ability to move audiences, and Republican governments had harnessed this power to an unprecedented extent from the early twentieth century onwards. Chen Duxiu made this clear in his 1904 essay "On Theater": "Theater is what people love to see and hear most. It is an art form that can easily get into people's heads and touch their [hearts]. Theater has the power to take possession of its audience, making it happy and joyful one moment and sad and mournful the next, making it dance in delirium the one moment and cry in a flood of tears the next. It doesn't take much to make incredibly great changes in people's mind[s]. . . . From this perspective

theater is in fact a great big school for all the people under heaven; theater workers are in fact influential teachers of the people." Cited in Fei, *Chinese Theories of
Theater*, 117.

81  Lanjun Xu, "Sentimentalism, Geopolitics, and Cosmopolitanism." Jin Jiang also
    writes of the popularity of love opera and the fact that urban audiences much
    preferred these operas over revolutionary drama; see Jiang, *Women Playing
    Men*, 185. Ying Du discusses the popularity of tabloids in the early 1950s, a
    genre often overlooked in early PRC historiography, in "Shanghaiing the Press
    Gang," 95–107.

82  Apter and Saich, *Revolutionary Discourse in Mao's Republic*, 78 and 263–64.
    Exegetical bonding, they argue, "results in an emotional and symbolic intensity
    that includes the consciousness of self in terms of others. The result of exegetical
    bonding then is prescriptive illumination. Its higher purpose is enlightenment
    by the transcendence of ordinary understanding."

83  Haiyan Lee, *Revolution of the Heart*, 283.

84  Zhou Yang, "Gaige he fazhan minzu xiqu yishu: 11 yue 14 ri zai Beijing di yi jie
    quanguo xiqu guanmo yanchu dahui bimu" [Reform and develop the national
    theatrical arts: The conclusion of the First National Congress on Theatrical Perfor-
    mances in Beijing on 14 November], GMRB, 27 December 1952. On this con-
    gress see the entry "Di yi jie quanguo xiqu guanmo yanchu dahui" [First Na-
    tional Congress on Theatrical Performances], 60.

85  SMA A22-2-143, 004–5.

86  Luohan coins are a type of ancient coin (with or without a hole) that was used
    as a martial arts weapon or as a lover's keepsake. Sometimes, these coins were
    also given as a New Year's gift. Some women would wear the coins as a necklace
    or as a bracelet in lieu of an engagement ring. Alternatively, Luohan coins would
    be placed at the bottom of a dowry trunk for a daughter. The name derives from
    the Luohan, the eighteen disciples of the Buddha who are believed to have forged
    these coins directly; see Yu and Yu, *Chinese Coins*, 47. The play also won several
    prizes at the National Congress on Theatrical Performances; see RMRB, 16 No-
    vember 1952, for a list of prize winners.

87  Zhao Shuli, "Dengji" [Registration], 27–45; On Zhao Shuli's role in the Commu-
    nist literature and arts world see also Feuerwerker, "Zhao Shuli," 100–145; and
    Birch, "Chao Shu-li," 185–95.

88  Wen Mu et al., *Luohan qian* [Luohan coins], 64.

89  SMA B172-1-70, 046–62.

90  Ibid., 052.

91  Dongbei daibiaotuan, *Xiao nüxu* [Little son-in-law].

92  "Di yi jie quanguo xiqu guanmo yanchu dahui."

93  "Xiang pingju 'xiao nüxu' xuexi" [Learning from the Ping Opera *Little Son-in-
    Law*], XWRB, 26 December 1952. For a discussion of different versions of the
    play see "Juxing 'Xiao nüxu' zuotan hui" [A discussion meeting on *Little Son-
    in-Law*], XMB, 27 March 1953.

94  This *hutong* was torn down in the 1980s to make way for the Chinese Educa-

tional Television building. For a discussion of the play see Chun Nian, "Xuan-chuan hunyinfa de hao juben: Jieshao 'Liushujing'" [Good plays to propagate the Marriage Law: Introducing *Liushujing*], XMB, 6 March 1953.

95  SMA A47-2-365, 099. On the play's adaptation see *Zhongguo xiqu zhi: Beijing juan* [Records of China's drama and opera: Beijing volume], 162. "Guanyu 'Liushujing' de ruogan wenti da duzhe" [A reply to readers on some problems regarding *Liushujing*], 96–97.

96  Tian Han, "Zuohao xiju gongzuo manzu renmin de xuyao" [Do dramas work well and satisfy people's needs], 4.

97  Chun Nian, "Xuanchuan hunyinfa de hao juben: Jieshao 'Liushujing.'"

98  "Guanyu 'Liushujing' de ruogan wenti da duzhe."

99  Ibid.

100  For a detailed study of this play and of Yue Opera in twentieth-century China, see Jiang, *Women Playing Men*.

101  See, for example, the advertisements in XWRB, 27 March 1953.

102  Juben yuekan bianjibu, *Liang Shanbo yu Zhu Yingtai* [Liang Shanbo and Zhu Yingtai].

103  SMA B172-4-209, 025–31.

104  Xu Qiyi, "'Liang Zhu' de jieshu" [The ending of "Liang Zhu"], XMB, 16 March 1953.

105  Lanjun Xu, "Sentimentalism, Geopolitics, and Cosmopolitanism."

106  There are different versions of the main characters' names. I have adoped the names used in *Juben* in 1953.

107  Ji Genyin, "Guanyu 'Lanqiaohui' de wenti" [On problems in Rendez-vous at Blue Bridge], Juben, no. 4 (1953): 90–91.

108  The minutes of the meeting were also published in *Dazhong ribao* [Masses daily], literature and arts section, 11 June 1952.

109  Ji Genyin, "Guanyu 'Lanqiaohui' de wenti," 91.

110  BMA 38-1-81, 012.

111  Jiang, *Women Playing Men*, discusses at length why opera and drama, despite different bureaucratic obstacles, continued to be a genre that local residents genuinely enjoyed.

112  SMA A59-1-298, 108.

113  Chen Kehan, "Guanyu xiuding 1953 nian jihua de yijian," 202.

114  "Chuban zongshu guanyu chuli 'Li Fengjin' deng lianhuanhua wenti gei Shanghai shi xinwen chubanchu de tongzhi" [General Publishing Administration notification to the Shanghai Municipal News and Publishing Office on administering the problem of *Li Fengjin* and other serial comics], 60–61; and "Chuban zongshu guanyu 'Li Fengjin' yishu bubi tingshou xiugai gei Shanghai shi xinwen chubanchu deng de tongzhi" General Publishing Administration notification to the Shanghai Municipal News and Publishing Office, etc., on not having to stop sales and revise the book *Li Fengjin*], 62.

115  "Chuban zongshu guanyu 'Li Fengjin' yishu bubi tingshou xiugai gei Shanghai shi xinwen chubanchu deng de tongzhi."

116  Ibid.

117  Zhongyang xuanchuanbu, "Tongsu shuji de xuyao he chuban qingkuang," 482.
118  "Guanyu xuanchuan hunyinfa de chubanwu de yixie quedian" [On some shortcomings in publications to propagate the Marriage Law], 37–40.
119  "Zhongyang xuanchuanbu guanyu ge di baozhi xuanchuan guanche hunyinfa de quedian he cuowu de tongbao" [Central Propaganda Department circular on shortcomings and mistakes of newspapers across the country in propagating and implementing the Marriage Law], 521–24.
120  Ibid., 523.
121  Ibid.
122  Zhongyang xuanchuanbu, "Tongsu shuji de xuyao he chuban qingkuang," 482.
123  "Guanyu xuanchuan hunyinfa de chubanwu de yixie quedian," 37. This was one of the examples that "traveled" through different criticism reports. The same problem was also mentioned in Zhongyang xuanchuanbu, "Tongsu shuji de xuyao he chuban qingkuang," 482. Suiyuan Province existed until 1954, and its area is today covered by the Inner Mongolia Autonomous Region.
124  Zhongyang xuanchuanbu, "Tongsu shuji de xuyao he chuban qingkuang," 484. Also see the March 1953 issue (no. 9) of *Xuanchuan tongxun*.
125  BMA 8-2-469, 007.
126  Zhongyang xuanchuanbu, "Tongsu shuji de xuyao he chuban qingkuang," 482.
127  In one example, *Fujian ribao* authors were criticized for responding to a reader's question about whether counterrevolutionaries could register marriages while under surveillance; they were told that they should have obtained advice from senior levels before answering solely on the basis of the printed law. See "Zhongyang xuanchuanbu pizhuan Huadongju xuanchuanbu guanyu guanche hunyinfa xuanchuan jiancha jieshu de tongbao" [The Central Propaganda Department transmits the East China regional office Propaganda Department's circular on the results of the investigation into propaganda to implement the Marriage Law], 4–6. For other examples of textbook criticisms see SMA C31-2-210, which gives insights into the Shanghai Women's Federation's criticism of a textbook for women that included discussions of the Marriage Law. On mistakes in *The Marriage Law Brings Happiness* see also RMRB, 1 April 1953.
128  Zhongyang xuanchuanbu, "Tongsu shuji de xuyao he chuban qingkuang," 484.
129  Here I follow Michael Schoenhals, who has argued that journalists "became the enablers of an entirely new political discourse centered on distinction." See Schoenhals, "Demonising Discourse," 467.
130  Timothy Cheek uses the concept of a "directed public sphere" to describe the role state institutions play in directing information flows and the formation of society; see Cheek, *Propaganda and Culture in Mao's China*, 15–17.
131  RMRB, 6 May 1953, 1; RMRB, 7 May 1953, 1; RMRB, 19 November 1953, 1.
132  RMRB, 19 November 1953, 1.
133  RMRB, 20 July 1954.
134  RMRB, 7 January 1955; RMRB, 6 March 1955.
135  SMA B168-1-821, 003.
136  SMA B168-1-223, 032–39.

137   On the dissemination of the Election Law see also Zhang Jishun, "Creating 'Masters of the Country'"; and Zhang Jishun, *Yuanqu de dushi*, 83–132.
138   NBCK, 27 July 1953, 385.
139   In the particular case of Putuo District, the Chinese term for elections (*pu-xuan*) contained a homophone "pu" which had people wondering whether the word actually meant "Putuo chooses." NBCK, 16 June 1953, 261.
140   NBCK, 16 June 1953, 261. For general responses to the Election Law in Shanghai see NBCK, 12 June 1953, 198–200.
141   NBCK, 27 July 1953, 384–85.
142   NBCK, 16 June 1953, 261.

# Chapter 4

1   Luo Longji, "On Human Rights," 138–51, 148. Luo would be attacked as one of the country's national "rightists" in 1957, and unlike many others he was never rehabilitated.
2   "Guanyu gongbu xianfa cao'an de baodao tishi" [Brief on reportage on prom-ulgation of the constitution draft], 265–70.
3   Ibid., 266.
4   The official translation can be found in Mao Zedong, "On the Draft of the Con-stitution of the People's Republic of China," 143.
5   Ibid., 144.
6   *Xin mingci cidian* [Dictionary of new terms], 2112.
7   The lexicon of "rights and duties," originating in nineteenth-century German jurisprudence, permeated Chinese socialist legislation via European civil law and Soviet law. Karl Marx, in his 1867 draft for the "Rules and Administrative Regulations of the International Workingmen's Association," wrote that "the struggle for the emancipation of the working classes means not a struggle for class privileges and monopolies, but for equal rights and duties." See Marx, "Rules and Administrative Regulations of the International Workingmen's Association." I thank Glenn Tiffert for pointing me to the larger legal history behind the notion of "rights and duties." In Cold War Europe, socialist countries blamed capitalist and "imperialist" countries for not fulfilling their promise of universal rights for all. Liberal-democratic countries meanwhile took socialist countries to task for human rights abuses, starting particularly in the 1960s. "Western publicists," Paul Betts writes, "used human rights as a cudgel with which to lambast Soviet despotism behind the Iron Curtain, and in doing so they helped consolidate a new Cold War anticommunist consensus." See Betts, "Socialism, Social Rights, and Human Rights," 409
8   Liu Shaoqi, *Report on the Draft Constitution of the People's Republic of China*, 15 September 1954, 42–43. The language was certainly not new to Chinese audi-ences, for they had been introduced to it in the third section of the Marriage Law, which stipulated the "Rights and Duties of Husband and Wife," yet pro-

nouncements on the constitution took this to a broader level, applying it to every aspect of life under socialism in China.

9  For two studies on constitution discussions in the Soviet Union, under Stalin and Brezhnev respectively, see Getty, "State and Society under Stalin"; and Nathans, "Soviet Rights-Talk in the Post-Stalin Era."

10  For a comprehensive history of the making of the 1954 constitution see Han Dayuan, *1954 nian xianfa yu Zhongguo xianzheng*; and Han Dayuan, *1954 nian xianfa zhiding guocheng* [Drafting the 1954 constitution]. Tiffert, "Epistrophy," details how the constitution was written and its contents negotiated at different levels of the party-state, showing both the international influences that shaped the constitution as well as the detailed and far from perfunctory discussions that took place during its drafting.

11  Sun Yatsen's ideas are discussed in Bergère, *Sun Yat-sen*; Fung, *In Search of Chinese Democracy*, 30–31, 66–71, 93–98; and Zarrow, *Educating China*, 36.

12  Li Huayu, "The Political Stalinization of China," 28–47.

13  RMRB, 15 June 1954, 1–3; the same text, issued by the Xinhua News Agency, appeared in *Xinwen ribao*, *Jiefang ribao*, *Beijing ribao*, and other papers.

14  For details of this first phase and how the discussion results fed into the creation of a second, revised constitution draft, see Han Dayuan, *1954 nian xianfa yu Zhongguo xianzheng*; and Tiffert, "Epistrophy," 68–70.

15  Throughout April and May 1954, RMRB featured a daily stream of longer articles and snippets on the discussion of the first draft, generally saying little about content and much about where it was discussed and by whom.

16  Diamant and Feng, "The PRC's First National Critique," 6. In his recollections, Dong Chengmei adds that another almost 6 million representatives from local people's congresses discussed this draft as well; see Dong Chengmei, "Zhiding 1954 nian xianfa ruogan lishi qingkuang huiyi" [Recollections on some historical circumstances in drafting the 1954 constitution], 2–4.

17  "Zhonggong zhongyang guanyu zai quanguo renmin zhong jinxing xianfa cao'an de xuanchuan he taolun de zhishi" [Party Central directive on carrying out propaganda for and discussion of the constitution draft among the people], 176.

18  BMA 1-6-957, 030.

19  "Zhongyang xuanchuanbu guanyu zai xianfa cao'an de xuanchuan he taolun zhong ying zhuyi sixiang de tongzhi" [Central Propaganda Department notification on the need to pay attention to thought during constitution draft propaganda and discussion], 207.

20  SMA A22-2-1525, 033.

21  BMA 14-2-57, 003.

22  Ibid.; and BMA 1-6-849, 011.

23  SMA A22-2-1525, 033.

24  Ibid.

25  XWRB, 18 June 1954, 4.

26  RMRB, 16 July 1954, 2.

27  RMRB, 18 July 1954, 1. See also RMRB, 16 July 1954, 2.

28  RMRB, 16 July 1954, 2.
29  RMRB, 18 July 1954, 1.
30  XWRB, 19 June 1954, 1.
31  XWRB, 19 June 1954, 1.
32  SMA A22-2-1525, 034.
33  Han Dayuan, "Guanyu zhiding 1954 nian xianfa ruogan lishi qingkuang de huiyi" [Recollections on some historical circumstances in drafting the 1954 constitution], 500–506.
34  "Zhonggong zhongyang guanyu zai quanguo renmin zhong jinxing xianfa cao'an de xuanchuan he taolun de zhishi," 177.
35  XWRB, 16 June 1954, 1.
36  BMA 1-6-957, 001.
37  Ibid., 002.
38  SMA A22-2-1525, 016–18.
39  Committees also paid for the printing of materials, the training of report-givers, and the report-givers' work fees. This discussion was, as Dong Chengmei remarked as well, an expensive undertaking; see his "Zhiding 1954 nian xianfa ruogan lishi qingkuang huiyi." Once laid out, reimbursement for these expenses could then be claimed from the central Ministry of Finance in Beijing, which, one report suggested, oversaw the finances for the discussion. See "Zhonggong zhongyang guanyu zai quanguo renmin zhong jinxing xianfa cao'an de xuanchuan he taolun de zhishi," 177.
40  Guanyu gongbu xianfa cao'an de baodao tishi," 265.
41  Copies of these briefings are compiled in SMA A22-2-1525.
42  SMA A22-2-1525, 018–20. Xinhua's reporters probably used a similar template. The layout of what they wrote for *Neibu cankao* mirrored the layout of the committee briefings.
43  Dong Chengmei, "Zhiding 1954 nian xianfa ruogan lishi qingkuang huiyi."
44  Tiffert, "Epistrophy," 70.
45  "Guanyu gongbu xianfa cao'an de baodao tishi," 265–67.
46  Ibid., 270.
47  "Zhongyang xuanchuanbu guanyu zai xianfa cao'an de xuanchuan he taolun zhong ying zhuyi sixiang de tongzhi," 207. The same advice was also given to local cadres. See for instance BMA 1-6-957, 034.
48  "Guanyu gongbu xianfa cao'an de baodao tishi," 270. There were further internal public security briefings, social investigation reports, and other internal reports written and circulated among different groups of people with their respective levels of access to internal government and internal party information.
49  BMA 1-6-957, 003.
50  Ibid., 029–30.
51  Ibid., 021.
52  Ibid.
53  "Guanyu gongbu xianfa cao'an de baodao tishi," 268–69.
54  BMA 1-6-849, 006.
55  SMA A22-2-1525, 136.

56  Ibid., 197–98. Uncertainty about how exactly to approach this work led the Shang-
    hai committee to belabor very fine points. It told cadres not to use the term
    "study" but to refer only to "discussion" and "propaganda" unless people talked
    about "studying" of their own volition, SMA A22-2-1525, 069.

57  Using reports on the draft discussion, Neil Diamant and Feng Xiaocai have
    argued that it was the first instance of organized engagement with the struc-
    ture of the Chinese state, the position of the party, and the role of citizens. They
    also show that the discussion was a forum for people to criticize the govern-
    ment and to point out inconsistencies in socialist rule. See Diamant and Feng,
    "The PRC's First National Critique."

58  Strauss, "Morality, Coercion and State Building," 37–58, argues that the mass cam-
    paigns of the early 1950s reinforced new social identities and class labels. See also
    U, "The Making of Chinese Intellectuals," and U, "The Making of *Zhishifenzi*."

59  SMA A22-2-1525, 131–32.

60  BMA 14-2-57, 008.

61  NBCK, no. 165, 24 July 1954, 401.

62  BMA 14-2-57, 021.

63  Ibid., 013.

64  Ibid.

65  NBCK, no. 163, 22 July 1954, 350.

66  Ibid.

67  NBCK, no. 165, 24 July 1954, 397.

68  Reports suggest that "capitalists" and public security and police officials were
    among the groups that responded most strongly to the constitution discus-
    sion. Xinhua reporters and draft discussion committees paid particularly
    careful attention to their responses. For a small selection of mentions about this
    part of the discussion on both the first and second drafts, see NBCK, no. 163, 22
    July 1954, 352; NBCK, no. 95, 28 April 1954, 285; NBCK, no. 99, 5 May 1954, 49;
    NBCK, no. 100, 6 May 1954, 58–59; NBCK, no. 113, 21 May 1954, 314–17; and
    BMA 14-2-57, 006.

69  NBCK, no. 165, 24 July 1954, 396.

70  BMA 14-2-57, 004.

71  BMA 14-2-57, 014.

72  BMA 14-2-57, 004.

73  The same problem occurred in Shanghai and other places; see NBCK, no. 165,
    24 July 1954, 397. It is also described in Diamant and Feng, "The PRC's First Na-
    tional Critique."

74  BMA 153-1-1267, 002.

75  Ibid.

76  SMA A22-2-1525, 204.

77  BMA 14-2-57, 007.

78  The English translation is taken from *The Constitution of the People's Republic
    of China*. For a memoir of the English edition of the constitution see Han Da-
    yuan, "Aipositan yu 1954 nian xianfa de yingwen ban" [Epstein and the English
    edition of the 1954 constitution], 492–99.

79  BMA 14-2-57, 062.

80  BMA 1-6-957, 032. There were other examples of this problem. In Heilongjiang Province, for instance, some people thought that every article of the constitution was a "law," meaning that the duty to work was a law and if one was unemployed then that would be a "violation of the law." NBCK, no. 165, 24 July 1954, 402.

81  "Guanyu gongbu xianfa cao'an de baodao tishi," 267.

82  Trying to make a connection to Stalin, they explained that a constitution should be a document of what is "now," not what will be in the "future." NBCK, no. 113, 21 May 1954, 316.

83  "Guanyu gongbu xianfa cao'an de baodao tishi," 266.

84  NBCK, no. 143, 29 June 1954, 350.

85  BMA 14-2-57, 010.

86  NBCK, no. 147, 3 July 1954, 43. See also NBCK, no. 146, 2 July 1954, 21; and NBCK, no. 165, 24 July 1954, 397.

87  NBCK, no. 143, 29 June 1954, 352-3. See also NBCK, no. 146, 2 July 1954, 26-27, for a report on an Indian newspaper's response to the draft; and NBCK, no. 193, 27 August 1954, 419-22, for a rebuttal to a US reporter's comments on the constitution cabled via the United States Information Service in Vienna. For another example from the Hong Kong *Sing Tao Daily* see NBCK, no. 152, 9 July 1954, 156.

88  Wang and Hao, "Zhonghua renmin gongheguo di yi bu xianfa de zhiding guocheng" [The compilation of the PRC's first constitution].

89  Dong Chengmei, "Zhiding 1954 nian xianfa ruogan lishi qingkuang huiyi," 2-4.

90  Ibid.

91  Lü's participation is mentioned in Tiffert, "Epistrophy," 68. Lü is famous for his 1951 lectures; see Lü and Zhu, *Yufa xiuci jianghua* [Lectures on grammar and rhetoric]. On national attempts to purify the Chinese language see Wagner, "Zhonggong 1940-1953 jianli zhengyu, zhengwen de zhengce dalüe" [A sketch of CCP policies to establish "incorrect speak" and "correct write' (1940-1953)]; and Volland, "A Linguistic Enclave," 470.

92  Yu Xuewen, "Renmin de xianfa, renmin de yuyan" [The people's constitution, the people's language], GMRB, 30 September 1954, 6.

93  BMA 14-2-57, 006.

94  NBCK, no. 165, 24 July 1954, 395.

95  Dong Chengmei, "Zhiding 1954 nian xianfa ruogan lishi qingkuang huiyi"; Han Dayuan, "Guanyu zhiding 1954 nian xianfa ruogan lishi qingkuang de huiyi," 505.

96  Some of the mistakes made during the meetings are discussed in Diamant and Feng, "The PRC's First National Critique," 19-21.

97  "Guanyu gongbu xianfa cao'an de baodao tishi," 269.

98  This was a fairly common problem; see for example SMA A22-2-1525, 065. For examples from Jiangxi Province see NBCK, no. 163, 22 July 1954, 352-54.

99  "Zhongyang xuanchuanbu guanyu gaijin baozhi shang guanyu xianfa cao'an he xianfa cao'an de quanmin taolun de xuanchuan he baodao de tongzhi" [Central Propaganda Department notification on improving propaganda and

newspaper reportage on the constitution draft and on the all-people discussion of the constitution draft], 235.

100  SMA A6-2-25, 151.

101  SMA A22-2-1525, 062.

102  Ibid., 068.

103  "Zhongyang xuanchuanbu guanyu gaijin baozhi shang guanyu xianfa cao'an he xianfa cao'an de quanmin taolun de xuanchuan he baodao de tongzhi," 234. This problem is also mentioned in SMA A22-2-1525, 068, which reminds readers that all Chinese persons are citizens and enjoy citizen rights.

104  *The Constitution of the People's Republic of China*, 11; and SMA A22-2-1525, 066.

105  "Zhongyang xuanchuanbu guanyu gaijin baozhi shang guanyu xianfa cao'an he xianfa cao'an de quanmin taolun de xuanchuan he baodao de tongzhi," 234.

106  Ibid.

107  SMA A22-2-1525, 066.

108  Ibid., 060. For a more extensive report that incorporates part of this report see SMA A6-2-25, 148–53.

109  SMA A22-2-1525, 061.

110  "Zhongyang xuanchuanbu guanyu gaijin baozhi shang guanyu xianfa cao'an he xianfa cao'an de quanmin taolun de xuanchuan he baodao de tongzhi," 233.

111  The divisions of different newspapers are discussed in Du, "Shanghaiing the Press Gang," 118. *Jiefang ribao* was the party daily, whereas *Wenhui bao* focused on intellectuals, teachers, and middle school pupils. *Xinwen ribao* was for people working in industry and commerce, while *Laodong bao* addressed workers and was the newspaper of the East China branch of the General Workers' Union and the Shanghai Workers' Union.

112  SMA A22-2-1525, 064.

113  *Zhonghua renmin gongheguo shi biannian: 1954 nian* [Annals of the history of the People's Republic of China: 1954], 425.

114  Ibid.

115  RMRB, 16 August 1954, 2.

116  Ibid.

117  Such images were printed almost daily in *Renmin ribao*, *Beijing ribao*, and *Jiefang ribao* in late June and July 1954. High-gloss versions of these images were reprinted in the July and August editions of *Renmin huabao* (People's pictorial); see for instance issue no. 7, 1954, and issue no. 8, 1954.

118  Apter and Saich, *Revolutionary Discourse in Mao's Republic*, 263–64.

119  SMA A22-2-1525, 114.

120  XWRB, 25 September 1954, 3; *Jiefang ribao*, 23 September 1954, 3.

121  GMRB, 25 September 1954, 6.

122  XWRB, 22 September 1954, 4.

123  GMRB, 28 September 1954, 3.

124  *Renmin huabao*, no. 10, October 1954, 2–3.

125  Diamant and Feng write, "We suggest that the constitution document was far less important than the prolonged exposure to the discussion about it." See "The PRCs First National Critique," 12. I would suggest both were important in

different ways, but they were crucially linked. The potency of the book symbol and slogans/formulations from the constitution provided a simple canvas and common denominator onto which state and non-state actors, with very different ideas about what a constitution was and should do, projected their interpretations. This goes some way to help explain why people would present physical copies of the constitution when making a complaint about government, a practice often reported in anecdotal evidence about conflicts between local officials and residents. This practice was also famously reported in elite struggles among the party leadership. In a well-known example from 1964, Mao countered Liu Shaoqi and Deng Xiaoping's attempt to delimit some of his influence within the party by holding copies of the party and state constitutions in hand during a meeting and asking why they had curtailed rights that each document granted him as a citizen and party member. See Dittmer, *Liu Shaoqi and the Chinese Cultural Revolution*. On other examples of "waving the constitution" as a political symbol, see also Yiching Wu, "The Great Retreat and Its Discontents."

126  RMRB, 26 October 1954, 3.

127  SMA A22-2-1525, 131. Penglai District became Huangpu District in 1956.

128  BMA 14-2-57, 003. Similar to the publication of the constitution draft in June 1954, copies of the final constitution, too, were in popular demand. In Shanghai, the municipal post office sent buses selling newspapers to People's Square to enable more people to purchase the constitution and to take some of the pressure off of bookstores and kiosks. XWRB, 22 September 1954, 4.

129  The manner in which the material form of the constitutional idea and the person of Mao Zedong were linked is suggestive of the cult of personality that would develop during the 1960s, though it was still bureaucratically managed in 1954. See Leese, *Mao Cult*.

130  SMA B123-3-332, 002; and SMA B6-2-103, 022–23.

131  SMA B123-3-332, 002.

132  Dong Biwu, "Dong Biwu zai di liu ci quanguo gongan huiyi shang guanyu zhengzhi falü sixiang gongzuo fangmian jige wenti de baogao" [Dong Biwu's report at the Sixth National Meeting on Public Security on some questions in political and legal thought work].

133  Yang Yuqing, "Lun zunshou falü" [On abiding by laws], 31.

134  Ibid., 31.

135  RMRB, 18 November 1954, 1.

136  Sun Guohua, *Tantan shoufa* [Talking about abiding by law]. Other volumes include Li Da, *Zhonghua renmin gongheguo xianfa jianghua* [An introduction to the PRC constitution]; and Wang and Wang, *Xianfa jiben zhishi jianghua* [An introduction to basic constitutional knowledge].

137  "Zhongyang gonganbu guanyu geji renmin gongan jiguan bixu yange zunshou xianfa he falü de zhishi" [Ministry of Public Security directive on the need for people's public security organs at all levels to abide by the constitution and laws], 2.

138  Ibid., 2–3.

139  Ibid., 3–5.

140  Ibid., 5.

141  "Jianxun: Gedi gongan bumen xuexi yu zunshou xianfa he falü de qingkuang" [News in brief: The situation of public security departments across the country studying and abiding by the constitution and laws], 14–16.

142  Ibid., 15.

143  See, for example, "Bixu jiaqiang gongan renyuan de shoufa jiaoyu" [Education to be law-abiding for public security staff must be strengthened], *Gongan jianshe*, no. 170 (28 August 1956), 10–13.

144  On the regularization of legal work in Beijing, see Tiffert, "Judging Revolution."

145  See, for example, "Jianxun: Gedi gongan bumen xuexi yu zunshou xianfa he falü de qingkuang," 15.

146  An indicative list of statements made by alleged "rightists" was collated in Dongbei gongxueyuan Ma-Lie zhuyi jiaoyanshi, "Baokan zhailu: Youpai dui minzhu, ziyou, zhuanzheng de waiqu" [Newspaper extracts: Rightists' distortions of democracy, freedom, and dictatorship].

147  "Mao Zedong zai shengshiwei zizhiqu dangwei shuji huiyi shang de zongjie" [Mao Zedong's summary at the meeting of provincial, municipal, and autonomous region party committee secretaries], 27 January 1957, CARCDB.

148  RMRB, 11 April 1957, 7. See also RMRB, 9 September 1957; RMRB, 12 September 1957; RMRB, 13 September 1957.

149  RMRB, 14 March 1957, 7.

150  Ibid. For a report on regular public law propaganda in the people's courts see RMRB, 30 June 1956, 6.

151  "Zhongyang gonganbu 1957 nian gongan xuanchuan gongzuo jihua yaodian" [Main points of the central Ministry of Public Security's 1957 public security propaganda work plan], 28.

152  "Zhonggong Liaoning shengwei guanyu 'kaizhan gongchan zhuyi daode jiaoyu he fazhi jiaoyu yanli daji xingshi fanzui huodong' de baogao" [CCP Liaoning Provincial Committee's report on "Launch Communist morality education and legal system education, strike severely against criminal activities"], 4–9.

153  SMA B168-1-821, 003.

154  Liu Binglin, "Guqi geming ganjin, zhengqu zai zhengfa gongzuo shang lai yi ge dayuejin" [Incite revolutionary vigor, fight for a Great Leap Forward in politico-legal work], 9.

155  RMRB, 27 January 1958.

156  On the work of the legal system following the closure of the Ministry of Justice see Bachman, "Aspects of an Institutionalizing Political System."

157  "Beijing shi Chaoyang qu kaizhan aishe baoliang shoufa de xuanchuan jiaoyu, shoudao xianzhu xiaoguo" [Beijing city Chaoyang district has launched "love the commune, protect the grain, abide by law propaganda and education," and has achieved notable results], 11.

158  Gong Jianmin, "Tigao zunshou zhengce, falü he jilü de zijuexing" [Raise consciousness to abide by policies, laws, and observe discipline], 8–10.

159  "Yiding yao zunshou falü, yifa banshi" [One must abide by laws, handle things according to law], 1–2.

160  Heilongjiang sheng gaoji renmin fayuan, "Guanyu sifa xuanchuan gongzuo cunzai de wenti he jinhou yijian" [On some problems in judicial propaganda work and suggestions for hereafter], 5–7.

161  Hebei sheng Luotian xian gonganju, "Women shi ruhe kaizhan fazhi xuanchuan jiaoyu de" [How we launched law propaganda and education], 11–12.

162  Amos, "Embracing and Contesting," 167n33. Nathans comments, "The official diagnosis of Stalin's crimes emphasized his failure to abide by 'socialist legality' rather than the content of socialist law itself." See Nathans, "Soviet Rights-Talk in the Post-Stalin Era," 173.

163  Schoenhals, "'Why Don't We Arm the Left?'"

164  Su, *Collective Killings*, 156–87.

165  RMRB, 31 January 1967, 6.

166  Non-Chinese scholars have frequently cited Xin Wu's article as the "editorial" that theorized "lawlessness." Yet it is perhaps noteworthy that the article was published on page 6 of the newspaper. The headline of the day was a reprint of an article from *Hongqi* [Red flag] magazine: "On the proletarian revolutionary struggle to seize power" (*Hongqi*, no. 3, 1967). On foreign ideas of Chinese lawlessness in the nineteenth and early twentieth centuries see Ruskola, *Legal Orientalism*, and for a theoretical discussion of this debate see in particular pages 1–29 and 42–50. Ruskola's insightful study unfortunately does not probe further or critically question Xin Wu's article and the idea of Cultural Revolution lawlessness, a point made by Fang in the book review "Teemu Ruskola, *Legal Orientalism*," 852.

167  The violence of the Cultural Revolution is reconstructed in detail in the recent book by Yang Su, including a chapter in which he engages the question of practical lawlessness; see Su, *Collective Killings*, 156–87.

# Chapter 5

1  Laws were central to Deng Xiaoping's "Four Modernizations" and "reform and opening" agenda. Laws have, therefore, mostly been placed either in an economic reforms / legal reforms nexus, a post-Mao criminal justice narrative, or in the context of post-Mao political change and the CCP's break with the past. Compared to other state projects of the Reform Era since 1978, law propaganda received only limited attention. For exceptions see Troyer, "Publicizing the New Laws," which argues—in line with CCP policy at the time—that legal education was a core component of social engineering; Exner, "Die Verbreitung der Gesetzeskenntnis unter den Bürgern der VR China," which was the first work to term these propaganda activities a "legal education campaign"; and Trevaskes, "Propaganda Work in Chinese Courts." Most scholarship on law does mention, in short sections, this law propaganda, but does not usually see it as much more than propaganda and publicity work without probing further into its structures and inherent contradictions. By comparison, there is a vast literature on the history of democracy, calls for democracy, and government

calls for "socialist democracy" in the aftermath of Mao's death. Two prominent contributions to this debate are Goldman, *Sowing the Seeds of Democracy in China*; and Nathan, *Chinese Democracy*.

2 The topics of democracy, democratic reforms, and socialist democracy in the post-1976 era have been widely debated. For some representative studies see David Goodman, *Beijing Street Voices*; Brodsgaard, "The Democracy Movement in China, 1978–1979"; Seymour, *The Fifth Modernization*; Kelliher, "Keeping Democracy Safe from the Masses"; Heilmann, *Sozialer Protest in der VR China*.

3 The link between law and literature in the Reform Era is explored in Kinkley, *Chinese Justice, the Fiction*.

4 The trial of the "Gang of Four" in 1981 served this function. The role of "transitional justice" is discussed in Cook, *The Cultural Revolution on Trial*.

5 *Renmin ribao* used the term "lawlessness" ever more frequently in reportage. See, for example, RMRB, 2 March 1978, 1; 29 October, 1978, 2; 7 January 1979, 1; 28 August 1979, 4; 26 January 1981, 3; 27 January 1981, 3; 22 June 1981, 1; 16 July 1982, 2; 4 December 1981, 2.

6 Weigelin-Schwiedrzik, "In Search of a Master Narrative," 226–32.

7 For a background history of the premise that "practice is the sole criterion of truth," see Schoenhals, "The 1978 Truth Criterion Controversy." On some of the broader context of the formulation of "seek truth from facts" see also Schram, "'Economics in Command?'"

8 Trevaskes, "Propaganda Work in Chinese Courts," 6.

9 This process is discussed under the example of legal system literature in Kinkley, *Chinese Justice, the Fiction*, 240–316.

10 Roberts and Westad, *China, Hong Kong, and the Long 1970s*.

11 "Zhonggong zhongyang guanyu zuzhi taolun xiugai xianfa de tongzhi" [Party Central notification on organizing the discussion of the revised constitution], *Zhongfa*, no. 53 (20 July 1970), CRDB. Party Central told committees that they could reproduce this notification for all work units and street-level committees and also use it to disseminate news about the upcoming discussion. The notification could not be printed on posters or copied onto blackboards, though, and newspapers and broadcasting stations could not publicize it. For a study of the 1970 draft see Yu Ruxin, "1970 nian xianfa xiugai cao'an jiedu" [Deciphering the 1970 constitution revised draft]. Yu participated in the discussion and wrote his article based on a copy of the draft he had personally retained. The copy I first accessed was in German translation via the East German Ministry of Foreign Affairs, which obtained a copy via the Soviet TASS. At the time, leaked copies also appeared in *Tokyo Shinbum* and in a Hong Kong newspaper. PA AA /MfAA C6585, Letter 16.12.1970, "Abteilung Ferner Osten." It is worth noting that the GDR department for the "Far East" commented that this draft only showed more clearly how much the PRC was distorting socialism.

12 Yu Ruxin, "1970 nian xianfa xiugai cao'an jiedu."

13 "Zhonggong zhongyang guanyu zuzhi taolun xiugai xianfa de tongzhi."

14 The momentous events surrounding the fallout between Mao and Lin Biao are discussed in Teiwes and Sun, *Riding the Tiger during the Cultural Revolution*;

Jin, *The Culture of Power*; and MacFarquhar and Schoenhals, *Mao's Last Revolution*. The brief discussion and study of the 1970 constitution, by contrast, has not featured much in the history of China's constitutions. Ladany, *Law and Legality in China*, mentions it in only one sentence (see p. 76).

15  SMA B123-8-295, 025.

16  Ibid.

17  Ibid., 027.

18  Ibid., 025.

19  Ibid., 001.

20  Ibid.

21  Ibid., 008–9.

22  Ibid., 031.

23  Ibid., 007.

24  Schoenhals, *Saltationist Socialism*, 111–27.

25  SMA B123-8-295, 031.

26  Ibid., 033.

27  Ibid.

28  Ibid., 032.

29  Ibid., 035.

30  Ibid., 036.

31  The discussion of the draft constitution, moreover, may also have been linked to the famous Li Yizhe protest posters episode in 1974 because it may have emboldened the group of three authors to put up a big-character poster calling for more socialist democracy, a reformed legal system, and a new constitution. The poster as well as relevant associated documents are collected in Chan et al., eds., *On Socialist Democracy and the Chinese Legal System*.

32  RMRB, 25 December 1976, 6.

33  *Hongqi*, no. 10, 1977, 81–84.

34  Cook, *The Cultural Revolution on Trial*.

35  SMA B123-10-101, 025–26.

36  The term "revolutionary legal system" had a brief renaissance in 1976; see for example a report from the Shanghai People's High Court Theory Group in RMRB, 15 July 1977, 3.

37  SMA A22-3-25, 002.

38  Ibid.

39  RMRB, 3 May 1978.

40  SMA A22-3-25, 017.

41  SMA B105-4-255. This is a notice from the Shanghai Municipal Bureau of Education Revolutionary Committee Office. Unfortunately, I have been unable to access any other records of this meeting in the archives.

42  SMA A22-3-25, 036–37.

43  SMA A22-4-20, 001.

44  For the program of the meeting see SMA A22-3-25, 035.

45  Ibid., 005.

46  SMA A22-3-24, 001–3.

47  SMA A22-4-20, 124.
48  SMA A22-3-24, 003. Shanghai renmin meishu chubanshe, ed. *Zhonghua Renmin gongheguo xianfa tujie.* [Illustrated explanations of the PRC constitution]
49  SMA A22-4-20, 122.
50  SMA A22-3-27, 002.
51  SMA A22-3-24, 008. On this problem see also SMA A22-4-21.
52  SMA A22-4-21, 066.
53  For a broader discussion of this process and the rebuilding of criminal justice structures after 1978 see Leng and Chiu, *Criminal Justice in Post-Mao China*, 38.
54  SMA A22-4-21, 069.
55  SMA A22-4-20, 023. The visual significance of the white worker's shirt as a marker of revolutionary distinction is discussed in Tina Mai Chen, "Proletarian White and Working Bodies in Mao's China."
56  SMA A22-3-24, 009.
57  RMRB, 13 July 1978, 1.
58  SMA A22-4-121, 001-2.
59  For an interpretation of the democracy walls in the context of the transition out of the Cultural Revolution, see Yiching Wu, *The Cultural Revolution at the Margins*, 212–16.
60  Leese, "Revising Verdicts in Post-Mao China," 102–28; RMRB, 22 December 1978.
61  On the estimated numbers of cases between 1979 and 1982 see Leese, "Revising Verdicts in Post-Mao China," 105–6.
62  Ibid.
63  SMA A22-4-266, 001–7.
64  Chen Jianfu, *Chinese Law*, 300.
65  SMA A22-4-266, 017–28.
66  Ibid.
67  Ibid., 025.
68  Schoenhals, "Demonising Discourse." The "dictatorship of the proletariat" was first included in the 1970 constitution draft and then enshrined in the 1975 state constitution.
69  I have adapted the fitting term "semantic surgery" from Schoenhals, "Demonising Discourse," 480.
70  Potter, *From Leninist Discipline to Socialist Legalism*, 110. In September 1979, Peng Zhen explained that the dictatorship of the proletariat and the people's democratic dictatorship were both needed, thereby remaining consistent with the 1978 constitution while also bringing back the people's democratic dictatorship. See "Peng Zhen tan fazhi xuanchuan wenti" [Peng Zhen on questions of legal system propaganda], 2. The 1982 constitution then only mentioned the people's democratic dictatorship.
71  Goldman, *From Comrade to Citizen*.
72  Schoenhals, "Demonising Discourse," 480.
73  SMA A22-4-266, 003.
74  Chen Jianfu, *Chinese Law*, 283; McCormick, *Political Reform in Post-Mao China*.

75 On 8 December cadres attended a national meeting on urban public order, only two days after authorities had decided to move the Beijing Xidan Democracy Wall. Shortly thereafter, the Shanghai Municipal Government organized cadre meetings. During their propaganda work, all work units were told to study closely their current issues with public order. See McCormick, *Political Reform in Post-Mao China*, 107–8.

76 SMA A22-4-266, 002–3.

77 "Peng Zhen tan fazhi xuanchuan wenti," 2.

78 Ibid., 3.

79 SMA A22-4-510, 006–9.

80 The original editors did not welcome the change in editorial policy. Details about this decision and the letter exchange that ensued when the editors filed a complaint with the municipal Propaganda Department are found in SMA A22-4-510, 006–9. See also SMA A22-4-290, 040–42.

81 ZFB, front cover, 1980.

82 Eliasoph and Grueneberg, "Law on Display in China," 671.

83 "Yao quanmian chanshu minzhu yu jizhong de guanxi" [One must comprehensively set out the relationship between democracy and centralism], 43.

84 Elizasoph and Grueneberg, "Law on Display in China," 669. Similar exhibitions were reported for the 1978 constitution propaganda week in the Shanghai Art Museum, the Shanghai Museum, and in the exhibition rooms of districts and counties. See SMA A22-3-27, 013–14.

85 Ho, *Curating Revolution*.

86 SMA A22-4-502, 002.

87 "Zhonggong zhongyang zhishi: Jianjue baozheng xingfa, xingshi susong fa qieshi shishi" [Party Central directive: Resolutely protect the practical implementation of the Criminal Code and the Criminal Procedure Law], 7.

88 Ibid., 7.

89 SMA A22-4-502, 002.

90 Smith, *Thought Reform and China's Dangerous Classes*, 213–32.

91 SMA A22-4-502, 006–7. See also Perry, *Patrolling the Revolution*.

92 SMA A22-4-502, 003.

93 "Zai qingnian zhong kaizhan 'daode fengxiang jingsai yue' deng huodong" [The launch of "morality competition month" and other activities among youth], 46.

94 ZFB, 16 July 1982, 2.

95 SMA A22-4-502, 004.

96 Ibid., 003.

97 Trevaskes, "Propaganda Work in Chinese Courts," 9.

98 Ibid.

99 SMA A22-4-266, 005.

100 "Ren yi ci gongkai shenpan kan sifa gongzuo zhong de wenti" [People's questions on seeing judicial work in an open trial], 33.

101 SMA A22-4-122, 034.

102 Ibid.

103 Ibid.

104 Ibid., 035. These trials against criminals were different from the revisions of "unjust, false, and wrong cases" administered by local courts and party committees. See Leese, "Revising Verdicts in Past-Mao China."

105 SMA A22-4-502, 003.

106 SMA A22-4-122, 032.

107 Ibid., 033.

108 SMA A22-4-134, 030.

109 SMA A22-4-502, 003.

110 Ibid., 005.

111 SMA A22-4-122, 032.

112 SMA B1-1-109, 196 to 197. Fan and He, *Zhonghua renmin gongheguo hunyinfa tujie* [Illustrated explanations of the PRC marriage law]. Propaganda departments also printed internal reference materials for report-givers and dedicated special issues of study materials to the Marriage Law; see for example "Xuexi cailiao: Xuanchuan xin hunyinfa zhuanji" [Study materials: Specially edited for the propagation of the new Marriage Law].

113 "Deng Xiaoping tongzhi tan xiugai xianfa, nongcun jingji he renmin gongshe zhidu" [Comrade Deng Xiaoping on revising the constitution, the rural economy, and the people's commune system], 2.

114 SMA B76-5-287, 072–74.

115 SMA B1-9-296, 036.

116 On the correlation between the 1981 resolution and the Gang of Four trial see Cook, *The Cultural Revolution on Trial*.

117 ZFB, 27 November 1982, 1.

118 "Guanyu 'Zhonghua renmin gongheguo xianfa xiugai cao'an' de xuanchuan tigang" [On the propaganda outline for the "PRC revised constitution draft"], 16.

119 "1981 nian xuanchuan gongzuo zhongdian" [Key points for 1981 propaganda work], 2.

120 The translation is taken from http://www.npc.gov.cn/englishnpc/Constitution /2007-11/15/content_1372964.htm. The 1982 constitution replicated much of the wording of Article 100 of the 1954 constitution, except that it added the duty to "keep state secrets" and "protect public property."

121 "1982 nian gongzuo yaodian" [Key points for 1982 propaganda work], 2–6.

122 This makeup of the first "internal" discussion more or less is found in all reports; see SMA B246-4-356.

123 SMA B248-4-705, 010.

124 "Lingdao hao xianfa xiugai cao'an de xuanchuan he taolun" [Lead well the propaganda and discussion on the revised constitution draft], 21.

125 Ibid., 22.

126 SMA B246-4-356, 143.

127 Ibid., 037 and 078.

128　Ibid., 143.

129　Ibid., 035.

130　Ibid., 144.

131　Strikes continued to take place, however; the history of post-Mao strikes in Shanghai is discussed in Perry, *Patrolling the Revolution*, 275–96.

132　SMA B246-4-356, 163.

133　Ibid., 144.

134　Ibid., 163.

135　SMA B248-4-705, 028.

136　"Lingdao hao xianfa xiugai cao'an de xuanchuan he taolun," 23.

137　Ibid.

138　MacFarquhar and Schoenhals include a discussion of this episode in *Mao's Last Revolution*, 325–32.

139　SMA B246-4-356, 145 and 006.

140　Ibid., 006.

141　Ibid., 163.

142　Ibid., 148–49.

143　Ibid., 145. Others commented that they "did not believe the articles of the constitution can be realized." See SMA B246-4-356, 037.

144　Ibid., 163.

145　SMA B246-4-356, 007, 149, and 116.

146　SMA B248-4-705, 011.

147　SMA B246-4-356, 078 and 118. People also asked if the law and party leadership were in contradiction.

148　Ibid., 164. See also SMA B248-4-705, 009–14.

149　SMA B246-4-356, 078 and 145.

150　SMA B248-4-705, 009–14.

151　Ibid., 034 and 164.

152　"Guanyu 'Zhonghua renmin gongheguo xianfa xiugai cao'an' de xuanchuan tigang."

153　SMA B246-4-356, 145.

154　SMA B76-5-287, 073.

155　Perry, *Anyuan*, 289.

156　For example, RMRB, 3 December 1984, 4; and RMRB, 18 June 1986, 8.

157　See, for example, ZFB, 7 June 1983, 4; ZFB, 30 July 1982, 4; ZFB, 21 May 1982, 3; and ZFB, 7 May 1986, 1.

158　The CCP's construction of private life after 1978 share many features in common with the GDR around the same time. See Betts, *Within Walls*.

159　See Schenk, *Der Chef*.

160　BArch, SAPMO, DP1/1773, "Vermerk: Vorbereitung der Teilnahme an einer europäischen Regionalkonferenz zur Auswertung des IV. UNO-Kongresses von Kyoto"; BArch, SAPMO DY 64/37, "Zentrale Schwerpunkte der Rechtspropaganda"; BArch, SAPMO DP2/720 for files concerning legal education during the 1970s.

161　In 1981, there was an entire conference devoted to the subject of "legal system literature" (by then an official term for a genre); see Kinkley, *Chinese Justice, the Fiction*, 257.

162  Ibid., 258.
163  Ibid., 257.
164  Ibid., 296 and 259.
165  "Shanghai yi pingbaozu dui baokan zhengfa xuanchuan de yijian" [Suggestions by a Shanghai newspaper review group on political and legal propaganda in newspapers and magazines].
166  Ibid., 99.
167  Ibid., 99–100.
168  Ibid., 100.
169  Ibid.
170  Ibid., 101.
171  Ibid., 102.

# Chapter 6

1  Party leaders such as Peng Zhen, as Pitman Potter writes, saw the science of law as "the study of law as the embodiment of policy—conceived, articulated, and enforced through the Party/state apparatus." See Potter, *From Leninist Disatpline to Socialist Legalism*, 111.

2  On popular responses to the implementation of law and legal reform see O'Brien and Li, *Rightful Resistance*; Perry, *Challenging the Mandate of Heaven*; Yan Sun, *The Chinese Reassessment of Socialism*, 235; Liebman, "Watchdog or Demagogue?"; and Diamant, Lubman, and O'Brien, eds., *Engaging the Law in China*. The question of whether these are examples of rights consciousness or rules consciousness is discussed in Li Liangjiang, "Rights Consciousness and Rules Consciousness in Contemporary China"; and Perry, "Chinese Conceptions of 'Rights.'"

3  Gallagher, "Mobilizing the Law in China," 783–85.

4  Ibid.

5  Yang Quanming, "Cengqiang shehui zhuyi xianfa yishi shi yi xiang poqie renwu" [Increasing and strengthening socialist constitutional consciousness is an urgent task], 5–8. For other discussions of constitutional consciousness see, for example, Wu Xieying, "Lun xianfa yishi" [On constitutional consciousness], 17–20; and Li Maoguan, "Shilun shehui zhuyi falü yishi" [On socialist legal consciousness], 61–64.

6  The term "constitutional consciousness" was not as prominent as "legal consciousness." In early 1987, the "Talk" column of the journal *Faxue* highlighted an article titled, "Something That Came to Mind While Reading the *Dictionary of Jurisprudence*" in which the author Sui Fu wrote: "I often leaf through the *Dictionary of Jurisprudence* lying on my desk . . . No matter whether it is to do research on theory of jurisprudence, law propaganda, or else 'law popularization' work, this reference work written by different specialists and authorities in the legal world is absolutely indispensable. I don't know how, but as of late as I have

been looking through this reference work, I have always felt that it is missing something. I've thought this over again and again, but I cannot avoid having doubts." Sui went on to explain that according to his understanding, dictionaries should include terms often seen and often used. Yet, he simply could not find entries on "civic consciousness," "constitutional consciousness," etc. In a dictionary published in 1980, and revised in 1984, Sui argued that these were major omissions. For Sui's article see Sui Fu, "Du 'Faxue cidian' xiang-dao de," 43. Constitutional consciousness also did not find inclusion in the Dazhong Press's 1986 *Small Dictionary on the Popularization of Legal Knowledge* compiled by the Legal Research Center at Tianjin's Nankai University and the *Newly Edited Handbook for Newspaper Reading*. See Nankai daxue faxue yanjiu suo, *Puji falü changshi xiao cidian* [Small dictionary on the popularization of legal knowledge].

7 Their findings were published in two articles that are in parts identical. Yan Xiansheng, "Gongmin xianfa yishi wenti de diaocha baogao" [Survey report on the question of citizens' constitutional consciousness], 61–69; and Yan Xiansheng, "Woguo gongmin 'xianfa zhishi' diaocha" [A survey of Chinese citizens' "constitutional knowledge"], 69–73.

8 Sleeboom-Faulkner, *The Chinese Academy of Social Sciences (CASS)*, discusses the role of CASS, affiliated to the Chinese government, during the political changes of the 1980s.

9 Yan received back 412 questionnaires, which he stated was a 91.6 percent response rate with 395 valid responses. Given other ratios of participation in surveys globally, this number suggests that work units required people to complete the survey. Of the valid responses, 196 participants were male and 199 female. Again, this is a surprising parity. In terms of age, 7.8 percent of the participants were younger than eighteen, 50.1 percent were between nineteen and thirty-five years of age, and 33.9 percent were between thirty-six and fifty-five. Only 8.1 percent were above fifty-five years of age, which suggests that the questionnaire mostly targeted the workforce. Political affiliation was seen as equally important: 33.7 percent of the respondents were party members, 32.9 percent were active in mass organizations, 3 percent had other party affiliations, 29.6 percent were not affiliated with any party, and 0.8 percent did not answer the question. Most respondents, according to Yan, had university, vocational, or high school educations; and 33.1 percent were cadres, 14.9 percent were workers, 8.4 percent were peasants, 7.8 percent were military personnel, 10.9 percent were researchers, and 17 percent were students. Overall, then, Yan's sample was highly skewed towards mostly educated, professional urban workforce. Yan Xiansheng, "Woguo gongmin 'xianfa zhishi' diaocha," 69.

10 Yan, "Gongmin xianfa yishi wenti de diaocha baogao," 63–64.

11 Ibid., 65–66.

12 Ibid., 66.

13 Ibid., 67–68.

14 Ibid., 63.

15 Li Yongfu, "Guanyu zai benshi gongmin zhong jiben puji falü changshi gong-

zuo de qingkuang huibao" [Situation report on the popularization of basic legal knowledge among the city's citizens], 60.

16 Gold, "Just in Time!"

17 Zhonggong zhongyang, Guowuyuan, "Guanyu xiang quanti gongmin jiben puji falü changshi de wu nian guihua' de tongzhi" [On the five-year plan to basically popularize common legal knowledge for all citizens], 1171.

18 RMRB, 9 June 1984, 4. See also Zou Yu, "Fazhi jiangzuo zoujin Zhongnanhai" [Legal lectures enter Zhongnanhai], 23.

19 Yang Qinglin, "Quanmin pufa shiyu Liaoning" [The popularization of law for all people began in Liaoning].

20 Ibid.

21 Ibid.

22 "Lingdao ganbu daitou xuefa shi gaohao pufa gongzuo de guanjian: Benxi shiwei fushuji Li Zhida" [Cadres setting an example in learning that law is the key to successful law popularization work: Benxi Party Committee Deputy Secretary Li Zhida], 18–19. On Benxi law propaganda work see also RMRB, 14 May 1991, 3; RMRB, 12 December 1985, 4.

23 "Lingdao ganbu daitou xuefa shi gaohao pufa gongzuo de guanjian."

24 Ibid., 18–19.

25 "Kaituo xin lu de ren: Fang quanguo fazhi xuanchuan jiaoyu gongzuo huiyi teyao daibiao, Benxi shi yuan shiwei shuji Xu Buyun tongzhi" [A man who developed a new way: Visiting the delegate by special invitation to the national law propaganda education work conference, Benxi city's former party committee secretary Comrade Xu Buyun], 4–6.

26 Zou Yu, "Fazhi jiangzuo zoujin Zhongnanhai," 23–24.

27 Harold Tanner provides many examples of petty theft and crime. Tanner argues that we should see the post-1978 anti-crime campaigns as "a modernity in which the heights of material production and the heights of moral perfection would be achieved simultaneously." See Tanner, Strike Hard!, 2.

28 Zou Yu, "Fazhi jiangzuo zoujin Zhongnanhai," 24.

29 Deng Liqun, "Zai quanguo xuanchuan buzhang huiyi shang de jianghua" [Speech given at the national meeting of Propaganda Department heads], 752.

30 "Zhongyang xuanchuanbu zhongyang zhengfa weiyuanhui guanyu dangqian baokan zai fazhi xuanchuan fangmian ying zhuyi de jige wenti de tongzhi" [CCP Central Propaganda Department and CCP Politics and Law Commission notification on the need to pay attention to some problems in the current legal system propaganda in newspapers and magazines], 688–89. The Sun Yonggen case is also reported in China Report: Political, Sociological and Military Affairs, no. CPS-86-78 (Foreign Broadcast Information Service, 1986), 12.

31 On the role of "authenticity" and "truthfulness" in propaganda work during the 1980s, see Cheek, "Re-defining Propaganda," 55.

32 Liebman, "Watchdog or Demagogue?"

33 "Zhongyang xuanchuanbu zhongyang zhengfa weiyuanhui guanyu dangqian baokan zai fazhi xuanchuan fangmian ying zhuyi de jige wenti de tongzhi," 689.

34 "Puji falü changshi de zongdongyuan" [General mobilization for the popularization of common legal knowledge], 4–5.

35 "Qieshi zuohao puji falü changshi de xuanchuan jiaoyu gongzuo" [Conscientiously perform propaganda and education work to popularize common legal knowledge], 255.

36 Ibid.

37 *Peng Zhen nianpu* [Chronicle of the life of Peng Zhen], vol. 5, 320.

38 "Puji falü changshi de zongdongyuan," 5.

39 The debate about the plan was then held at the thirteenth meeting of the sixth National People's Congress Standing Committee. See Xinhua tongxunshe Zhongguo nianjian bianjibu, *Zhongguo nianjian: 1985* [China Yearbook: 1985], 344.

40 Ibid.

41 On youth being encouraged to "nurture a habit of consciously respecting discipline and obeying laws," see "Dui 'guanyu jiaqiang fazhi xuanchuan jiaoyu zai gongmin zhong puji falü changshi de jueyi (cao'an)' de shuoming" [An explanation of the "Decision to strengthen law propaganda and education and popularize common legal knowledge among citizens (draft)"], 4–5.

42 "Zhonggong zhongyang guanyu jinyibu jiaqiang qingshaonian jiaoyu yufang qingshaonian weifa fanzui de tongzhi" [CCP Central notification on gradually strengthening youth education to prevent youth crime], 1355.

43 Ibid.

44 "Xianzai dui quanju lai shuo shi zhua fazhi" [All departments should now stress the law], 9.

45 On the idea of the "scientific" in Chinese political discourse see Schoenhals, *Doing Things with Words*, 20–29.

46 Zou Yu, "Puji falü changshi yao miqie lianxi shiji" [The popularization of law should closely connect to practice], 78.

47 Zou Yu, "Fazhi jiangzuo zoujin Zhongnanhai," 24.

48 *Xinbian dubao shouce* [Newly edited newspaper readers' handbook].

49 The transition away from the language of mass campaigning is discussed in Perry, "From Mass Campaigns to Managed Campaigns."

50 On the conflicts over economic and political reforms that took place in the course of 1985 and 1986 see Sullivan, "Assault on the Reforms."

51 "Pufa jie fu" [Guard against excesses in law popularization], 1.

52 Thorgensen and Clausen, "New Reflections in the Mirror." On gazetteers in the imperial period see Zurndorfer, *China Bibliography*, 190.

53 Peerenboom, *China's Long March toward Rule of Law*, 6–7.

54 "Beijing shi 'fazhi xuanchuan zhou' huodong jinru gaochao" [Beijing municipality's "law propaganda week" activities are entering a high tide], 1.

55 Beijing shi Haidian qu difangzhi bianzuan weiyuanhui, *Beijing shi Haidian quzhi* [Beijing city Haidian district gazetteer], 334–35.

56 Beijing shi Fengtai qu difangzhi bianzuan weiyuanhui, *Beijing shi Fengtai quzhi* [Beijing city Fengtai district gazetteer], 261.

57 Beijing shi Xicheng qu difangzhi bianzuan weiyuanhui, *Beijing shi Xicheng quzhi* [Beijing city Xicheng district gazetteer], 311–12.

58 Beijing shi Chaoyang qu difang zhi bianzuan weiyuanhui, *Beijing shi Chaoyang quzhi* [Beijing city Chaoyang district gazetteer], 573.

59 Beijing shi Dongcheng qu difang zhi bianzuan weiyuanhui, *Beijing shi Dongcheng quzhi* [Beijing city Dongcheng district gazetteer], 317–18.

60 Beijing shi Xuanwu qu difang zhi bianzuan weiyuanhui, *Beijing shi Xuanwu quzhi* [Beijing city Xuanwu district gazetteer], 304–5.

61 Ibid., 305.

62 Qu Jun, *Jing'an quzhi* [Jing'an district gazetteer], 732.

63 Ibid., 733.

64 Hu and Shanghai shi Luwan qu difang bianzuan weiyuanhui, *Luwan quzhi* [Luwan district gazetteer].

65 Zhang Yilei, *Putuo quzhi* [Putuo district gazetteer].

66 Qu Jun, *Jing'an quzhi*, 733.

67 Li Yongfu, "Guanyu shenru jinxing yi xianfa wei zhongdian de pufa jiaoyu de qingkuang baogao" [Situation report on thoroughly conducting popularization of law education taking the constitution as a focus], 8.

68 Volland, "The Control of the Media"; Brady, *Marketing Dictatorship*; Shambaugh, "China's Propaganda System."

69 Cheek, "Re-defining Propaganda," 70.

70 Kinkley, "Chinese Crime Fiction."

71 BFB, 13 April 1985, 1.

72 Schmalzer, *Red Revolution, Green Revolution*, 178–79 and 258n68.

73 "Fazhi xuanchuan zhongyao zhuyi de wuge wenti" [Five issues one should pay attention to during law propaganda], 29.

74 "Yunyong gezhong shouduan jiaqiang fazhi xuanchuan deng wuze" [Use all sorts of methods to strengthen law propaganda, and five other principles], 18–19.

75 Zhonggong zhongyang Guowuyuan, "Guanyu xiang quanti gongmin jiben puji falü changshi de wu nian guihua de tongzhi," 1174.

76 "Yunyong gezhong shouduan jiaqiang fazhi xuanchuan deng wuze," 18–19. However, an article in the same bulletin, published in the next issue two weeks later, replicated almost verbatim some of the comments in this piece, thus perhaps somewhat undermining the original article's call for diversity in propaganda materials in unintentional and ironic ways.

77 Shi Qiubo, ed., *Shanghai sifa xingzheng zhi* [Shanghai Judicial Administration gazetteer], 239.

78 Ibid.; "Zhonggong zhongyang bangongting, Guowuyuan bangongting zhuanfa zhongyang xuanchuanbu 'guanyu zhengdun neirong bu jiankang baokan de qingshi' de tongzhi" [CCP General Office, State Council General Office notification to the Central Propaganda Department on the "Request for instructions on rectifying the content of unhealthy newspapers and periodicals], 1383–86.

79 Li Maoguan, "Jiaqiang fazhi de xuanchuan baodao" [Strengthen law propaganda reportage], 16.

80 "Fazhi xuanchuan zhongyao zhuyi de wuge wenti," 29.

81 "Yunyong gezhong shouduan jiaqiang fazhi xuanchuan deng wuze," 19.

82 Ibid.

83 Popular materials (*populärwissenschaftlich*, in essence the same as Chinese *tongsu* materials though presuming better educational and literacy levels) produced for popular legal education in the GDR were designed in cooperation with URANIA, an institution with a long history of disseminating scientific knowledge to a wider audience since the first half of the nineteenth century. See Olbertz, "Zwischen Systemgebundenheit und Variabilität," 311–15.

84 Sonnenkalb, "Sozialistische Rechtserziehung als ständiger Prozess innerhalb der Persönlichkeitsentwicklung," 553–55; Palwezig, "Kolloquium über populärwissenschaftliche Vermittlung von Rechtskenntnissen," 458–59; Hebig, "Rechtspropaganda in den Jugendklubs," 268–69; Christoph, "Rechtspropaganda—wirksames Instrument der politischen Massenarbeit," 398–400.

85 Beijing shi Dongcheng qu difang zhi bianzuan weiyuanhui, *Beijing shi Dongcheng quzhi*, 317.

86 Beijing shi Xuanwu qu difang zhi bianzuan weiyuanhui, *Beijing shi Xuanwu quzhi*, 305. For other contests across town see Li Yongfu, "Guanyu shenru jinxing yi xianfa wei zhongdian de pufa jiaoyu de qingkuang baogao," 7.

87 Shi Qiubo, ed., *Shanghai sifa xingzheng zhi*, 237.

88 Ibid.

89 Xiao and Shanghai shi Xuhui qu difang bianzuan weiyuanhui, *Xuhui quzhi* [Xuhui district gazetteer], 329.

90 Ye Li, "'Zhili jingsai' weihe shenshou guanzhong huanying?" [Why are "knowledge contests" well received by audiences?], 37.

91 "Fazhi zhishi xuexi jingsai jiexiao" [Announcement of the legal knowledge study contest], 4.

92 "Pengbo xingqi de qunzhongxing de 'fazhi re'" [A vigorously rising mass-character "legal fever"], 8. I have elected to translate this as "legal fever" though it should, strictly speaking, be translated as "legal system fever," following the English translations of magazines such as *Minzhu yu fazhi*. The report also contains the answers to the test questions; see pp. 8–9.

93 "Zai fazhi zhishi xuexi jingsai zhong" [In the legal knowledge study contest], inside cover.

94 "Pengbo xingqi de qunzhongxing de 'fazhi re,'" 8.

95 "Jingsai youshengzhe jiangpin [Contest winner prizes], 7.

96 He Wannan, "'Women jia zhen chu 'faguan' le" [Our family has really produced a "judge"], 10–11. The stories of other winners are retold on pp. 11–14.

97 He Wannan, "'Women jia zhen chu 'faguan' le," 10.

98 Ibid.

99 Ibid., 11.

100 Ibid.

101 "Benkan di er jie fazhi zhishi jingsai jiang yu ming chun juxing" [This magazine's second legal knowledge contest will take place next spring], 1.

102 An overview of Shanghai legal knowledge contests is given in Shi Qiubo, ed., *Shanghai sifa xingzheng zhi*, 237–38.

103 Ma Wanli, "Falü hanshou jiaoyu jie shouguo" [Legal education by correspondence bears great fruit], 78–79.

104 Xiao Yihua and Shanghai shi Xuhui qu difang bianzuan weiyuanhui, *Xuhui quzhi*, 329.

105 See, for example, RMRB, 23 November 1985, 1; and RMRB, 10 June 1985, 1.

106 Zou Yu, "Puji falü changshi yao miqie lianxi shiji," 73–79, 74 and 78.

107 SMA B323-1-65, 074–75.

108 Nathans, "Soviet Rights-Talk in the Post-Stalin Era."

109 Eastern European socialist governments and the Soviet Union paid increased attention to the distribution of law propaganda through state mass media, always emphasizing the role of the state. See BArch, SAPMO, DP1/20190, Abt. Rechtspropaganda, "Informationen über die Konferenz der Justizministerien der sozialistischen Länder in Budapest am 13. und 14. Mai 1975 zur Rechtserziehung der Bürger."

110 Mazower, *Governing the World*, 273–305.

111 Gehrig, *Legal Nation* and Keys, *Reclaiming American Virtue*, 103–27.

112 On the rise of human rights debates in Western countries see, for example, Moyn, *The Last Utopia*; Moyn and Eckel, *The Breakthrough*; Eckel, *Die Ambivalenz des Guten*; Hoffmann, *Human Rights in the Twentieth Century*; Snyder, *Human Rights Activism and the End of the Cold War*; Keys, *Reclaiming American Virtue*; Wildenthal, *The Language of Human Rights in West Germany*; Betts, "Socialism, Social Rights, Human Rights."

113 Nathans, "Soviet Rights-Talk in the Post-Stalin Era," 166–90; Donert, "Whose Utopia?" 68–87.

114 Simons, "Introduction," xii.

115 Bolle, "Rechtspropaganda in den Massenmedien der DDR," 175. On the popularization of legal knowledge through discussions of human rights see Nathans, "Soviet Rights-Talk in the Post-Stalin Era."

116 Billinsky, *Rechtsentwicklung in der Sowjetunion*, 12–13.

117 BArch, SAPMO, DP1/20190, letter Mihaly Korom (Minister of Justice, Hungary) to Hans Joachim Heusinger (Minister of Justice, GDR), 28 February 1975, Appendix: "Arbeitsdokument des Ministeriums der Justiz der Volksrepublik Ungarn zur Budapester Konferenz der Ministerien der Justiz der sozialistischen Länder zum Thema 'Rechtserziehung der Bürger.'"

118 BArch, SAPMO, DP3/572, "Diskussionsbeitrag zum Thema 'Rechtserziehung und Rechtspropaganda,'" 2.

119 Akademie für Staats - und Rechtswissenschaft der DDR, ed., *Wörterbuch zum Sozialistischen Staat*, 257.

120 BArch, SAPMO, DP3/572, "Referierender Bericht über den Inhalt der wesentlichen Ereignisse der 2. Konferenz der Minister der Justiz der sozialistischen Länder vom 27.-29.11.1973 in Moskau," 3.

121 Ibid., 8.

122 Ibid., 9.

123  Ibid., 19–20. See also BArch, DP2/20190, letter Heusinger to Korom, 21 April 1975.
124  Ullmann, "Wirksame Rechtspropaganda in den Massenmedien," 497ff.
125  BArch, SAPMO, DP3/225 Rechtspropaganda. In German, law and right both translate as "Recht," so this title has an intentional double meaning.
126  BArch, SAPMO, DY31/1068, Ehe und Familie in der DDR.

# Conclusion

1  See Feldbrugge and Simons, *Perspectives on Soviet Law for the 1980s*.
2  Middell, "1989," 170–84; Engel, *The Fall of the Berlin Wall*; Muueller, Gehler, and Suppan, eds., *The Revolutions of 1989*.
3  BArch, SAPMO, DP1/21861, "Vermerk über ein Gespräch des Genossen Botschafter Rolf Berthold mit dem stellvertretenden Minister der Justiz der VR China, Zhen Xiwen, am 07.02.1985." See also Betts, "Socialism, Social Rights, and Human Rights," 420–21. This basic agreement on the role of the party also becomes apparent in the notes prepared for Egon Krenz with the PRC Minister of Justice, Cai Cheng. See BArch, SAPMO, DP1/21861, "Empfehlungen und Informationen für des Gespräch des Mitglieds des Politbüros des ZK der SED, Egon Krenz, mit dem Minister der Justiz der VR China Cai Cheng."
4  BArch, SAPMO, DP2/2586, "Anlage 2: Vermerk über das Gespräch mit dem Generalstaatsanwalt der VR China, Genossen Liu Fuzhi."
5  BArch, SAPMO, DP1/21861, "Ministerium der Justiz, Empfehlungen und Informationen für das Gespräch des Mitglieds des Politbüros und Sekretär des ZK der SED, Egon Krenz mit dem Minister der Justiz der VR China, Cai Cheng," 4.
6  Ibid.
7  Wasserstrom and Perry, *Popular Protest and Political Culture*; Calhoun, *Neither Gods nor Emperors*; Zhang, *The Tiananmen Papers*; Sänger, "Einfluss durch Öffentlichkeit?" 165. See also Eckel, *Die Ambivalenz des Guten*, 711–65.
8  Zhang, *The Tiananmen Papers*.
9  *Die Welt*, 28 September 1989.
10  Peng Zhen, "Yong xianfa he falü tongyi sixiang" [Unite thought using the constitution and law], 875.
11  Ibid., 877.
12  Liebman, "A Return to Populist Legality?" 165–200.
13  Kotkin, *Magnetic Mountain*, 200.
14  Gallagher, "Mobilizing the Law in China."
15  Liang Luo, *The Avantgarde and the Popular*
16  Stolleis, *Geschichte des öffentlichen Rechts in Deutschland, Erster Band*.
17  Tuck, *Hobbes: Leviathan*, 190.
18  Sherwin, *When Law Goes Pop*; Sarat and Kearns, *Law in Everyday Life*; Sarat and Kearns, *Law in the Domains of Culture*; Burgess, *The Founding Fathers, Pop Culture and Constitutional Law*.
19  Bryna Goodman, "Law Is One Thing"; and Zarrow, *Educating China*.

20 For studies that examine how citizens have used legal knowledge they obtained in part as a result of this education, see Stern, *Environmental Litigation in China*; Liebman, "Watchdog or Demagogue?"; O'Brien and Li, *Rightful Resistance*; and van Rooij, "Implementation of Chinese Environmental Law," 57–74.

21 For a recent discussion of media and law dissemination see Liebman, "Watchdog or Demagogue?"; and Stockmann and Gallagher, "Remote Control."

22 Stockmann and Gallagher, "Remote Control," 446.

23 Creemers, "China's Constitution Debate," 91–109; Hand, "Constitutionalizing Wukan," 5–9.

# Chinese Character List for Selected Terms, Titles, and Names

The list is ordered alphabetically. Personal names are ordered by surname. Most entries are first listed in pinyin, followed by characters and English translation. In the few instances where I have used English translations of publisher names or publication titles in the chapters, these are first listed in English, followed by characters and pinyin. Names of books, periodicals, and plays are italicized.

Abulaomofu 阿布劳莫夫
aiguo shoufa jiaoyu 爱国守法教育   patriotic education to abide by laws

ba fa 八法   eight laws
Baode xian 保德县   Baode County
*Beijing fazhi bao* 北京法制报   *Beijing Legal Daily*
*Beijing ribao* 北京日报   *Beijing Daily*
Beijing shi renmin fating 北京市人民法庭   Beijing People's Municipal Court
bu hefa 不合法   unlawful

Cai Cheng 蔡诚
Cangzhou 沧州
Caoyang xin cun 曹杨新村   Caoyang New Village
changshi 常识   common knowledge
Chegongzhuang ditie zhan 车公庄地铁站   Chegongzhuang Subway Station
Chen Kehan 陈克寒
China Youth Press 中国青年出版社 Zhongguo qingnian chubanshe
Chuban zongshu 出版总署   General Publishing Administration
Commercial Press 商务印书馆   Shangwu yinshuguan
cuowu 错误   error

da yundong 大运动 great campaign
dafa 大法   great laws

*Dajia lai shixing hunyinfa* 大家来实行婚姻法　*Everybody Come Implement the Marriage Law*

danghua 党化　partification

danxingbeng 单行本　edition/volume

daode shang de yaoqiu 道德上的要求　moral demands

daoxuan 倒悬　be in dire straits / hanging upside down

Dazhong chubanshe 大众出版社　Mass Press

*Dazhong ribao* 大众日报　*Masses Daily*

De Wei 德威

Deng Liqun 邓力群

Deng Xiaoping 邓小平

Deng Yingchao 邓颖超

*Dengji* 登记　*Registration*

difangzhi 地方志　local gazetteer

dizhu 地主　landlord

Dong Biwu 董必武

Dong Chengmei 董成美

*Dongbei ribao* 东北日报　*North-East Daily*

Dongdan qu 东单区　Dongdan District

dubaoyuan 读报员　newspaper reader

*Dushu yuebao* 读书月报　*Dushu Monthly*


fa 法　law, method, standard

falü 法律　law

falü changshi 法律常识　common legal knowledge

falü xuanchuan 法律宣传　law propaganda

falü yaoqiu 法律要求　legal demands

*Falü yu shenghuo* 法律与生活　*Law and Life*

famang 法盲　blind to the law

Fan Jin 范瑾

Fan Shijie 范世杰

Fan Xiaolan 范小兰

fan'an 翻案　reversal of verdicts

Fanyoupai yundong 反右派运动　Anti-Rightist Campaign

*Faxue* 法学　*Jurisprudence*

fazhi 法制　legal system

fazhi 法治　rule of law

fazhi jiaoyu 法制教育　legal education

fazhi re 法制热　legal fever

Fazhi weiyuanhui 法制委员会　Legal System Committee

fazhi wenxue 法治文学　legal system literature

fazhi xuanchuan 法制宣传　legal system propaganda

fazhi xuanchuan yundong 法制宣传运动　legal propaganda campaign

fazhi yishi 法制意识　legal consciousness

fei renmin 非人民　non-People

jiben 基本　basic
jiben jingshen 基本精神　basic spirit
*Jiefang ribao* 解放日报　*Liberation Daily*
jieji 阶级　class
jiji fenzi 积极分子　activist
*Jilin ribao* 吉林日报　*Jilin Daily*
jilü 纪律　discipline
Jingju 京剧　Peking Opera
jingshen wuran 精神如染　spiritual pollution
jiu faguan 旧法观　old legal outlooks
*Juben* 剧本　*Plays*

Kaiming Bookstore 开明书店　Kaiming shudian
kantu shizi 看图识字　see the images, know the characters
kepu 科普　science dissemination
kexuede 科学地　scientific
kongsu hui 控诉会　mass accusation meeting

Lan Ruilian 蓝瑞莲
*Lanqiao hui* 蓝桥会　*Rendezvous at Blue Bridge*
lao jiefang qu 老解放区　old liberated areas
Lao She 老舍
*Laodong bao* 劳动报　*Labor Daily*
*Law and Order: The Suppression of Counterrevolutionaries Songbook* 有法有天：镇
　　压反革命唱本　*Youfa youtian: Zhenya fangeming changben*
Law Press 法律出版社　Falü chubanshe
Lei Jieqiong 雷洁琼
Li Fengjin 李风金
Li Yizhen 李宜珍
Li Yongfu 李庸夫
Li Zhaodi 李招第
Liang Shanbo 梁山伯
*Liang Shanbo yu Zhu Yingtai* 梁山伯与祝英台　*Liang Shanbo and Zhu Yingtai*
Liang Sicheng 梁思成
Liaodong 辽东
*Liaoning fazhi bao* 辽宁法制报　*Liaoning Legal Daily*
*Liaoning xuanchuan dongtai* 辽宁宣传动态　*Liaoning Propaganda Trends*
*Liaoxi ribao* 辽西日报　*Liaoxi Daily*
lifa fangfa 立法方法　legislative principle
*Lilun jialiu* 理论交流　*Theory Exchange*
Liu Binglin 刘秉琳
Liu Fuzhi 刘复之
Liu Jingfan 刘景范
liudong gongying 流动供应　mobile supply
Liufa quanshu 六法全书　Six Codes

*Liushujing* 柳树井
Lu Dingyi 陆定一
Lü Shuxiang 吕叔湘
Luo Longji 罗隆基
Luo Qiong 罗琼
*Luohan qian* 罗汉钱　*Luohan Coins*
Luwan qu 卢湾区　Luwan District

Ma Xiwu 马锡五
mafan 麻烦　trouble
Mai Guo 迈国
maimai hunyin 买卖婚姻　buy and sell marriages
*Manhua yuebao* 漫画月报　*Cartoon Monthly*
maozi 帽子　label
Miao Peishi 苗培时
Minzhengju 民政局　Civil Affairs Bureau
minzhu yu fazhi 民主与法制　democracy and legal system
*Minzhu yu fazhi* 民主与法制　*Democracy and Legal System*
*Minzhu yu fazhi huabao* 民主与法制画报　*Democracy and Legal System Pictorial*
mufa 母法　mother law

Nanshi qu 南市区　Nanshi District
neibu 内部　internal
*Neibu cankao ziliao* 内部参考资料　*Internal Reference Materials*
New Tide Press 新潮出版社　Xinchao chubanshe

People's Press 人民出版社　Renmin chubanshe
Peng Zhen 彭真
Penglai qu 蓬莱区　Penglai District
*Popular Introduction to the Suppression of Counterrevolutionaries* 镇压反革
　命讲话　Zhenya fangeming jianghua
Popular Culture Press 通俗文化出版社　Tongsu wenhua chubanshe
Popular Readings Press 通俗读物出版社　Tongsu duwu chubanshe
puji 普及　popularize
puji falü changshi de chuntian 普及法律常识的春天　springtime for the
　popularization of law
puji falü / pufa 普及法律　popularization of law
Putuo qu 普陀区普法　Putuo District

qi fa 七法　seven laws
Qian Duansheng 钱端升
Qianmen qu 前门区　Qianmen District
*Qingdao ribao* 青岛日报　*Qingdao Daily*
Qingnian tuan 青年团　Youth League
qunzhong 群众　the masses

qunzhong jiedai 群众接待    people's reception room
qunzhong luxian 群众路线    the mass line
qunzhong yundong 群众运动    mass campaign

renmin 人民    the People
renmin fazhi 人民法制    the People's legal system
*Renmin gongan* 人民公安    *People's Public Security*
*Renmin huabao* 人民画报    *People's Pictorial*
renmin minzhu zhuanzheng 人民民主专政    people's democratic dictatorship
*Renmin qianzike: Hunyin dashi*    人民千字课: 婚姻大事    *People's Thousand-*
    *Character Lesson: The Great Event of Marriage*
*Renmin ribao* 人民日报    *People's Daily*
*Renmin xuexi cidian* 人民学习词典    *People's Study Dictionary*

sanfan 三反    Three Antis
Shaanxi People's Press 陕西人民出版社    Shaanxi renmin chubanshe
Shanghai People's Art Press 上海人民美术出版社    Shanghai renmin meishu
    chubanshe
Shanghai yingxiong youxian gongsi 上海英雄有限公司    Shanghai Hero Pen
    Company
*Shanxi ribao* 山西日报    *Shanxi Daily*
shehui zhuyi 社会主义    socialism
shehui zhuyi fazhi 社会主义法制    socialist legal system
shehui zhuyi minzhu 社会主义民主    socialist democracy
Shen Junru 沈钧儒
Shen Tiancheng 沈天呈
shenpan 审判    trial
shenpanguan 审判官    judge
Shi Liang 史良
shidian 试点    test site
Shihezi 石河子
Shijingshan 石景山
shinian dongluan 十年动乱    ten years of turmoil
shishi qiu shi 实事求是    to seek truth from facts
*Shishi shouce* 时事手册    *Current Affairs Handbook*
shoufa 守法    to abide by laws / to obey the law
shoukandian 收看点    watching stations
*Shuoshuo changchang* 说说唱唱    *Recite and Sing*
si pa san bu xuanchuan 四怕三不宣传    four fears and three do not propagates
si ren bang 四人帮    Gang of Four
sifa gaige 司法改革    judicial reform
sifa gaige yundong 司法改革运动    Judicial Reform Movement
Sifabu 司法部    Ministry of Justice
Sifaju 司法局    Bureau of Justice
sixiang douzheng 思想斗争    thought struggle
South-West People's Press 西南人民出版社    Xi'nan renmin chubanshe

Suiyuan People's Press 绥远人民出版社   Suiyuan renmin chubanshe
suku 诉苦   speak bitterness
Sun Guohua 孙国华

*Tantan shoufa* 谈谈守法   *Talking about Abiding by Law*
tewu 特务   anyone suspected of maintaining links with perceived external
　　enemies of the PRC
Tian Han 田汉
Tian Jiaying 田家英
Tian Xi'er 田喜儿
Tongli Press 通力出版社   Tongli chubanshe
tongsu 通俗   popular
*Tongsu bao* 通俗报   *Popular News*
Tongsu duwu chubanshe 通俗读物出版社   Popular Readings Press
tongsu yidong 通俗易懂   easy to understand
"tongsu yidong, renren nengji, bianyu yunyong" 通俗易懂人人能记便于运用
　　"popular and easy to understand, memorable for everyone, convenient to use"
Tongsu wenhua chubanshe 通俗文化出版社   Popular Culture Press
tudi gaige 土地改革   Land Reform
Tudi gaigefa 土地改革法   Agrarian Reform Law

Wan Li 万里
Wang Feiran 王斐然
Wang Ruqi 王汝琪
Wang Ziye 王子野
wanjiu 挽救   remedy
Wei Jingsheng 魏京生
Wei Shengyuan 魏生元
Wei Wenbo 魏文伯
wei xianfa 违宪法   violate the constitution
weifa luanji 违法乱纪   violations of law and discipline
Wen Mu 文牧
*Wenhui bao* 文汇报   *Wenhui Daily*
wenming 文明   civilized, civilization
*Wenyibao* 文艺报   *Literature and Art*
Workers' Press 工人出版社   Gongren chubanshe
wu fa wu tian 无法无天   lawless, without law
wufan 五反   Five Antis
wuqi 武器   weapon

Xia Yan 夏炎
xian 限   restrict
xianfa 宪法   constitution
xianfa cao'an taolun 宪法草案讨论   constitution draft discussion
xianfa moxing 宪法模型   constitution model
xianfa yishi 宪法意识   constitutional consciousness

*Xiao nüxu* 小女婿    *Little Son-in-Law*
*Xiaofei bao* 消费报    *Consumer Report*
Xie Juezai 谢觉哉
Xin Dao 辛稻
Xin dazhong chubanshe 新大众出版社    New Masses Press
xin faguan 新法观    new legal outlooks
*Xin guancha* 新观察    *New Observer*
*Xin jianshe* 新建设    *New Construction*
xin jiefang qu 新解放区    new liberated areas
Xin minzhu zhuyi 新民主主义    New Democracy
Xin minzhu zhuyi hunyin zhidu 新民主主义婚姻制度    New Democratic
    marriage system
xin sanfan 新三反    new three antis
xin shiqi de zong renwu 新时期的总任务    general task for the new period
Xin Wu 辛午
*Xin Zhongguo funü* 新中国妇女    *Women of New China*
Xing Zhi 幸之
Xinhua she 新华社    New China/Xinhua News Agency
Xinhua shudian 新华书店    Xinhua (New China) Bookstore
*Xinmin bao* 新民报    *New People's Daily*
xinwen 新闻    news
*Xinwen ribao* 新闻日报    *News Daily*
xu 须    must
xuanchuan 宣传    propaganda/propagate
*Xuanchuan dongtai* 宣传动态    *Propaganda Trends*
*Xuanchuan tongxun* 宣传通讯    *Propaganda Bulletin*
xuanchuan zhou 宣传周    propaganda week
xuanchuanbu 宣传部    Propaganda Department
*Xuanchuanyuan shouce* 宣传员手册    *Handbook for Propagandists*
xuanjiaoke 宣教科    propaganda and education sections
Xuanjufa 选举法    Election Law
"xue fa, dong fa, zhi fa" 学法懂法执法    learn law, understand law, enforce law


Yan Xiansheng 严显生
Yang Shangkun 杨尚昆
Yang Shu 杨述
Yang Xiaocao 杨小草
Yang Zhihua 杨之华
Ye Laishi 叶籁士
Ye Shengtao 叶圣陶
yi fa ban shi 依法办事    to handle matters according to the law
yi fa zhi guo 以法治国    to govern the country according to the law
yiding xiaoguo 一定效果    a definitive effect
ying 应    should
youguan wenjian 有关文件    relevant document
yu 与    and

Yu Yunjie 俞云阶
Yuanchang Press 元昌印书馆   Yuanchang yinshuguan
yuan jia cuo an 冤假错案   unjust, false, and wrong cases
yuanze 原则   general principle
Yueju 越剧   Yue Opera
yundong 运动   campaign
*Yunnan ribao* 云南日报   *Yunnan Daily*

Zhang Aiai 张艾艾
Zhang Peng 张彭
Zhang Youyu 张友渔
Zhao Shuli 赵树理
Zhen Hua 振华
zhengfa 政法   politics and law
*Zhengfa yanjiu* 政法研究   *Political-Legal Research*
zhengzhi quanli 政治权利   political rights
Zhenya fangeming yundong 镇压反革命运动   Campaign to Suppress
    Counterrevolutionaries
zhishi 知识   knowledge
Zhonggong zhongyang 中共中央   Party Central
*Zhongguo fazhi bao* 中国法制报   *China Legal Daily*
*Zhongguo funü* 中国妇女   *Women of China*
Zhonghua renmin gongheguo chengzhi fangeming tiaoli 中华人民共和国
    惩治反革命条例   Regulations of the PRC for the Punishment of
    Counterrevolutionaries
*Zhonghua renmin gongheguo chengzhi fangeming tiaoli: Tujie tongsuben* 中华
    人民共和国惩治反革命条例: 图解通俗本 *Regulations for the Punishment
    of Counterrevolutionaries: Illustrated Popular Explanations*
Zhonghua Bookstore 中华书店   Zhonghua shudian
*Zhongyang zhengfa gongbao* 中央政法公报   *Central Bulletin on Politics
    and Law*
Zhou Enlai 周恩来
Zhou Qiang 周强
Zhou Yang 周扬
Zhu Yingtai 祝英台
zichan jieji falü 资产阶级法律   bourgeois law
zichan jieji youfa youtian 资产阶级有法有天   bourgeois lawfulness
zichan jieji ziyou zhuyi 资产阶级自由主义   bourgeois liberalization
zijuede 自觉地   consciously
Zong Hua 宗华
Zou Yu 邹瑜
zunji shoufa 遵纪守法   respect discipline, abide by law
Zuzhifa 组织法   Organic Laws

# List of Archival Files

Notes cite archival documents by file number followed by either the page range or a specific page. A note will cite a specific page only if it references a selected quotation or passage. Titles and dates (where available) for all documents cited are given in this list.

## Beijing Municipal Archives (BMA)

BMA 1-5-105, 001 to 005. "Guanyu guanche hunyinfa yundong zhunbei gongzuo jihua he jinxing qingkuang de baogao" 关于贯彻婚姻法运动准备工作计划和进行情况的报告 (Report on the situation of planning and carrying out preparatory work for the Campaign to Implement the Marriage Law). 10 January 1953.

BMA 1-5-105, 010 to 014. "Guanyu guanche hunyinfa yundong yue de zongjie baogao" 关于贯彻婚姻法运动月的总结报告 (Summary report on the Marriage Law implementation campaign month). 10 July 1953.

BMA 1-6-442, 033 to 041. "Deng Yingchao tongzhi baogao 'Guanyu xin hunyinfa'" 邓颖超同志报告'关于新婚姻法' (Comrade Deng Yingchao's report 'On the New Marriage Law'). 1951.

BMA 1-6-753, 039 to 053. "Beijing shi guanche hunyinfa yundong zongjie" (chugao) 北京市贯彻婚姻法运动总结 (初稿)" (Beijing municipal summary of the Campaign to Implement the Marriage Law [first draft]). 1953.

BMA 1-6-753, 055 to 056. Letter from the Beijing Municipal Marriage Law Implementation Committee Party Group (北京市贯彻婚姻法委员会党组) to the Beijing Municipal Party Committee (北京市委). 22 December 1952.

BMA 1-6-753, 057 to 061. "Beijing shi wei zhankai dazhangqigu guanche hunyinfa yundong de zhunbei gongzuo jihua" 北京市为展开大张旗鼓贯彻婚姻法运动的准备工

作计划 (Beijing municipal work plan for the preparations to launch the Campaign to Implement the Marriage Law on a grand scale). December 1952.

BMA 1-6-849, 001 to 007. "Beijing shi xianfa cao'an taolun weiyuanhui guanyu Beijing xuanchuan taolun xianfa cao'an gongzuo de baogao" 北京市宪法草案讨论委员会关于北京市宣传讨论宪法草案工作的报告 (Beijing Constitution Draft Discussion Committee report on constitution draft propaganda and discussion work in Beijing municipality). August 1954.

BMA 1-6-849, 008 to 011. "Beijing shi xianfa cao'an xuanchuan taolun gongzuo baogao (cao'an)" 北京市宪法草案宣传讨论工作报告(草案) (Beijing municipal report on constitution draft propaganda and discussion work [draft]). 1954.

BMA 1-6-957, 001 to 003. "Zhonggong Beijing shiwei Beijing shi xuanchuan he taolun xianfa cao'an de jihua" 中共北京市委北京市宣传和讨论宪法草案的计划 (CCP Beijing Party Committee plan for propagating and discussing the constitution draft in Beijing). 30 May 1954.

BMA 1-6-957, 009 to 015. "Guanyu Beijing shi xuanchuan, taolun xianfa cao'an gongzuo de zongjie baogao" 关于北京市宣传，讨论宪法草案工作的总结报告 (Summary report on propagating and discussing the constitution draft in Beijing). September 1954.

BMA 1-6-957, 018 to 023. "Beijing shi xianfa cao'an taolun weiyuanhui guanyu xuanchuan he taolun xianfa cao'an de jihua (cao'an)" 北京市宪法草案讨论委员会关于宣传和讨论宪法草案的计划(草案) (Beijing Municipal Constitution Draft Discussion Committee plan for propagating and discussing the constitution [draft]). 15 June 1954.

BMA 1-6-957, 029 to 035. "Beijing shi xianfa cao'an xuanchuan taolun gongzuo baogao (caogao)" 北京市宪法草案宣传讨论工作报告(草稿) (Beijing municipal report on constitution draft propaganda and discussion work [draft]). 1954.

BMA 1-12-128, 001 to 002. "Beijing shi ganbu xuexi hunyinfa jihua" 北京市干部学习婚姻法计划 (Beijing municipal cadres' Marriage Law study plan). 20 February 1953.

BMA 1-12-128, 003 to 009. "Qunzhong dui hunyinfa ji ci ci guanche hunyinfa yundong de renshi ji fanying" 群众对婚姻法及此次贯彻婚姻法运动的认识及反映 (The masses' knowledge of and responses to the Marriage Law and this Campaign to Implement the Marriage Law). 19 January 1953.

BMA 2-4-37, 001 to 009. "Beijing shi sifa gaige yundong zongjie baogao" 北京市司法改革运动总结报告 (Beijing municipal summary report on the Judicial Reform Movement). December 1952.

BMA 2-4-37, 012 to 018. "Benshi sifa gaige yundong di san jieduan de gongzuo qingkuang baogao" 本市司法改革运动第三阶段的工作情况报告 (Situation report on the work for the third phase of the Judicial Reform Movement in this city). 6 December 1952.

BMA 2-4-37, 019 to 026. "Guanyu sifa gaige yundong di er jieduan jinxing qingkuang de baogao" 关于司法改革运动第二阶段进行情况的报告 (Report on the situation of carrying out the second phase of the Judicial Reform Movement). 11 November 1952.

BMA, 2-5-58. Peng Zhen. "Guanyu zhengzhi falü gongzuo de baogao" 关于政治法律工作的报告 (Report on political and legal work). 16 September 1953.

BMA 2-20-314, 027 to 028. "Jiuqu shenpanting jiya anjian qingkuang" 九区审判庭积压案件情况 (Delayed cases at the Ninth district court). 26 April 1952.

BMA 8-2-469, 001 to 002. "Qing pishi jinzhi Beijing Xinghua shudian chuban de 'Gechang hunyinfa' yi shu fashou" 请批示禁止北京兴华书店出版的歌唱婚姻法一书发售 (Request for instructions on banning sales of Xinghua Bookstore's volume *Singing the Marriage Law*). 19 August 1953.

BMA 8-2-469, 007 to 008. "Guanyu 'Gechang hunyinfa' yi shu de cuowu" 关于'歌唱婚姻法'一书的错误 (On the mistakes in the book *Singing the Marriage Law*). 14 August 1953.

BMA 8-2-469, 011 to 012. Letter from the Central People's Publishing Administration (中央人民政府出版总署) to the Beijing News and Publishing Bureau (北京市新闻出版处) Beijing News and Publishing Bureau. 14 September 1953.

BMA 8-2-699. "Zhongyang renmin zhengfu chuban zongshu guanyu zuohao xuanchuan hunyinfa de shukan he chuban faxing gongzuo de zhishi" 中央人民政府出版总署关于做好宣传婚姻法的书刊和出版发行工作的指示 (Central People's Government Publishing Administration directive on completing books for propagating the Marriage Law and on publishing and distribution work). 8 December 1952.

BMA 14-2-57, 003 to 005. "Zhonggong Beijing shi wei xuanchuanbu 1954 nian xianfa taolun sixiang qingkuang jianbao (2): xianfa gongbu dangri de qunzhong fanying" 中共北京市委宣传部1954年宪法讨论思想情况简报(2)：宪法草案公布当日的群众反映 (CCP Beijing Party Committee Propaganda Department bulletin on the thought situation during the 1954 constitution discussion: Reactions from the masses on the day of the promulgation of the constitution draft). 15 June 1954.

BMA 14-2-57, 006 to 007. "Zhonggong Beijing shi wei xuanchuanbu 1954 nian xianfa taolun sixiang qingkuang jianbao (3): xianfa cao'an gongbu dangri de qunzhong fanying" 中共北京市委宣传部1954年宪法讨论思想情况简报(3)：宪法草案公布当日的群众反映 (CCP Beijing Party Committee Propaganda Department bulletin on the thought situation during the 1954 constitution discussion: Reactions from the masses on the day of the promulgation of the constitution draft). 16 June 1954.

BMA 14-2-57, 008 to 010. "Zhonggong Beijing shi wei xuanchuanbu 1954 nian xianfa taolun sixiang qingkuang jianbao (4): xianfa cao'an gongbu dangri de qunzhong fanying" 中共北京市委宣传部1954年宪法讨论思想情况简报 (4)：宪法草案公布当日的群众反映 (CCP Beijing Party Committee Propaganda Department bulletin on the thought situation during the 1954 constitution discussion: Reactions from the masses on the day of the promulgation of the constitution draft). 16 June 1954.

BMA 14-2-57, 013. "Zhonggong Beijing shi wei xuanchuanbu 1954 nian xianfa taolun sixiang qingkuang jianbao (6): Ganbu taolun xianfa cao'an zhong baolu de jiufa guandian de yi ge lizi" 中共北京市委宣传部1954年宪法讨论思想情况简报(6)：干部讨论宪法草案中暴露的旧法观点的一个例子 (CCP Beijing Party Committee Propaganda Department bulletin on the thought situation during the 1954 constitution discussion: An example of old legal outlooks revealed during cadres' discussion of the constitution draft). 25 June 1954.

BMA 14-2-57, 014 to 016. "Zhonggong Beijing shi wei xuanchuanbu 1954 nian xianfa taolun sixiang qingkuang jianbao (7): xianfa cao'an gongbu hou de qunzhong fanying" 中共北京市委宣传部1954年宪法讨论思想情况简报(7): 宪法草案公布后的群众反映 (CCP Beijing Party Committee Propaganda Department bulletin on the thought situation during the 1954 constitution discussion: Responses from the masses following the promulgation of the constitution draft). 25 June 1954.

BMA 14-2-57, 019 to 021. "Zhonggong Beijing shi wei xuanchuanbu 1954 nian xianfa taolun sixiang qingkuang jianbao (9): Youxie ganbu dui xianfa cao'an de xuexi taidu bu zhengque" 中共北京市委宣传部1954年宪法讨论思想情况简报 (9):有些干部对宪法草案的学习态度不正确 (CCP Beijing Party Committee Propaganda Department bulletin on the thought situation during the 1954 constitution discussion: Some cadres' attitudes on the study of the constitution draft are incorrect). 2 July 1954.

BMA 14-2-57, 061 to 063. "1954 nian xianfa cao'an xuanchuan yu taolun gongzuo jianbao (8): Qunzhong xuanchuan gongzuo jingyan diandi" 1954年宪法草案宣传与讨论工作简报(8): 群众宣传工作经验点滴 (Work bulletin on the 1954 constitution draft propaganda and discussion work: Some experiences from propaganda work among the masses). 3 July 1954.

BMA 27-2-59, 002 to 004. "Guanyu peihe jinxing sifa gaige yundong de zhishi" 关于配合进行司法改革运动的指示 (Directive on support for carrying out the Judicial Reform Movement). 7 August 1952.

BMA 38-1-81, 001 to 017. "Qianmen qu guanche hunyinfa gongzuo zongjie" 前门区贯彻婚姻法工作总结 (Qianmen District work summary on the implementation of the Marriage Law). 1953.

BMA 153-1-1267. "Guanyu Beijing shi zhengfu gaojizu taolun xuexi xianfa cao'an qingkuang jianbao" 关于北京市政府高级组讨论学习宪法草案情况简报 (Bulletin on the situation of the Beijing Municipal Government high-ranking group discussion and study of the constitution draft). 10 July 1954.

BMA 196-2-470. "Zhongyang renmin zhengfu neiwubu, sifabu 'jixu guanche hunyinfa de zhishi'" 中央人民政府内务部，司法部 "继续贯彻婚姻法的指示" (Central People's Government Ministry of Internal Affairs and Ministry of Justice "Directive on continuing the implementation of the Marriage Law"). 24 September 1952.

BMA 196-2-473. "Hunyinfa xuanchuan cankao cailiao" 婚姻法宣传参考材料 (Marriage Law propaganda reference material). 19 May 1950.

## Bundesarchiv Berlin-Lichterfelde (BArch)

BArch, SAPMO, DP1/1773. "Vermerk: Vorbereitung der Teilnahme an einer europäischen Regionalkonferenz zur Auswertung des IV. UNO-Kongresses von Kyoto."

BArch, SAPMO, DP1/20190. "Informationen über die Konferenz der Justizministerien der sozialistischen Länder in Budapest am 13. Und 14. Mai 1975 zur Rechtserziehung der Bürger."

BArch, SAPMO, DP1/20190. "Arbeitsdokument des Ministeriums der Justiz der Volksrepublik Ungarn zur Budapester Konferenz der Ministerien der Justiz der sozialistischen Länder zum Thema 'Rechtserziehung der Bürger.'" 28 February 1975.

BArch, SAPMO, DP1/21861. "Vermerk über ein Gespräch des Genossen Botschafter Rolf Berthold mit dem stellvertretenden Minister der Justiz der VR China, Zhen Xiwen, am 07.02.1985."

BArch, SAPMO, DP1/21861. "Empfehlungen und Informationen für das Gespräch des Mitglieds des Politbüros und Sekretär des ZK der SED, Egon Krenz mit dem Minister der Justiz der VR China, Cai Cheng."

BArch, SAPMO, DP2/2586. "Anlage 2: Vermerk über das Gespräch mit dem Generalstaatsanwalt der VR China, Genossen Liu Fuzhi."

BArch, SAPMO, DP2/20190. Letter Heusinger to Korom. 21 April 1975.

BArch, SAPMO, DP3/225. "Rechtspropaganda–Artikel, Referate, Vorträge, Interviews," 1971–83.

BArch, SAPMO, DP3/572. "Diskussionsbeitrag zum Thema 'Rechtserziehung und Rechtspropaganda.'"

BArch, SAPMO, DP3/572. "Referierender Bericht über den Inhalt der wesentlichen Ereignisse der 2. Konferenz der Minister der Justiz der sozialistischen Länder vom 27.–29.11.1973 in Moskau."

BArch, SAPMO, DY31/1068. "Ehe und Familie in der DDR," 1965–81.

BArch SAPMO DY31/1117. "Gesetz über den Mutter-und Kinderschutz und die Rechte der Frau.–Zeitungsausschnitte." 1950–1959.

BArch, SAPMO DY64/37. "Zentrale Schwerpunkte der Rechtspropaganda."

## Shanghai Municipal Archives (SMA)

SMA A6-2-25, 112 to 114. "Guanyu zai quanshi jinxing xianfa cao'an xuanchuan he taolun de jihua" 关于在全市进行宪法草案宣传和讨论的计划 (Plan for carrying out constitution draft propaganda and discussion across town). 29 June 1954.

SMA A6-2-25, 146 to 153. "Guanyu yi ge yue lai benshi ge bao xuanchuan xianfa cao'an de qingkuang baogao" 关于一个月来本市各报宣传宪法草案的情况报告 (Situation report on last month's propaganda on the constitution in this city's newspapers). 23 July 1954.

SMA A22-1-92, 001 to 005, "Guanyu 'guanche hunyinfa yundong yue' xuanchuan gongzuo jihua" 关于'贯彻婚姻法运动月'宣传工作计划 (On the propaganda work plan for the 'campaign month to implement the Marriage Law'). 24 January 1953.

SMA A22-2-143, 004 to 008, "Zhongyang xuanchuanbu guanyu du cui geji dangwei xuanchuanbu buzhi guanche hunyinfa xuanchuan yue gongzuo de zhishi" 中央宣传部关于督催各级党委宣传部布置贯彻婚姻法宣传月工作的指示 (Central Propaganda Department directive on supervising and urging each party committee propaganda department to arrange work for the Campaign to Implement the Marriage Law month). January 1953.

SMA A22-2-1525, 016 to 018. "Shanghai shi xianfa cao'an xuanchuan taolun fenhui zuzhi jigou chengli qingkuang" 上海市宪法草案宣传讨论分会组织机构成立情况 (Situation of setting up an organizational structure for the Shanghai municipal constitution draft propaganda and discussion branches). 23 June 1952.

SMA A22-2-1525, 018 to 020. "Guanyu ge fenhui xianfa cao'an xuanchuan taolun qingkuang huibao de guiding" 关于个分会宪法草案宣传讨论情况回报的规定 (Regulations on each branch reporting back on the situation of the constitution draft propaganda and discussion). 23 June 1952.

SMA A22-2-1525, 032 to 038. "Jiaotong lianlun gongren relie huanying xianfa cao'an" 交通链轮工人热烈欢迎宪法草案 (Transportation chainwheel workers ardently welcome the constitution draft). 6 July 1954.

SMA A22-2-1525, 060 to 065. "Zuijin Shanghai baozhi dui xianfa cao'an xuanchuan zhong yousuo cunzai de jige wenti" 最近上海报纸对宪法草案宣传中有所存在的几个问题 (A few issues in Shanghai newspapers' recent propaganda on the constitution draft). 14 July 1954.

SMA A22-2-1525, 065 to 069. "Guanyu xianfa cao'an de yixie mingci jieshi he shiyong de guiding" 关于宪法草案的一些名词解释和使用的规定 (Regulations on explaining and using some of the terms in the constitution draft). 1954.

SMA A22-2-1525, 069 to 078. "Xianfa cao'an xiang qunzhong xuanchuan de zhunbei gongzuo zonghe qingkuang" 宪法草案向群众宣传的准备工作综合情况 (Overall situation of the preparatory work for propagating the constitution draft among the masses). 1954.

SMA A22-2-1525, 110 to 114. "Guanyu zuzhi xianfa chuandaoxing xuanchuan huodong de jige wenti" 关于组织宪法传导性宣传活动的几个问题 (On a few problems in organizing constitution transmission propaganda activities). 20 July 1954.

SMA A22-2-1525, 131 to 138. "Xianfa cao'an gongbu hou gongren qunzhong de sixiang fanying" 宪法草案公布后工人群众的思想反映 (Reflections on the thought of the working masses following the promulgation of the constitution draft). 22 July 1954.

SMA A22-2-1525, 197 to 201. "Zenyang zai gongren zhong zuzhi xianfa cao'an de xiaozu taolun" 怎样在工人中组织宪法草案的小组讨论 (How to organize a small group discussion on the constitution draft among workers). 3 August 1954.

SMA A22-2-1525, 203 to 210. "Jingguo xianfa cao'an xuanchuan taolun Yimiao qu gongren qunzhong sixiang renshi tigao" 经过宪法草案宣传讨论邑庙区工人群众思想认识提高 (Having undergone the constitution draft propaganda and discussion, the Yimiao District working masses' thought and understanding has been raised). 1954.

SMA A22-3-24, 001 to 013. "Zai xuanchuan zhou jingyan jiaoliu hui shang de jianghua (er gao)" 在宣传周经验交流会上的讲话(二稿) (Speech at the meeting to exchange propaganda week experiences [second draft]). 1978.

SMA A22-3-25, 002 to 016. "Guanyu juban xin shiqi zong renwu he xin xianfa xuanchuan zhou de tongzhi" 关于举办新时期总任务和新宪法宣传周的通知 (Notification on conducting the propaganda week on the general task for the new period and the new constitution). 1978.

SMA A22-3-25, 017. "Xuanchuan kouhao" 宣传口号 (Propaganda slogans). 1978.

SMA A22-3-25, 035. "Shanghai shi 'Xin shiqi zong renwu he xin xianfa xuanchuan zhou' kaimushi dahui chengxu" 上海市'新时期总任务和新宪法宣传周'开幕式大会程序 (Procedures for the Shanghai municipal opening ceremony of the "Propaganda week for the general task for a new period and the new constitution"). 27 May 1978.

SMA A22-3-25, 036 to 037. "Xuanchuan zhou kaimushi gongzuo chengxu" 宣传周开幕式工作程序 (Sequence of work for the propaganda week opening ceremony). 27 May 1978.

SMA A22-3-27, 001 to 019. "Guanyu xuanchuan xuexi xin shiqi zong renwu he xianfa de qingkuang baogao (xiugaigao)" 关于宣传学习新时期总任务和宪法的情况报告 (修改稿) (Situation report on propagating and studying the general task for the new period and the constitution [revised draft]). August 1978.

SMA A22-4-20, 001 to 002. "Dui shiwei juxing xuanchuan zhou kaimushi de fanying" 对市委举行宣传周开幕式的反应 (Responses to the municipal party committee's organization of the propaganda week opening ceremony). 20 May 1978.

SMA A22-4-20, 023 to 024. "Xin shiqi zong renwu he xin xianfa xuanchuan zhou qingkuang" 新时期总任务和新宪法宣传周情况 (Situation of the propaganda week on the general task for the new period and the new constitution). 29 May 1978.

SMA A22-4-20, 122 to 124. "Gequ zai xuanchuan zhou zhong yunyong duozhong xingshi xiang qunzhong xuanchuan" 各区在宣传周中运用多种形式向群众宣传 (Each district is using a variety of forms to propagate to the masses during the propaganda week). 31 May 1978.

SMA A22-4-21, 001 to 004. "Xin shiqi zong renwu he xin xianfa xuanchuan zhou qingkuang" 新时期总任务和新宪法宣传周情况 (Situation of the propaganda week on the general task for the new period and the new constitution). 1 June 1978.

SMA A22-4-21, 066 to 069. "'Xin shiqi zong renwu he xin xianfa xuanchuan zhou' qingkuang" 新时期总任务和新宪法宣传周情况 (Situation of the propaganda week on the general task for the new period and the new constitution). 3 June 1978.

SMA A22-4-121, 001 to 002. "Daxuesheng xie de jipian heibanbao wenzhang" 大学生写的几篇黑板报文章 (A few blackboard articles written by university students). 9 November 1979.

SMA A22-4-122, 032 to 035. "Sixiang dongxiang" 思想动向 (Thought trends). 21 December 1979.

SMA A22-4-134, 027 to 033. "Xuanchuan gongzuo jianbao" 宣传工作简报 (Propaganda work bulletin). 3 December 1979.

SMA A22-4-266, 002 to 007. "Guanyu kaizhan shehui zhuyi minzhu yu fazhi xuanchuan jiaoyu huodong de yijian" 关于开展社会主义民主与法制宣传教育活动的意见 (Suggestions on launching socialist democracy and legal system propaganda and education activities). 5 September 1979.

SMA A22-4-266, 017 to 028. "Jiaqiang shehui zhuyi minzhu he fazhi, wei ba women jianshe chengwei yi ge shehui zhuyi xiandaihua qiangguo er douzheng (xuanchuan tigang)" 加强社会主义民主和法制，为把我们建设成为一个社会主义现代化强国而斗争 (宣传提纲) (Strengthening socialist democracy and the legal system, struggle for our country to become a socialist modernized powerful country [propaganda outline]). September 1979.

SMA A22-4-290, 040 to 042. "Guanyu huifu chuban 'Minzhu yu fazhi' yuekan de qingshi baogao" 关于恢复出版'民主与法制'月刊的请示报告 (Report and request for instructions on resuming publication of the monthly magazine "Democracy and Legal System"). 14 May 1979.

SMA A22-4-502, 001 to 009. "Shanghai shi kaizhan minzhu yu fazhi xuanchuan huodong de baogao" 上海市开展民主与法制宣传活动的报告 (Report on the launch of democracy and legal system propaganda activities in Shanghai). 7 March 1980.

SMA A22-4-510, 006 and 008. "Guanyu 'minzhu yu fazhi' zazhi de lingdao guanxi wenti de huibao" 关于‘民主与法制’杂志的领导关系问题的汇报 (Report on leadership relation problems in "Democracy and Legal System" magazine) 2 December 1980.

SMA A47-1-160, 002. "Fangzhi dangwei xuanchuanbu: tongzhi" 纺织党委宣传部: 通知 (Textile Industry Party Committee's Propaganda Office: Notification) 20 February 1953

SMA A47-1-161, 033 to 040. "Guo mian qi chang xuanchuan guanche hunyinfa yundong zhongdian shiyan zongjie" 国棉七场宣传贯彻婚姻法运动重点试验总结 (No. 7 State Cotton Factory summary report on focal experiments for propagating the Campaign to Implement the Marriage Law). March 1953.

SMA A47-1-161, 042 to 047. "Shanghai shi guanche hunyinfa baongongshi: Tongzhi" 上海市贯彻婚姻法办公室: 通知 (Shanghai Municipal Marriage Law Implementation Office: Notification). 23 March 1953.

SMA A47-1-161, 049. "Guanyu Shanghai shi guanche hunyinfa yundong weiyuanhui bangongshi de tongzhi" 关于上海市贯彻婚姻法运动委员会办公室的通知 (Notification on the Shanghai Municipal Implement the Marriage Law Campaign Office). 18 March 1953.

SMA A47-1-161, 077 to 079. "Guang zhong ranzhi chang guanche hunyinfa yundong weiyuanhui gongzuo baogao" 光终染织厂贯彻婚姻法运动委员会工作报告 (Guangzhong Cloth Making and Dyeing Factory Campaign to Implement the Marriage Law work report). 19 March 1953.

SMA A47-1-161, 080. "Guanche hunyinfa yundong richengbiao" 贯彻婚姻法运动日程表 (Daily schedule for the Campaign to Implement the Marriage Law). 1953.

SMA A47-2-364, 017 to 027. "Shuang manyi" 双满意 (Double satisfaction). 1953.

SMA A47-2-364, 109. "Tongzhi" 通知 (Notification). 27 March 1953.

SMA A47-2-365, 001 to 002. "Dangwei guanche hunyinfa bangongshi: tongzhi" 党委贯彻婚姻法办公室: 通知 (Party Committee Marriage Law Implementation Office: Notification). 27 March 1953.

SMA A47-2-365, 004. "Xinwen mishu tongzhimen: tongzhi" 新闻秘书同志们: 通知 (News secretary comrades: notification). 3 April 1953.

SMA A47-2-365, 011. "Fangzhi dangwei guanyu guanche hunyinfa yundong yue gongzuo zhong muqian cunzai wenti de jinji zhishi" 纺织党委关于贯彻婚姻法运动月工作中目前存在问题的紧急指示 (Textile Industry Party Committee urgent directive on current problems in the work for the Campaign to Implement the Marriage Law month). 4 April 1953.

SMA A47-2-365, 023 to 026. "Guanyu guanche hunyinfa yundong yue jinru qunzhong xuanchuan jieduan gongzuo de yijian" 关于贯彻婚姻法运动月进入群众宣传阶段工作的意见 (Suggestions on the work to be done during the phase of going to the masses and propagating the Campaign to Implement the Marriage Law month). 1953.

SMA A47-2-365, 097 to 098. "Guanche hunyinfa gongzuo huibao" 贯彻婚姻法工作汇报 (Work report on the implementation of the Marriage Law). April 1953.

SMA A47-2-365, 099 to 100. "Hunyinfa gongzuo huibao" 婚姻法工作汇报 (Work report on the Marriage Law). 13 April 1953.

SMA A47-2-365, 130 to 131. "Hunyinfa diaocha tigang" 婚姻法调查提纲 (Outline for Marriage Law investigations). 26 March 1953.

SMA A47-2-365, 183 to 184. "Guanche hunyinfa yundong xuanchuanwang gongzuo zongjie" 贯彻婚姻法运动宣传网工作总结 (Summary work report on the propaganda network for the Campaign to Implement the Marriage Law). 21 April 1953.

SMA A59-1-298, 108. "Zhonggong Shanghai shi gongyongshiye weiyuanhui xuanchuanbu guanyu xuanchuan hunyinfa tui cun tushu, huandeng, xiju, lianhuanhua de tongzhi" 中共上海市公用事业委员会宣传部关于宣传婚姻法推存图书，幻灯，戏剧，连环画的通知 (CCP Shanghai Public Utility Committee Party Committee Propaganda Department notification on promoting and gathering books, shadow plays, theatre plays, and serial comics for Marriage Law propaganda). 20 March 1953.

SMA A59-1-302, 077 to 082. "Gongjiao guanyu guanche hunyinfa yundong de gongzuo zongjie" 公交关于贯彻婚姻法运动的工作总结 (Public transportation sector summary report on work for the Campaign to Implement the Marriage Law). 17 April 1953.

SMA A71-2-915, 115 to 119. "Gaoqiao qu cheng xiang wuzi jiaoliu dahui hunyinfa zhanlanhui qingkuang zongjie baodao" 高桥区城乡物资交流大会婚姻法展览会情况总结报告 (Summary report on the Gaoqiao district town and country material exchange meeting Marriage Law exhibition). 4 October 1952.

SMA B1-1-109, 196 to 197. "Guowuyuan guanyu renzhen guanche zhixing xin hunyinfa de tongzhi" 国务院关于认真贯彻执行新婚姻法的通知 (State Council notification on earnestly implementing and enforcing the new Marriage Law). 10 December 1980.

SMA B1-1-1862, 011 to 012. "Zhongyang renmin zhengfu zhengwuyuan guanyu gaijin he fazhan quanguo chuban shiye de zhishi" 中央人民政府政务院关于改进和发展全国出版事业的指示 (Central People's Government Administrative Council directive on improving and developing the national publishing industry). 28 October 1950.

SMA B1-1-1864, 008. "Quanguo Xinhua shudian chuban gongzuo huiyi guanyu tongyi quanguo gongying chuban shiye de jueyi" 全国新华书店出版工作会议关于统一全国供应出版事业的决议(Decision of the national Xinhua Bookstore publishing work meeting on unifying the national supply and publishing industry). 18 October 1949.

SMA B1-1-1944, 011. "Chuban fenlei shuoming" 出版分类说明 (Explanation of publication classifications). 1951.

SMA B1-2-3591, 011. Letter from the East China Publishing Committee (华东出版委员会) to all shop owners across the East China region. 15 January 1950.

SMA B1-9-296, 034 to 035. "Dui xiugai xianfa de yixie yijian" 对修改宪法的一些意见 (Some opinions on the revised constitution). 11 December 1980.

SMA B6-2-103, 022 to 023. "Benshi youguan lingxiuxiang, guoqi, xianfa tiaowen, guoge deng wupin chuli banfa chubu yijian qing shenhe zhishi" 本市有关领袖像，国旗，宪法条文，国歌等物品处理办法初步意见请审核指示 (Preliminary suggestions on this city's method for dealing with goods [featuring] leaders' portraits, the national flag, the articles of the constitution, the national anthem, etc, with a request for examination, verification, and instructions). 26 November 1955.

SMA B76-5-287, 072 to 074. "Zhonggong zhongyang xuanchuanbu guanyu xuanchuan xin xianfa de tongzhi"中共中央宣传部关于宣传新宪法的通知 (CCP Central Propaganda Department notification on propagating the new constitution). 26 November 1982, 10 December 1982.

SMA B92-2-77, 001 to 002. "Sifa gaige yundong de baodao jihua" 司法改革运动的报导计划 (Plan for reporting on the Judicial Reform Movement). 25 August 1952.

SMA B92-2-77, 003. Letter from the Shanghai Party Committee Propaganda Department (中央上海市委宣传部) to the Shanghai Broadcasting Station (上海广播电台). 2 September 1952.

SMA B105-4-255. "Shanghai shi jiaoyuju geweihui bangongshi - tongzhi" 上海市教育局革委会办公室- 通知 (Shanghai Municipal Bureau of Education Revolutionary Committee Office: Notification). 20 January 1978.

SMA B123-3-332, 002 to 003. "Wei guiding jinhou bijiben, guanggao, baozhuangzhi ji shangpin jun buzhun yin lingxiuxiang, guoqi, xianfa tiaowen, guoge, Guojige he yulu dengyou" 为规定今后笔记本，广告，包装纸及商品均不准印领袖像，国旗，宪法条文，国歌，国际歌和语录等由(From today on diaries, advertisements, wrapping paper, and merchandise are without exception forbidden from printing leaders' portraits, national flags, constitution articles, the national anthem, the Internationale, quotations, etc.). 19 January 1956.

SMA B123-8-295, 001 to 010. "Guanyu taolun xiugai Zhonghua renmin gongheguo xianfa ruogan wenti de yijian" 关于讨论修改中华人民共和国宪法若干问题的意见

(Suggestions on some questions in the discussion on the revision of the PRC constitution). 4 August 1970.

SMA B123-8-295, 025 to 036. "Guanyu xianfa xiugai cao'an xuexi taolun qingkuang de zonghe baogao" 关于宪法修改草案学习讨论情况的综合报告 (Overall report on the situation of studying and discussing the revised constitution draft). 22 September 1970.

SMA B123-10-101, 025 to 031. "Guanyu jiaqiang geming fazhi zhengdun shehui zhi'an zhixu de xuanchuan tigang" 关于加强革命法制整顿社会治安秩序的宣传提纲 (Propaganda outline on strengthening the revolutionary legal system and rectifying social order). [no date].

SMA B168-1-223, 032 to 039. "Shanghai shi minzhengju dangzu, Shanghai shi gaoji renmin fayuan dangzu guanyu xuanchuan guanche hunyinfa de qingshi baogao" 上海市民政局党组，上海市高级人民法院党组关于宣传贯彻婚姻法的请示报告 (Shanghai Municipal Bureau of Civil Affairs Party Cell, Shanghai Municipal People's High Court Party Cell report and request for instructions on propagating and implementing the Marriage Law). 10 February 1964.

SMA B168-1-821, 003. "Guanyu jiaqiang guojia fazhi zhengque guanche zhixing hunyinfa de han" 关于加强国家法制正确贯彻执行婚姻法的函 (Letter on strengthening the country's legal system and correctly implementing and enforcing the Marriage Law). 26 August 1957.

SMA B172-1-70, 046 to 062. "Wei tigao xiqu chuangzuo shuiping er nuli gaibian Huju 'Luohan Qian,' 'Bai Maonü,' Huaiju 'Wang Gui yu Li Xiang Xiang' he zhengli, gaibian Huaiju 'Shuman Lanqiao,' 'Qian Li Song Jing niang' de gongzuo zongjie" 为提高戏曲创作水平而努力改编沪剧'罗汉钱'，'白毛女'，淮剧'王贵与李香香'和整理改编淮剧'舒曼蓝桥'，'千里送京娘'的工作总结 (Summary work report on making great efforts to revise the Hu opera 'Luohan qian,' 'Bai Maonü,' the Huai Opera 'Wang Gui and Li Xiangxiang' and rearranging the Huai Opera 'Shuman Lanqiao,' 'Qian Li Song Jing Niang' in order to raise the standards of operatic productions). 22 January 1952.

SMA B172-4-209, 025 to 031. "1952 nian yi yue dao 1953 nian ba yue 'Liang Shanbo yu Zhu Yingtai' yanchu qingkuang tongji" 1952年1月到1953年8月'梁山伯与祝英台'演出情况统计 (Performance statistics on 'Liang Shanbo and Zhu Yingtai' from January 1952 until August 1953). 1953.

SMA B172-4-209, 032. "Shanghai shi san nian lai xiqu chuangzuo yanchang jumu qingkuang tongji biao" 上海市三年来戏曲创作演唱剧目情况统计表 (Statistical chart on theatrical productions, performances, and repertoires in Shanghai over the past three years). April 1953.

SMA B246-4-356, 004 to 008. "Jingwei xitong xuexi taolun xianfa xiugai cao'an de qingkuang huibiao" 经委系统学习讨论宪法修改草案的情况汇报 (Economic commission situation report on the study and discussion of the revised constitution draft). 14 July 1982.

SMA B246-4-356, 031 to 034. "Guanyu taolun xianfa xiugai cao'an de qingkuang baogao" 关于讨论宪法修改草案的情况报告 (Situation report on the discussion of the revised constitution draft). 24 July 1982.

SMA B246-4-356, 035 to 037. "Guangda zhigong dui xianfa cao'an de fanying" 广大职工对宪法草案的反映 (Reflections of workers on the constitution draft). 11 May 1982.

SMA B246-4-356, 078 to 079. "Guanyu 'xianfa xiugai cao'an' taolun de qingkuang fanying" 关于'宪法修改草案'讨论的情况反映 (Reflections on the discussion of the 'revised constitution draft'). 17 July 1982.

SMA B246-4-356, 116 to 118. "Yiyaoju xuexi taolun 'xianfa xiugai cao'an' zhong tichu de yixie kanfa he jianyi" 医药局学习讨论'宪法修改草案' 中提出的一些看法和建议 (Some views and suggestions raised during the Bureau of Medicine study and discussion of the 'revised constitution draft'). 20 July 1982.

SMA B246-4-356, 143 to 145. "Shanggang sanchang dangwei xuanchuan ke: qingkuang fanying" 上钢三厂党委宣传科: 情况反映 (Shanghai No. 3 Steel Plant Party Committee Propaganda Section: Report on the situation). 5 May 1982.

SMA B246-4-356, 146 to 150. "Shanghai di san gangtie chang dangwei xuanchuan ke: qingkuang fanying" 上海第三钢铁厂党委宣传科: 情况反映 (Shanghai No. 3 Steel Plant Party Committee Propaganda Section: Report on the situation). 6 July 1982.

SMA B246-4-356, 160 to 164. "Yidian qingkuang: zhigong xuexi, taolun 'xianfa xiugai cao'an de fanying" 一点情况: 职工学习讨论宪法修改稿草案的反映 (Some circumstances: Report on workers' study and discussion of the revised constitution draft). 22 May 1982.

SMA B248-4-705, 009 to 014: "Shanghai shi renmin zhengfu caimao bangongshi guanyu xuexi, taolun xianfa xiugai cao'an de qingkuang huibao" 上海市人民政府财贸办公室关于学习, 讨论宪法修改草案的情况汇报 (Shanghai Municipal Finance and Trade Office situation report on the study and discussion of the revised constitution draft). 23 July 1982.

SMA B248-4-705, 024 to 028. "Shi caimao xitong xuexi xianfa de qingkuang" 市财贸系统学习宪法的情况 (Municipal finance and trade system study of the constitution). 22 December 1982.

SMA B323-1-65, 074 to 075. "'Zhonghua renmin gongheguo xiugai cao'an' xiugai yijian" '中华人民共和国宪法修改草案'修改意见 ("Revised PRC constitution draft" revision suggestions). 14 July 1982.

SMA C31-2-60, 001 to 002. "Hunyinfa zhanlanpeng gongzuo jihua" 婚姻法展览棚工作计划 (Marriage Law exhibition canopy work plan). 1951.

# Bibliography

"1981 nian xuanchuan gongzuo zhongdian" [Key points for 1981 propaganda work]. *Xuanchuan tongxun*, no. 1 (1981): 2–3.

"1982 nian gongzuo yaodian" [Key points for 1982 propaganda work]. *Xuanchuan tongxun*, no. 4 (1982): 2–6.

Akademie für Staats- und Rechtswissenschaft der DDR, ed. *Wörterbuch zum Sozialistischen Staat*. Berlin, DDR: Dietz Verlag, 1974.

Alford, William P. "Double-edged Swords Cut Both Ways: Law and Legitimacy in the People's Republic of China." *Daedalus* 122, no. 2 (1993): 45–69.

———. "Law, Law, What Law? Why Western Scholars of Chinese History and Society Have Not Had More to Say about Its Law." *Modern China* 23, no. 4 (1997): 398–419.

———. "Zhu Qiwu and the Development of Criminal Law in the People's Republic of China." *Pacific Basin Law Journal* 2, no. 60 (1983): 61–64.

Altehenger, Jennifer. "A Socialist Satire: *Manhua* Magazine and Political Cartoon Production in the PRC, 1950–1960." *Frontiers of History in China* 8, no. 1 (2013): 78–103.

———. "Between State and Service Industry: Group and Collective Weddings in Communist China, 1949–1956." *Twentieth-Century China* 40, no. 1 (2015): 48–68.

———. "Simplified Legal Knowledge in the Early PRC: Explaining and Publishing the Marriage Law." In *Chinese Law. Knowledge, Practice and Transformation, 1530s to 1950s*, edited by Li Chen and Madeleine Zelin, 342–66. Leiden: Brill, 2015.

Amos, Jennifer. "Embracing and Contesting: The Soviet Union and the Universal Declaration of Human Rights, 1948–1958." In *Human Rights in the Twentieth Century*, edited by Stefan-Ludwig Hoffmann, 147–65. Cambridge: Cambridge University Press, 2011.

Apter, David E., and Tony Saich. *Revolutionary Discourse in Mao's Republic*. Cambridge, MA: Harvard University Press, 1994.

Asen, Daniel. *Death in Beijing: Murder and Forensic Science in Republican China*. Cambridge: Cambridge University Press, 2016.

Autorenkollektiv. *Recht im Alltag*. 3rd edition. Leipzig: Verlag für die Frau, 1977.

Bachman, David. "Aspects of an Institutionalizing Political System: China, 1958–1965." *The China Quarterly*, no. 188 (2006): 933–58.

Bailey, Paul. *Reform the People: Changing Attitudes toward Popular Education in Early Twentieth Century China*. Edinburgh: Edinburgh University Press, 1990.

Balmé, Stéphanie, and Michael E. Dowdle, eds. *Building Constitutionalism in China*. London: Palgrave Macmillan, 2009.

de Bary, William Theodore. *Asian Values and Human Rights: A Confucian Communitarian Perspective*. Cambridge, MA: Harvard University Press, 1998.

Bastid, Marianne. *Educational Reform in Early Twentieth-Century China*. Ann Arbor: Center for Chinese Studies, University of Michigan, 1988.

Beijing shi Chaoyang qu difang zhi bianzuan weiyuanhui. *Beijing shi Chaoyang quzhi* [Beijing city Chaoyang district gazetteer]. Beijing: Beijing chubanshe, 2007.

"Beijing shi Chaoyang qu kaizhan aishe baoliang shoufa de xuanchuan jiaoyu, shoudao xianzhu xiaoguo" [Beijing city Chaoyang district has launched "love the commune, protect the grain, abide by law propaganda and education," and has achieved notable results]. *Renmin gongan*, no. 1 (1961): 11.

Beijing shi Dongcheng qu difang zhi bianzuan weiyuanhui. *Beijing shi Dongcheng quzhi* [Beijing city Dongcheng district gazetteer]. Beijing: Beijing chubanshe, 2005.

"Beijing shi 'fazhi xuanchuan zhou' huodong jinru gaochao" [Beijing municipality's "law propaganda week" activities are entering a high tide]. BFB, 27 May 1983, 1.

Beijing shi Fengtai qu difangzhi bianzuan weiyuanhui. *Beijing shi Fengtai quzhi* [Beijing city Fengtai district gazetteer]. Beijing: Beijing chubanshe, 2001.

Beijing shi Haidian qu difangzhi bianzuan weiyuanhui. *Beijing shi Haidian quzhi* [Beijing city Haidian district gazetteer]. Beijing: Beijing chubanshe, 2004.

Beijing shi Xicheng qu difangzhi bianzuan weiyuanhui. *Beijing shi Xicheng quzhi* [Beijing city Xicheng district gazetteer]. Beijing: Beijing chubanshe, 1999.

Beijing shi Xuanwu qu difang zhi bianzuan weiyuanhui. *Beijing shi Xuanwu quzhi* [Beijing city Xuanwu district gazetteer]. Beijing: Beijing chubanshe, 2004.

"Benkan di er jie fazhi zhishi jingsai jiang yu ming chun juxing" [This magazine's second legal knowledge contest will take place next spring]. *Minzhu yu fazhi*, no. 11 (1985): 1.

Bennett, Gordon A. *Yundong: Mass Campaigns in Chinese Communist Leadership*. Berkeley: Center for Chinese Studies, University of California, 1976.

Bergère, Marie-Claire. *Sun Yat-sen*. Stanford: Stanford University Press, 1998.

Bernhardt, Kathryn. *Women and Property in China, 960–1949*. Stanford: Stanford University Press, 1999.

Bernhardt, Kathryn, and Philip C. C. Huang, eds. *Civil Law in Qing and Republican China*. Stanford: Stanford University Press, 1994.

Betts, Paul. "Socialism, Social Rights, and Human Rights: The Case of East Germany." *Humanity: An International Journal of Human Rights, Humanitarianism, and Development* 3, no. 3 (2012): 407–26.

———. *Within Walls: Private Life in the German Democratic Republic*. Oxford: Oxford University Press, 2010.

Billinsky, Andreas. *Rechtsentwicklung in der Sowjetunion* (Berichte des Bundesinstituts für ostwissenschaftliche und internationale Studien 36). Cologne: Bundesinstitut für ostwissenschaftliche und internationale Studien, 1975.

Birch, Cyril. "Chao Shu-li: Creative Writing in a Communist State." *New Mexico Quarterly*, no. 25 (1955): 185–95.

"Bixu jiaqiang gongan renyuan de shoufa jiaoyu" [Education to be law-abiding for public security staff must be strengthened]. *Gongan jianshe*, no. 170 (28 August 1956): 10–13.

Bolle, Hans Jürgen. "Rechtspropaganda in den Massenmedien der DDR." In *Publizistik und der Journalismus in der DDR*, edited by Rolf Geserick and Arnulf Kutsch, 173–92. Munich: K. G. Saur, 1988.

Bourgon, Jerome. "Abolishing 'Cruel Punishments': A Reappraisal of the Chinese Roots and Long-term Efficiency of the Xinzheng Legal Reform." *Modern Asian Studies* 37, no. 3 (2003): 851–62.

Brady, Anne-Marie. *Marketing Dictatorship: Propaganda and Thought Work in Contemporary China*. Lanham, MD: Rowman & Littlefield, 2008.

Bray, David. *Social Space and Governance in Urban China: The Danwei System from Origins to Reform*. Stanford: Stanford University Press, 2005.

Brodsgaard, Kjeld Erik. "The Democracy Movement in China, 1978–1979: Opposition Movement, Wall Poster Campaigns, and Underground Journals." *Asian Survey* 21, no. 7 (1981): 747–74.

Brown, Jeremy. *City Versus Countryside in Mao's China: Negotiating the Divide*. Cambridge: Cambridge University Press, 2012.

Brown, Jeremy, and Matthew Johnson, eds. *Maoism at the Grassroots: Everyday Life in China's Era of High Socialism*. Cambridge, MA: Harvard University Press, 2015.

Brown, Jeremy, and Paul G. Pickowicz, eds. *Dilemmas of Victory: The Early Years of the People's Republic of China*. Cambridge, MA: Harvard University Press, 2010.

Burbank, Jane. "Lenin and the Law in Revolutionary Russia." *Slavic Review* 54, no. 1 (1995): 23–44.

Burgess, Susan. *The Founding Fathers, Pop Culture and Constitutional Laws: Who's Your Daddy?* London: Routledge, 2009.

Calhoun, Craig. *Neither Gods nor Emperors. Students and the Struggle for Democracy in China*. Berkeley: University of California Press, 1994.

Carlitz, Katherine. "Genre and Justice in Late Qing China: Wu Woyao's Strange Case of Nine Murders and Its Antecedents." In *Writing and Law in Late Imperial China: Crime, Conflict, and Judgment*, edited by Robert E. Hegel and Katherine N. Carlitz, 234–59. Seattle: University of Washington Press, 2007.

Cassel, Pär K. *Grounds of Judgment: Extraterritoriality and Imperial Power in Nineteenth-Century China and Japan*. Oxford: Oxford University Press, 2012.

Cell, Charles P. *Revolution at Work: Mobilization Campaigns in China*. New York: Academic Press, 1977.

Chan, Anita, Stanley Rosen, and Jonathan Unger, eds. *On Socialist Democracy and the Chinese Legal System: The Li Yizhe Debates*. Armonk, NY: M. E. Sharpe, 1985.

Chang, Julian. "The Mechanics of State Propaganda: The People's Republic of China and the Soviet Union in the 1950s." In *New Perspectives on State Socialism in China*, edited by Timothy Cheek and Tony Saich, 76–124. Armonk, NY: M.E. Sharpe, 1997.

"Chedi suqing jiufa guandian he jiu sifa zuofeng" [Thoroughly eliminate old legal outlooks and old styles of judicial work]. *Xin jianshe*, no. 10 (October 1952): 35–38.

Cheek, Timothy. *Propaganda and Culture in Mao's China: Deng Tuo and the Intelligentsia*. Oxford: Clarendon Press, 1997.

———. "Redefining Propaganda: Debates on the Role of Journalism in Post-Mao Mainland China." *Issues and Studies* 25, no. 2 (1989): 47–74.

Chen, Beiou. *Renmin xuexi cidian* [People's study dictionary]. Shanghai: Guangyi shuju, 1951.

Chen, Jianfu. *Chinese Law: Context and Transformation*. Leiden: Martinus Nijhoff Publishers, 2008.

Chen, Kehan. "Chen Kehan jiancha Huadong, Zhongnan chuban gongzuo zhi youguan bumen ji fuzeren de xin" [Chen Kehan's letters to relevant departments and leading cadres on the investigation into publishing work in East China and South-Central China]. 25 March to 23 April 1953. In CBSL, vol. 5, 138–70.

———. "Chuban zongshu dangzu guanyu xiuding 1953 nian gongzuo jihua zhi zhongyang de baodao" [General Publishing Administration party group report to Party Central on revising the 1953 work plan]. 8 January 1953. In CBSL, vol. 5, 23–29.

———. "Guanyu chubanshe gongzuo de mouxie wenti" [On a few problems in publishing work]. June 1954. In CBSL, vol. 6, 318–28.

———. "Guanyu xiuding 1953 nian jihua de yijian" [Suggestions on revising the 1953 plan]. 27 May 1953. In CBSL, vol. 5, 200–212.

Chen, Li. *Chinese Law in Imperial Eyes: Sovereignty, Justice, and Transcultural Politics*. New York: Columbia University Press, 2016.

———. "Legal Specialists and Judicial Administration in Late Imperial China, 1651–1911." *Late Imperial China* 33, no. 1 (2012): 1–54.

———. "Regulating Private Legal Specialists and the Limits of Imperial Power in Qing China." In *Chinese Law: Knowledge, Practice and Transformation, 1530s to 1950s*, edited by Li Chen and Madeleine Zelin, 254–86. Leiden: Brill, 2015.

———. "Zhishi de liliang: Qingdai muyou miben yu gongkai chuban de lüxue zhuzuo dui qingdai sifa changyu de yingxiang" [Power of knowledge: The role of secret and published treatises by private legal specialists in the Qing juridical field]. *Zhejiang daxue xuebao* 45, no. 1 (January 2015): 13–32.

Chen, Li, and Madeleine Zelin, eds. *Chinese Law: Knowledge, Practice and Transformation, 1530s to 1950s*. Leiden: Brill, 2015.

———. "Rethinking Chinese Law and History: An Introduction." In *Chinese Law: Knowledge, Practice and Transformation, 1530s to 1950s*, edited by Li Chen and Madeleine Zelin, 1–14. Leiden: Brill, 2015.

Chen, Tina Mai. "Proletarian White and Working Bodies in Mao's China." *Positions: east asia cultures critique* 11, no. 2 (2003): 361–93.

Chinese Anti-Rightist Campaign Database (CARCDB). Edited by Song Yongyi. Hong Kong: Chinese University Press / Universities Services Center, 2013.

Chinese Political Campaigns in the 1950s Database (CPCDB). Edited by Song, Yongyi et al. Hong Kong: Chinese University Press / Universities Services Center, 2014.

Christoph, Karl-Heinz. "Rechtspropaganda—wirksames Instrument der politischen Massenarbeit." *Neue Justiz (DDR)* (1977): 398–400.

"Chuban zongshu bangongting guanyu zai baoshang deng fanyin Jiefangshe, Xinhua shudian shuji qishi de tongzhi" [Notification from the office of the General Publishing Administration on giving notice on reprinting *Liberation Daily*'s news agency and New China Bookstore's books in newspapers]. 3 January 1950. In CBSL, vol. 2, 1–2.

"Chuban zongshu dangzu xiaozu guanyu chengli tongsu duwu chubanshe de qingshi baogao" [Report and request for instructions by the small group of the General Publishing Administration party group on establishing a popular readings press]. In CBSL, vol. 5, 474–78.

"Chuban zongshu guanyu chubu jiancha qiangpo tanpai shukan de baogao" [Report of the General Publishing Administration on the first investigations into forced allotments of books and periodicals]. 5 March 1953. In CBSL, vol. 5, 8.

"Chuban zongshu guanyu chuli 'Li Fengjin' deng lianhuanhua wenti gei Shanghai shi xinwen chubanchu de tongzhi" [General Publishing Administration notification to the Shanghai Municipal News and Publishing Office on administering the problem of *Li Fengjin* and other serial comics]. 6 June 1952. In CBSL, vol. 4, 60–61.

"Chuban zongshu guanyu jianjue jiuzheng shukan faxing gongzuo zhong qiangpo tanpai cuowu de zhishi" [General Publishing Administration directive on resolutely correcting the mistake of forced allotments in book and periodical distribution]. 3 January 1953. In CBSL, vol. 5, 1–5.

"Chuban zongshu guanyu 'Li Fengjin' yishu bubi tingshou xiugai gei Shanghai shi xinwen chubanchu deng de tongzhi" [General Publishing Administration notification to the Shanghai Municipal News and Publishing Office, etc., on not having to stop sales and revise the book *Li Fengjin*]. 11 June 1952. In CBSL, vol. 4, 62.

"Chuban zongshu guanyu siying zazhishe, chubanshe bu de fabiao he chuban xianfa cao'an de wenzi de tongzhi" [General Publishing Administration notification on private magazines and publishers not being permitted to issue or publish interpretations of the words in the constitution draft]. 21 May 1954. In CBSL, vol. 6, 301.

"Chuban zongshu guanyu xianzhi siying feifa chuban tushu de tongbao" [General Publishing Administration circular on restricting private businesses' illegal publication of books]. 28 June 1954. In CBSL, vol. 6, 339–41.

Chun, Nian. "Xuanchuan hunyinfa de hao juben: Jieshao 'Liushujing'" [Good plays to propagate the Marriage Law: Introducing *Liushujing*]. XMB, 6 March 1953.

Cohen, Jerome A. "China's Changing Constitutions." *The China Quarterly*, no. 76 (December 1978): 794–841.

———. *The Criminal Process in the People's Republic of China 1949–1963: An Introduction*. Cambridge, MA: Harvard University Press, 1968.

———. "The Party and the Courts: 1949–1959." *The China Quarterly*, no. 38 (June 1969): 120–57.

———, ed. *Contemporary Chinese Law: Research Problems and Perspectives*. Cambridge, MA: Harvard University Press, 1970.

"The Common Program of the Chinese People's Political Consultative Conference, 1949." In *The Important Documents of the First Plenary Session of the Chinese People's Political Consultative Conference*, 1–20. Beijing: Foreign Languages Press, 1949. Translation available via http://www.lawinfochina.com/display.aspx?lib=law&id=13212&CGid= (last accessed 25 February 2017).

Cong, Xiaoping. "From 'Freedom of Marriage' to 'Self-Determined Marriage': Recasting

Marriage in the Shaan-Gan-Ning Border Region of the 1940s." *Twentieth-Century China* 38, no. 3 (2013): 184–209.

———. "Ma Xiwu's Way of Judging: Villages, the Masses and Legal Construction in Revolutionary China in the 1940s." *The China Journal*, no. 72 (July 2014): 29–52.

———. *Marriage, Law, and Gender in Revolutionary China, 1940–1960*. Cambridge: Cambridge University Press, 2016.

"Cong falü de jieji xing tan suqing jiufa guandian" [Discussing the elimination of old legal standpoints on the basis of the class character of law]. *Xin jianshe*, no. 9 (September 1952): 3–5.

Conner, Allison W. "Lawyers and the Legal Profession during the Republican Period." In *Civil Law in Qing and Republican China*, edited by Kathryn Bernhardt and Philip C. C. Huang, 215–48. Stanford: Stanford University Press, 1994.

———. "Legal Education during the Republican Period: Soochow University Law School." *Republican China* 19, no. 1 (1993): 84–112.

*The Constitution of the People's Republic of China: Adopted on 20 September 1954 by the First National People's Congress of the People's Republic of China, at Its First Session*. Beijing: Foreign Languages Press, 1954.

Cook, Alexander C. *The Cultural Revolution on Trial: Mao and the Gang of Four*. Cambridge: Cambridge University Press, 2016.

Creemers, Rogier. "China's Constitution Debate: Context, Content, and Implications." *The China Journal*, no. 74 (2015): 91–109.

Croll, Elisabeth. *Feminism and Socialism in China*. London: Routledge, 1978.

———. *The Politics of Marriage in Contemporary China*. Cambridge: Cambridge University Press, 1981.

Culp, Robert C. *Articulating Citizenship: Civic Education and Student Politics in Southeastern China, 1912–1940*. Cambridge, MA: Harvard University Press, 2007.

———. "Culture Work: Industrial Capitalism and Socialist Cultural Production in Mao-Era China." Unpublished paper presented at the 2014 AAS annual meeting, cited with the author's permission.

The Cultural Revolution Database (CRDB). Edited by Song Yongyi. Hong Kong: Chinese University Press / Universities Services Center, 2013.

Davin, Delia. *Woman-Work: Women and the Party in Revolutionary China*. Oxford: Clarendon Press, 1976.

DeMare, Brian. *Mao's Cultural Army: Drama Troupes in China's Rural Revolution*. Cambridge: Cambridge University Press, 2015.

Deng, Liqun. "Zai quanguo xuanchuan buzhang huiyi shang de jianghua" [Speech given at the national meeting of Propaganda Department heads]. 2 December 1984. In DXGHGW, 737–54.

"Deng Xiaoping tongzhi tan xiugai xianfa, nongcun jingji he renmin gongshe zhidu" [Comrade Deng Xiaoping on revising the constitution, the rural economy, and the people's commune system]. *Xuanchuan tongxun*, no. 22 (1981): 2.

Deng, Yingchao. "Guanyu 'Zhonghua renmin gongheguo hunyinfa' de baogao" [Report on the "PRC Marriage Law"]. In *Cai Chang, Deng Yingchao, Kang Keqing funü jiefang wenti wenxian* [Selected documents by Cai Chang, Deng Yingchao, and Kang Keqing on the question of women's liberation]. Beijing: Renmin chubanshe, 1983.

"Di yi jie quanguo chuban huiyi yilai Xinhua shudian de gongzuo" [Xinhua Book-store's work since the first national meeting on publishing]. 1 September 1951. In CBSL, vol. 3, 281–305.

"Di yi jie quanguo xiqu guanmo yanchu dahui" [First National Congress on Theatrical Performances]. In *Zhongguo da baike quanshu: Xiyu & quyi* [Great encyclopedia of China: Theater and vocal art], 60. Beijing: Zhongguo dabaike quanshu chubanshe, 1983.

Diamant, Neil J. "Making Love 'Legible' in China: Politics and Society during the Enforcement of Civil Marriage Registration, 1950–66." *Politics and Society* 29, no. 3 (2001): 447–80.

———. "Re-Examining the Impact of the 1950 Marriage Law: State Improvisation, Local Initiative, and Rural Family Change." *The China Quarterly*, no. 161 (2000): 171–98.

———. *Revolutionizing the Family: Politics, Love, and Divorce in Urban and Rural China, 1949–1968*. Berkeley: University of California Press, 2000.

Diamant, Neil J., and Xiaocai Feng. "The PRC's First National Critique: The 1954 Campaign to 'Discuss the Draft Constitution.'" *The China Journal*, no. 73 (2015): 1–37.

Diamant, Neil J., Stanley B. Lubman, and Kevin O'Brien, eds. *Engaging the Law in China. State, Society, and Possibilities for Justice.* Stanford: Stanford University Press, 2005.

Dikötter, Frank. *Crime, Punishment, and the Prison in Modern China.* London: Hurst, 2002.

Dillon, Nara. *Radical Inequalities: China's Revolutionary Welfare State in Comparative Perspective.* Cambridge, MA: Harvard University Asia Center, 2015.

Dittmer, Lowell. *Liu Shaoqi and the Chinese Cultural Revolution.* Armonk, NY: M. E. Sharpe, 1998.

———. "Reconstructing China's Cultural Revolution." *China Information* 11, no. 2/3 (Autumn/Winter 1996): 1–20.

Donert, Celia. "Whose Utopia? Gender, Ideology and Human Rights at the 1975 World Congress of Women in East Berlin." In *The Breakthrough: Human Rights in the 1970s*, edited by Jan Eckel and Samuel Moyn, 68–87. Philadelphia: University of Pennsylvania Press, 2014.

———. "Women's Rights in Cold War Europe: Disentangling Feminist Histories." *Past and Present*, supplement 8 (2013): 180–202.

Dong, Biwu. "Dong Biwu zai di liu ci quanguo gongan huiyi shang guanyu zhengzhi falü sixiang gongzuo fangmian jige wenti de baogao" [Dong Biwu's report at the sixth national meeting on public security on some questions in political and legal thought work]. 2 June 1954. In *Gongan huiyi wenjian xuanbian, 1949.10–1957.9.* CARCDB.

Dong, Chengmei. "Zhiding 1954 nian xianfa ruogan lishi qingkuang huiyi" [Recollections on some historical circumstances in drafting the 1954 constitution]. *Faxue*, no. 5 (2000): 2–4.

Dongbei daibiaotuan. *Xiao nüxu* [Little son-in-law]. Shanghai: Zhongyang wenhuabu diyijie quanguo xiqu guanmo yanchu dahui, 1952.

Dongbei gongxueyuan Ma Lie zhuyi jiaoyanshi. "Baokan zhailu: Youpai dui minzhu, ziyou, zhuanzheng de waiqu" [Newspaper extracts: Rightists' distortions of democracy, freedom, and dictatorship]. November 1957. In *Yuopai yanlun xuanji* [Selected speeches of rightists], edited by Shehui zhuyi sixiang jiaoyu cankao ziliao zhi er, Dongbei gongxueyuan Ma-Lie zhuyi jiaoyanshi, November 1957. CARCDB.

Du, Ying. "Shanghaiing the Press Gang: The Maoist Regimentation of the Shanghai Popular Publishing Industry in the Early PRC (1949–1956)." *Modern Chinese Literature and Culture* 26, no. 2 (Fall 2014): 89–141.

DuBois, Thomas. "Inauthentic Sovereignty: Law and Legal Institutions in Manchukuo." *Journal of Asian Studies* 69, no. 3 (2010): 749–70.

"Dui 'guanyu jiaqiang fazhi xuanchuan jiaoyu zai gongmin zhong puji falü changshi de jueyi (cao'an)' de shuoming" [An explanation of the "Decision to strengthen law propaganda and education and popularize common legal knowledge among citizens" (draft)]. *Falü yu shenghuo*, no. 1 (January 1986): 4–5.

Dutton, Michael. *Policing Chinese Politics: A History*. Durham, NC: Duke University Press, 2005.

Ecke, Felix. "Der Film 'Jud Süß': Über die Popularisierung eines inhumanen Gesetzes." In *Recht-Idee-Geschichte: Beispiele zur Rechts- und Ideengeschichte*, edited by Rolf Lieberwirth, Heiner Lück, and Bernd Schildt, 275–99. Cologne: Böhlau Verlag, 2000.

Eckel, Jan. *Die Ambivalenz des Guten: Menschenrechte in der internationalen Politik seit den 1940er Jahren*. Göttingen: Vandenhoeck & Ruprecht, 2014.

Edwards, Louise. *Gender, Politics, and Democracy: Women's Suffrage in China*. Stanford: Stanford University Press, 2008.

Eliasoph, Ellen R., and Susan Grueneberg. "Law on Display in China." *The China Quarterly*, no. 88 (1981): 669–85.

Engel, Jeffrey A., ed. *The Fall of the Berlin Wall: The Revolutionary Legacy of 1989*. Oxford: Oxford University Press, 2009.

Exner, Mechthild. "Die Verbreitung der Gesetzeskenntnis unter den Bürgern der VR China." *Zeitschrift für Gesetzgebung* 10 (1995): 54–79.

Eyferth, Jacob. *Eating Rice from Bamboo Roots: The Social History of a Community of Handicraft Papermakers in Rural Sichuan, 1920–2000*. Cambridge, MA: Harvard University Asia Center, 2009.

Fan, Ruoyou, and He Jin, eds. *Zhonghua renmin gongheguo hunyinfa tujie* [Illustrated explanations of the PRC Marriage Law]. Shanghai: Shanghai renmin meishu chubanshe, 1980.

Fan, Zhongxin et al., eds. *Zhongguo fazhishi* [A history of the Chinese legal system]. Beijing: Beijing daxue chubanshe, 2007.

Fang, Qiang. "Teemu Ruskola. *Legal Orientalism: China, the United States, and Modern Law*." *The American Historical Review* 119, no. 3 (June 2014): 851–52.

"Fazhi xuanchuan zhongyao zhuyi de wuge wenti" [Five issues one should pay attention to during law propaganda]. *Liaoning xuanchuan dongtai*, no. 10 (1986): 29.

"Fazhi zhishi xuexi jingsai jiexiao" [Announcement of the legal knowledge study contest]. *Minzhu yu fazhi*, no. 3 (1985): 4.

Fei, Faye Chunfang. *Chinese Theories of Theater and Performance from Confucius to the Present*. Ann Arbor: University of Michigan Press, 1999.

Feldbrugge, Ferdinand, and William B. Simons, eds. *Perspectives on Soviet Law for the 1980s*. Leiden: Brill, 1982.

Feng, Xiaocai. "Shenfen dingyi yu shehui fanying: Zhonggong jianzheng chuqi de 'renmin' yu 'guomin.'" Unpublished paper, cited with the author's permission.

Feuerwerker, Yi-tsi Mei. "Zhao Shuli: The 'Making' of a Model Peasant Writer." In *Ideology, Power, Text: Self-Representation and the Peasant 'Other' in Modern Chinese Literature*, edited by Yi-tsi Mei Feuerwerker, 100–145. Stanford: Stanford University Press, 1998.

Finkelstein, David. "The Language of Communist Chinese Criminal Law." *Journal of Asian Studies* 27, no. 3 (1968): 503–21.

Fitzgerald, John. *Awakening China: Politics, Culture, and Class in the Nationalist Revolution*. Stanford: Stanford University Press, 1996.

Fung, Edmund S. K. *In Search of Chinese Democracy: Civil Opposition in Nationalist China, 1929–1949*. Cambridge: Cambridge University Press, 2006.

Gallagher, Mary E. "Mobilizing the Law in China: 'Informed Disenchantment' and the Development of Legal Consciousness." *Law and Society Review* 40, no. 4 (December 2006): 783–816.

Gao, Deming, ed. *Jiating falü changshi* [Common legal knowledge for the family]. Shanghai: Zhonghua shuju, 1948.

Gao, James Z. *The Communist Takeover of Hangzhou: The Transformation of City and Cadre, 1949–1954*. Honolulu: University of Hawaii Press, 2004.

Gehrig, Sebastian. *Legal Nation: The Politics of Law and Sovereignty in Divided Germany, 1949–1989*. Unpublished manuscript, cited with the author's permission.

Gerth, Karl. "Compromising with Consumerism in Socialist China: Transnational Flows and Internal Tensions in 'Socialist Advertising.'" *Past and Present* 218, suppl. 8 (2013): 203–32.

Getty, J. Arch. "State and Society under Stalin: Constitutions and Elections in the 1930s." *Slavic Review* 50, no. 1 (Spring 1991): 18–35.

Gilmartin, Christina. *Engendering the Chinese Revolution: Radical Women, Communist Politics, and Mass Movements in the 1920s*. Berkeley: University of California Press, 1995.

Glosser, Susan L. *Chinese Visions of Family and State, 1915–1953*. Berkeley: University of California Press, 2003.

Gold, Thomas. "Just in Time! China Battles Spiritual Pollution on the Eve of 1984." *Asian Survey* 24, no. 9 (September 1984): 947–74.

Goldman, Merle. "Hu Feng's Conflict with the Communist Literary Authorities." *The China Quarterly*, no. 12 (October 1962): 102–37.

———. *Literary Dissent in Communist China*. Cambridge, MA: Harvard University Press, 1967.

———. *Sowing the Seeds of Democracy in China: Political Reform in the Deng Xiaoping Era*. Cambridge, MA: Harvard University Press, 1994.

Gong, Jianmin. "Tigao zunshou zhengce, falü he jilü de zijuexing" [Raise consciousness to abide by policies, laws, and observe discipline]. *Renmin gongan*, no. 7 (12 May 1961): 8–10.

"Gongtong gangling shi woguo xianshi de genben dafa" [The Common Program is our country's current fundamental great law]. *Xin jianshe*, no. 9 (September 1952): 1–2.

346 Bibliography

Goodman, Bryna. "'Law Is One Thing, and Virtue Is Another': Vernacular Readings of Law and Legal Process in 1920s Shanghai." In *Chinese Law. Knowledge, Practice and Transformation, 1530s to 1950s*, edited by Li Chen and Madeleine Zelin, 148–75. Leiden: Brill, 2015.

Goodman, David S. G. *Beijing Street Voices: The Poetry and Politics of China's Democracy Movement*. London/Boston: Marion Boyars, 1981.

Gross, Miriam. *Farewell to the God of Plague: Chairman Mao's Campaign to Deworm China*. Berkeley: University of California Press, 2016.

Guangming ribao she bianjisuo. *Dubao shouce* [Handbook for reading newspapers]. Beijing: Guangming ribao she, 1951.

"Guanli shukan chubanye yinshuaye faxingye zanxing" [Provisional regulations on the administration of the publication of books and periodicals, the printing industry, and the distribution trades]. 21 December 1951. In CBSL, vol. 3, 433–35.

"Guanyu guanche hunyinfa yundong yue de baodao tishi" [Briefing on the Campaign to Implement the Marriage Law month]. 26 January 1953. In *Xinhuashe wenxian ziliao xuanbian* [Selected New China News Agency documents and materials], edited by Xinhuashe xinwen yanjiu bu, vol. 2, 347–51.

"Guanyu gongbu xianfa cao'an de baodao tishi" [Brief on reportage on promulgation of the constitution draft]. 16 June 1954. In *Xinhuashe wenjian ziliao xuanbian*, edited by Xinhuashe xinwen yanjiubu, vol. 3, 265–70.

"Guanyu 'Liushujing' de ruogan wenti da duzhe" [A reply to readers on some problems regarding *Liushujing*]. *Juben* no. 5 (1953).

"Guanyu xiuding 1953 nian jihua de yijian" [Suggestions on revising the 1953 plan]. Report by Chen Kehan at the publishing construction planning meeting, 27 May 1953. In CBSL, vol. 5, 200–212.

"Guanyu xuanchuan hunyinfa de chubanwu de yixie quedian" [On some shortcomings in publications propagating the Marriage Law]. *Xuanchuan tongxun*, no. 9 (March 1953): 37–40.

"Guanyu 'Zhonghua renmin gongheguo xianfa xiugai cao'an' de xuanchuan tigang" [On the propaganda outline for the "PRC revised constitution draft"]. *Xuanchuan tongxun*, no. 8 (1982): 2–18.

Guo, Pixiang. *Zhongguo de fazhi xiandaihua* [The modernization of Chinese law]. Beijing: Zhongguo zhengfa daxue chubanshe, 2004.

Habermas, Jürgen. *Theorie des kommunikativen Handelns*, vol. 2. Frankfurt/M.: Suhrkamp, 1981.

Han, Dayuan. *1954 nian xianfa yu xin Zhongguo xianzheng* [The 1954 constitution and New China's constitutionalism]. Changsha: Hunan renmin chubanshe, 2004.

———. *1954 nian xianfa zhiding guocheng* [Drafting the 1954 constitution]. Beijing: Falü chubanshe, 2014.

———. "Aipositan yu 1954 nian xianfa de yingwen ban [Epstein and the English edition of the 1954 constitution]. Appendix to *1954 nian xianfa yu xin Zhongguo xianzheng* [The 1954 constitution and New China's constitutionalism], by Han Dayuan, 492–99. Changsha: Hunan renmin chubanshe, 2004.

———. "Guanyu zhiding 1954 nian xianfa ruogan lishi qingkuang de huiyi—Dong Chengmei jiaoshou fangtan lu" [Recollections on some historical circumstances in drafting the 1954 constitution—An interview with Professor Dong Chengmei]. Appendix to *1954 nian xianfa yu xin Zhongguo xianzheng* [The 1954 constitution and New China's constitutionalism], by Han Dayuan, 500–506. Changsha: Hunan renmin chubanshe, 2004.

Han, Yanlong. *Zhonghua renmin gongheguo fazhi tongshi (1949–1995)* [A General History of the PRC legal system (1949–1995)]. Beijing: Zhonggong zhongyang dangxiao chubanshe, 1998.

Hand, Keith. "Constitutionalizing Wukan: The Value of the Constitution outside the Courtroom." *China Brief* 12, no. 3 (2012): 5–9.

Hao, Tiechuan. "Zhongguo jindai faxue liuxuesheng yu fazhi jindaihua" [Modern China's law students who studied abroad and the modernization of the legal system]. *Faxue yanjiu*, no. 6 (1997): 3–27.

———. "Zhongguo jindai faxue liuxuesheng yu xin Zhongguo chuqi da fazhi jianshe" [Modern China's law students who studied abroad and the construction of the legal system in the early years of New China]. *Faxue yanjiu*, no. 2 (2000): 136–53.

Havel, Václav. "The Power of the Powerless." In *The Power of the Powerless: Citizens Against the State in Central-Eastern Europe*, edited by Václav Havel et al., 23–96. London: Routledge, 2009.

He, Wannan. "'Women jia zhen chu 'faguan' le" [Our family has really produced a "judge"]. *Minzhu yu fazhi*, no. 5 (1985): 10–11.

Hebei sheng Luotian xian gonganju. "Women shi ruhe kaizhan fazhi xuanchuan jiaoyu de" [How we launched law propaganda and education]. *Renmin gongan*, no. 9 (7 June 1962): 11–12.

Hebig, Wolfgang. "Rechtspropaganda in den Jugendklubs." *Neue Justiz (DDR)* (1978): 268–69.

Hegel, Robert E., and Katherine Carlitz, eds. *Writing and the Law in Late Imperial China*. Seattle: University of Washington Press, 2007.

Heilmann, Sebastian. *Sozialer Protest in der VR China: die Bewegung vom 5. April 1976 und die Gegen-Kulturrevolution der siebziger Jahre*. Hamburg: Institut für Asienkunde, 1994.

Heilongjiang sheng gaoji renmin fayuan. "Guanyu sifa xuanchuan gongzuo cunzai de wenti he jinhou yijian" [On some problems in judicial propaganda work and suggestions for hereafter]. *Renmin gongan*, no. 8 (8 June 1961): 5–7.

Hershatter, Gail. *The Gender of Memory: Rural Women and China's Collective Past*. Berkeley: University of California Press, 2011.

Hill, Joshua. "Voting as a Rite: Changing Ideas of Elections in Early Twentieth-Century China." Unpublished PhD diss., Harvard University, 2011.

Hinton, William. *Fanshen: A Documentary of Revolution in a Chinese Village*. New York: Monthly Review Press, 1966.

Ho, Denise. *Curating Revolution: Politics on Display in Mao's China*. Cambridge: Cambridge University Press, 2017.

Hoffmann, Stefan-Ludwig, ed. *Human Rights in the Twentieth Century*. Cambridge: Cambridge University Press, 2010.

———. "Introduction: Genealogies of Human Rights." In *Human Rights in the Twentieth Century*, edited by Hoffmann, 1–26. Cambridge: Cambridge University Press, 2011.

Hsia, Tao-tai. "Chinese Legal Publications: An Appraisal." In *Contemporary Chinese Law: Research Problems and Perspectives*, edited by Jerome A. Cohen, 20–83. Cambridge, MA: Harvard University Press, 1970.

Hsiao, Ching-chang, and Timothy Cheek. "Open and Closed Media: External and Internal Newspapers in the Propaganda System." In *Decision-Making in Deng's China: Perspectives from Insiders* edited by Carol Lee Hamrin and Suisheng Zhao, 76–88. Armonk, NY: M.E. Sharpe, 1995.

Hsiao, Kung-Chuan. *Rural China: Imperial Control in the Nineteenth Century*. Seattle: University of Washington Press, 1960.

Hu, Ruirong, and Shanghai shi Luwan qu difang bianzuan weiyuanhui, eds. *Luwan quzhi* [Luwan district gazetteer]. Shanghai: Shanghai shehui kexue chubanshe, 1998.

Hu, Xia, and Huang Yan, eds. *Susong changshi* [Basic knowledge about lawsuits]. Shanghai: Shangwu yinshuguan, 1922.

Hu, Yingxi. *Hunyinfa sanzijing* [Marriage Law three-character classic]. Shanghai: Tongli chubanshe, 1951.

Hu, Yuzhi. "Chuban gongzuo wei guangda renmin qunzhong fuwu" [Publishing work serves the broad masses of the people]. 25 September 1952. In CBSL, vol. 4, 228–32.

———. "Hu Yuzhi ni gedi chuban zhengfu wenjian de fangzhen yu banfa gao jiao chuban zongshu bangongting banli de xin" [Hu Yuzhi's letter on the draft for the guiding principles and regulations on publishing government documents, transmitted to the General Publishing Administration's office for processing]. 27 April 1950. In CBSL, vol. 2, 159–61.

Huabei tushuguan, ed. *Guanche hunyinfa yundong cankao ziliao mulu suoyin* [Index and catalogue to reference material on the Campaign to Implement the Marriage Law]. 25 February 1953.

"Huabei xingzheng weiyuanhui dangzu guanyu sifa gaige yundong xiang huabeiju de baogao" [North China regional administrative committee party group report to the North China Office on the Judicial Reform Movement], 26 January 1953." In *Zhonggong zhongyang huabeiju zhongyao wenjian huibian* 15, no. 3 (March 1954): 457–59.

Huadong renmin chubanshe, ed. *Hunyinfa tujie tongsuben* [The Marriage Law: Illustrated popular explanations]. Shanghai: Huadong renmin chubanshe, 1951.

Huadong renmin chubanshe. *Zhonghua renmin gongheguo chengzhi fangeming tiaoli: Tujie tongsuben* [The Regulations of the People's Republic of China for the Punishment of Counterrevolutionaries: Illustrated popular explanations]. Shanghai: Huadong renmin chubanshe, 1951.

Huadong wenhuabu yishu shiye guanlichu, ed. *Huyinfa gequ ji* [Anthology of Marriage Law songs]. Shanghai: Wanye shudian, 1953.

Huang, Chuanhui. *Tianxia hunyin: Gongheguo sanbu hunyinfa jishi* [Chinese marriage: A chronicle of the People's Republic's three marriage laws]. Shanghai: Wenhui chubanshe, 2004.

Huang, Philip C. C. *Chinese Civil Justice: Past and Present*. Lanham, MD: Rowman & Littlefield, 2010.

———. *Civil Justice in China: Representation and Practice in the Qing*. Stanford: Stanford University Press, 1996.

———. *Code, Custom and Legal Practice in China: The Qing and the Republic Compared.* Stanford: Stanford University Press, 2001.

Huang, Qijie. "Wutaiju jilupian 'Zhao Xiaolan': Yi bu peihe hunyinfa xuanchuan de yingpian" [The stage play documentary *Zhao Xiaolan*: A film for the propagation of the Marriage Law]. XMB, 23 March 1953.

Hung, Chang-tai. *Mao's New World: Political Culture in the Early People's Republic of China.* Ithaca: Cornell University Press, 2011.

Ji, Genyin. "Guanyu 'Lanqiaohui' de wenti" [On problems in *Rendezvous at Blue Bridge*]. *Juben* no. 4 (1953): 90–91.

Jiang, Jin. *Women Playing Men: Yue Opera and Social Change in Twentieth-Century Shanghai.* Seattle: University of Washington Press, 2009.

"Jianxun: Gedi gongan bumen xuexi yu zunshou xianfa he falü de qingkuang" [News in brief: The situation of public security departments across the country studying and abiding by the constitution and laws]. *Gongan jianshe*, no. 128 (5 June 1955): 14–16.

"Jianxun: Shanghai shi yi zhankai sufan douzheng" [News in brief: Shanghai has already launched the struggle to eliminate counterrevolutionaries]. *Gongan jianshe*, no. 137 (30 August 1955): 13–15.

Jin, Jian. *Zhao Xiaolan.* Beijing: Renmin wenxue chubanshe, 1953.

Jin, Qiu. *The Culture of Power: The Lin Biao Incident in the Cultural Revolution.* Stanford: Stanford University Press, 1999.

"Jingsai youshengzhe jiangpin" [Contest winner prizes]. *Minzhu yu fazhi*, no. 3 (1985): 7.

Johnson, David G., Andrew J. Nathan, and Evelyn S. Rawski, eds. *Popular Culture in Late Imperial China.* Berkeley: University of California Press, 1985.

Johnson, Kay Ann. *Women, the Family, and Peasant Revolution in China.* Chicago: University of Chicago Press, 1983.

Johnson, Matthew. "Beneath the Propaganda State: Official and Unofficial Cultural Landscapes in Shanghai, 1949–1965." In *Maoism at the Grassroots: Everyday Life in China's Era of High Socialism*, edited by Jeremy Brown and Matthew Johnson, 199–229. Cambridge, MA: Harvard University Press, 2015.

Juben yuekan bianjibu. *Liang Shanbo yu Zhu Yingtai* [Liang Shanbo and Zhu Yingtai]. Shanghai: Renmin wenxue chubanshe, 1953.

Judge, Joan. *Print and Politics: 'Shibao' and the Culture of Reform in Late Qing China.* Stanford: Stanford University Press, 1996.

"Juxing 'Xiao nüxu' zuotan hui" [A discussion meeting on *Little son-in-law*]. XMB, 27 March 1953.

"Kaituo xin lu de ren: Fang quanguo fazhi xuanchuan jiaoyu gongzuo huiyi teyao daibiao, Benxi shi yuan shiwei shuji Xu Buyun tongzhi" [A man who developed a new way: Visiting the delegate by special invitation to the national law propaganda education work conference, Benxi city's former party committee secretary Comrade Xu Buyun]. *Falü yu shenghuo*, no. 9 (September 1985): 4–6.

Kelliher, Daniel. "Keeping Democracy Safe from the Masses: Intellectuals and Elitism in the Chinese Protest Movement." *Comparative Politics* 25, no. 4 (July 1993): 379–96.

Keys, Barbara J. *Reclaiming American Virtue: The Human Rights Revolution of the 1970s.* Cambridge, MA: Harvard University Press, 2014.

Kiely, Jan. *The Compelling Ideal: Thought Reform and the Prison in China, 1901–1956.* New Haven: Yale University Press, 2014.

Kinkley, Jeffrey C. "Chinese Crime Fiction." *Society* (May/June 1993): 51–62.

———. *Chinese Justice, the Fiction: Law and Literature in Modern China.* Stanford: Stanford University Press, 2000.

Kirby, William C., ed. *Realms of Freedom in Modern China.* Stanford: Stanford University Press, 2004.

Kotkin, Stephen. *Magnetic Mountain: Stalinism as a Civilization.* Berkeley: University of California Press, 1995.

Kuo, Margaret. *Intolerable Cruelty: Marriage, Law, and Society in Early Twentieth-Century China.* Lanham, MD: Rowman & Littlefield, 2012.

Kushner, Barak. *Men to Devils, Devils to Men: Japanese War Crimes and Chinese Justice.* Cambridge, MA: Harvard University Press, 2015.

———. *The Thought War: Japanese Imperial Propaganda.* Honolulu: University of Hawaii Press, 2006.

Ladany, Laszlo. *Law and Legality in China: The Testament of a China-watcher.* London: Hurst & Company, 1992.

Lean, Eugenia. *Public Passions: The Trial of Shi Jianqiao and the Rise of Popular Sympathy in Republican China.* Berkeley: University of California Press, 2007.

Lee, Haiyan. *Revolution of the Heart: A Genealogy of Love in China 1900–1950.* Stanford: Stanford University Press, 2006.

Lee, Lily Xiao Hong, ed. *Biographical Dictionary of Chinese Women: The Twentieth Century.* Armonk, NY: M. E. Sharpe, 2003.

Leese, Daniel. *Mao Cult: Rhetoric and Ritual in China's Cultural Revolution.* Cambridge: Cambridge University Press, 2011.

———. "Revising Verdicts in Post-Mao China: The Case of Beijing Fengtai District." In *Maoism at the Grassroots: Everyday Life in China's Era of High Socialism,* edited by Jeremy Brown and Matthew Johnson, 102–28. Cambridge, MA: Harvard University Press, 2015.

———. "A Single Spark: Origins and Spread of the Little Red Book in China." In *Mao's Little Red Book: A Global History,* edited by Alexander C. Cook, 23–42. Cambridge: Cambridge University Press, 2014.

Leng, Shao-chuan. *Justice in Communist China: A Survey of the Judicial System of the Chinese People's Republic.* New York: Oceana Publications, 1967.

Leng, Shao-chuan, and Hungdah Chiu. *Criminal Justice in Post-Mao China: Analysis and Documents.* Albany: SUNY Press, 1985.

Li, Da, ed. *Zhonghua renmin gongheguo xianfa jianghua* [An introduction to the PRC constitution]. Beijing: Renmin chubanshe, 1956.

Li, Honghe. "Xin Zhongguo chengli chuqi guanche 'hunyinfa' yundong zhong de shehui wenti ji qi jiejue—yi Henan wei zhongxin de lishi kaocha" [Social problems in the implementation of the Marriage Law in Henan Province in the early days of New China and their solution]. *Zhonggong dangshi yanjiu,* no. 7 (2009): 96–103.

Li, Huayu. "The Political Stalinization of China: The Establishment of One-Party Constitutionalism." *Journal of Cold War Studies* 3, no. 2 (Spring 2001): 28–47.

Li, Lianjiang. "Rights Consciousness and Rules Consciousness in Contemporary China." *The China Journal* no. 64 (2010): 47–68.

Li, Maoguan. "Jiaqiang fazhi de xuanchuan baodao" [Strengthen law propaganda reportage]. *Lilun jiaoliu*, 10 March 1986, 16–17.

———. "Shilun shehui zhuyi falü yishi" [On socialist legal consciousness]. *Xuexi yu tansuo*, no. 3 (1983): 61–64.

Li, Victor. "The Role of Law in Communist China." *The China Quarterly*, no. 44 (October 1970): 66–111.

Li, Xiaobing. "The Dragon's Tale: China's Efforts toward the Rule of Law." In *Modern Chinese Legal Reform: New Perspectives*, edited by Xiaobing Li and Qiang Fang, 83–108. Lexington: University Press of Kentucky, 2013.

Li, Yi. "Buyao mangmu chuban shuji" [Do not blindly publish books]. *Dushu yuebao*, no. 11 (November 1956): 1.

Li, Yizhen. *Hunyinfa yu hunyin wenti* [Marriage law and marriage problems]. Shanghai: Zhengzhong shuju, 1931.

Li, Yongfu. "Guanyu shenru jinxing yi xianfa wei zhongdian de pufa jiaoyu de qingkuang baogao" [Situation report on thoroughly conducting popularization of law education taking the constitution as a focus]. *Shanghai shi renmin daibiao dahui changwu weiyuanhui gongbao* (August 1987): 7–8.

———. "Guanyu zai benshi gongmin zhong jiben puji falü changshi gongzuo de qingkuang huibao" [Situation report on the popularization of basic legal knowledge among the city's citizens]. *Shanghai shi renmin daibiao dahui changwu weiyuanhui gongbao*, no. 2 (1989): 60.

Liang, Yongkai. *Hunyinfa qizige* [Marriage Law seven-character song]. Changsha: Hunan renmin chubanshe, 1952.

Liebman, Benjamin L. "A Return to Populist Legality? Historical Legacies and Legal Reform." In *Mao's Invisible Hand: The Political Foundations of Adaptive Governance in China*, edited by Sebastian Heilmann and Elizabeth J. Perry, 165–200. Cambridge, MA: Harvard University Asia Center, 2011.

———. "Watchdog or Demagogue? The Media in the Chinese Legal System." *Columbia Law Review* 105, no. 1 (2005): 1–157.

Lin, Shipu, and Tang Guohua, eds. *Dubao cidian* [Newspaper readers' dictionary]. Shanghai: Shixue chubanshe, 1954.

"Lingdao ganbu daitou xuefa shi gaohao pufa gongzuo de guanjian—Benxi shiwei fushuji: Li Zhida" [Cadres setting an example in learning law is the key to successful law popularization work: Benxi Party Committee Deputy Secretary Li Zhida]. *Liaoning xuanchuan tongxun*, no. 7 (1986): 18–19.

"Lingdao hao xianfa xiugai cao'an de xuanchuan he taolun" [Lead well the propaganda and discussion on the revised constitution draft]. *Xuanchuan tongxun*, no. 11 (1982): 19–24.

Link, Perry. *An Anatomy of Chinese: Rhythm, Metaphor, Politics*. Cambridge, MA: Harvard University Press, 2013.

Liu, Alan P. *Communications and National Integration in Communist China.* Berkeley: University of California Press, 1975.

Liu, Binglin. "Guqi geming ganjin, zhengqu zai zhengfa gongzuo shang lai yi ge dayue-jin" [Incite revolutionary vigor, fight for a Great Leap Forward in politico-legal work]. *Gongan jianshe,* no. 228 (3 April 1958): 7–10.

Liu, Shaoqi. *Report on the Draft Constitution of the People's Republic of China.* Beijing: Foreign Languages Press, 1954.

"Lu Dingyi zai zhongxuanbu tongsu baokan tushu chuban huiyi shang de zongjie baogao" [Lu Dingyi's summary report at the Central Propaganda Department's meeting on popular newspaper, magazine, and book publishing]. 27 April 1951. In CBSL, vol. 3, 132–37.

Lu, Qi. *Hunyin yao zizhu* [Marriage should be self-determined]. Beijing: Huabei ren-min chubanshe, 1950. Reprinted in Shanghai: Huadong renmin chubanshe, 1953.

Lü, Shuxiang, and Zhu Dexi, eds. *Yufa xiuci jianghua* [Lectures on grammar and rheto-ric]. Shanghai: Kaiming shudian, 1951.

Lubman, Stanley B. *Bird in a Cage: Legal Reform in China after Mao.* Stanford: Stanford University Press, 1999.

Luo, Liang. *The Avant-garde and the Popular in Modern China: Tian Han and the Inter-section of Performance and Politics.* Ann Arbor: University of Michigan Press, 2014.

Luo, Longji. "On Human Rights." In *The Chinese Human Rights Reader: Documents and Commentary 1900–2000,* edited by Stephen C. Angle and Marina Svensson, 138–51. Armonk, NY: M. E. Sharpe, 2001.

Luo, Pinghan. *Tudi gaige yundong shi* [A history of the Land Reform Campaign]. Fu-zhou: Fujian renmin chubanshe, 2005.

Ma, Wanli. "Falü hanshou jiaoyu jie shouguo" [Legal education by correspondence bears great fruit]. *Falü xuexi yu yanjiu,* no. 6 (1987): 78–79.

Ma, Zhao. *Runaway Wives, Urban Crimes, and Survival Tactics in Wartime Beijing, 1937–1949.* Cambridge, MA: Harvard University Asia Center, 2015.

Macauley, Fiona. "Taking the Law into their Own Hands: Women, Legal Reform and Legal Literacy in Brazil." In *Gender and the Politics of Rights and Democracy in Latin America,* edited by Nikki Craske and Maxine Molyneux, 79–101. London: Palgrave Macmillan, 2002.

Macauley, Melissa A. *Social Power and Legal Culture: Litigation Masters in Late Impe-rial China.* Stanford: Stanford University Press, 1998.

MacFarquhar, Roderick, and Michael Schoenhals. *Mao's Last Revolution.* Cambridge, MA: Harvard University Press, 2006.

Mackerras, Colin. *Chinese Theater: From Its Origins to the Present Day.* Honolulu: Uni-versity of Hawaii Press, 1981.

Mäding, Klaus. *Strafrecht und Massenerziehung in der Volksrepublik China.* Frankfurt/M.: Suhrkamp, 1979.

McCormick, Barrett. *Political Reform in Post-Mao China: Democracy and Bureaucracy in a Leninist State.* Berkeley: University of California Press, 1990.

McDougall, Bonnie S., and Paul Clark, eds. *Popular Chinese Literature and Performing Arts in the People's Republic of China, 1949–1979.* Berkeley: University of California Press, 1984.

Mao, Zedong. "Be a True Revolutionary." 23 June 1950. In *Selected Works of Mao Tse-tung*, vol. 5, 37–40. Beijing: Foreign Languages Press, 1977.

———. "On New Democracy." January 1940. In *Selected Works of Mao Tse-tung*, vol. 4, 339–84. Beijing: Foreign Languages Press, 1975.

———. "On the Draft of the Constitution of the People's Republic of China." 14 June 1954. In *Selected Works of Mao Tse-tung*, vol. 5, 141–47. Beijing: Foreign Languages Press, 1977.

———. "On the People's Democratic Dictatorship." In *Selected Works of Mao Tse-tung*, vol. 4, 411–24. Beijing: Foreign Languages Press, 1969.

———. "Some Questions Concerning Methods of Leadership." 1 June 1943. In *Selected Works of Mao Tse-tung*, vol. 3, 117–22. Beijing: Foreign Languages Press, 1965.

———. "Zhongshi dianxing baodao" [Pay attention to model reports]. 15 March 1953. In ZGXGWX, vol. 3, 520.

"Mao Zedong zai shengshiwei zizhiqu dangwei shuji huiyi shang de zongjie" [Mao Zedong's summary at the meeting of provincial, municipal, and autonomous region party committee secretaries]. 27 January 1957. CARCDB.

Marx, Karl. "Rules and Administrative Regulations of the International Workingmen's Association," online copy available at https://www.marxists.org/history/international/iwma/documents/1867/rules.htm (last accessed 1 November 2015).

Mazower, Mark. *Governing the World: The History of an Idea*. London: Allen Lane, 2012.

Meijer, Marinus J. *Marriage Law and Policy in the Chinese People's Republic*. Hong Kong: Hong Kong University Press, 1971.

Miao, Peishi. *Hunyin ziyouge* [Freedom of marriage song]. Beijing: Xin dazhong chubanshe, 1951.

Middell, Matthias. "1989." In *The Oxford Handbook of the History of Communism*, edited by Steven A. Smith, 171–84. Oxford: Oxford University Press, 2014.

Mittler, Barbara. *A Continuous Revolution? Making Sense of Cultural Revolution Culture*. Cambridge, MA: Harvard University Asia Center, 2012.

Moyn, Samuel. *The Last Utopia: Human Rights in History*. Cambridge, MA: Harvard University Press, 2010.

Moyn, Samuel, and Jan Eckel, eds. *The Breakthrough: Human Rights in the 1970s*. Philadelphia: University of Pennsylvania Press, 2014.

Mueller, Wolfgang, Michael Gehler, and Arnold Suppan, eds. *The Revolutions of 1989: A Handbook*. Vienna: Verlag der Österreichischen Akademie der Wissenschaften, 2014.

Mühlhahn, Klaus. *Criminal Justice in China: A History*. Cambridge, MA: Harvard University Press, 2009.

Nankai daxue faxue yanjiusuo, ed. *Puji falü changshi xiao cidian* [Small dictionary on the popularization of legal knowledge]. Tianjin: Dazhong chubanshe, 1986.

Nathan, Andrew J. *Chinese Democracy: An Investigation into the Nature and Meaning of "Democracy" in China Today, with a Report on the Remarkable but Short-lived Democracy Movement*. New York: Alfred A. Knopf, 1985.

Nathans, Benjamin. "Soviet Rights-Talk in the Post-Stalin Era." In *Human Rights in the Twentieth Century*, edited by Stefan-Ludwig Hoffmann, 166–90. Cambridge: Cambridge University Press, 2011.

O'Brien, Kevin J., and Lianjiang Li. *Rightful Resistance in Rural China*. Cambridge: Cambridge University Press, 2006.

Ocko, Jonathan. "I'll Take It All the Way to Beijing: Capital Appeals in the Qing." *Journal of Asian Studies* 47, no. 2 (May 1988): 291–315.

Olbertz, Jan H. "Zwischen Systemgebundenheit und Variabilität—Erwachsenenbildung in der DDR." In *Pädagogik und Erziehungsalltag in der DDR: Zwischen Systemvorgaben und Pluralität*, edited by Heinz-Hermann Krüger and Winfried Marotzki, 295–320. Opladen: Leske + Budrich, 1994.

Palwezig, Jürgen. "Kolloquium über populärwissenschaftliche Vermittlung von Rechtskenntnissen." *Neue Justiz (DDR)* (1982): 458ff.

Pashukanis, Evgeny. "Lenin and the Problems of Law." In *Pashukanis, Selected Writings on Marxism and Law* edited by Piers Beirne and Robert Sharlet, 132–64. London: Academic Press, 1980.

Peerenboom, Randall. *China's Long March toward Rule of Law*. Cambridge: Cambridge University Press, 2002.

Peng, Zhen. "Yong xianfa he falü tongyi sixiang" [Unite thought using the constitution and law]. In ZGXGWX, vol. 4, 875–78.

*Peng Zhen nianpu* [Chronicle of the life of Peng Zhen]. 5 vols. Beijing: Zhongyang wenxian chubanshe: 2012.

"Peng Zhen tan fazhi xuanchuan wenti" [Peng Zhen on questions of legal system propaganda]. 16 September 1979. *Xuanchuan tongxun* (Shanghai edition), no. 2 (1979): 2.

"Pengbo xingqi de qunzhongxing de 'fazhi re'" [A vigorously rising mass-character "legal fever"]. *Minzhu yu fazhi*, no. 2 (1985): 8.

"People's Court Status Reports" 法院情况简报. Social History of China, 1949–1976. http://projekt.ht.lu.se/rereso/sources/peoples-court-status-reports/ (last accessed 13 July 2017).

People's Daily Online. "Jianguo hou woguo banbu de diyibu falü 'Zhonghua renmin gongheguo hunyinfa'" [The PRC Marriage Law: The first law China promulgated after liberation]. http://dangshi.people.com.cn/GB/17650634.html (last accessed 20 October 2017).

Perry, Elizabeth J. *Anyuan: Mining China's Revolutionary Tradition*. Berkeley: University of California Press, 2012.

———. *Challenging the Mandate of Heaven: Social Protest and State Power in China*. Armonk, NY: M. E. Sharpe, 2003.

———. "Chinese Conceptions of 'Rights': From Mencius to Mao—and Now." *Perspectives on Politics* 6, no. 1 (March 2005): 37–50.

———. "From Mass Campaigns to Managed Campaigns: 'Constructing a New Socialist Countryside.'" In *Mao's Invisible Hand: The Political Foundations of Adaptive Governance in China*, edited by Sebastian Heilmann and Elizabeth J. Perry, 30–61. Cambridge, MA: Harvard University Asia Center, 2011.

———. "Introduction: Chinese Political Culture Revisited." In *Popular Protests and Political Culture in Modern China*, edited by Jeffrey N. Wasserstrom and Elizabeth J. Perry, 1–14. Boulder, CO: Westview Press, 1994.

———. *Patrolling the Revolution: Worker Militias, Citizenship, and the Modern Chinese State*. Lanham, MD: Rowman & Littlefield, 2007.

————. "Studying Chinese Politics: Farewell to Revolution?" *China Journal*, no. 57 (2007): 1–22.

————. Trends in the Study of Chinese Politics: State-Society Relations." *The China Quarterly*, no. 139 (September 1994): 704–13.

Peterson, Glen. *The Power of Words: Literacy and Revolution in South China, 1949–95.* Vancouver: UBC Press, 1997.

Pollard, Vincent K. "Marriage, Children, and Chinese Law: Transformation and Diversity during War and Revolution." *E-AsPac* (2008): 1.

Potter, Pitman. *From Leninist Discipline to Socialist Legalism: Peng Zhen on Law and Political Authority in the PRC.* Stanford: Stanford University Press, 2003.

"Pufa jie fu" [Guard against excesses in law popularization]. ZFB (7 May 1986): 1.

"Puji falü changshi de zongdongyuan" [General mobilization for the popularization of common legal knowledge]. *Falü yu shenghuo*, no. 8 (1984): 4–5.

Qian, Qinfa. *Haipai da lüshi* [Famous Shanghai lawyers]. Shanghai: Wenhui chubanshe, 2008.

"Qieshi zuohao puji falü changshi de xuanchuan jiaoyu gongzuo" [Conscientiously perform propaganda and education work to popularize common legal knowledge]. 30 June 1985. In *Xuanchuan dongtai xuanbian 1985* [Selections from *Propaganda Trends 1985*], 255–56. Beijing: Zhongguo shehui kexue chubanshe, 1986.

Qingdao renmin tushuguan, ed. *Guanche hunyinfa cankao ziliao suoyin* [Index to reference materials on implementation of the Marriage Law]. 25 March 1953.

Qu, Jun, ed. *Jing'an quzhi* [Jing'an district gazetteer]. Shanghai: Shanghai shehui kexue chubanshe, 1996.

Ransmeier, Johanna. *Sold People: Traffickers and Family Life in North China.* Cambridge, MA: Harvard University Press, 2017.

Reed, Christopher A. *Gutenberg in Shanghai: Chinese Print Capitalism, 1876–1937.* Honolulu: University of Hawaii Press, 2004.

Renmin chubanshe. *Renmin chubanshe 50 nian dashiji: 1950–2000* [The People's Press: a chronicle of fifty years: 1950–2000]. Beijing: Renmin chubanshe, 2000.

————. *Hunyinfa jianghua* [Introduction to the Marriage Law]. Beijing: Renmin chubanshe, 1953.

*Renmin qianzike: Hunyin dashi* [People's thousand-character lesson: The great event of marriage]. Shanghai: Yuanchang yinshuguan, 1951.

"Ren yi ci gongkai shenpan kan sifa gongzuo zhong de wenti" [People's questions on seeing judicial work in an open trial]. *Xuanchuan tongxun*, no. 4 (October 1979): 33.

Richardson-Little, Ned. "Dictatorship and Dissent: Human Rights in East Germany in the 1970s." In *The Breakthrough: Human Rights in the 1970s*, edited by Jan Eckel and Samuel Moyn, 49–67. Philadelphia: University of Pennsylvania Press, 2013.

Roberts, Priscilla, and Odd Arne Westad, eds. *China, Hong Kong and the Long 1970s: Global Perspectives.* London: Palgrave Macmillan, 2017.

Ruskola, Teemu. "Law, Sexual Morality, and Gender Equality in Qing and Communist China." *Yale Law Journal* 103, no. 8 (1994): 2531–65.

————. *Legal Orientalism: China, the United States, and Modern Law.* Cambridge, MA: Harvard University Press, 2013.

Sänger, Eva. "Einfluss durch Öffentlichkeit? Zur Bedeutung des Zentralen Runden

Tisches im Umbruch der DDR." In *Die demokratische Revolution 1989 in der DDR*, edited by Eckard Conze, Katharina Gajdukowa, and Sigrid Koch-Baumgarten, 154–69. Cologne: Böhlau, 2009.

Sarat, Austin, and Thomas R. Kearns, eds. *Law in Everyday Life*. Ann Arbor: University of Michigan Press, 1995.

———. *Law in the Domains of Culture*. Ann Arbor: University of Michigan Press, 2000.

Schenk, Dieter. *Der Chef: Horst Herold und das BKA*. Hamburg: Hoffmann und Campe Verlag, 1998.

Schmalzer, Sigrid. "The Appropriate Use of Rose-Colored Glasses: Reflections on Science in Socialist China." *Isis* 98, no. 3 (2007): 571–83.

———. *The People's Peking Man: Popular Science and Human Identity in Twentieth-Century China*. Chicago: University of Chicago Press, 2008.

———. *Red Revolution, Green Revolution: Scientific Farming in Socialist China*. Chicago: University of Chicago Press, 2016.

Schneewind, Sarah. *Community Schools and the State in Ming China*. Stanford: Stanford University Press, 2006.

Schoenhals, Michael. "The 1978 Truth Criterion Controversy." *The China Quarterly*, no. 126 (1991): 243–68.

———. "China's 'Great Proletarian Information Revolution' of 1966–1967." In *Maoism at the Grassroots: Everyday Life in China's Era of High Socialism*, edited by Jeremy Brown and Matthew Johnson, 230–58. Cambridge, MA: Harvard University Press, 2015.

———. "Demonising Discourse in Mao Zedong's China: People vs. Non-People." *Totalitarian Movements and Political Religions* 8, no. 3–4 (2007): 465–82.

———. *Doing Things with Words in Chinese Politics: Five Studies*. Berkeley: Institute of East Asian Studies, University of California, 1992.

———. "Elite Information in China." *Problems of Communism* 34 (1985): 65–71.

———. "The Global War on Terrorism as Meta-Narrative: An Alternative Reading of Recent Chinese History." *Sungkyun Journal of East Asian Studies* 8, no. 2 (2008): 179–201.

———. *Saltationist Socialism: Mao Zedong and the Great Leap Forward, 1958*. Stockholm: Skrifter utgivna av Foeringen foer Orientaliska Studier, vol. 19, 1987.

———. *Spying for the People: Mao's Secret Agents, 1949–1967*. Cambridge: Cambridge University Press, 2013.

———. "Talk About a Revolution: Red Guards, Government Cadres, and the Language of Political Discourse." *Indiana East Asian Working Paper Series on Language and Politics in Modern China*, no. 1 (June 1993).

———. "'Why Don't We Arm the Left?' Mao's Culpability for the Cultural Revolution's 'Great Chaos' of 1967." *The China Quarterly*, no. 182 (2005): 277–300.

Schoenhals, Michael, ed. and trans. "Reactions to Executions in Beijing (1951)." *Contemporary Chinese Thought* 38, no. 3 (2007): 10–24.

Schram, Stuart R. "'Economics in Command?' Ideology and Policy since the Third Plenum, 1978–84." *The China Quarterly*, no. 99 (1984): 417–61.

Schültzke, Steffi. *Propaganda für Kleinbürger: Heitere Dramatik im DDR-Fernsehen*. Leipzig: Leipziger Universitätsverlag, 2009.

Schurmann, Franz. *Ideology and Organization in Communist China*. Berkeley: University of California Press, 1971.

Scott, James C. *Seeing Like a State: How Certain Schemes to Improve the Human Condition Have Failed*. New Haven: Yale University Press, 1998.

Seifert, Andreas. *Bildergeschichten für Chinas Massen*. Cologne: Böhlau, 2008.

Seymour, James D. *China: The Politics of Revolutionary Reintegration*. New York: Thomas Y. Crowell Company, 1976.

———, ed. *The Fifth Modernization: China's Human Rights Movement, 1978–1979*. Stanfordville, NY: Earl M. Coleman Enterprises, 1980.

Sha, Lin. *Hunyinfa sizijing* [Marriage Law four-character classic]. Shanghai: Zhenli shudian, 1951.

Shambaugh, David. "China's Propaganda System: Institutions, Processes and Efficacy." *The China Journal*, no. 57 (2007): 25–58.

Shandong sheng tushuguan, ed. *Guanche hunyinfa yundong cankao tushu mulu* [Catalogue of reference readings on the Campaign to Implement the Marriage Law]. 10 March 1953.

Shanghai renmin meishu chubanshe, ed. *Zhonghua renmin gongheguo xianfa tujie* [Illustrated explanations of the PRC constitution]. Shanghai: Shanghai renmin meishu chubanshe, 1978.

Shanghai renmin meishu chubanshe, ed. *Zhonghua renmin gongheguo xingfa tujie* [Illustrated explanations of the PRC Criminal Law]. Shanghai: Shanghai renmin meishu chubanshe, 1979.

Shanghai shi Hongying tushuguan, ed. *Guanche hunyinfa yundong qikan cankao ziliao suoyin* [Index to periodical reference materials on the Campaign to Implement the Marriage Law]. 8 March 1953.

"Shanghai yi pingbaozu dui baokan zhengfa xuanchuan de yijian" [Suggestions by a Shanghai newspaper review group on political and legal propaganda in newspapers and magazines]. 21 April 1982. In *Xuanchuan dongtai xuanbian 1982* [Selections from Propaganda Trends 1982], 99–102. Beijing: Zhongguo shehui kexue chubanshe, 1983.

Sherwin, Richard K. *When Law Goes Pop: The Vanishing Line between Law and Popular Culture*. Chicago: University of Chicago Press, 2000.

Shi, Liang. "Zhongyang renmin zhengfu sifabu buzhang Shi Liang guanyu chedi gaizao he zhengdun guojia renmin fayuan de baogao" [Central People's Government Minister of Justice Shi Liang's report on thoroughly transforming and rectifying the country's people's courts]. 13 August 1952. CPCDB.

Shi, Qiubo, ed. *Shanghai sifa xingzheng zhi* [Shanghai judicial administration gazetteer] Shanghai: Shanghai shehui kexue chubanshe, 2003.

Shi, Shouyun, and Ge Xiumin. *Hunyinfa tongsu jianghua* [Popular Introduction to the Marriage Law]. Shanghai: Huadong qingnian chubanshe, 1953.

Shu, Bo. *Dajia lai shixing hunyinfa* [Everyone come help implement the Marriage Law]. Nanchang: Jiangxi renmin chubanshe, 1952.

Shue, Vivienne. "Epilogue: Mao's China: Putting Politics in Perspective." In *Maoism at the Grassroots: Everyday Life in China's Era of High Socialism*, edited by Jeremy Brown and Matthew Johnson, 365–79. Cambridge, MA: Harvard University Press, 2015.

Silbey, Susan S. "After Legal Consciousness." *Annual Review of Law and Social Science*, no.1 (2005): 323–68.

Simons, William B. "Introduction." In *The Constitutions of the Communist World*, edited by William B. Simons, ix–xvi. Alphen aan den Rijn: Sijthoff & Noordhoff, 1980.

Sleeboom-Faulkner, Margaret. *The Chinese Academy of Social Sciences (CASS): Shaping the Reforms, Academia and China (1977–2003)*. Leiden: Brill, 2007.

Smith, Aminda M. *Thought Reform and China's Dangerous Classes: Reeducation, Resistance, and the People*. Lanham, MD: Rowman & Littlefield, 2012.

Snyder, Sarah. *Human Rights Activism and the End of the Cold War: A Transnational History of the Helsinki Network*. Cambridge: Cambridge University Press, 2011.

Sommer, Matthew. *Polyandry and Wife-Selling in Qing Dynasty China: Survival Strategies and Judicial Interventions*. Berkeley: University of California Press, 2015.

———. *Sex, Law, and Society in Late Imperial China*. Stanford: Stanford University Press, 2000.

Sonnenkalb, Edith. "Sozialistische Rechtserziehung als ständiger Prozess innerhalb der Persönlichkeitsentwicklung." *Neue Justiz (DDR)* (1977): 553–55.

Stacey, Judith. *Patriarchy and Socialist Revolution in China*. Berkeley: University of California Press, 1983.

Steinmetz, Willibald. "New Perspectives on the Study of Language and Power in the Short Twentieth Century." In *Political Languages in the Age of Extremes*, edited by Willibald Steinmetz, 3–51. Oxford: Oxford University Press, 2011.

Stern, Rachel E. *Environmental Litigation in China: A Study in Political Ambivalence*. Cambridge: Cambridge University Press, 2013.

Stockmann, Daniela, and Mary E. Gallagher. "Remote Control: How the Media Sustains Authoritarian Rule in China." *Comparative Political Studies* 44, no. 4 (2011): 436–67.

Stolleis, Michael. *Geschichte des öffentlichen Rechts in Deutschland, Erster Band: Reichspublizistik und Policeywissenschaft 1600–1800*. Munich: C. H. Beck, 2012.

Stranahan, Patricia. *Molding the Medium: The Chinese Communist Party and the Liberation Daily*. Armonk, NY: M. E. Sharpe, 1990.

———. *Yan'an Women and the Communist Party*. Berkeley: University of California Press, 1983.

Strauss, Julia. "Morality, Coercion, and State Building by Campaign in the Early PRC: Regime Consolidation and After, 1949–1956." In *The History of the PRC (1949–1976)*, edited by Julia Strauss, 37–58. Cambridge: Cambridge University Press, 2007.

———. "Paternalist Terror: The Campaign to Suppress Counterrevolutionaries and Regime Consolidation in the People's Republic of China." *Comparative Studies in Society and History* 44, no. 1 (2002): 80–105.

———, ed. *The History of the PRC (1949–1976)*. The China Quarterly Special Issues New Series, no. 7. Cambridge: Cambridge University Press, 2007.

Su, Yang. *Collective Killings in Rural China during the Cultural Revolution*. Cambridge: Cambridge University Press, 2011.

Sui, Fu. "Du 'Faxue cidian' xiangdao de" [Something that came to mind while reading the *Dictionary of Jurisprudence*]. *Faxue*, no. 3 (1987): 43.

Sullivan, Lawrence R. "Assault on the Reforms: Conservative Criticism of Political and Economic Liberalization in China, 1985–86." *The China Quarterly*, no. 114 (1988): 198–222.

Sun, Guohua. *Tantan shoufa* [Talking about abiding by law]. Beijing: Tongsu duwu chubanshe, 1955.

Sun, Yan. *The Chinese Reassessment of Socialism, 1976–1992*. Princeton: Princeton University Press, 1995.

Svarverud, Rune. *International Law as World Order in Late Imperial China: Translation, Reception and Discourse, 1847–1911*. Leiden: Brill, 2007.

Tanner, Harold M. *Strike Hard! Anti-crime Campaigns and Chinese Criminal Justice, 1979–1985*. Ithaca: Cornell University Press, 1999.

Teiwes, Frederick C. *Politics and Purges in China: Rectification and the Decline of Party Norms, 1950–1965*. Armonk, NY: M. E. Sharpe, 1993.

Teiwes, Frederick C., and Warren Sun. *Riding the Tiger during the Cultural Revolution: The tragedy of Lin Biao*. Honolulu: University of Hawaii Press, 1996.

Thorgensen, Stig, and Soren Clausen. "New Reflections in the Mirror: Local Chinese Gazetteers (*Difangzhi*) in the 1980s." *The Australian Journal of Chinese Affairs*, no. 27 (1992): 161–84.

Thornton, Patricia. *Disciplining the State: Virtue, Violence, and State-Making in Modern China*. Cambridge, MA: Harvard University Asia Center, 2007.

Tian, Han. "Zuohao xiju gongzuo manzu renmin de xuyao" [Do drama work well and satisfy people's needs]. *Juben*, no. 10 (October 1953): 3–9.

Tianjin shi renmin tushuguan, ed. *Guanche hun-yinfa youguan ziliao suoyin* [Index to relevant materials for the implementation of the Marriage Law]. 10 March 1953.

Tiffert, Glenn D. "The Chinese Judge: From Literatus to Cadre (1906–1949)." In *Knowledge Acts in Modern China: Ideas, Institutions, and Identities*, edited by Eddy U, Robert Culp, and Wen-hsin Yeh. Berkeley: Institute of East Asian Studies, University of California, 2016.

———. "Epistrophy: Chinese Constitutionalism and the 1950s." In *Building Constitutionalism in China*, edited by Stephanie Balmé and Michael Dowdle, 59–67. London: Palgrave Macmillan, 2009.

———. "An Irresistible Inheritance: Republican Judicial Modernization and Its Legacies to the People's Republic of China." *Cross-Currents: East Asian History and Culture Review*, no. 7 (2013): 84–112.

———. "Judging Revolution: Beijing and the Birth of the PRC Judicial System (1906–1958)." Unpublished PhD diss., University of California, Berkeley, 2015.

Tran, Lisa. *Concubines in Court: Marriage and Monogamy in Twentieth-Century China*. Lanham, MD: Rowman & Littlefield, 2015.

Trevaskes, Susan. "Propaganda Work in Chinese Courts: Public Trials and Sentencing Rallies as Sites of Expressive Punishment and Public Education in the People's Republic of China." *Punishment and Society* 6, no. 1 (2004): 5–21.

Troyer, Ronald J. "Publicizing the New Laws: The Public Legal Education Campaign." In *Social Control in the People's Republic of China*, edited by Ronald J. Troyer, John P. Clark, and Dean G. Rojek, 70–83. New York: Praeger, 1989.

Tuck, Richard, ed. *Hobbes: Leviathan*. Cambridge: Cambridge University Press, 1996.

U, Eddy. "The Hiring of Rejects: Teacher Recruitment and Crises of Socialism in the Early PRC Years." *Modern China* 30, no. 1 (2004): 46–80.

————. "The Making of Chinese Intellectuals: Representations and Organization in the Thought Reform Campaign." *The China Quarterly*, no. 192 (2007): 971–89.

————. "The Making of *Zhishifenzi*: The Critical Impact of the Registration of Unemployed Intellectuals in the Early PRC." *The China Quarterly*, no. 173 (March 2003): 100–121.

Ullmann, Klaus. "Wirksame Rechtspropaganda in den Massenmedien." *Neue Justiz (DDR)* (1997): 497ff.

Unger, Susanne. "Priorities of Law: A Conversation with Judith Scheele, Daniel Lord Smail, Bianca Premo, and Bhavani Raman." 5 July 2017. *Comparative Studies in Society and History*. http://cssh.lsa.umich.edu/2017/07/05/priorities-of-law/ (last accessed 15 July 2017).

van de Valk, Marius. "Previous Chinese Legal Language." *Monumenta Serica* 29, no. 1 (1971): 589–630.

van der Burg, Wibren. *The Dynamics of Law and Morality: A Pluralist Account of Legal Interactionism*. London: Routledge, 2016.

van Rooij, Benjamin. "Implementation of Chinese Environmental Law: Regular Enforcement and Political Campaigns." *Development and Change* 37, no. 1 (2006): 57–74. Volland, Nicolai. "The Control of the Media in the People's Republic of China." Unpublished PhD diss., University of Heidelberg, 2003.

————. "Cultural Entrepreneurship in the Twilight: The Shanghai Book Trade Association, 1945–57." In *The Business of Culture: Cultural Entrepreneurs in China and Southeast Asia, 1900–1965*, edited by Christopher Rea and Nicolai Volland, 234–58. Vancouver: University of British Columbia Press, 2015.

————. "A Linguistic Enclave: Translation and Language Policies in the Early People's Republic of China." *Modern China* 35 no. 5 (2009): 467–94.

————. "Translating the Socialist State: Cultural Exchange, National Identity, and the Socialist World in the Early PRC." *Twentieth-Century China* 33, no. 2 (2008): 51–72.

van Slyke, Lyman P. *Enemies and Friends: The United Front in Chinese Communist History*. Palo Alto: Stanford University Press, 1967.

Wagner, Rudolf. "The *Shenbao* in Crisis: The International Environment and the Conflict between Guo Songtao and the *Shenbao*." *Late Imperial China* 20, no. 1 (1999): 107–38.

————. "Shenbaoguan zaoqi de shuji chuban" [The early publishing activities of the Shenbaoguan]. In *Wan Ming yu wan Qing: Lishi chuancheng yu wenhua chuangxin* [The late Ming and the late Qing: Historical dynamics and cultural innovation], edited by Chen Pingyuan, Wang Dewei, and Gao Wei, 169–78. Wuhan: Hubei jiaoyu chubanshe, 2002.

————. "Zhonggong 1940–1953 jianli zhengyu, zhengwen de zhengce dalüe" [A sketch of CCP policies to establish "correctspeak" and "correctwrite" (1940–1953)]. In *Wenyi lilun yu tongsu wenhua*, edited by Peng Xiaoyan, 11–38. Taipei: Zhongyang yanjiuyuan Zhongguo wen zhe yanjiusuo zhoubeichu, 1999.

Wakeman, Frederic. "'Clean-up': The New Order in Shanghai." In *Dilemmas of Victory: The Early Years of the People's Republic of China*, edited by Jeremy Brown and Paul G. Pickowicz, 21–58. Cambridge, MA: Harvard University Press, 2007.

Walder, Andrew G. *China under Mao: A Revolution Derailed.* Cambridge, MA: Harvard University Press, 2015.

Waley-Cohen, Joanna. "Politics and the Supernatural in Mid-Qing Legal Culture." *Modern China* 19, no. 3 (1993): 330–53.

Wan, Margaret. "Court Case Ballads: Popular Ideals of Justice in Late Qing and Republican China." In *Knowledge, Practice, and Transformation, 1530s to 1950s,* edited by Li Chen and Madeleine Zelin, 287–320. Leiden: Brill, 2015.

Wang, Bo. *Jichengfa ABC* [Inheritance law ABC]. Shanghai: Shijie shuju, 1930.

———. *Qinshufa ABC* [Family law ABC]. Shanghai: Shijie shuju, 1931.

Wang, Dechang, and Hao Heguo. "Zhonghua renmin gongheguo di yi bu xianfa de zhiding guocheng" [The compilation of the PRC's first constitution]. *Gongheguo licheng* [The historical process of the Republic]. Beijing: Guangming chubanshe, 1997.

Wang, Feiran. "Youguan hunyinfa de wenti" [On the question of the Marriage Law]. *Xin jianshe* 2, no. 6 (7 May 1950): 16–17.

Wang, Min, and Wang Shuwen. *Xianfa jiben zhishi jianghua* [An introduction to basic constitutional knowledge]. Beijing: Zhongguo qingnian chubanshe, 1962.

Wang, Zheng. *Finding Women in the State: A Socialist Feminist Revolution in the People's Republic of China, 1949–1964.* Berkeley: University of California Press, 2017.

Wasserstrom, Jeffrey N., and Elizabeth J. Perry, eds. *Popular Protest and Political Culture in Modern China.* Boulder, CO: Westview Press, 1994.

"Wei tigao chubanwu de zhiliang er fendou" [Struggle to raise the quality of publications]. 27 August 1951. In CBSL, vol. 3, 217–44.

Weigelin-Schwiedrzik, Susanne. "In Search of a Master Narrative for Twentieth-Century Chinese History." In *The History of the PRC (1949–1976),* edited by Julia Strauss, 59–76. Cambridge: Cambridge University Press, 2007.

Weitz, Eric D. "Self-determination: How a German Enlightenment Idea Became the Slogan of National Liberation and a Human Right." *American Historical Review* 120, no. 2 (2015): 462–96.

Wen, Mu, Xing Zhi, and Zong Hua. *Luohan qian* [Luohan coins]. Shanghai: Huadong qu yanchu daibiaotuan, 1952.

Wildenthal, Lora. *The Language of Human Rights in West Germany.* Philadelphia: University of Pennsylvania Press, 2013.

Wolf, Margery. *Revolution Postponed: Women in Contemporary China.* Stanford: Stanford University Press, 1985.

Wu, Xieying. "Lun xianfa yishi" [On constitutional consciousness]. *Faxue yanjiu,* no. 6 (1986): 17–20.

Wu, Yanhong. "The Community of Legal Experts in Sixteenth- and Seventeenth-Century China." In *Chinese Law: Knowledge, Practice and Transformation, 1530s to 1950s,* edited by Li Chen and Madeleine Zelin, 207–30. Leiden: Brill, 2015.

———. "To Teach and To Entertain: The Production of Legal Culture in 16th and 17th Century China." Unpublished PhD diss., Oklahoma State University, 2008.

Wu, Yiching. *The Cultural Revolution at the Margins: Chinese Socialism in Crisis.* Cambridge, MA: Harvard University Press, 2014.

———. "The Great Retreat and Its Discontents: Re-examining the Shengwulian Episode in the Cultural Revolution." *The China Journal,* no. 72 (July 2014): 1–28.

Wu, Yuenong. "Wang Ming yu xin Zhongguo di yi bu 'hunyinfa'" [Wang Ming and New China's first Marriage Law]. *Yanhuang chunqiu*, no. 5(2001).

"Xiang pingju 'xiao nüxu' xuexi" [Learning from the Ping Opera *Little Son-in-Law*]. XWRB, 26 December 1952.

"Xianzai dui quanju lai shuo shi zhua fazhi" [All departments should now stress the law]. *Liaoning xuanchuan dongtai*, no. 16 (1986): 9.

Xiao, Yihua, and Shanghai shi Xuhui qu difang bianzuan weiyuanhui, eds. *Xuhui quzhi* [Xuhui district gazetteer]. Shanghai: Shanghai shehui kexue chubanshe, 1997.

Xie, Juezai. "Yao xuexi falü yu xuanchuan falü" [One should study law and propagate law]. *Xin guancha*, no. 17 (1952): 9.

*Xin mingci cidian* [Dictionary of new terms]. Shanghai: Chunming chubanshe, 1955.

*Xinbian dubao shouce* [Newly edited handbook for newspaper reading]. Hangzhou: Zhejiang jiaoyu chubanshe, 1986.

"Xinhua shudian zongdian chubu jiancha qiangpo tanpai shukan qingkuang de baogao" [New China Bookstore main branch report on the first investigations into the situation of forced allotments of books and periodicals]. 5 March 1953. In CBSL, vol. 5, 9–15.

Xinhua tongxunshe Zhongguo nianjian bianjibu. *Zhongguo nianjian: 1985* [China yearbook: 1985]. Beijing: Xinhua chubanshe, 1985.

Xiong, Xianjue. "Feichu 'liufa quanshu' de yuanyou ji yingxiang" [The reasons and impact of the abrogation of the "Complete Book of Six Codes"]. *Yanhuang chunqiu*, no. 3 (2007): 10–13.

————. "Lüshi zhidu de tuohuangzhe Wang Ruqi" [Wang Ruqi, a pioneer of the lawyer system]. In *Xiong Xianjue faxue wenji* [Xiong Xianjue's collected works on jurisprudence], 458–64. Beijing: Beijing yanshan chubanshe, 2004.

Xu, Lanjun. "Sentimentalism, Geopolitics, and Cosmopolitanism: The Liang-Zhu Fever and Yue Opera in 1950s China." Unpublished paper presented at the workshop "The Cultures of Emergency: Cultural Production in Times of Turmoil," NUS, August 2009, cited with the author's permission.

Xu, Qiyi. "'Liang Zhu' de jieshu" [The ending of 'Liang Zhu']. XMB, 16 March 1953.

Xu, Xiaoqun. *Chinese Professionals and the Republican State: The Rise of Professional Associations in Shanghai, 1912–1937*. Cambridge: Cambridge University Press, 2000.

————. "The Fate of Judicial Independence in Republican China." *The China Quarterly*, no. 149 (March 1997): 1–28.

————. *Trial of Modernity: Judicial Reform in Early Twentieth-Century China, 1901–1937*. Stanford: Stanford University Press, 2008.

Xu, Zhong. "Deng Yingchao yu xin Zhongguo shoubu 'hunyinfa'" [Deng Yingchao and New China's first Marriage Law]. *Shihai guanlan*, no. 3 (2010).

Xuanchuan tongxun bianjibu. "Xuanchuan gongzuozhe zhuyi" [For the attention of propaganda workers]. 16 August 1952. *Xuanchuan tongxun*, no. 26. CPCDB.

"Xuexi cailiao: Xuanchuan xin hunyinfa zhuanji" [Study materials: Specially edited for the propagation of the new Marriage Law]. November 1980.

"Xuexi gongtong gangling, xuexi Mao Zedong sixiang" [Study the Common Program, study Mao Zedong Thought]. *Xin jianshe*, no. 8 (August 1952): 1–4.

Yan, Xiansheng. "Gongmin xianfa yishi wenti de diaocha baogao" [Survey report on the question of citizens' constitutional consciousness]. *Beijing daxue xuebao*, no. 4 (1985): 61–69.

———. "Woguo gongmin 'xianfa zhishi' diaocha" [A survey of Chinese citizens' "constitutional knowledge"]. *Zhengfaxue yanjiu*, no. 1 (1986): 69–73.

Yan, Yunxiang. *Private Life under Socialism: Love, Intimacy, and Family Change in a Chinese Village, 1949–1999*. Stanford: Stanford University Press, 2003.

Yang, Guichang, and Lin Jin. *Tantan hunyinfa* [Talking about the Marriage Law]. Beijing: Qingnian chubanshe, 1951.

Yang, Kuisong. "Reconsidering the Campaign to Suppress Counterrevolutionaries." *The China Quarterly*, no. 193 (March 2008): 102–21.

Yang, Qinglin. "Quanmin pufa shiyu Liaoning" [The popularization of law for all people began in Liaoning]. *Liaoning fazhi bao*, 12 October 2012.

Yang, Quanming. "Cengqiang shehui zhuyi xianfa yishi shi yi xiang poqie renwu" [Increasing and strengthening socialist constitutional consciousness is an urgent task]. *Xiandai faxue*, no. 4 (1985): 5–8.

Yang, Shaoxuan. "Zhongguo falü bianqian shilüe yu xin faxue guan" [A brief history of changes in Chinese law and the new view on jurisprudence]. *Xin jianshe* 2, no. 6 (7 May 1950): 12–16.

Yang, Yuqing. "Lun zunshou falü" [On abiding by law]. *Zhengfa yanjiu*, no. 3 (1954): 31–35.

"Yao quanmian chanshu minzhu yu jizhong de guanxi" [One must comprehensively set out the relationship between democracy and centralism]. *Xuanchuan tongxun*, no. 4 (1979): 43–44.

Ye, Li. "'Zhili jingsai' weihe shenshou guanzhong huanying?" [Why are "knowledge contests" well received by audiences?]. *Xinwen jizhe*, no. 5 (May 1986): 37.

"Yiding yao zunshou falü, yifa banshi" [One must abide by laws, handle things according to law]. *Renmin gongan*, no. 8 (8 June 1961): 1–2.

You, Chenjun. *Falü zhishi de wenzi chuanbo: Ming-Qing riyong leishu yu shehui richang shenghuo* [The written dissemination of legal knowledge: Ming-Qing reference works for everyday usage and everyday social life]. Shanghai: Shanghai renmin chubanshe, 2013.

"You xitongde xuexi Mao Zedong sixiang lai jinyibu gaizao sixiang" [Systematically study Mao Zedong Thought to further reform thinking]. *Xin jianshe*, no. 2 (February 1952): 8–12.

Yu, Liu. "Maoist Discourse and the Mobilization of Emotions in Revolutionary China." *Modern China* 36, no. 3 (2010): 329–62.

Yu, Liuliang, and Hong Yu. *Chinese Coins: Money in History and Society*. San Francisco: Long River Press, 2004.

Yu, Ruxin. "1970 nian xianfa xiugai cao'an jiedu" [Deciphering the 1970 constitution revised draft]. China News Digest, no. 692, 9 March 2009 (www.cnd.org/CR/ZK09/cr524.gb.html).

Yu, Xuewen. "Renmin de xianfa, renmin de yuyan" [The people's constitution, the people's language]. GMRB, 30 September 1954.

"Yunyong gezhong shouduan jiaqiang fazhi xuanchuan deng wuze" [Use all sorts of methods to strengthen law propaganda, and five other principles]. *Xuanchuan tongxun* (Zhejiang Province edition), no. 10 (16 May 1986): 18–19.

"Zai fazhi zhishi xuexi jingsai zhong" [In the legal knowledge study contest]. *Minzhu yu fazhi*, no. 2 (February 1985).

"Zai qingnian zhong kaizhan 'daode fengxiang jingsai yue' deng huodong" [The launch of "morality competition month" and other activities among youth]. *Xuanchuan tongxun*, no. 4 (1979): 46–47.

Zarrow, Peter. *After Empire: The Conceptual Transformation of the Chinese State, 1885– 1924*. Stanford: Stanford University Press, 2012.

———. *Educating China: Knowledge, Society, and Textbooks in a Modernizing World, 1902–1937*. Cambridge: Cambridge University Press, 2015.

Zelin, Madeleine. *The Merchants of Zigong: Industrial Entrepreneurship in Early Modern China*. New York: Columbia University Press, 2005.

Zhang, Chengji, and Mo Hongwei. "Xin Zhongguo diyibu 'hunyinfa' xuanchuan yu guanche hunyinfa yundong shilun" [A discussion of the propaganda and implementation campaign of New China's first "Marriage Law"]. *Henan shifan daxue xuebao* 35, no. 1 (2008): 120–23.

Zhang, Jishun. "Creating 'Masters of the Country' in Shanghai and Beijing: Discourse and the 1953–54 Local People's Congress Elections." *The China Quarterly*, no. 220 (2014): 1071–91.

———. *Yuanqu de dushi: 1950 niandai de Shanghai* [A city displayed: Shanghai in the 1950s]. Beijing: Shehui kexue wenxian chubanshe, 2015.

Zhang, Liang. *The Tiananmen Papers: The Chinese Leadership's Decision to Use Force against Their Own People*, edited by Andrew J. Nathan and Perry Link. New York: Public Affairs, 2008.

Zhang, Min. "Shilun 1952 nian sifa gaige yundong" [On the judicial movement in 1952]. *Falü shiyong*, no. 8 (2004): 55–58.

Zhang, Ning. "The Political Origins of Death Penalty Exceptionalism: Mao Zedong and the Practice of Capital Punishment in Contemporary China." *Punishment & Society* 10, no. 2 (2008): 117–36.

Zhang, Qingfu, and Han Dayuan, eds. *1954 nian xianfa yanjiu* [Research on the 1954 constitution]. Beijing: Zhongguo renmin gongan daxue chubanshe, 2005.

Zhang, Ting. "Marketing Legal Information: Commercial Publications of the *Great Qing Code, 1644–1911*." In *Chinese Law: Knowledge, Practice and Transformation, 1530s to 1950s*, edited by Li Chen and Madeleine Zelin, 231–53. Leiden: Brill, 2015.

Zhang, Xipo, and Han Yanlong, eds. *Zhongguo geming fazhishi* [A history of China's revolutionary legal system]. Beijing: Zhongguo shehui kexue chubanshe, 1987.

Zhang, Yilei, ed. *Putuo quzhi* [Putuo district gazetteer]. Shanghai: Shanghai shehui kexue chubanshe, 1994.

Zhang, Youyu. *Zhongguo faxue sishinian* [Forty years of Chinese jurisprudence]. Shanghai: Shanghai renmin chubanshe, 1989.

Zhao, Shuli. "Dengji" [Registration]. *Shuoshuo changchang*, no. 6 (1950): 27–45.

"Zhengwuyuan banfa 'qikan dengji zanxing banfa,' 'guanli shukan chubanye yinshuaye faxingye zanxing tiaoli' ji pizhun 'guowai yinshuapin jinkou zanxing banfa,' de mingling" [Government Administrative Council order on the promulgation of the 'Provisional Regulations for the Registration of Periodicals," the "Provisional Regulations on the Administration of Book and Periodical Publishing, the Printing

Industry, and the Distribution Trades," and the ratification of the "Provisional Regulations on the Import of Foreign Print Products"], 16 August 1952. In CBSL, vol. 4, 172.

Zhonggong dangshi renwu yanjiuhui, eds. *Zhonggong dangshi renwu zhuan* [Biographies of personalities in Chinese Communist party history]. Vol. 82. Xi'an: Shaanxi renmin chubanshe, 2002.

"Zhonggong Liaoning shengwei guanyu 'kaizhan gongchan zhuyi daode jiaoyu he fazhi jiaoyu yanli daji xingshi fanzui huodong' de baogao" [CCP Liaoning provincial committee's report on "Launch Communist morality education and legal system education, strike severely against criminal activities"]. *Gongan jianshe*, no. 193 (10 July 1957): 4–8.

"Zhonggong zhongyang bangongting, Guowuyuan bangongting zhuanfa zhongyang xuanchuanbu 'guanyu zhengdun neirong bu jiankang baokan de qingshi' de tongzhi" [CCP General Office, State Council General Office notification to the Central Propaganda Department on the "Request for instructions on rectifying the content of unhealthy newspapers and periodicals"]. 6 June 1985. *Zhongbanfa*, no. 35 (1985). In DXGWX, vol. 3, 1383–86.

"Zhonggong zhongyang guanyu guanche hunyinfa de zhishi" [Party Central directive on implementing the Marriage Law], 26 November 1952. In ZGXGWX, vol. 3, 461–66.

"Zhonggong zhongyang guanyu jinyan jiuju wenti gei dongbeiju de zhishi" [Directive of the CCP Central Committee to the North-East China Bureau on the matter of banning performances of old plays], 13 March 1950. *Jianguo yilai zhongyao wenxian*. Beijing: Zhongyang wenxian chubanshe, 1992.

Zhonggong zhongyang guanyu jinyibu jiaqiang qingshaonian jiaoyu yufang qingshaonian weifa fanzui de tongzhi" [CCP Central notification on gradually strengthening youth education to prevent youth crime], 4 October 1985. *Zhongfa*, no. 20 (1985). In DXGWX, vol. 3, 1353–61.

"Zhonggong zhongyang guanyu qingzhu 'wu yi' laodongjie de kouhao" [Party Central on the slogans to celebrate "May 1st" Labor Day], 26 April 1950." CPCDB.

"Zhonggong zhongyang guanyu Xinhuashe jizhe caixie Neibu cankao ziliao de guiding" [Party Central regulations on employing Xinhua New Agency journalists to produce coverage for *Internal Reference*]. July 1953. In DXGWX, vol. 1, 138–39.

"Zhonggong zhongyang guanyu zai quanguo renmin zhong jinxing xianfa cao'an de xuanchuan he taolun de zhishi" [Party Central directive on carrying out propaganda for and discussion on the constitution draft among the people]. May 1954. In DXGWX, vol. 1, 176–78.

"Zhonggong zhongyang guanyu zuzhi taolun xiugai xianfa de tongzhi" [Party Central notification on organizing the discussion of the revised constitution]. *Zhongfa*, no. 53 (20 July 1970). CRDB.

Zhonggong zhongyang, Guowuyuan. "Guanyu xiang quanti gongmin jiben puji falü changshi de wu nian guihua de tongzhi" [On the five-year plan to basically popularize common legal knowledge for all citizens]. *Zhonghua renmin gongheguo guowuyuan gongbao*, no. 36 (1985): 1171.

Zhonggong zhongyang huabeiju bangongting. "Huabeiju guanyu sifa gaige yundong xiang Zhongyang de baogao" [North China office report to Party Central on the Judicial Reform Movement]. 7 October 1952. In *Zhonggong zhongyang huabeiju zhuyao wenjian huibian*, edited by Zhonggong zhongyang huabeiju bangongting, vol. 2 (1954), 823–25.

Zhonggong zhongyang wenxian yanjiu shi. *Mao Zedong nianpu (1949–1976)* [Chronicle of the life of Mao Zedong (1949–1976)]. 6 vols. Beijing: Zhongyang wenxian chubanshe, 2013.

Zhonggong zhongyang xuanchuanbu bangongting, Zhongyang dang'anguan bianyanbu, eds. *Zhongguo gongchandang xuanchuan gongzuo wenxian xuanbian* [Selected documents on CCP propaganda work]. 4 vols. Beijing: Xuexi chubanshe, 1996.

"Zhonggong zhongyang xuanchuanbu guanyu chuban gongzuo xiang zhonggong zhongyang de baogao ji Mao Zedong de pishi" [Central Propaganda Department report to Party Central on publishing work and Mao Zedong's memo]. 10 October 1951. In CBSL, vol. 3, 349–53.

"Zhonggong zhongyang zhishi: Jianjue baozheng xingfa, xingshi susong fa qieshi shishi" [Party Central directive: Resolutely protect the practical implementation of the Criminal Law and the Criminal Procedure Law]. *Xuanchuan tongxun*, no. 4 (16 October 1979): 7–8.

Zhongguo chuban kexue yanjiusuo and Zhongyang dang'anguan, eds. *Zhonghua renmin gongheguo chuban shiliao*. 11 vols. Beijing: Zhongguo shuji chubanshe, 1995–2007.

*Zhongguo dangdai mingrenlu* [Who's who in contemporary China]. Shanghai: Renmin chubanshe, 1991.

*Zhongguo xiqu zhi: Beijing juan* [Chinese drama and opera gazetteer: Beijing volume]. Beijing: Xinhua shudian, 1999.

"'Zhonghua renmin gongheguo chengzhi fangeming tiaoli tujie tongsuben': Shanghai 500 wan ren, du le 62 wan ce" ["Regulations of the People's Republic of China for the Punishment of Counterrevolutionaries: Illustrated popular explanations": Shanghai's five million people read 620,000 copies]. *Lianhe shibao*. http://www.shszx.gov.cn/node2/node4810/node4851/wswh/u1ai58671.html (last accessed 20 July 2017).

*Zhonghua renmin gongheguo shi biannian: 1954 nian* [Annals of the history of the People's Republic of China: 1954]. Beijing: Dangdai Zhongguo chubanshe, 2004.

Zhongnan minzhu fulian chouweihui, ed. *Hunyin wenti wenda* [Marriage law questions and answers]. Hankou: Zhongnan renmin chubanshe, 1952.

"Zhongnan qu guanche hunyinfa shidian xuanchuan gongzuo jingyan" [Propaganda work experiences of the Marriage Law implementation pilot tests in the South-Central region]. 1 April 1953. In ZGXGWX, vol. 3, 543–48.

"Zhongyang dui quanzong dangzu guanyu zai gongkuang qiye zhong xuanchuan guanche hunyinfa yundong de baogao de pishi" [Party Central memorandum on the Trade Union party group's report regarding propaganda on the Campaign to Implement the Marriage Law in industry, factories, and enterprises]. 13 April 1953. In ZGXGWX, vol. 3, 541–42.

"Zhongyang gonganbu 1957 nian gongan xuanchuan gongzuo jihua yaodian" [Main points of the central Ministry of Public Security's 1957 public security propaganda work plan]. *Gongan jianshe*, no. 190 (14 May 1957): 27–28.

"Zhongyang gonganbu guanyu geji renmin gongan jiguan bixu yange zunshou xianfa he falü de zhishi" [Ministry of Public Security directive on the need for people's public security organs at all levels to abide by the constitution and laws]. January 1955. *Gongan jianshe*, no. 117 (4 March 1955): 2–6.

Zhongyang guanche hunyinfa yundong weiyuanhui. "Guanche hunyinfa xuanchuan tigang" [Implement the Marriage Law propaganda outline]. In *Guanche hunyinfa yundong de zhongyao wenxian* [Important documents on the Campaign to Implement the Marriage Law], 12–22. Beijing: Renmin chubanshe, 1953.

"Zhongyang guanyu jiuzheng Shanxi qingnianbao faqi suowei 'Ziyou lianai' taolun de cuowu de zhishi" [Directive from Party Central on correcting *Shanxi Youth Daily's* mistake to start a discussion on so-called "free love"]. March 1953. CPCDB.

"Zhongyang renmin zhengfu jiaoyubu guanyu jiaqiang jinnian dongxue zhengzhi shishi jiaoyu de zhishi" [Ministry of Education of the Central People's Government directive on strengthening political and current affairs education during this year's winter study]. 11 November 1951. CPCDB.

Zhongyang xuanchuanbu. "Tongsu shuji de xuyao he chuban qingkuang. [The publishing situation and demand for popular works]. In CBSL, vol. 5, 470–86.

Zhongyang xuanchuanbu bangongting, ed. *Dang de xuanchuan gongzuo huiyi gaikuang he wenxian* [Overview of and documents related to party propaganda work meetings]. Beijing: Zhonggong zhongyang dangxiao chubanshe, 1994.

Zhongyang xuanchuanbu bangongting, ed. *Dang de xuanchuan gongzuo wenjian xuanbian* [Selection of documents on party propaganda work]. 4 vols. Beijing: Zhonggong zhongyang dangxiao chubanshe, 1994.

"Zhongyang xuanchuanbu guanyu chengli tongsu duwu chubanshe de jueding" [Central Propaganda Department decision on establishing a popular readings press]. December 1953. In DXGWX, vol. 1, 165–66.

"Zhongyang xuanchuanbu guanyu chengli tongsu duwu chubanshe de jueding" [Central Propaganda Department decision on establishing a popular readings press], 8 December 1953, CBSL, vol. 5, 487–88.

"Zhongyang xuanchuanbu guanyu gaijin baozhi shang guanyu xianfa cao'an he xianfa cao'an de quanmin taolun de xuanchuan he baodao de tongzhi" [Central Propaganda Department notification on improving propaganda and newspaper reportage on the constitution draft and on the all-people discussion of the constitution draft]. August 1954. In DXGWX, vol. 1, 233–37.

"Zhongyang xuanchuanbu guanyu ge di baozhi xuanchuan guanche hunyinfa de quedian he cuowu de tongbao" [Central Propaganda Department circular on shortcomings and mistakes of newspapers across the country in propagating and implementing the Marriage Law]. 18 March 1953. In ZGXGWX, vol. 3, 521–24.

"Zhongyang xuanchuanbu guanyu muqian chuban gongzuo de zhishi" [Central Propaganda Department directive on current publishing work]. July 1950. In DXGWX, vol. 1, 58–61.

"Zhongyang xuanchuanbu guanyu zai xianfa cao'an de xuanchuan he taolun zhong ying zhuyi sixiang de tongzhi" [Central Propaganda Department notification on the need to pay attention to thought during constitution draft propaganda and discussion]. 11 June 1954. In DXGWX, vol. 1, 206–8.

"Zhongyang xuanchuanbu pizhuan Huadongju xuanchuanbu guanyu guanche hunyinfa xuanchuan jiancha jieshu de tongbao" [The Central Propaganda Department
transmits the East China regional office Propaganda Department's circular on the
results of the investigation into propaganda to implement the Marriage Law]. February 1953. *Xuanchuan tongxun*, no. 9 (19 March 1953), 4–6.

"Zhongyang xuanchuanbu zhongyang zhengfa weiyuanhui guanyu dangqian baokan
zai fazhi xuanchuan fangmian ying zhuyi de jige wenti de tongzhi" [CCP Central
Propaganda Department and CCP Politics and Law Commission notification on
the need to pay attention to some problems in the current legal system propaganda
in newspapers and magazines]. 27 March 1985. In ZGXGWX, vol. 4, 688–89.

Zhongyang zhengfa jiguan sifa gaige bangongshi. *Sifa gaige yu sifa jianshe cankao wenjian* [Reference documents on juridical reform and judicial construction]. April
1954, undated, no publication information.

Zhou, Wu. "Cong quanguoxing dao difanghua: 1945 zhi 1956 nian Shanghai chubanye
de bianqian" [From national to localization: Changes in Shanghai's publishing industry, 1945–1956]. *Shilin*, no. 6 (2006): 80–88.

Zhou, Yang. "Gaige he fazhan minzu xiqu yishu: 11 yue 14 ri zai Beijing di yi jie quanguo xiqu guanmo yanchu dahui bimu" [Reform and develop the national theatrical
arts: The conclusion of the First National Congress on Theatrical Performances at
Beijing on 14 November]. GMRB, 27 December 1952.

Zhu, Caizhen, *Falüxue ABC* [Jurisprudence ABC]. Shanghai: Shijie shuju, 1929.

Zhu, Hongxia. "Xin Zhongguo chengli liushinian lai de hunyinfa yanjiu" [Marriage
law research in the sixty years since the founding of New China]. *Xueshu jiaoliu*,
no. 3 (2010): 49–52.

Zhu, Jinping. *Zhongguo gongchandang dui siying chubanye de gaizao, 1949–1956* [The
CCP's transformation of the private publishing industry, 1949–1956]. Beijing: Zhongyang dangxiao chubanshe, 2008.

Zou, Yu. "Fazhi jiangzuo zoujin Zhongnanhai" [Legal lectures enter Zhongnanhai].
*Bainian chao*, no. 4 (2009): 23–25.

———. "Puji falü changshi yao miqie lianxi shiji" [The popularization of law should
closely connect to practice]. 13 May 1986. In *Xuanchuan dongtai xuanbian 1986* [Se-
lections from *Propaganda Trends 1986*], 73–79. Beijing: Zhongguo shehui kexue
chubanshe, 1987.

Zurndorfer, Harriet T. *China Bibliography: A Research Guide to Reference Works about
China Past and Present*. Leiden: Brill, 1995.

———. "Contracts, Property and Litigation: Intermediation and Adjudication in the
Huizhou Region (Anhui) in Sixteenth-Century China." In *Law and Long-Term Economic Change: A Eurasian Perspective*, edited by Debin Ma and Jan van Zanden, 91–
114. Stanford: Stanford University Press, 2011.

# Index

# Harvard East Asian Monographs
(most recent titles)